W9-ADM-452

THE OHIO RIVER VALLEY SERIES

Rita Kohn
Series Editor

American Grit

A Woman's Letters
from the Ohio Frontier

~

Edited by
Emily Foster

UNIVERSITY PRESS OF KENTUCKY

Publication of this volume was made possible in part
by a grant from the National Endowment for the Humanities.

Copyright © 2002 by The University Press of Kentucky
Scholarly publisher for the Commonwealth,
serving Bellarmine University, Berea College, Centre
College of Kentucky, Eastern Kentucky University,
The Filson Historical Society, Georgetown College,
Kentucky Historical Society, Kentucky State University,
Morehead State University, Murray State University,
Northern Kentucky University, Transylvania University,
University of Kentucky, University of Louisville,
and Western Kentucky University.
All rights reserved.

Editorial and Sales Offices: The University Press of Kentucky
663 South Limestone Street, Lexington, Kentucky 40508–4008

07 06 05 04 03   5 4 3 2 1

Frontispiece: Anna Briggs Bentley, 1796–1890. Courtesy Virginia Niles Taylor.

Library of Congress Cataloging-in-Publication Data

Bentley, Anna Briggs, 1796-1890.
American grit : a woman's letters from the Ohio frontier / edited by
Emily Foster.
p. cm. — (Ohio River Valley series)
Includes bibliographical references and index.
ISBN 0-8131-2265-1 (cloth : alk. paper)
1. Bentley, Anna Briggs, 1796-1890—Correspondence. 2. Frontier and
pioneer life—Ohio River Valley. 3. Ohio River Valley—Social life and
customs—19th century. 4. Pioneer women—Ohio River Valley—
Correspondence. 5. Pioneers—Ohio River Valley—Correspondence.
I. Foster, Emily, 1945- II. Title. III. Series.
F518 .B46 2002
977.1'6303'092—dc21   2002011431

This book is printed on acid-free recycled paper meeting
the requirements of the American National Standard
for Permanence in Paper for Printed Library Materials.

Manufactured in the United States of America.

Contents

Illustration insert follows page 158

Series Foreword

The Ohio River Valley Series, conceived and published by the University Press of Kentucky, is an ongoing series of books that examine and illuminate the Ohio River and its tributaries, the lands drained by these streams, and the peoples who made this fertile and desirable area their place of residence, of refuge, of commerce and industry, of cultural development and, ultimately, of engagement with American democracy. In doing this, the series builds upon an earlier project, "Always a River: The Ohio River and the American Experience," which was sponsored by the National Endowment for the Humanities and the humanities councils of Illinois, Indiana, Kentucky, Ohio, Pennsylvania, and West Virginia, with a mix of private and public organizations.

Each book's story is told through men and women acting within their particular time and place. Each directs attention to the place of the Ohio River in the context of the larger American story and reveals the rich resources for the history of the Ohio River and of the nation afforded by records, papers, artifacts, works of art and oral stories preserved by families and institutions. Each traces the impact the river and the land have had on individuals and cultures and, conversely, the changes these individuals and cultures have wrought on the valley with the passage of years.

The letters of Anna Bentley and her family provide drama and insights beyond fictionalized sagas. Emily Foster's *The Ohio Frontier,* her best-selling first book with the University Press of Kentucky, proved regional history can be a page turner. Now, *American Grit: A Woman's Letters from the Ohio Frontier,* as a story of the Quaker religion, its evolution during the nineteenth century and its impact on the emerging nation's social, political, and feminist issues, equally offers a unique understanding of pioneer daily life in eastern Ohio.

Ordinary people engaged in ordinary living makes for extraordinary reading, be it with a meticulous listing of items lovingly received by a frontier family destitute of clothing and household goods such as sewing needles and tablecloths, or with the fulsome itinerary of goings and comings where distant neighbors are creating a new social order. We experience the myriad illnesses and homemade remedies including medicinals and herbals that we now are revisiting as part of holistic health care. In direct relation to the nation's evolving economy we witness the downsizing of families from that of Anna Bentley's generation to that of her children and grandchildren. We observe values and relationships in transformation.

But most important, Anna Bentley's story flies in the face of the stereotypical presentation of the wife being wrenched from her comfortable eastern home by a husband bent on conquering the frontier. Rather, we witness a partnership where suffering hardships is gender equal. To survive, Anna clearly understood and advanced the need to find arable land. Hearing Anna's views is refreshing and revelatory. Foster is not immodest in stating that this is about as honest a report as we're likely to get—no artifice, no posturing—it's straight from the heart. Human beings emerge, warts and all.

While reading someone else's mail may seem voyeuristic, doing so is perfectly acceptable nearly two hundred years later. Wrestling and finally wresting sustenance from a place not initially suited to be farmed in the European tradition becomes a repeated story across this nation. That the Maryland soil was depleted so early proves how out of sync the initial Atlantic seaboard settlers were with land use. We come to appreciate the understandings the Nanticokes had, which the Europeans lacked. While Foster has done extensive research to verify and provide context, she skillfully allows the original words to convey their narrative. Ultimately, we see Anna, the Ohio frontierswoman who begged goods and money from her Maryland family, become the matriarch-giver of goods and money to her own children who move ever westward. Here we have a universal story of living on the fringe of poverty. Letter after letter, we experience history unfolding, consequently providing context for pressing contemporary issues.

Rita Kohn
Series Editor

Acknowledgments

Since I first looked at the collection of Anna Briggs Bentley's letters housed in the Maryland Historical Society archives in 1998, many people have helped me. Some were hardly aware they were assisting a research project, but they helped nonetheless. I owe gratitude to more people than I can name.

To begin at the moment I saw Anna Bentley's letters, I would like to thank Jennifer Bryan, Mary Herbert, and the other staff at the Maryland Historical Society for their patience, expertise, and good will. The same might be said of staff at other archives, who without exception helped make my visits both efficient and fruitful. Among them, Lauren Brown at the University of Maryland Libraries; Frances Pollard of the Virginia Historical Society archives; Richard Dinsmore of the Ritter Library, Baldwin-Wallace College; Fran Parker, Jean Snyder, and Lee Halper of the Sandy Spring Museum; Daisy Hagan-Bolen at the Columbus Metropolitan Library; and staff at the Ohio Historical Society archives and the Salem Public Library. I would also like to note the friendly assistance of Rebecca Hankins of the Amistad Research Center, Tulane University.

Kathleen Schmidt helped immeasurably by editing the manuscript. I am indebted to her sharp eyes and red pencil. I am also grateful to Roger Antolik, the flintlock gun expert who explained to me how Granville Bentley exploded a powder horn trying to light a candle.

I would like to extend my thanks to many descendants of Anna and Joseph Bentley, who unstintingly shared family stories, genealogy, and photographs, and, just as important, a delighted interest in the project. My gratitude goes to Anna Chavelle (who was named for her ancestor), William Henderson, Virginia Niles Taylor, Don McArtor, Larry Preston, Joan Blosser, Warwick Miller Tompkins, Richard Lyman, John T. Lyman, Alice Gibson, Paul Heston, Lindy Marohn, Bill Sprague, and Paul and Linda Waste.

Several people in Columbiana County lent their generous assistance in various ways, for which I am deeply grateful: Earl and the late Helen Chilson; Paul Stanley, Don Lane and others from the Damascus Historical Society; Josephine Rupp of the Salem Historical Society; Sue Scharf, who grew up on the Bentley farm; historian Dale Shaffer; and Margaret Starbuck of the old Quaker meeting house in Salem.

And for his enthusiastic embrace of this project from the beginning, when I first drove up to his door, special thanks go to Steve Smith, for whom no kind of help was too much trouble, up to and including an aerial search for the Bentley family graveyard. His appreciation of the history of West Township, Columbiana County, runs deep. He and his wife Susan were good friends throughout my work.

Finally, I would like to thank my husband, Lee Brown, who hung in there for the long haul.

Introduction

In the panorama of human events, the story of Anna Briggs Bentley occupies a quiet corner. In 1826, Anna and her husband, Joseph, left a close-knit settlement in Maryland for the sparsely populated frontier of Columbiana County, Ohio, where they raised a large family and Anna worked as she had never worked before. Circumscribed by geography and the demands of a nineteenth-century farm and a house full of children, their lives were simple and unremarkable.

Things might have been otherwise.

Anna came from a prominent Maryland family that once owned thousands of acres in Montgomery County. Her father, Isaac, was closely acquainted with two U.S. presidents. But when he died in 1825, he left the family in debt and his children struggling to make ends meet. So like many other Americans, Anna and Joseph sought new opportunities in the West.

Unlike earlier pioneers to Ohio, they didn't battle Indians or wild beasts, but they had to carve a homestead out of virgin forest with the sweat of their labors. They lived beyond the reach of comforts that Anna had known all her life, such as abundant servants, good society, schools, shops, and ready money. They encountered other newcomers who couldn't cope with frontier life and primitive conditions.

But Anna was armed with grit, determination, a sense of humor, and a resolve to make a better life in Ohio for her children and her children's children. Starting on the road in 1826, she wrote voluminous, detailed letters to her family in Maryland about life on the frontier. No inadequacies of grammar, spelling or punctuation ever stood between Anna and a lively account of her daily affairs. She followed a philosophy of letter writing that she frequently recommended to correspondents: "Don't fear a repetition, but just give daily concerns, the affairs of the neighbourhood, the sayings and doings of the children, how little Henry looks, your garden, your cows, horses, chickens, and pigs, and even Ajax . . . so that as I am journeying on through time in my distant habitation I may keep up a kind of accquaintance and not feel like a stranger in my own dear native land, if ever I should visit it again." Anna's letters poured unedited from her pen during stolen moments of her busy life, often late at night after everyone else in the house was asleep. Anna addressed them primarily to her mother and sister at Sharon, the family home in Sandy Spring. She knew it would be years, if ever, before she would see them again. Her letters became her lifeline to Maryland, a strong, binding cord made of stories, jokes, descriptions, gossip, hopes, and fears that would keep her tied to them for life, even from far away.

Afraid of being forgotten, Anna created letters that would inform and amuse. They pleased her family mightily. Passing along one of Anna's stories about a family acquaintance, her sister Elizabeth wrote, "Oh! how shall I compose myself to tell it, please be patient till I wipe my eyes." Tied as she was to her farm and a succession of babies, Anna transported herself in letters back over the mountains to smoke a pipe and share a laugh with her beloved mother. They were like visits from Anna herself. Thanks to their power and warmth, she now travels through time, bringing back to life the farm and family at Green Hill, West Township, Columbiana County, Ohio.

Although she describes herself caring for sick children in a cold, drafty Ohio cabin, bending over a washtub doing the laundry for eight or nine people, or up to her elbows in grease making sausage, Anna Bentley wasn't a born pioneer. She came from a well-educated, genteel family and had her father's enterprise and her mother's practicality.

On her mother's side, Anna's first American ancestor, Robert Brooke, emigrated in 1650 from England in his own ship with his wife, ten children, twenty-seven servants, and a pack of foxhounds. Cecil Calvert, Lord Baltimore, immediately appointed him commander of Charles County, Maryland, and Lieutenant of the Province. Robert Brooke's son married into a Catholic family. His grandson, James, adopted the Quaker religion when he married the Quaker daughter of one of the largest landowners in the area of present-day Laurel, Maryland. James and Deborah Snowden Brooke moved onto 889 acres James had inherited in Sandy Spring. Over the next forty years, he accumulated no less than 22,000 acres in the area.

As James and Deborah Brooke's six children matured, they were each given land for themselves and their families. Eventually they established their own homes: Basil at Falling Green, Richard at Fair Hill, and Roger Brooke IV at Brooke Grove. Roger and his wife, Mary Matthews, a fellow Quaker, raised nine children (Samuel, Mary, James, Deborah, Margaret, Sarah, Hannah, Roger, and Dorothy) at Brooke Grove. They and their children intermarried several times with Maryland or Pennsylvania Quaker families, including the Garrigueses, Thomases, Bentleys, Gilpins, and Hopkinses.

Born in 1770, Hannah, the seventh of the bunch, grew up in the shadow of the Revolutionary War, when the political climate severely tested the pacifist Quakers. Not only were they objects of suspicion to their neighbors, but they also faced internal conflict brought on by the war. Hannah's uncle, Richard Brooke, served as a delegate to the rebellious Maryland Convention, then defied Quaker teaching by joining the Continental Army, where he rose to the rank of colonel. The Society of Friends immediately disowned him for engaging in military pursuits. Her father and oldest brother, Samuel, were disowned for "taking the test," or swearing an oath of allegiance to the new state government. They were reinstated years later.

In August 1794, Hannah married Isaac Briggs, a young Quaker farmer, engineer, and surveyor from Haverford, Pennsylvania. Briggs, a graduate of the University of Pennsylvania, had come to the Sandy Spring area the year before to assist Andrew Ellicott, the surveyor who completed Pierre L'Enfant's plans for the new capital city of Washington, D.C. A man of wide-ranging talents and scientific interests, Briggs was a member of the Society of Useful Knowledge and the American Philosophical Society.

The young couple moved into the log house Isaac and his father, Samuel Briggs, built on land Hannah inherited outside Sandy Spring. They called their farm Sharon, after the fertile Plain of Sharon in Israel. They began housekeeping surrounded by Hannah's nearby brothers and sisters: Samuel, married to Sarah Garrigues; Deborah, married to Richard Thomas, founder of Brookeville; Mary and her husband, Thomas Moore, at Longwood near Brookeville; and Sarah, who was married to Caleb Bentley, Brookeville's long-time postmaster. Sister Dorothy, who married Gerard Hopkins in 1796, moved to Baltimore.

Aunts, uncles, and cousins abounded in the neighborhood of Sandy Spring. Uncle Basil Brooke and his wife, Elizabeth Hopkins Brooke, had inherited Falling Green farm, part of James Brooke's original land. When they died in 1794, Basil Jr. took it over. In 1793, first cousin Deborah Pleasants Stabler and her family came from Leesburg, Virginia, to live on property she inherited from her mother, Elizabeth, the only daughter of James and Deborah Brooke.

Life centered on the Quaker meetinghouse. The Brookes were pillars of the Sandy Spring community of Friends. As such, they set themselves apart from the rest of the world both theologically and culturally. The Society of Friends had been founded in the mid-seventeenth century by the English religious reformer George Fox, who hated the pomp and trappings of the Roman Catholic and Anglican churches. Salaried ministers and ornate churches interfered in the relationship between a Christian and his God, Fox argued. He rejected the sacraments and the outward manifestations of faith, such as statuary, liturgical singing, elaborate ritual, even Bible reading. He espoused instead a mystical concept called the Inner Light, a direct communication between God and man that brought the faithful to a personal experience of God in their hearts. Quakers had little interest at this point in the divinity of Jesus, the status of Mary, the existence of saints or miracles, or the fine points of baptismal rites; much later, however, conflicting theories of revelation and doctrine formed a battleground in the church.

Fox's followers adopted "plain" clothing and speech that distinguished them from worldly sects. Women wore simply constructed gowns, unadorned bonnets, and subdued colors. Men favored single-breasted, collarless coats and broad-brimmed hats. Both sexes addressed each other as Friend; their refusal to recognize worldly titles occasionally got them into trouble in class-conscious England. They referred to each other as "thee" and "thou," adopting the archaic usage of the Bible. They numbered the months and days of the week to avoid using names derived from Norse or Roman mythology. (January was first month, Sunday was first day, and so on.) They refused to swear oaths or take up arms.

Intolerance and discrimination in England eventually drove many members of the sect to the New World. They settled in Maryland, which had a history of religious freedom; New Jersey, where a couple of Quakers owned about half the state; and Pennsylvania, founded by the rich English Quaker, William Penn. They also moved to the Carolinas, Virginia, and Georgia and even dominated the whaling industry in Nantucket, Massachusetts.

Although they were widely respected by non-Quakers, Friends largely lived, traded, and socialized among themselves. They married within the Society or risked censure. The penalty for infractions could be disownment.

In some ways they were remarkably liberal. Quakers not only valued education—as Sandy Spring historian William H. Farquhar (Anna Bentley's brother-in-law) put it, "giving to intellectual pursuits the preference to all amusements that are in conflict with them"—they opened schools to children of both sexes. Quaker marriages were unions of equals. A young woman was not "given" to her husband, nor did she promise to obey him. Instead, they jointly announced their intention to marry. If, after a careful investigation, elders found no obstructions to the union, the couple was joined in a ceremony unique among Christian sects in demonstrating that man and woman came together as free agents on an equal footing.

Women participated fully in running the church. They held church business meetings that were counterparts of the men's and served as ministers (the Quaker ministry always being a volunteer position), occasionally traveling to other meetings on priestly missions. It was no coincidence that Quaker women like Lucretia Mott and Abby Kelly played prominent roles in the anti-slavery and women's rights movements of the nineteenth century. Such movements sprang naturally from the Friends' moral principles, and the skills Quaker women had learned in running meetings, handling finances, and speaking in public made them natural leaders.

The Society of Friends was also among the first groups in America to take steps to discourage slavery among its members. According to Howard Brinton in his classic Quaker history, *Friends for 300 Years,* "The first protest in America against slavery was made by German Quakers in Germantown, Pennsylvania, in 1688." In 1772, both the Virginia and North Carolina Yearly Meetings condemned slavery. Theirs wasn't a popular position in slave-owning states, especially as they began to free their own slaves and encourage others to do likewise. In 1780, the Indian Springs Monthly Meeting in Maryland (which met alternately with Sandy Spring) formed a committee "to treat with such amongst us as kept slaves" and try to persuade them to see the light. A year later, a member named Elizabeth Johns was disowned for "the unjust practise of slave keeping." Anna Bentley therefore grew up detesting slavery, although Maryland remained a slave-owning state until the Civil War.

Born on May 18, 1796, Anna was Hannah and Isaac Briggs's oldest child (after a first-born died in infancy). She was followed by Mary (1798), Deborah (1799), and Sarah (1801).

With two of his brothers-in-law, Isaac Briggs brought fresh energy and ambition into the Brooke family, whose fortunes had somewhat diminished since the days of James Brooke. Isaac's talent and intellect soon made him stand out in the small, educated society of the Eastern seaboard. Thomas Jefferson, who knew him well, called Isaac "second to no man in the United States" in science, astronomy, geometry, and mathematics. He also respected Briggs's personal gifts, praising "the candor, modesty and simplicity of his manners."

Isaac's brother-in-law, Thomas Moore, was just as ambitious and multitalented. Moore not only helped engineer the National Road from Cumberland, Maryland, to Ohio (now US 40), but also invented an early refrigerator. Thomas Jefferson was so taken by the idea of Moore's icebox (a cedar chest covered with cloth and rabbit fur) that he paid Isaac $13 for a model and diagram of it.

The two brothers-in-law also were ardent agriculturists who strove to reverse the destructive farming practices that had depleted the soil in Montgomery County, Maryland. In 1799, they founded the Sandy Spring Farmers Society to promote scientific farming. James Madison, the future president—whose wife, Dolly, came from a respected Quaker family of North Carolina and Virginia—was made an honorary member. When President Jefferson took office, one of the first things he did was to enlist the help of Madison and Isaac Briggs to form a national coalition of these societies.

Before the turn of the century, Isaac Briggs started a school at Sandy Spring and served for a time as the schoolmaster. According to Thomas McCormick, who was then living with his uncle, Thomas Moore, and attending the log school, the pupils also included Isaac's daughters, Anna and Mary, along with Richard and John Brooke, Thomas Pleasants, Edward Stabler, and three "Garriguez" brothers from Philadelphia. McCormick described Isaac the teacher as "kind-hearted" and "fond of exercise."

"Though rather a stout man," McCormick wrote, "he was active on the foot, could run very fast for a moderate distance, enjoying it very much when time would admit." So enthusiastically did Isaac participate in foot races with his pupils that he once fell and broke his collarbone, McCormick remembered.

When Isaac traveled, as he did often and for extended periods, he worried about his daughters' progress in their schooling. In 1803, he and Hannah spoke by letter of their concern that nine-year-old Anna's disposition be "curbed" and that she be prodded to read and write. Isaac promised to address a note specifically to Anna so that she must learn to write well enough to reply.

Using his powerful contacts in Washington, Isaac Briggs busied himself at an array of jobs trying to support his growing family. President Jefferson, who outlined a plan for Merriwether Lewis to lead an expedition northwest across the continent, also appointed Isaac Surveyor General of the Mississippi and Orleans territories. In May 1803, Isaac set off southwest, taking along his youngest brother, Joseph, as a clerk, and carrying a certificate from the Sandy Spring meeting which attested to his membership in the Society of Friends. He was gone for months.

On this first extensive trip Isaac established a pattern he would follow later: He kept track of the number of letters he received from home. Considering how often letters went astray, that practice was not a bad idea. Misunderstandings were likely to arise as letters crept slowly to their destination, often crossing replies to previous letters on their way. But there was a less attractive side to Isaac's habit—he also complained repeatedly that his family didn't write often enough.

Hannah was pregnant when Isaac left. In October 1803, she gave birth to a son, writing to Isaac afterward, "I hope thou wilt have nothing against his bearing thy own [name] as it is dearer to me, than all others; I felt it hard at first to depart from what I knew <u>had</u> been thy choice, but I found that others would name him, if I did not; as it was the cry with the Doctor, and all who had a say in it, that it must be ISAAC BRIGGS Junior." Isaac Senior responded in December, when he first heard the news, that he had preferred William, but "peradventure, he may make us <u>to laugh</u> in our old age."[1]

Anna's younger brother grew up the favored son of the family, a feckless charmer. His every move in an increasingly eccentric life was recorded by his sisters with great interest. An amusing raconteur, Isaac Junior made many people laugh during his lifetime.

From Natchez and New Orleans Isaac Senior sent dispatches back to Jefferson on the political and social situation in the West. He wasn't favorably impressed. "The Divine Author of Nature has indeed made this Country a Paradise—but man has converted it into a <u>Pandemonium</u>," he wrote. He was most disturbed by the institution of slavery. Writing frankly, as he always did to his patron, Briggs ventured to express the dictates of his Quaker conscience: "The number of slaves in this country is already great, and the infatuated inhabitants are in the habit of increasing it by large importations. . . . Oh! my friend—may I not call thee the friend of Man!—is there no way of putting a stop to this crying, dangerous, national sin?" Isaac had a point. Nearly half the inhabitants of the Orleans Territory were slaves at that time.

In March 1804, Isaac returned east for a visit of a few months, meeting his son for the first time. On his way back to New Orleans in August he stopped for dinner with James Madison at his home, Montpelier, and visited Jefferson at Monticello. At Jefferson's request he then traveled through Georgia to look for an overland postal route to New Orleans. (While in Georgia he apparently bought some land; many years later, Isaac Jr. went there to try to make a legal claim on it.) Unfortunately, Congress did not authorize this part of Isaac Senior's trip, and though the postal route was adopted, Isaac spent years trying to get Congress to reimburse him for his expenses.

The second leg of Isaac's extended business trip proved to be far harder on him and his family than the first had been. While Isaac was wracked with homesickness and separation anxiety, Hannah felt abandoned. His compulsion to tick off the letters he had sent and received, showing a balance sheet to his credit and Hannah's debit, backfired. Her letters—at least, the ones that have come down in the family papers—are few, brief, uninformative and distant. Often she hid behind the children, writing only part of each letter with the excuse that she was too busy or (in July) that there were too many flies in the house and too much noise. She would let the children fill in the rest. Saddled with the responsibilities of keeping the household running, disciplining and educating the children, and making ends meet, Hannah may have felt the marital bond stretched to the breaking point. Even at a distance of two centuries the strain that the next couple of years put on their marriage is palpable in their letters.

On top of that, Isaac's brother Joseph, who had become the private secretary of William C.C. Claiborne, the governor of Orleans Territory, died in September during one of New Orleans's recurrent yellow fever epidemics. Scarcely had Isaac sent the "melancholy tidings" back to Maryland than he too came down with the fever and was so sick he stopped writing home altogether. It was the end of January 1805, after a couple of anxious letters from Hannah wondering at the long silence, before Isaac was well enough to take up his pen again.

During these worrisome times, little Anna remained on a prolonged visit to her Briggs relatives in Philadelphia, where her father apparently had dropped her off. There was nothing unusual in those days about visits that lasted weeks or months. Travel was arduous and expensive, especially, in this case, when the traveler was a child and could not return home until an adult accompanied her. Still, Hannah's daughter was expected to remember whose child she was, and obviously Anna hadn't yet become the prolific correspondent of her adulthood. Three months into her visit Hannah complained to Isaac, "to think I have never heard but <u>twice</u> since thou left her." She threatened to make Anna come home if the child didn't keep in touch more regularly. Whether Anna did or didn't come up to the mark, she stayed away almost a year, returning to Sharon in May 1805.

As spring turned to summer and then fall, Isaac stayed on and on in the West, growing increasingly unhappy with the "party cabals" and political intrigues of New Orleans and Natchez. All around him were undercurrents of unrest and murmurs of plots to separate the territories west of the Alleghenies and form a new government. There was dark talk of invading Mexico. At the center of such disturbing gossip were the former vice president of the United States, Aaron Burr, and the governor of Louisiana Territory, General James Wilkinson, a genial scoundrel whom Isaac apparently trusted. Along with his other duties, Isaac became Jefferson's unofficial informant about the rumors swirling around him. Governor Claiborne wrote to Jefferson in late 1805 that Isaac "has lately been the object of abuse and like all others, who are unused to attacks of the kind, he discovers a Share of mortification." Claiborne added, "I believe him to be a faithful Officer and an honest man and of his ability to discharge the trust committed him, there can be no doubt."

Unable to break away from his work, Isaac urged Hannah to travel out and join him. She declined, girding up her refusal by adding that "everyone" agreed with her decision.

During this period Isaac suffered serious financial reverses. His brother Samuel, a heavy drinker, entered into a contract with Evan Jones, a New Orleans lawyer, to build a steam-powered sawmill. Isaac signed as surety for his brother. When Samuel failed to complete the contract, Jones took Isaac to court and got a judgment for $5,096. He agreed to release Isaac from the debt only if the job were completed by July. Distraught, Isaac wrote to President Jefferson in December laying out the whole depressing situation and explaining that he wouldn't neglect his other work while trying to dig out from under this misfortune. "I long for the time to come when I can leave this Country forever, which I hope will be next spring," he groaned.

It wouldn't be for more than a year. In the meantime, Isaac started a drumbeat of petitions for money he thought Congress owed him for the surveying jobs. It is possible he never fully recovered from the financial damage his brother inflicted. Years later, during the War of 1812, even though Jefferson had paid some of the surveying costs out of his own pocket, Isaac was still appealing to Congress and trying to reconstruct accounts that had been lost when the British burned Washington. He never felt financially secure the rest of his life.

Isaac left New Orleans abruptly in late 1806 "without previous arrangement and brought with me no papers, except those relating to the enterprise of Burr," he reminded Jefferson some years later. Isaac's bit part in the so-called Burr Conspiracy was to carry to Washington letters from General Wilkinson, which Isaac delivered to the White House during the president's New Year celebrations.

He continued to travel in the interests of business for the rest of his life, but he never again stayed away from his family for as long as he had in the period 1804 to 1807. While Isaac was in Maryland, of course, the number of family letters diminished, so there is no running account of Anna Briggs's early adolescence with her younger sisters Mary, Sarah, and Deborah and brother Isaac. Her sister Elizabeth was born in 1807, the same year Caleb Bentley, a widower since his wife Sarah died, married Henrietta Thomas from a local Quaker family. He remained close to Sarah's sister, Hannah Briggs, and her family.

In 1809, he went into partnership with his former brothers-in-law, Thomas Moore and Isaac Briggs, to build the town of Triadelphia northeast of Sandy Spring and Brookeville on the Patuxent River. With a grist mill, cotton factory and other enterprises, it grew to several hundred inhabitants, but it didn't bring the return the partners anticipated. As Isaac put it later to Thomas Jefferson, his compensation for this project, in the form of a share of profits, "was <u>nothing</u>—and my family had been enabled to live but just decently, by the absorption of most of my wife's little property, made independently hers before the marriage." Triadelphia eventually declined. It was largely swept away by floods in 1889 and now lies at the bottom of the Triadelphia Reservoir.

While Triadelphia was still in its formative years, events of great moment to the fragile young republic were unfolding not far away. America was being drawn into England's war with Napoleonic France. One of England's highest military priorities was to try to cut off France's foreign trade. At sea the Royal Navy pursued this policy aggressively. British ships freely stopped and searched American vessels, looking for deserters or goods on their way to help the French cause.

In 1807, HMS *Leopard* stopped the USS *Chesapeake*, and when the captain of the American ship refused to allow the British to search, the *Leopard* opened fire, killing or wounding twenty-one American crew members. Then they boarded, took four sailors, and later hanged one and impressed the others into the Royal Navy. American public opinion was outraged. Politicians and newspapers roared for revenge. But the infant government and minuscule navy were ill-equipped to exact it.

In the Northwest Territory the British maintained fur trading posts on America's doorstep and competed with American traders. The Indians of that region deeply resented the floods of American settlers who poured across the Ohio River after the 1795 Treaty of Greeneville, and Americans resented British support for the Indians there. Into this volcanic situation stepped Tecumseh, a charismatic Shawnee warrior from Ohio bent on forming a tribal confederation to stop the expansion of white settlements. The British in Canada encouraged and abetted him. In June 1812, Congress declared war on Britain for impressing American sailors, interfering with trade and encouraging the Indians to attack American settlements.

Just sixteen miles away from Washington, with war about to descend on an unprepared country, sixteen-year-old Anna Briggs took a serious step of her own. In a letter dated August 1, 1812, her cousin Edward Garrigues (son of Isaac's sister Hannah) wrote to Isaac from Haverford, Pennsylvania that he had heard Anna was going to be "settled" and would be setting up housekeeping near her parents. The rumor was true. That month Anna married twenty-three-year-old Joseph Bentley, son of Ellis and Alice Edmunds Bentley and a nephew of Caleb Bentley, Anna's uncle by marriage. Only a month later, Hannah Briggs gave birth to Margaret, the last of the Briggs girls.

Joseph and Anna Bentley started married life in and around Sandy Spring while Joseph took whatever jobs came along, such as postmaster of Triadelphia, a position he undoubtedly got through his uncle and his father-in-law. In October 1813, Anna gave birth to a boy they named Granville Sharp after the famous English abolitionist who had died in July.

As close as they were to Washington, Anna's family must have received constant bulletins about the progress of the war. Things hadn't been going terribly well. Sixty wounded American soldiers had been massacred on the River Raisin in Michigan in January. With the help of the British, Tecumseh and his forces also captured Detroit and burned Fort Dearborn.

But the defeat of British ships at the Battle of Put-In Bay by young Commodore Oliver Hazard Perry set the stage for the American recapture of Detroit and the invasion of Canada. In October 1813, British and Indian forces were defeated by the Americans under William Henry Harrison on the Thames River in Ontario. With Tecumseh's death on the battlefield, the idea of an Indian confederation was extinguished, and Indian resistance ended in the Northwest Territory. American settlers could move unhindered across the virgin landscape. And they did.

But in the East the young government faced one of its darkest moments. Under General Robert Ross, the British navy landed at the mouth of the Potomac River in August 1814 and marched on Washington, brushing aside the Virginia and Maryland militias as they went. President Madison, who had ridden out to encourage the troops, raced back to Washington when it was clear the British couldn't be stopped. He found that his wife had fled with valuable state papers and a full-length portrait of George Washington. Madison escaped, but by the time his ferry had reached the Virginia bank of the Potomac, the public buildings in the city behind him, including the White House, were in flames.

The second night after the burning of the capital, Madison and his entourage made their way to Brookeville, Maryland, where they found shelter with Anna's Uncle Caleb and Aunt Henrietta Bentley. Novelist and essayist Margaret Bayard Smith, a friend of the Madisons who also stayed in the house that night, wrote that she had "never seen more benevolent people." The next day, the British having left for their ships, Madison returned to the capital. The Treaty of Ghent ended the war just four months later.

In 1815, Isaac packed up the younger members of his family, including the new baby, William Henry, the youngest Briggs child, and moved to Wilmington, Delaware. From there he wrote to Anna that he had dined recently with the president and Dolly Madison "by particular invitation—family dinner—or, as the President called it, potluck," and sat next to Dolly.

In October, Anna gave birth to her second child, Franklin Hamilton, a few months younger than his Uncle William Henry. Over the next few years, as Anna's little family grew (with Maria, born in 1817, and Edward in 1819), the Briggses and Bentleys continued to look for settled employment. For whatever reason, they couldn't seem to shake the specter of debt. Isaac and his son-in-law, Joseph, shared a restless and frustrated ambition. Isaac even wrote to Jefferson asking him to sit down with James Madison and try to think of some job that would suit both Briggs and the country.

The retired president agreed in early 1816 to try to get Isaac compensation from Congress for the long-ago surveying trip to the Mississippi Territory. Isaac replied with obsequious gratitude. He quoted from a gushing letter written (at Isaac's prompting?) by his daughter, Mary, in which she called Jefferson "Great and excellent man!" The flattery worked. Jefferson offered to recommend Isaac as surveyor of the state of Virginia.

By May of the following year, though, Isaac landed himself a different job. Governor DeWitt Clinton of New York made him the chief engineer of the Erie Canal. Isaac wrote Jefferson, "Yesterday afternoon, when about every hope had fled, the information of this prospect in New York broke suddenly and unexpectedly upon me like a light from Heaven." He immediately set about trying to get his brother-in-law, Thomas Moore, appointed a sort of co-engineer of the project, at $10,000 a year, and asked Jefferson to write on his behalf. Isaac worked on the canal until at least 1819. (Moore took the Virginia job, which put him in charge of the James River Canal project, and later hired Isaac.)

At the same time, Joseph Bentley started talking about going to Ohio. It would have been a natural destination for him and Anna, following the route of many other Quaker emigrants. Aunt Dorothy's husband, Gerard T. Hopkins, had traveled there on his way to Fort Wayne as early as 1804. Members of the Society of Friends from Georgia, New Jersey, Pennsylvania, and the Carolinas had been drifting into Ohio since before the turn of the century. The first monthly meeting was established in 1801 by Friends from Wrightsborough, Georgia. Other Friends went down the Ohio River and then up into present Clinton County. Still others settled in Ross and Highland counties. The Quakers Zadok Street and John Straughan formed the village of Salem in Columbiana County in 1806. Quakers settled in villages and on farms from the county seat of New Lisbon to the western border and into neighboring Stark County, establishing meetings as soon as they formed a community. Among them was a cousin of Anna's, James Brooke, and his family.

Ohio seemed like a land of opportunity, but Anna didn't share Joseph's readiness to abandon family and friends. Her mother had nearly died of typhus in 1816, and Anna's baby daughter Maria from a childhood ailment in 1817. (Anna had her inoculated for smallpox as soon as she recovered.) She wrote to her father in New York, while Joseph was looking for work in Georgetown, "Pray do not say any thing to encourage his going where thou art now, it would be a trial too great for me to bear a separation so distant from my dear parents. . . ."

In reply, Isaac came down on her hard, chiding her for a "prejudice" that might "if indulged have a damping and chilling influence on the energies of her husband's mind." Clearly worked up at his daughter's timidity, saying that he had lain awake all night thinking about it, Isaac went on, "My wishes point to, and my exertions have in view, if the Lord will, a place where my whole family, for a generation or two to come, may sit down, in one neighborhood, in peace, competence, and humble virtue. Your part of the world, in every view I can take of it as respects my family, presents to my mind in prospect, division and scattering. And I firmly believe those who decide for it, if they should succeed, would find, when too late, that they had decided, in effect, for such scattering and division; and had cast away opportunities perhaps never to return."

Hannah Briggs worried about what she feared was her son-in-law's "unsettled, roving disposition, which seldom fails of bringing anguish and bitterness of soul." Poor Anna must have felt oppressed by all these different pressures. To add to her troubles, Joseph took to drink and began to stay away from Quaker meetings. In 1819, he was required to defend himself before a church committee. "With contrition of heart," he wrote, "I confess the crime of which I am charged, and I feel it to be a duty to acknowledge also that I have been in the use of ardent Spirits. . . ." He vowed "never again to wet my lips with ardent Spirits." And he appears to have kept his word.

Anna's father continued to struggle with debt. In 1818, the family sold furniture, Hannah took in sewing, and the Georgia property was sacrificed for taxes (although Isaac later insisted that a fraud had been committed). An agricultural recession and banking panic in 1819 may have made things even worse. Isaac's pursuit of patronage went into high gear about that time. He visited both Madison at Montpelier and Jefferson at Monticello in 1820. Jefferson took Isaac on a tour of his architectural masterpiece, the University of Virginia. In a letter describing that visit, Isaac related a long conversation he had had with Jefferson about slavery. Some of those who sought to abolish it were taking a moral stance to cloak their lust for power, Isaac had argued. This argument was such a departure from the views Isaac had expressed in 1804 it seems as though, after years of playing supplicant to the great man, he was pandering shamelessly to the slaveholding ex-president out of financial need.

Isaac never completely extricated himself from debt. He was employed for a time assisting Thomas Moore in Virginia, but not long after Moore's death in 1822 Isaac, too, began to fail. In February 1824, Mary Briggs wrote to her sister Deborah that "our dear father's health continues so precarious," and "he appears not often to anticipate a return of health, or even a long continuance with us." Anna, who was living in Triadelphia, buried her young child Edward in August. Hannah wrote that she seemed "resigned."

After a long illness characterized by "patience, calmness & affectionate mildness," Isaac succumbed, at age sixty-one, the following January. His youngest child, William Henry, was only nine years old. Before the family recovered from this blow, in late April or early May, Anna's sister Deborah, wife of Joseph Bond, died after giving birth to a baby boy. The family at Sharon took in the infant Isaac Bond, named for his grandfather. They remained on good terms with Joseph Bond even after he remarried and reclaimed the child. Isaac Bond, for his part, retained special ties to his Sandy Spring relatives for the rest of his life.

The death of Isaac Briggs may have brought things to a head for Anna and Joseph. Isaac's legacy consisted mainly of debts, and the land had become so poor in Montgomery County that many families were migrating west. Uncle Samuel Brooke and his family had already packed up and moved to Pennsylvania, on their way eventually to Ohio. In Sandy Spring the monthly meeting minutes record the "division" and "scattering" that Isaac

Briggs had feared. After his father's death Isaac Jr. took over the running of the Sharon farm, but as his mother wrote a year later, "He often suffers great discouragement from not being able to make from the place over our living what would defray some debts due from the estate to persons in the neighbourhood I suppose to the amount of seven or eight hundred dollars."

Whatever objections Anna might have raised to emigration must have collapsed in the year following the deaths of her father and sister. She now had six children. Thomas Moore had been born in 1821, Hannah in 1823, and Deborah Bond in 1825. There were too many mouths to feed, and not enough prosperity in her beloved Sandy Spring. Joseph prevailed.

In May 1826, Joseph and Anna, with their children and a black servant named Henry, started on their long journey to eastern Ohio. Their destination: an established Quaker community in the rolling hills of Columbiana County where Uncle Caleb Bentley had bought property in 1806. Like other pioneers who had preceded them, they would carve a farm out of the forest and make a new home. Anna left with an aching heart and high hopes. She wouldn't see her mother or Sandy Spring again for twenty-one years.

Anna's inability to forget them, and her determination not to be forgotten, sowed a harvest of warm, chatty, garrulous letters as she sought to maintain her ties with the loved ones at Sharon. With thousands of words over the next half-century, she drew vivid pictures of her life and family. "Here I am, in the flesh, your very own Anna," each one essentially said. "I defy you to forget me."

They didn't. And though her letters eventually lay for many years almost forgotten by subsequent generations in the Maryland Historical Society archives, they emerge today as fresh and immediate as the living presence of Anna Briggs Bentley, who wrote, "I just will put down things as they come in my mind, and mix up soap and whitewash and peach orchards, mountain tea and weddings in one mess."

The Sharon family

When Anna began addressing letters to her family at Sharon, the household there included her mother, her unmarried sisters Sarah, Elizabeth, and Margaret—Mary had wedded Richard Brooke in 1824—and her brothers Isaac and William Henry. For a time Sharon also housed the infant

Isaac Bond, her sister Deborah's child. Two servants, an orphan girl and a black boy, took care of the house.

In 1830, Sarah married her cousin, James P. Stabler, and moved out of Sharon. About that time Anna's crippled Aunt Polly Moore, the widow of Thomas, moved in with her sister Hannah Briggs. She spent the last years of her life at Sharon, dying there in 1840 at age eighty-one. That was the same year Sarah, newly widowed and nearly destitute, returned home with her children and spent the rest of her life there. Although the spinster sister, Elizabeth, always made Sharon her home, too, it was Sarah who became Anna's chief correspondent after the death of their mother.

Isaac Briggs Jr. mostly sought his livelihood outside Sandy Spring, as did his younger brother, William Henry Briggs. They both pursued an array of jobs. Isaac practiced botanical medicine for years, then became an itinerant daguerreotypist. William Henry taught school, preached the gospel, and sold patent medicine. Their brother-in-law, James P. Stabler, repaired watches, helped engineer the building of the B&O railroad, practiced botanical medicine, raised silkworms, and served as the postmaster of Sandy Spring. Not one of them ever achieved financial stability.

Anna very likely wrote to members of her family apart from Sharon, but those letters are not extant. They may have been few. She frequently asked for news of other family members, implying that she wasn't in regular correspondence with them. Her most faithful correspondents over fifty years were her mother and her sister Sarah, with whom she felt the deepest bonds. Because they stayed on at Sharon, they also represented home to her.

Notes on the editing of the letters

I first became interested in Anna Briggs Bentley when gathering material for my anthology *The Ohio Frontier*, published in 1996 by the University Press of Kentucky. One of her letters had been transcribed and reprinted with notes by Bayly Ellen Marks of the Maryland Historical Society. Marks noted that there were many more letters by Anna in the Maryland archives.

In 1998, I traveled to Maryland to see them for myself. Despite Anna's crabbed handwriting—and her practice of saving paper by turning the page ninety degrees and writing across earlier lines—her words leaped from the crumbling pages. Anna Bentley had a rare knack for making her daily routine compelling. She extended an invitation back through history into her family circle at Green Hill.

The letters needed to be put in their historical context, of course, but my main interest was to ensure that they could be read and enjoyed much as they were by the people who received them. Anna's originals present a number of obstacles to modern readers outside the Bentley/Briggs family circle, however. The trick was to remove the obstacles without processing the life out of Anna's highly personal style.

For instance, as a child of the eighteenth century, Anna always used the symbol that looks to us like "f" to indicate "ss." She kept this anachronism long after it had disappeared from conventional usage. I make no attempt to reproduce it here.

She usually referred to children and relatives by their initials; after all, her correspondents knew whom she meant. She also wasted little space on punctuation and none on paragraphing. I didn't want anything to diminish the pleasure of reading Anna's stories or descriptions, so I have freely punctuated and paragraphed her letters to suit modern tastes. I have put in commas, periods and quotation marks, and added apostrophes to indicate contractions.

In most cases I have printed people's names in full, even when Anna referred to them in her letters by initial or abbreviation. The exceptions: Her husband usually appears as "Jos" and her cousin Margaret Garrigues as either "Cousin Margaret" or "MEG." "RHG" and "the RHGs" are MEG's husband, Robert H. Garrigues, and the Garrigues household. It was so habitual for Anna to refer to these loved ones in this way that Jos and MEG served as equivalents of their real names. On the other hand, whenever I had to make an informed guess as to whose initials Anna was using, I have added the names in brackets.

Where Anna wrote "to day," I substituted "today," and "another" for her "an other," and so on. I left many of Anna's misspellings unchanged (she never consistently followed the rule of "i before e except after c"), but freely correct many that were clearly a slip of the pen, or would cause the reader to be confused or even to pause in the flow of reading. Suffice it to say she was a worse speller than she appears here, but not by a great deal. I saved brackets for occasions when I had to guess at a word or phrase or when a meaningful word had been left out in the original. Nevertheless, I tried to leave Anna's underlining intact, even when the emphasis may seem odd to our ears.

Let me give an example. Here is the start of her first letter, penned on the road in 1826, as she wrote it:

> Well <u>this</u> day has passed, and my poor tired children and their father all asleep it goes harder with Thomas than any of them he wants to go back to live at uncle Richards" and his <u>modesty</u> is an <u>affliction</u> to him he has been crying ever since we stopped and eat no supper— complains of soreness &c D <u>laughed</u> and slept all the way H is good. G more fatigued than F. he is a <u>valient</u> walker M walked 2 miles.

Here is the same passage as I edited it:

> Well <u>this</u> day has passed, and my poor tired children and their father all asleep. It goes harder with Thomas than any of them. He wants to "go back to live at Uncle Richard's," and his <u>modesty</u> is an <u>affliction</u> to him. He has been crying ever since we stopped, and eat no supper—complains of soreness, &c. Deborah <u>laughed</u> and slept all the way. Hannah is good, Granville more fatigued than Franklin— he is a <u>valient</u> walker. Maria walked 2 miles.

Relationships were complicated in Anna's Quaker community. The large families often intermarried from one generation to the next, to the confusion of genealogists and historians. And they recycled Christian names from family to family and generation to generation. Take Robert Humphrey Garrigues, for instance. He and his wife moved to Ohio in 1828 and lived within a mile of the Bentleys the rest of their lives. They were "Cousin Robert" or "RHG" and "Cousin MEG" to Anna. If the genealogies are correct, they were related in several ways.

MEG was born Margaret E. Thomas, the daughter of Anna's Aunt Deborah Brooke and her husband, Richard Thomas. Robert Garrigues's mother was Isaac Briggs's sister, Hannah (who began life with the same name Anna's mother acquired by marriage). Hannah Briggs Garrigues's sons Robert and William both emigrated to Ohio, Robert to Columbiana County and William to Marlborough (now Marlboro) in Stark County. Their father, William Garrigues, had been married previously. His daughter, Sarah, their half-sister, married Samuel Brooke, Anna's "Uncle Sammy." They too moved to Marlborough, along with most or all of their children, including their five sons, who were active in the abolition movement.

William Garrigues, Robert's older brother, married Margaret Humphreys and had a large family in Marlborough. Three of them eventually married their second cousins, Anna Bentley's children.

Another complicated relationship existed among the Brookes, Garrigueses and Lukens. In 1834, Hannah Luken married Edward Brooke of Marlborough. Edward was the son of Anna's Uncle Samuel Brooke and Sarah (Garrigues) Brooke. Hannah Luken was the daughter of Samuel Luken and his first wife, Hannah Tompkins. Samuel Luken's second wife, Hannah's stepmother, was Anna's Aunt Betsy (Elizabeth) Luken, another sister of Isaac Briggs.

And so it went. I try to clarify these relationships in footnotes. Where I might fail, let me say in defense that even Anna got confused. When a family named Farquhar bought property near her in Ohio, she wrote home asking if they were related to her or not.

Notes to Introduction

1. The name Isaac means "laughter."

ONE

1826–1827

~

Joseph, thirty-seven, Anna, thirty, their children, and a black servant named Henry left Maryland for Ohio in the spring of 1826. The six Bentley children were Granville, twelve, Franklin, ten, Maria, eight, Thomas, four, Hannah, three, and Deborah, an infant. They took turns walking over the mountains, probably along the well-used Cumberland Trail across Maryland and western Pennsylvania with their belongings in an ox-drawn wagon. They headed for Columbiana County, Ohio, a destination of Quakers from the beginning of the century. There the Bentleys looked forward to finding comradeship and assistance as well as religious kinship. One of Hannah's cousins, James Brooke, already lived in the area.

After staying with a Quaker family in the county seat of New Lisbon (now Lisbon), they pushed on to the forested rolling hills of West Township, near the village of Hanover (now Hanoverton), where other Quakers had prepared a temporary cabin for them to live in until a house could be built on their own land a couple of miles away. They shared the cabin with Benjamin and Mary Higgins and their two children,[1] who had traveled with them from Maryland, making thirteen all told in the cramped space. While the men and older boys soon went out all day to ready the land for a first crop, the women stayed at home tending the young children, cooking, and trying to make do without adequate furniture or utensils. The noise and chaos wore on Anna's nerves. Worse, perhaps, she now faced life for the first time without the support of an extended family, the underpinnings of an established social structure, and the ready availability of servants to do the hardest work of the household.

1. Benjamin Higgins married Mary Thomas in 1822. They were Anna's cousins through Mary's family.

∾

On the way to Ohio, 1826
My dear mother,

Well, <u>this</u> day has passed, and my poor tired children and their father all asleep. It goes harder with Thomas than any of them. He wants to "go back to live at Uncle Richard's," and his <u>modesty</u> is an <u>affliction</u> to him. He has been crying ever since we stopped, and eat no supper—complains of soreness &c. Deborah <u>laughed</u> and slept all the way. Hannah is good, Granville more fatigued than Franklin. He is a <u>valient</u> walker. Maria walked 2 miles. I am very tired, have but little milk for Deborah, and my back very weak and aching, but I find so much call for <u>all</u> my energies that my mind cannot <u>dwell</u> on what is <u>behind</u> but has to look forward.

It was so late when we got here, Joseph bespoke coffee and 2 <u>beds</u>. Everything is nice and comfortable. I think <u>the Higgins</u> obliging, kind, proper, and though not of the class I have heretofore associated with, <u>think we shall be gainers by their company.</u> He appears as tender a husband and father as I ever saw, I have <u>no</u> remains of doubt. His oldest child is much smaller than Deborah, 20 months old, his youngest 4 weeks.

When Kirk[1] came to bid us farewell, he went to speak to Thomas but was overcome and wept aloud, which he continued to do, and we left him leaning against a tree. Thomas has cried about it this evening and asked, "Mother, did Kirk cry because he would never see me again?" Poor little one, he is sobbing so in his sleep and has a fever.

I must bid thee farewell. Oh, how often I think of you all. I am, affectionately, Anna

1. This name possibly is Kink, although there was a Kirk family in Sandy Spring. It may refer to the young black servant at Sharon, who took care of the house along with an orphan girl.

∾

A cabin 2 miles from our land
5th mo 22 1826
My beloved friends,

How often do I wish that you could peep in at us and hear the sound of cheerful voices issuing from our <u>lowly cabin</u>? I have not yet sufficient leisure to tell you <u>how</u> we got here, but it was without accident, though we suffered great fatigue and the children were much disordered with the limestone water and had colds, and my back suffered much and still does. We got to Lisbon on last 4th day, slept 5th day with Ben Hanna.[1] They are very clever and have all the comforts and the elegancies anybody need wish. We went to the cabinet makers and got some furniture: a <u>very</u> large walnut dining table (the handsomest I ever saw; I could not tell it from mahogany) for 6 dollars, a case of drawers as large as Aunt D Thomas's (more modern in appearance) made of walnut for $10, a larger dough trough (walnut) $2 1/2, a walnut cradle, $4 for bedsteads and truckle bedstead. I was really astonished to find so much nice walnut and cherry furniture and so much cheaper than with you. They find walnut and cherry cheaper than pine, and I don't see any cabin, however poor its outside, but has its own walnut or cherry tables.

We went to the chair maker's and to our great surprise found him a very genteel-looking fellow: Joseph Gillingham, brother to John.[2] We got 6 brown chairs intending to get splay-bottomed ones, which we can for 25 cents. We left all to be sent for when our house is finished, which will be a large commodious log house.

On 6th day we arrived at Levi Miller's,[3] found he had a house for us to come in on his farm 1/4 of a mile from his own house. We dined there and they said so much about the house, and the children, Granville and Franklin, and Henry, who had been to see it, gave such an account, that I dreaded to look up when we came to it as we are obliged to take Benjamin Higgins's family till they can put up a cabin on their land.

6th mo 4th day night: This is the first leisure time I have had, where I have not been too tired to sit up to write. I will go on with a description of our house and affairs. It stands on the brow of a beautiful hill at the foot of which the Sandy River winds its way through a meadow of the richest [?], a mill and 2 dwelling houses, one within sight and hearing. . . . The spring down a hill about 30 yds from the door as pure and cold as can be. It is nicely walled round with brick. A large springhouse, also a small garden of rich black mold the boys have worked up and planted for me. A building stands in the yard, once a meat house, we use as a stone house cellar.

And now for the house. It is a cabin with 1 only room to it. Though the door is not too low for <u>Granville's high head</u>, it has 2 12–light windows, board floor, brick hearth, and has been whitewashed. It is as long nearly as the room at Hebron.[4] There is a kind of a loft with no window that I have lines hung to hold the clothing that I have no room for downstairs. All our trunks, boxes, and beds are piled one on the other round the room. I have hung a curtain for a partition as Benjamin and his wife are still here, and it is likely will be for 2 or 3 weeks to come.

I will give an inventory of our household and kitchen furniture: 1 frying pan, 2 skillets, 1 Dutch oven of Cousin Mary, a brass kettle, 2 teakettles, gridiron, ladle and flesh fork, coffee mill, 2 small tin buckets with covers and 2 tin buckets that hold 1 gallon, 1 iron-bound bucket for water, 1 small tub (lent), 1 larger iron sugar kettle (lent), a few cups and saucers and bowls and plates, and a few other things I brought along constitute all the conveniences both familys have to cook with or in. I forgot the pothooks (we brought them). The little chair and crickets and one stool are all the seats we have except trunks and boxes. We have brought in a sugar trough for a cradle. We have a large common table with leaves and 2 drawers, finished, which we have not got home yet. We have done without since we came. I don't speak of our inconveniences to complain. It is wholly because the men have been too busy to take time to go after the things that can all be had for much less than we sold ours for at the sale.

We are sometimes visited by a swarm of musquitos, and the fly that is so troublesome to horses in our woods often draws the blood from my sweet good Deborah. She would sit on the floor and play happily and eat bread, meat, and potatoes all day. I often take her up out of pity. Of all good babys she is one of the best. I have left off her caps, that it may not add to the washing which I am compelled to undertake. Thomas is very hard of hearing and is very troublesome teasing the children and is not so willing to rough it as the others.

Cousin Mary's babe is quiet, but the oldest (Caroline) is troublesome. She is 23 months old, weighs 16 lbs and has never been used to being with other children, and Thomas and Henry, finding her easily teased, delight in making her squall, so we almost always have music; but no shade of unpleasantness has ever arisen between the parents on the children's account. Cousin Mary and Benjamin try all they can to lighten the trouble their being here unavoidably occasions, and I do strive after resignation, as I know if we can only get through this summer the worst will be over. I will not deny that I do find it hard to do for all with so few conveniences and no help, but I have all reason to expect better times soon.

The men and boys all went immediately to grubbing and clearing a place for the house, for which the logs are all ready, and they have 2 or 3 acres grubbed and are clearing off the brush, so they could not take the time to go out to get pots, pans, chairs, &c, but will in a day or 2. Joseph finds plenty of sugar trees on our land for a sugar camp; the hop vine, the black currant and gooseberry in abundance grow wild. . . .

The <u>pains</u> I used to feel all center in my back and sometimes I am almost ready to give out. Not having a seat with a back to it makes it worse, but my appetite is very good and I sleep so sound that I have waked several times and found how little Deborah had cried herself sick almost. . . .

Oh, that wearisome, trying journey—it would be <u>no</u> hardship without little children, but we were so crowded and overloaded. I had thought I should have written such <u>pretty letters</u> to you as I came along, but I little knew how harassed the mind would feel and wearied the body when each day's travel was ended and after much bustle the supper was over and the poor children put to bed.

The neighbors are very kind and sociable. Many have called to see us and proffered kindnesses. A son of Levi Miller, Maurice Miller, is our nearest neighbor. His wife, Ann, came this day week to see us. She appears to be a lovely woman. She has two children, Oliver and <u>little Isaac</u>. They have supplied us with milk ever since we came.[5]

A very clever old man formerly of Pennsylvania, Seth Hoopes, lives at Levi Miller's. He knew all Father's family and many of our relations in Philadelphia. He has taken a great liking to Joseph. Another neighbour spent most of this afternoon here, James Snode; he is an intelligent man, quite agreeable. Levi Miller spent an hour on trees. Also Maurice Miller, our nearest neighbour, came over with a bucket of milk in his hand. They press us to come and see them, but I think my first outing must be to meeting. . . .

For the last week we have had a good deal of rain in showers accompanied with thunder every day and all day. I never saw more dreadful looking clouds. They seemed to come from every quarter and meet overhead, descending in torrents. I had to clamber up in the loft and take the clothes off the lines and find a <u>dry</u> corner to pile them. The men and boys were away. At first I felt much alarm, but some reflection made me calm; but it was less serious than the appearance seemed to indicate.

3rd day night. Jos has bought a nice new tub. Maria is very useful to me. She washed some of Deborah's clothes very well, minds Deborah and brings nearly all the water, washes all the dishes, &c. Thomas's hearing is <u>much</u> worse than I ever knew it. He has a cold, but I am very uneasy.

One of Levi Miller's daughters will wash for me this week; they did last week. At 25 the men and boys make their clothes very dirty. I wish they had waited till we got here, for shirts' cotton takes dirt so easy, and nice, wide, fine flax linnen can be got here for 25 [cents], white and thick, the yellow striped for pantaloons the same.

6th day night. Well, the work begins to go lighter with me. Maria is very useful. She irons the clothes as well as anybody. . . . I have made a pair of trousers for Henry this week. Jos and Henry are so good in helping me . . . fry meat, lift oven lids, pare potatoes, fill the kettle, and sometimes make tea or coffee. Henry is more obliging than ever and entirely sober at all times. He is so fond of the children and us. Granville and he slept in the waggon.

I could fill another sheet, but I have no time to write but at night and after a hard day's work, without a chair to rest my back upon. . . . How anxiously I look fourward to the fall in expectation of my dear brother's visit. I cannot yet say when it is probable our own house will be done, but they are hard at work. Joseph's hands are sorely blistered, but he is resolute. We have plenty of good provisions and excellent appetites and all in good spirits. . . .

They are all very kind and I do not regard the difference in customs, but there is a blank, a void, as yet. Mary is a clever little woman in her own way, but I cannot feel any nearness or intimacy with her. They are, if I must speak the truth, much in our way and might, if she would, be less so—that is, if they were as ready to help as to be helped. That is in confidence. . . . I pity them but think they might try to get a small cabin put up quick to themselves.

Please send letters to New Garden, Columbiana County, and fill all the paper and say all you can of all I love. Oh, can it be that I am so far from you? I think of it sometimes and fall to wondering how I ever could have consented to it, but still as yet I never have repented it. . . .

I am your own affectionate Anna

1. Benjamin Hanna (1779–1853), the grandfather of Ohio businessman and politician Marcus Hanna, came to Columbiana County with his Quaker family in 1801. He was president of the Sandy & Beaver Canal Company for twenty-five years.
2. Joseph Gillingham, a Windsor chair maker, had a shop on East Washington Street in New Lisbon. He possibly came from a well-known Philadelphia family of furniture makers. The John Gillingham Anna refers to was an acquaintance and fellow Quaker from Sandy Spring Monthly Meeting in Maryland.
3. Levi Miller (1774–1838) came to Ohio in 1810. His first wife, Deborah Morris Miller, having died in 1816, he married Ann Hole three years later. In 1832, he built near Hanover the first fulling mill and sawmill in the area to be run by steam power.
4. This was property left to Hannah and Isaac Briggs by Hannah's father, Roger Brooke. Later, Hannah's daughter Margaret Briggs Farquhar and her husband owned most of the land and built a house they called The Cedars.

5. Morris (or Maurice) Miller (1799–1883), Levi's son, and his wife, the former Ann Votaw, were Pennsylvania Quakers. Over the years they had a large family, including the two oldest mentioned here. Anna underlined Isaac's name to call attention to the fact that it is the same as her father's, her brother's, and little Isaac Bond's.

∾

6th mo 14th 1826
4th day
My beloved friends,

Having a <u>few moments</u> of leisure, <u>I have stolen from the children</u> to the only <u>private</u> place I can find suitable for the purpose of beginning another letter to you (the waggon, which yet stands near the yard gate and is Henry and Granville's lodging room), and so many things arise in my mind to say to thee I know not what to begin with. The men and boys leave at daybreak and return at sundown. . . . They are engaged in felling, grubbing, mauling, and burning and expect <u>very</u> shortly to have 3 or 4 acres fenced in and planted in potatoes, turnips, &c. They have men getting shingles, and I hope by fall we shall be fixed comfortably. They have hived a fine swarm of bees in the woods.

   Joseph went to work a <u>little</u> on 3rd day and Granville staid to wait on me as on that day <u>I made my first attempt at the washtub.</u> Some of their clothing was <u>literally black</u>. I had no soft soap or lye, my only stool was too low, but I stuck to it resolutely till I got all laid in the last rinsing water. . . . How my back felt (and still does) <u>I need not tell you.</u> I did say once, "Oh, how glad I am Mother cannot know how I feel just at this moment". . . .

   Well, Maria had made a pone, Granville had baked it and made coffee and brought milk from neighbors when Jos came home. He threw down his load of wood, and when he looked at my full tubs and pale face covered with a cold sweat he began to <u>scold</u> me for undertaking all at once. "It is just like thee overdoing the matter and then good for nothing." He and Henry scoured their hands and set the table, took up the pone, helped the children, &c. Supper over, Henry and Granville went home (as they call it) to the waggon. Jos fed Deborah, helped Maria clean the table, <u>spread the beds,</u> and <u>I was too tired to sleep for a long</u> time.

   Yesterday I got the clothes [?] in the morning, got dinner, scoured some things, and sat down, saying I was too tired to make rolls which I had intended for supper.

"Let me, Mother," said Maria. "I can, and Grandmother would be so pleased."

Well, she scoured her hands, got the flour and materials, and with my directions made up and worked 4 ovens full. She tended them and they rose beautifully. I baked them for supper. While they were getting light, she folded all the clothes, which I sprinkled for her. . . . Her father praised the rolls and said, "Well, Maria, for every time thee does all the ironing thyself I will give thee a fine penny bit."

"Well, wake me soon, Father, and I will tomorrow."

And this morning the first sight I saw when I woke and turned over was her standing at the table ironing her father's shirt. . . . We soon eat, she cleaned up the table, and she actually finished entirely herself—and as well as I could have done it—every piece of a large washing by 12 o'clock. I did not know how much she was capable of doing, and little Deborah cries after her and is very fond of her.

But I must not hide her faults. She teases the younger children too much. She sometimes pouts very ugly at me, though I think not so much as she did, and I hope my next letter may inform you she is striving to conquer the habit. I know you love her and will be rejoiced if I can give a good account of her. She is also in the habit of speaking too cross to her brother and sister.

Granville is the same affectionate dear child he always was, and Franklin the wild one, plagues me often. Thomas is of an age to give much trouble. He [is] so fond of teasing he makes Hannah and Caroline twice the trouble they would be, and, poor fellow, he is very hard of hearing—indeed, more so than I ever saw him in Montgomery [County]. Deborah is so good and sweet. . . . Oh, dear Elizabeth, I wish thou most here this minute, for there are 2 pretty doves and a blackbird picking up the corn I am throwing them from the waggon, and they are looking in my face all the time. The birds are very sociable here. Every day the doves come to the door to gather our crumbs, and the red-winged blackbirds walk about like chickens. And the sweet little snakes. Thomas trod on one yesterday coming from the spring and says it felt soft and cold to his foot, and he ran one way and the snake the other.

I enquired of Levi Miller's daughter, Mary, what esteem I Lambourne[1] was held in here. "Oh, dear, he has been very troublesome. He has such a memory that he gets other people's sermons by heart and did try to preach, but they would not let him. He has attempted it several times, and they have had to lead him out of meeting."

The neighbors are all very friendly and I am affraid will think me

unsociable, but I cannot visit till <u>my family is smaller</u>. I could bear
patiently every other inconvenience I am subjected to if I had a little
more room and stillness, and would be <u>to myself like</u>. I never shall feel at
home till then. We have got our own common table, and I have
borrowed a chair. We have bought several hams and shoulders of
excellent bacon (as good as Sharon or Falling Green) for 4 cents per lb,
butter and lard 6 1/4. We can get a fresh cow in calf for 8 dollars, a first-
rate one for 10—.

I now look forward to receiving letters from you as one of the
highest pleasures I shall ever enjoy in this world, and I have not heard
one word since I left you. Don't let any trifle prevent your writing.
Sometimes perhaps dear Cousin JPS[2] may, out of the compassionate
feelings of his own heart, think it worthwhile [to] contribute his share
towards sweetening a bitter cup by writing to me. I could then hear from
you all; and he writes with so much ease to himself. . . .

Did I ever tell you that we staid a day and night at Cousin Samuel
Thomas's in Cumberland, were treated with the most affectionate
kindness by all the family? He found us out when we first arrived and
stuck by us till we left it. Thomas was so ill with a cold we had to lay by a
day. His wife shows a countenance familiar with affliction but shows the
dignity of a mind struggling for resignation and consoling itself with its
own good intentions. . . .

I must go and get supper. I have buiscuits to bake.

6th day night. This morning my awakening eyes were delighted with
the view of my dear mother's handwriting on your letter. I sat up in the
bed and read it with many tears. I had not missed any of the articles left
except the meat, and as to the nightcap felt quite indifferent about it.
Only I wished it had been a better one since I did leave it. You must try
to tell me <u>all you can</u> when you write of yourselves, of other dear friends,
too, that here in our Cabin I may have you brought before me and for a
little moment forget the mountains, the rivers, the long road that lies
between us. . . .

Cousin Mary took [Caroline] and spent this afternoon at Levi
Miller's. . . . I like them [the Higginses] very much. He is a most
indulgent, kind husband and a very fond father. We have lived in the
strictest harmony, and I can make allowances for want of thought in
helping as they are young, has children—one troublesome to him—and
she, as well as myself, has been used to servants to put things in order
and clean up after.

Well, Jos is grumbling about the candle, and as he goes to Lisbon

early in the morning, this must be finished now. . . . Farewell, all of you.
Oh, farewell. Your own Anna Bentley
[P.S.] My dearest love to you all. JEB

1. Israel Lambourne (1807–1891) was from the Quaker Lambourne (or Lamborn) family
of Chester County, Pennsylvania, some of whom eventually emigrated to Columbiana County
in the late 1830s. Levi Lamborn, of the next generation, was one of the founders of Alliance, Ohio, a well-known public speaker, politician, and abolitionist, and the editor of
Alliance's first newspaper, the *Ledger*.
2. James P. Stabler, a cousin who later became Anna's brother-in-law.

~

The Cabin
6th mo 20th 1826
3rd day night
My beloved friends,

Indisposition obliges me to be up while all the rest are fast locked in the
arms of sleep. My dear little Deborah and self have something of
dysentery. She don't appear to suffer much pain as yet but is as good and
playful almost as usual. I shall have the red mixture prepared tomorrow. I
have suffered much pain today and sickness, but a dose of Epsom [salts]
has been some relief to me. No wonder that at this time my thoughts
should dwell on you, so long my dependence, my comforters in sickness
or affliction.

I must tell you of my dear Granville. I had prepared this morning for
washing, and feeling weak, only put out a change for all, round 20 pieces
in all. He insisted on beginning it. And he actually accomplished the
whole as well as I could have done it, with nothing but my directions for
assistance. He seems to feel much for me and is a great comfort. Maria
also is a great help, and but for the dreadful propensity to tease and
domineer over the younger ones, I should be able to tell you she also was
a great comfort. (Please give a word of advice when you write. They every
day almost say, "Wouldn't it please Grandmother to see me doing this?"
and "What would Grandmother say if she saw thee being so bad? How
sorry it would make her.") Thomas often says, "Mother, oh how I do
want to see my Aunt Mary and Uncle Richard. I wish they would of let
me stay. Mother, can't I never get there any more?"

Well, as I did not commence this immediately after sending my last,
I must go back a little. Last 4th and 5th day I accomplished a very large
washing, was so outdone that I could scarcely hold out to finish, which I
did about 1 o'clock. A dark awful-looking cloud had been rising

sometime before I finished, which did not strengthen me in the least. The storm came on with a tremendous roaring. A young married man, Evan Cooper, was ploughing near and ran in. (He had been here before.) For a moment I felt joyful to see him but soon found I was fainting, which I did to the great alarm of all of them. He held me on my chair with one arm and Cousin Mary's baby with his other. She and Granville were looking for camphor. Cousin Mary got part way to me with a bottel of snuff, which she mistook for it. Granville ran with another. It was snuff too. At last it was found and my face bathed. When I came to I felt comical to find a stranger supporting me and exclaiming (as my eyes opened), "My dear creature, don't be alarmed. The worst is over." I could scarcely hear him for the hail and wind. Dear Cousin Mary and the children were so scared at me they heeded not the storm. I had some symptoms of convulsions or maybe <u>hysteric spasms</u>, and my right arm became numbed and useless for about 15 minutes. They rubbed it with vinegar and camphor. The storm was soon over and was not as bad as I expected, but I had heard such dreadful accounts of the hurricanes here that I feel more dread than I <u>used</u> to even.

7th mo, 9th; 1st day. Well, this is the first leisure I have had when I have not felt too weary to collect my thoughts to write, and I am affraid I never shall be able to tell you all that would interest you except some little <u>aches</u> relieved by salt and water and 2 or 3 doses of salts divided amongst us. We enjoy good health and from great to small the most wonderful appetites and could all sleep, I beleive, on the hard floor if it was not for fear of snakes and the <u>largest spiders I ever beheld</u>. Though we have killed 4 snakes near the door, none have come in, and they would not have injured us if they had. But they brought a rattlesnake home with them from the woods, which was within a few feet of one of the workmen when its rattle gave notice of its <u>terrific presence</u>. He killed it with his axe. It was a young one, a yd long with but 4 rattles.

On the 5th of this month Benjamin Higgins and family left us. He has purchased a peice of land within 3 miles of us and given up his first plan of building on ours after clearing 2 acres and getting logs and shingles all ready for a house. We all concurred with him in thinking it best, when this chance offered, to make a purchase before his money was all spent. He got 82 acres for 102 dollars and has gone to live with a family 1/2 a mile from the spot he will build on it. Felt sorrowful to part with them after being together so long. I love them. They are amiable. He is a very kind husband, and there never was the least unpleasantness between us, though their Caroline was very fretful and the most mischiefous little creature I ever saw. And their removal gives me a chance to arrange my furniture a little and keep things a little in order, for I never saw as much and as many crowded in as small a space as was here for awhile.

I begin to be naturalized to this cabin now that I can turn myself around in it. It looks right comfortable. The roof juts over in front and a platform of hewn boards forms a kind of porch. The door is in the width of the house, the front window on the right hand. It looks [she draws a picture of it]. Ain't it a pretty little house?

Now, for its inside. On the right hand of the door as you enter stands a large poplar dining table. Under the window on the left, 8 shelves or dressers (my only cupboard). The lower shelf, broad and low, holds the bucket of water, tea board, waiters, some pans, & some handsome Liverpool teapots. Sugar dis[h], cream pot, plates, &c, in addition to what I brought, sit on the other shelves. The fireplace is on the left of the door (placed wrong in the picture), the size of the kitchen one at Sharon. A recession each side of the wall of it holds my flatirons, coffee mill, box, and pot. Little nails drove to one side hold the gridiron and pothooks and sometimes the dishcloth when I have not got it under my arm, as I often do by mistake when I am betried and don't know what I am about. The right hand of the fireplace, the ladder stands.

Now we have got to the back of the house. The window is not right in the middle but nearer the fireplace, has a shelf over it filled with books. Nearly under it a very nice walnut dough trough which we eat off. It holds our cold victuals. And in the corner parallel with it a handsome low post bedstead, under it the nicest trundle bed that I ever saw anywhere—has head, foot, and side boards and runs on wheels. A large trunk stands at the head and next a very large case of drawers, 6 very handsome brown chairs, and an elegant armed rocking chair with a high back. I have swung a pole across the wall at the back of the house and there display pantaloons, petticoats, frocks, waistcoats, and divers other clothing. I have the comfit down and the floor clean and white. It is a very large brick hearth.

Oh, I forgot the cradle. It is a beautiful walnut one, varnished, cost 2 dollars.

I have been to meeting twice. It is quite a large meeting. The young people with not any exception are plain, and many of them neat—though I saw no black bonnets amongst them—and some of the largest old women I ever saw. We have no minister. Many came forward to speak to the stranger. They looked kind and I felt as if some pitied me to be there a stranger and no relative near me. I looked from one face to another to see if I could trace anything there that would feel like mother to me if I was sick or in affliction, and at last I turned to Ann Miller (Levi's wife), a dear, kind, valuable woman.

When coming home I found Henry had dinner ready. I took Maria, Franklin, and Deborah and went soon after to Levi Miller's and spent the afternoon agreeably. There are 3 girls grown, 3 sons—young men, 1 of them married to a fine woman who has been twice here. Ann is her name, Maurice is her husband. Robert is a widower and lost his wife in this house 14 months ago, left an infant 10 days old which followed her in a week, and Isaac. They have 5 more boys and girls. This [Ann Hole Miller] is a second wife to whom he has been married 8 years. She never had any children but is an excellent stepmother. I am thus particular in describing them because they feel nearer and more like relatives than any others, though all are kind and seem anxious to do us favours. They have such a cordial, affectionate way of doing a kindness or giving advise and it seems to come from the heart, without guile. They seem to stand high in the esteem of friends. Both he and his wife sit the second in the gallery. They sent me a nice peice of veal today, and Levi took tea with us.

Jos and he have been to look at the land Uncle Sammy Brooke wants. Jos likes it better than any he has seen since we came. The improvements are considerable, enough cleared in cultivation to support a large family. An orchard, sugar trees, and a great many large walnut trees, a great deal of fine meadow land. But I expect Jos will write to Uncle immediately. I hope no one will discourage him from coming. Oh, how I wish some more of you were here. The people are so kind & hospitable, so much more so to strangers than with you, so much less pride, though all I have seen are remarkable for neatness and cleanliness.

Our nearest neighbor, Samuel Holland, formerly of Philadelphia, often comes over. His wife is a very fine woman. They were once wealthy, but misfortune drove them to the West. They have been very pressing for me to come over. They have had the advantage of a good education. Susan, their daughter, is a very fine, neat girl, has been over once. They give us a bucket of rich milk every evening and press me to send my cream pot.

4th day night. Well, yesterday I undertook the washing. I had to bathe my face in vinegar and water after I got all the white clothes hung out and a pair of coarse linnen trowsers, the towels, tea cloths, &c boil'd, when I was so outdone I was obliged to throw them in the tub and go to bed. . . . [The letter ends here. On the side of page 1 Anna wrote, "One little sheet of paper won't pay for this"]

~

7th mo 20th 1826
My dear friends,

Well, when I was just thinking of Cousin BM and TSS[1] and concluding they had certainly passed us by, I heard the sound of thier carriage last 5th day morning, 8 o'clock AM. I cannot express the joy I felt. They appeared equally pleased with our beautiful situation on the hill. I met them without even thinking of the <u>fuss</u> I should once have thought it necessary to make with such a visitor as Cousin BM. (Thomas I was better acquainted with.) I never thought of being flustered, but told them they looked more <u>beautiful</u> to me than they had ever done before. Thomas and I had an abundance of chat, and Benjamin would sit and smile <u>so</u> sweetly to hear our tongues run. I, or we, entertained them as well as we knew how, and they seemed pleased with all.

They will tell you the most, I expect, but they will not tell you of thier generosity. Thomas came to me in the morning and said, "Now, Cousin Anna, I am going to take a liberty with thee as if thee was my own sister, and thee won't be offended. Here is a pair of Benjamin's pantaloons (fine cassemere). They are getting a little thin at the knees and will be of no use to him. We both wish thee to accept of them for Granville." I did accept them. They are an exellent pair and just fit him. He gave me a vial of Ess[ence] of lemon, one of opedeldoc (which to smell of is the very best thing for the headache I ever tried), and the most beautiful new brown silk handkerchief I ever saw, and neck ribbons for the boys, several yds braid, a paper of needles. He also left his (something to wear round the neck), which Joseph will prefer <u>wearing</u> to saving for an opportunity to return him. (Tell him so.) Cousin Benjamin called me to one side just before he started and gave me a dollar 6 1/4 cent to divide amongst the 4 younger children. He had given Granville and Franklin 50 cents each. "And here is a little present I wish thee to accept." It was 5 dollars. They also inquired where anything <u>sent to us</u> would be most convenient to get, from Salem or Lisbon.

This generous supply came at a more seasonable time than they were aware of, for they did not know that the coffee they praised so was all I had. . . . They left us on 6th day morning. . . . They both expressed a strong wish to settle here, but Benjamin feared his wife would never consent. Cousin Thomas thought you could do much better here than where you are. There is an elegant farm near Lisbon for sale at 15 or 16 hundred dollars. Cousin Benjamin has the disposal of it. He often repeated, "I don't know any person whose situation in all respects would be so much bettered by a removal here as Uncle Sammy Brooke's.[2] They could get along with so much more ease than they do."

I would have written by them, but thier stay was so short and I had written so lately. . . . Your letters were all acceptable. I must notice more particularly Sister Elizabeth's. What makes she so <u>poison</u> diffident of her own powers? What dost thou think would interest me in a letter? <u>Big words and fine sentiments</u>? No. If thou wilt only delineate thy own affectionate feelings and just plain matter-of-fact occurences, and not take up time in telling fibs about thy "higher insignificance," &c, thee could interest me as much as any one of them and maybe improve thyself. I wish they would send thee to <u>me</u>. Would thee come?

7th mo 23rd. Yesterday I went home from meeting with Susan. I staid all night and spent the day. I had intended [coming] home in the morning, but rain prevented. About 4 Granville came for me, told me Deborah had been very sick in the night but seemed right smart now. My uneasiness was so great as to produce a <u>violent pain in my back</u>. I hurried off. Susan accompanied me. Half way my pain became very severe accompanied with symptoms of dysentery. When I arrived at home I found my sweet babe asleep, her countenance pale and ghastly, and was informed that she had in the night a long violent convulsion fit attended with high fever. They were much alarmed. The fever at last yielded to bathing in warm water and essence of peppermint. We think she has worms, and one of her stomach teethe is coming through. She has been very languid today, and I am now (near 1 o'clock) watching with painful anxiety her restless slumbers. Joseph and Granville, Seth and Nancy [Hoopes] sat up all last night and are now all asleep. Oh, that you were near. This dear babe is so engaging, so dear to me. Oh, if I should lose her, how could I bear it? She has no fever but is quite cool.

8th mo 4th. My dear child seems now restored to health, has had no return of convulsions, has had the dysentery, but the bene cured her as well as myself.[3] Nancy has been ill for a week past with errisypelas in her ankle and face and head. She is now much better. Seth brought Dr Robertson, a very handsome, genteel-looking young married man, about the same size and dresses like Dr Palmer. They say he is very skilfull.[4]

I have had my <u>hands full this week: poultices to make, 2 a day,</u> <u>medicine every hour, and many other attentions, and to cook for</u> <u>harvesters.</u> Jos is making the hay in McNeely's meadow next [to] the road, Isaac, a very heavy crop. They are hauling it home. I had thier dinners—that is, 5 of them—to cook and send off by 11 o'clock and to get all Nancy's meals separate from the rest <u>for she craves something better</u>.

But *Alice Jackson is the kindest creature. She came twice and insisted on taking flour home and made and baked bread for me, 3 loaves each time. She came over today, washed a large washing, then scoured both rooms and the steps and passage and dressers. She got done at 4—when I looked out and saw dear Sarah Holland and Susan coming.

After we had chatted a while, Sarah expressed a wish to look about at the garden and other improvements. Alice said to me, "Well, go out with her and I will attend to all in the house." We were not gone long, but when we came in we found an exellent supper waiting on the table that Susan and Alice had prepared. Sarah made a request of me which she ended with, "Now, my dear, if there is any feeling of pleasantness or sweetness in complying, do it, but not without." It was that I would try to get thee to procure for her a <u>large plain colored</u> cotton shawl—not a high-priced one—for she could not anywhere here procure one. She is a very large woman. If thou could get one in Baltimore and keep it to send by the next opportunity, no matter where thee is, and let me settle with thee, how obliged I would be. She said if I would make the request she would with her own wool mix and have spun stocking yarn enough for my family this winter, besides paying for the shawl when it comes. I believe I will make an end of this and begin another as I just hear of a private opportunity.

You[r] affectionate A

*Please, dear Isaac, don't mention her name with ridicule in any other letter to Sally, for I have heard her repeat thy message before several and have felt much uneasiness for fear she would get to hear it, and though rather unpolished, has proved a real friend in need to me.

1. Benjamin Moore and Thomas S. Stabler, who had traveled out to Ohio in June.
2. Hannah Brooke Briggs's brother, who was married to Sarah Garrigues.
3. Bene (or benne) seed is sesame seed. Erisypelas, or St. Anthony's Fire, was a streptococcal infection characterized by red, itchy, burning skin and blotches, with fever and delirium. It generally broke out from a wound, insect bite or other lesion. Before antibiotics were discovered, it was sometimes fatal.
4. "The best known man in the county," according to one local history James R. Robertson served Hanover as doctor for forty-five years from 1823. Along with many of his Quaker neighbors, the Presbyterian doctor was also active in the Underground Railroad.

[To Isaac Briggs]
The Cabin 7th mo 30th 1826
First day night, 12 o'clock

Dear Brother <u>Isaac's</u> letter (as he occupied the most of it) came to hand
this morning and was cordially welcomed by us all. Thy account of your
difficulties is nothing new to me. It is a subject long dwelt on with
painful anxiety by me, and I also <u>think</u> I can see how greatly your
situation might be bettered by a removal here, but notwithstanding this I
feel a check on my mind against urging you to move without light. I
would with that the pillar of fire might guide you through this
wilderness, and then hard things would be made easy. But do not be
rash. . . . As to what would be the most profitable thing to bring here for
sale, we think leather would be (sole leather) or 40 or 50 dollars laid out
here in linnen that would cost 25 cents would with you bring 45 cents
per yd readily. Jos says if he ever takes any produce there, it will be
linnen, he thinks. A tanner might make a fortune here in a little time,
leather being the scarcest and leaving the highest price of any article we
have. . . .

    This afternoon for the first time I took a walk with Jos to our land. I
cannot describe my feelings as I sat on a log and cast my eyes around on
the beautiful hills, the majestic Oaks, and the traces of labour arround
me. A <u>feeling of thankfulness arose in my heart</u> as I thought, here <u>is</u> my
home, <u>here is an inheritance for my children</u> where they <u>may</u> earn their
bread if it <u>is</u> by the sweat of their brow.

    They have cleared 5 or 6 acres. It is a fine piece of land. There is 80
acres adjoining it for sale, real shell bark trees and a handsome tree with
broad leaves called linn [linden] trees grow on ours.

    1st day. Well, a week has passed since I commenced this. <u>I find but
little leisure for writing, and the children's noise in the daytime prevents
me when I might steal a few minutes.</u> I have made a pr of trousers for Jos
and Granville and felt as tired of sitting as I used to be to run about. It
has become comparitively easy to me (all but washing) to do the work.
<u>My back is getting stronger</u>, my health excellent, my appetite invariably
good for anything almost. Toil gives the best relish to a frugal repast. Our
garden affords us as yet no vegetables, but then our neighbours send us
cucumbers, beans, potatoes in <u>abundance</u>, and I make an <u>abundance</u> of
nice puddings and pies. We have a cow that supplies us with excellent
milk, and a capital spring house keeps it cool.

    The children all are as hearty as they can be. Maria never complains now except when she gets lazy and wants an excuse to get hold of a book. Dr scarcely gets a living here. I feel confident if Elizabeth could with suitable company be got here she would become strong and healthy, and Oh, how rejoiced her poor sister would be to have her here. But Bro Iky, I don't advise <u>compulsion</u>.

Yesterday I had a visit from dear Sarah Holland. There is a something in her that powerfully draws my affections. She is the one that in this neighbourhood by the old and young is looked up to in sickness and in sorrow—as our dear Cousin D Stabler,[1] a mother in Israel. She seems to feel a great interest for us, says they will assist me in the great undertaking of cooking for the raisers—30 or 40, it is probable, dinner and supper. It will be in the course of 3 or 4 weeks at furthest. The people here have a great many different kinds of preserves, puddings, pies, pickles, &c and always have some on a tea table. They are all Pennsylvanians or Virginians and have their manners.

Levi Miller's daughter, Hannah, and neice, Prudence Gammel, spent an afternoon and evening here last week. Dear Levi comes in every few days with the affectionate freedom of a relative. He said the other day, "Anna, there is one thing I have had on my mind to advise thee against in writing to thy friends, not to be too extravagant in praise or urgent in thy entreaties for them to come, so that if they should see right to come (at which I should rejoice) they might be disappointed and consequently disatisfied." I answered, "I think I have always been sufficiently on my guard. I feel a check against using any persuasion. I wish to try and prove more before I would advise my dear mother to do so, and I believe when it is right she will give up."

I was talking with him and several others about what would be the most profitable commodity for Bro Isaac to bring out. All said Leather. Samuel Holland says, "Tanning is certainly without exception far the most profitable trade in this country. Bro Jos, we have an exelent situation for a tan yard on our land."

A neighbour called a few days since and said Cousin James Brooke sent his love to us and said he had not been able to travel for some time but was mending, and as soon as he could, would come and see us, and begged we would try to come and see them. He owns a large, rich farm 15 miles from here and lives in plentiful ease. . . .[2]

They have a custom here in harvest or other busy times to collect as many neighbours as they can, and they will pay back in work. Joseph and Henry have been out several days and will get in return help from one of the finest hands in the county. They all seem bent on having Jos for a schoolmaster this winter. Many think we could get all our provisions and a great deal of work on the land, as they prefer that to paying money.

I feel so anxious to hear from Uncle Sammy Brooke. There could not be a better time for moving than now, provisions are so cheap. Yesterday I baked in the Dutch 6 bread puddings, 4 pies, 2 loaves of bread, 3 spiders full of biscuits, pared and cut and stewed apples, got supper for company, entertained here, too, and a great many other things. "Wasn't I smart?"

Oh, the people here make pies out of elderberries (of which there are immense quantities). They mostly add a few dried currants and a little vinegar and very little sugar, and they make very good pies. I have tried them. Well, farewell. It is late and I must go to bed.

1st day morning. I find there is a chance to send this to the post office presently, and though I have not said half yet, I must leave the rest for another letter. We are all enjoying excellent health and have no time to spare for desponding, if there was any cause. The separation from you is now my heaviest affliction, for there is a certain something in our air and <u>exercise</u> that has wonderfully braced up my spirits as well as body.

Ann Miller (Maurice's wife) with her two sweet little children spent her 6th day afternoon here. She is a lovely woman 1 year younger than I. After a day's work <u>now</u>, when I am fatigued and stiff in every limb, I do not feel as I used to do, but I often sit down at night and while all are sleeping around me cast my eyes around this humble cabin with an overflowing heart filled with love, first to Him who has led us through many difficulties, and then spreading towards those who surround me and those dear, dear far distant friends. Oh, Lord bless them and guide them and comfort them in all their trials. My tears are flowing now, but they are not tears of sorrow.

Jos is hurrying me. We all anxiously look forward to Bro Isaac's visit and have a strong wish for him to come in some way that he could bring a few things for us. I wish he would write often. Do, please, be particular in telling me every little thing. I churned 3 lb of butter yesterday without any churn, and buckwheat is elegant and our potatoes, cabbage, beets, &c very fine. It is no trouble to raise a garden here, the soil is so light, and oh, how luxuriantly things grow.

We have been striving on bravely at the new ground. 8 or 10 men passed over it like a <u>whirlwind</u> grubbing. We have 10 acres grubbed and 6 quite cleared and expect to raise week after next. The children talk of you incessantly, Hannah especially. She talks very swiftly and not any plainer. Jos says, "I do wish they would let Elizabeth come this fall and

stay till spring," and the more I think of it the more earnestly I wish it.
Do give it all consideration. . . . Jos won't let me write more. The
children are all round me with messages of love to all of you, to WH[3]
especially.

1. Deborah Pleasants Stabler, born 1763, was the granddaughter of James and Deborah
Brooke by their daughter Elizabeth, and therefore was Anna's second cousin once removed.
She was also the mother of James P. Stabler, who married Anna's sister Sarah.
2. The son of Anna's uncle, Basil Brooke, and his wife, the former Elizabeth Hopkins. James
married Hester Boone, daughter of Isaac and Hannah Boone, in 1797. They had eight
children.
3. William Henry Briggs, Anna's youngest sibling, age eleven.

~

The Cabin 8th mo 17th 1826
5th day night
My dear friends,

This I expect will be forwarded by a private conveyance and save you the
postage, for if I get time I could make it as lengthy a letter as one I wrote
lately to you. This has been a most laborious week to me, washing,
baking, scouring, cooking, &c. I have been constantly on my feet; and I
feel very tired now and look forward to tomorrow as a treat, for I have a
great pile of patching to do that I can set down to—and I have 4 and 1/2
loaves baked and pies enough. I have had many calls from neighbors
since 1st day: Susan Holland and her sister that I had not seen before—
Catherine, a fine, interesting girl just recovered from a Salivation[1] for the
liver complaint—A Miller (of Maurice), Levi's daughter, Mary, and
neice, Prudence, and I don't know how many men, but 3 took supper
last night.

It is customary here for the neighbors to go out and help at what
they call a log-rolling—that is, rolling in large heaps with levers the
largest saw logs and then piling on the brush and firing it. All their pay is
to go home and take supper with them.

3rd day the 22nd. Well, I get on slowly with my letter, but you can
have no idea of the constant variety of engagements I have, and I now
know how to make allowances for the poor black people who cannot
keep awake when they sit down of an evening. But I sometimes shed
tears of thankfulness when I find how much I am made capable of doing
cheerfully. My beloved mother, thy prayers have been heard—the hearts
of strangers have indeed seemed to be turned towards us in a manner
wonderful to me, not in empty proffessions but in real substantial acts of

kindness. I will give some instances. My cow, in jumping a low fence, tore open one of her teats the whole length. We could not milk her at night. In the morning I went over to friend Miller's, 1/4 of a mile, for a little tallow to grease it and to know what to do. Friend Miller was very busy, but she immediately left all and came through the dew to milk her, which she accomplished in spite of her kicking by making a kind of pen in a fence corner. One of the girls came and milked her in the evening.

Friend Miller says let them know whenever I have more work to do than I can easily get through with and some of them will come and help. They supply me with beans, potatoes, and roasting ears. This is the way she talks: "Now, do send over for any vegetable or anything thee stands in need of. Thee must not be any ways backward with us more than thy own <u>people</u>. I know just how it is with you. New begginers <u>have all</u> to <u>buy till they can make for themselves, and I want thee to feel welcome</u> <u>and always at home here. I want our intercourse to ripen into a</u> <u>friendship, not of a day but permanent.</u>"

"Come, that is thy hen and chickens. I will have them and a roaster caught and sent over, and I have a tub of soap for thee when I can get it over."

She was looking at the wool thee gave me, Mother. She said, "I have just got some wool dyed black. Thee shall have half a lb of it, and I will bring it over and pick thine and mix it for thee, and we will spin it for thee." Well, this morning Sally Miller came over she said to help me wash, for "I know thee stands in need of help and I will be very willing to come and help thee every week, but I won't take pay." The tears gushed from my eyes as I thanked the kind-hearted girl. (She is 16 years old.)

Last 1st day morning they sent a pressing invitation for Joseph and me, Maria and Deborah and Henry to go over and spend the afternoon. We found a good deal of company. (They entertain as much as Brooke Grove.) Among them was two fine girls from New Garden 5 miles from here—Margaret and Hannah Grizzle—and Eliza Galbraith. There was 18 in all. There is a sort of feeling that don't suit my awkward diffidence to find myself an object of general attention whenever I go, and I feel more at ease with a few in a family circle than in a crowd. In our own neighborhood, where our insignificance was known, we were treated with no more regard than we merited by some. (This is no reflection; I cherish with grateful remembrance numberless acts of kindness, I know beyond my merits.) But here they as yet all seem to be looking <u>up</u> to us. May it be a strong inducement to us to establish our characters so as to keep the respect and affection of these dear kind people.

As our exellent friend, Levi Miller, was sitting with us one evening lately, I was, as I often before had done, noticing something in the sound of his voice so like Father's, my eye happened to rest on his profile on the wall. It was instantly rivetted there, for it is as exactly like our father's. I called to Joseph, just telling him to look. He and all the children were struck with the likeness in an instant, before I mentioned it. . . .

1st day 27th. 6th day was our monthly meeting. I attended for the first time and was surprised to find about <u>30 babies attended</u>. There were more monstrous fat women than I ever saw at once. One couple passed meeting and another handed in their intentions (which they do one month, and the next appear and say, "Friends, I continue my intentions of marriage with" &c). The clerk was a neat young woman very much like Hannah Carlisle, and the assistant clerk is a lovely looking woman with exactly such a face as Hannah Wilson's, a fine delicate complexion; she has been married 4 years and has no children.

Dear old Sarah Holland walked part way home with me. I told her I had received a letter from home and mentioned some of the particulars of poor Cousin J Kersey. She seemed much affected, for she had known him. The rumour had reached us some weeks since, but it seemed beyond belief he that could so well point out to others the danger of giving way to temptation. Oh, can he ever attain to the exellence he has fallen from?[2]

In the afternoon, Susan Holland came in. "Anna," she said, "my sister Catherine takes me to task for using so much freedom with thee as to make no change in my dress when I come over, but I tell her she has not found thee out yet as well as I have. When she has been as much with thee, she will discover that thee is one that would not value a person less for being dressed in homespun." She is perfectly neat always.

Soon after her mother came in. "Well, I cannot be satisfied. If thee has no objection, I want thee to read thy letters to me, or the parts relating to J Kersey." I did so. The tears rolled down her cheeks as she exclaimed, "Alas! poor human nature." And when I read what dear Sister Mary and Mother said of my neighbors, she again strove to conceal the tears, but they would come. And she stretched out her hand and took mine in hers. . . .

Joseph went down to the clearing (i.e. our [corral]) today and found some person had stolen our hive which was nearly full of honey. Botheration to them. We cannot raise till next week, and Oh, then the work to cook for these pie-eating people. S[usan] Holland and Hannah Miller will help, and I shall bake in Friend Holland's oven. It is not near so far as from Sharon to Hebron.

How I have feasted on plums for 2 or 3 weeks past. So large and delicious they grow in the greatest abundance about 50 yds from the house—large trees almost breaking down with them. And wild cherries are here used for pies. They grow larger here than with you and resemble black heart cherries in taste. I make a great many pies and puddings and try some experiments with them. I mostly bake 15 or 20 a week. I stew peaches, not dried, or apples, and make a custard and mix with them, seasoning it nicely, and make puff paste and bake them in. I do all my baking in a Dutch oven and spider. They have taught me to scour tin ware with bullrushes and soap brighter than with sand.

We have heard there was a house raised a mile from here day before yesterday. A man got his head between the logs. When it was extricated he was bled, and he soon conversed with those arround telling them he was not seriously injured, they need not have sent for the Dr. When the physician examined his head, he instantly pronounced it fractured and no hope of saving him. He died yesterday. Ours will be such a <u>heavy</u> raising that I dread accidents.

I believe my account of the children might as well be stuck in here, as I am so bothered I can hardly think of anything. I am at this moment, and have been all the time I have been writing this side, singing "bye a baby" as loud as I can baul, and Deborah won't go to sleep. She is a sweet good babe. It has been some time since she could get up in the floor and stand alone, but she does not walk yet. . . . She does not look as fat or as clumsy as when I left you, but quite enough so. Maria's teasing has had an effect on her temper and she is a little fractious sometimes. She has 4 teeth. And our little Indian-looking Hannah is as fat and hearty as need be. She will not wear a bonnet, and her neck is like a mulatto. She don't talk any plainer but talks a great deal about you. . . . Last week she was leaning on my washtub; she saw me raise up to ease my back and looked concerned and said, "Me wit me wud big enouf to help de wats."

Thomas's hearing is quite restored. He dwells upon "my dear Uncle Richard and Aunt Mary," says sometimes, "Mother, it seems as if I loved them <u>most better</u> than thee. I wish they had of let me stay. . . ."

What shall I say for Maria? She is very useful, and I would be glad to say she strove to conquer her temper, was always respectful to me, and did not tease her brothers and sisters. But she gives me a great deal of trouble by teasing them and disputing with them, and they follow her example with each other. I hope I shall have a better account next letter. Franklin and Granville are mostly good boys. They work very hard and enjoy the hours of rest. Granville grows rappidly. They talk of you every day and of William Henry. They often wonder if he loved them as much as they did him.

I wish you would tell me if you really think Uncle Sammy will come and how soon. Jos does not get time to write as he would write you. . . . Oh, I am so anxious for our certificates. Sandy Spring is the name of our monthly meeting here. . . .[3]

I have not seen one black person since I came to this place. Henry has been invariably steady and always about home. On first days he goes nowhere but among Friends. He has not heard from his friends since he came except Bro Isaac's message. I wish my love to be given to Cousins EP & SB Thomas and MEG.[4] . . . Dear friends, so many of whom my eyes will behold no more in this life. . . . Give my love to Cousin D[eborah] Stabler, to dear uncles Sammy and Roger Brooke and their families, but I need not particularize. . . . I also wish my love to be given to Flora Powel, Polly Pumphrey, Dorcas, and Billy.[5] Oh, all of your dear faces come so plain before me that I closed my eyes and kept them before my mental view, forgetting that it is past midnight and a toilsome day approaching; trying, too, to forget the mountains, the long, long road. But I must not cherish useless regrets.

Why does not Sister Sarah let me hear more of the Poetry she did promise to?[6] In your distribution of love, don't forget M Howard, and tell Aunt Henny[7] Jos has worn no other coat (except first days) than the one she gave him since he left you. . . .

Your own affectionate Anna Bentley

1. An increase in the flow of saliva from taking large doses of mercury as a medical treatment.
2. Jesse Kersey (1768–1845) was a famous Quaker preacher from Chester County, Pennsylvania, and a follower of Elias Hicks. He eventually overcame the addiction to laudanum he had acquired during an attack of typhus. One of his daughters married Benjamin Hanna in 1852.
3. To join the local monthly meeting of the Society of Friends, Joseph and Anna needed certificates, or recommendations, from their home meeting, Sandy Spring Monthly Meeting in Maryland, and were waiting for them to arrive at the Sandy Spring Monthly Meeting in Hanover.
4. MEG was Margaret E. Garrigues, born Margaret Thomas, the daughter of Richard and Deborah Brooke Thomas. Her mother was Hannah Briggs's sister. Cousins EP and SB Thomas probably are her older sisters, Elizabeth and Sarah B. Thomas.
5. These were all freed slaves who lived in Sandy Spring, Maryland. Anna particularly asked after Dorcas Pumphrey over the years. She was a former slave who adopted Quaker ways, bore sixteen children, and died at a great age in 1891.

6. Sarah Briggs was always known as the poetess in the family. In Sandy Spring she was solicited to write poetry commemorating local events.

7. Henrietta Bentley, the second wife of Caleb Bentley, Anna's former brother-in-law. President James Madison stayed at their house in Brookeville after fleeing the burning of Washington by the British in 1814.

∼

9th month 18th 1826
My dear friends,

Can it be true, my very dear sister, <u>Sarah Bentley Briggs</u>, that I have heretofore omitted the mention of thy name in my letters? I assume thee notwithstanding, that you are all, as it were, embodied in <u>one mass</u> on which the fond affection of my heart dwells with equal tenderness. Each one must take my letters as individually to themselves. And one thing you must all guard against—that is being uneasy when letters do not come as often as you wish from us. I will just tell you how it is. <u>My time is so entirely taken up, day and night, that unless I steal the time my wearied frame requires for sleep, I get little leisure for writing</u> and <u>then</u>, when I am hurried and tired, I omit many things I would wish to say.

I very often have <u>boarders</u>, and in the course of a week or two shall have a constant one till our house and outbuildings are all finished, which will take up the winter and summer at least. He is an old man, Seth Hoopes.

This is the dreaded week. The <u>raising is</u> now decidedly fixed (no unforeseen event occurring) to be on the fifth day. <u>I shall have 40 hands to provide for.</u>

I cannot make you sensible of the gratification we had in the company of dear Uncle and Aunt Steer and his brother Joseph.[1] To think of their coming so far to see us. Oh, she is such a dear, affectionate woman. They all expressed great satisfaction and said they felt themselves paid for their trouble. We spent a day at John Battin's, a worthy elder. I wish you could see the overflowing abundance apparent there, the orchards bending down with the finest fruit (apples and peaches), the barns full, herds, flocks, swine, and poultry, the garden flourishing, and with it all such simplicity and open-hearted hospitality and kindness—Oh, this is a favored spot.

The day after they left us I felt more <u>alone</u> than usual, and having some sewing that I could take abroad, I went off to S Holland's. It had been so long since my other visit, the place looked altered to me. The whole front of the house is entirely covered with the most luxuriant vines—the Nasturtium, the sweet-scented pea, balloon pea, convolvulus, purple flowering bean—the little kitchen detached from the house also covered to the roof. I never saw so lovely and romantic a spot. And the dear inmates—they are the people, Mother, that I feel the most like rellatives. They seem so interested for us, and so do our first kind friends, the Millers.

You never took any notice of what I said about Elizabeth. Oh, if it could be so that you could spare her and she could be got here, I fully believe her health would be entirely restored. Joseph so often expresses a strong wish that it could be so. I want Bro Isaac to say more about <u>his</u> coming. If he does in the carriole, Henry wanted to know if he could buy his greatcoat and boots. . . .

Money is so scarce we try to be very careful in our expenditures as our little stash is running out very fast. I have sometimes thought I would get you to procure me plaid enough for 2 dresses, a peice for Maria, Hannah, and self with our money for Brother to bring out. I am getting a flannel frock made and shall alter my linsey petticoat into a gown, and if I can't get a bombazet,[2] as I don't expect to be able, shall wear them to meetings. Tell Aunt Henny I did send the bundle by a friend from Smithfield some time ago. It was a good while before an opportunity allowed.

It is now 1 o'clock at night and a laborious day approaching. . . . Tell dear Sister Mary to arouse her lazy pen once more. For she well can manage it to gratify the heart of her poor far-distant sister. Oh, if you could hear me sometimes as I am busily employed and painful thoughts of our separation comes over my heart. I repeat aloud, and it seems a relief, "Oh, my dear, dear mother," and Oh, my sisters."

We received a letter from Uncle Sammy requesting more particular information about the land. It is a mile and a half from each meeting, Sandy Spring and Augusta.[3] It is considered very healthy, none more so—the low grounds dry, the spring very near the door, a spring house, &c. Apples <u>are plenty</u>. He does not recollect what other fruit trees [are] there. The water is not limestone.

This morning the trustees of the school called to see Joseph, and he is under an engagement to take the school to commence the 1st of the 12 mo. You never expressed your sentiments with regard to his taking it.

2nd day night. Last night Deborah was suddenly attacked with croup. It yielded to wine drops. She has seemed playful today though still hoarse. Maria has been very poorly today, a good deal like the commencement of Ague.

4th day morning. The children are all much better, and while I am
taking time to <u>breathe</u> a little I will devote it to you. (I shall write to the
bottom of the page and then begin to cross the lines, and after that is
done commence on the back. I give these directions that you may not be
puzelled.)[4]

Yesterday my dear, sisterly friend Susan Holland came over and
helped me wash all day, nursed and fed Deborah, put her to sleep,
roasted coffee; and I could allmost fancy her Sister Sarah in manners and
affectionate deportment to me and mine. She insisted on having the fruit
[and] flour sent to her this day, and she would make and bake all my pies
for the raisers tomorrow. I went over just now to help the children carry
it. Aunt Sarah says, "Poor thing . . . You [go] home and season thy meat
and send it to me, and I will roast it for thee and Susan will come over by
daybreak tomorrow and help thee get breakfast."

There will be 11 or 12 to breakfast by sunrise, and all our meat and
pies must be done today. I sent as she desired 4 roasting pieces of the
most ellegant mutton I ever saw—that is, half of the sheep except the
legs. Well, Hannah Miller came and insisted on taking the flour to make
and bake the bread, and her mother would make the applesauce. Friend
Battin sent word one of her daughters would come and assist me, if I
wished it. . . .

6th day night. Yesterday we arose before day and got breakfast for 6
of the raisers, which we sat at table. Ann Battin, a very amiable, smart
girl, came in and said, "I have come to aid, if I can assist in any way
today." I thanked her and she threw off her bonnet and went to work
washing dishes, pots, ovens, sweeping, and putting things in order just as
if she had always been living here. Hannah Miller and dear Sarah
Holland came and boiled a ham, a half bushel of potatoes, the same of
beets, in addition to the half of a sheep and 2 large pieces of beef cooked
the day before, 7 loaves of bread, and 30 pies and 2 gallons applesauce. I
did all the packing up in tubs and baskets, and we were ready by 10
o'clock to follow the waggon—that is, Ann, Hannah, and myself—to the
<u>woods</u>. (You won't help me to a name.)

39 sturdy sons of the forest, including Granville and Henry, were
exerting their strength to the utmost. They formed a table of the joists,
we arranged it, and they surround it with keen appetites. At 12 o'clock
43 of us dined there. We washed all the dishes, collected the remains,
packed up the dishes leaving the pies &c for them to eat for supper, and,
after looking at them till my blood chilled me, came home. Ann went to
her own home, Hannah with me. We got there by 5 o'clock. Sarah soon

came over. "Dear child," she said, "I am so affraid thee will be outdone, and I am so anxious to hear how you made out."

She went home and sent Susan to assist Hannah in getting supper for 10 who returned. I enquired of William Holland (Susan's brother) if any accident had occured. He very seriously replied, "Why, none more serious than W Reeder getting his toe badly smashed."

Oh, how did it happen?

"He let a piece of pie fall on it."

The girls washed all the things, put all in order, Susan took a tin of her own accord, boil'd victuals, and fed Deborah, put her to sleep and in the cradle, setting William to rock it. Her behavior to me and the children and her freedom about the house is constantly reminding me of Sister Sarah, though no poetess. The children often say Susan seems like Aunt Sarah. She laughs and says, "How can that be? I'm only a simple backwoods girl."

There is one more round and the rafters to put up yet, and in a few days I shall have a supper to get for 20 hands. But don't be uneasy. They won't let me do it myself.

My head is much composed. I have been in a kind of stupor all day. I went over to Levi's to carry plates, dishes, &c. In returning, I sat down under a peach tree and went fast to sleep and waked in a fright thinking I was frying chickens and the fat in [the] pan was on fire. It was only the wind blowing the leaves. Franklin was sitting by laughing and watching me.

A few days since while at breakfast the log at the eaves that supports the roof of our cabin being rotten broke in two and followed by 2 others that kept the roof on came rolling down, breaking 3 panes of glass and a milk pan. I had been standing there a few moments before. If there comes a smart wind, it will take half our roof off, but I am not uneasy. It can soon be repeared.

Please write particularly and write longer ones. I am confident it cannot be as difficult where there are so many of you to fill a sheet as for me. . . . Please write more of thy visit, dear Bro Isaac, and if thou wilt only bring one of my sisters I will love thee better than ever I did. Susan Holland and Hannah Miller requested me to send their love to you. Joseph also sends his to all our dear friends and says there are several he wants to write to but cannot yet. Mother, does thee ever look forward to a visit here? For it would be misery to me if I thought we never more should meet. And what of your promised visit, dear Bro and Sister Brooke? I wish dear Sister Sarah would answer her muse in behalf of an absent sister, and my dear Elizabeth and Margaret and William Henry, I love you all and think of you all many times in the day. Oh, Elizabeth, if they would but spare thee. It is late. Give my love to dear Aunt P Moore[5] and all my friends.

Your tenderly affectionate AB

1. Aunt Jane Steer appears several times in Anna's letters. I have not been able to identify her. Perhaps she was another sister of Isaac Briggs. The Steers lived in Salem.
2. Silk or silk-wool blend fabric.
3. Sandy Spring Monthly Meeting was outside Hanover in Hanover Township; Augusta Monthly Meeting was south of the Bentley farm on the Carroll County border.
4. The reader of this letter would have the idea long before getting to these lines. Several times, when paper was scarce and Anna had a great deal to say, she filled pages side to side and top to bottom, then turned the sheet ninety degrees and wrote over her previous lines. The result is surprisingly legible. Paper was both rare and costly on the frontier. The *Salem Gazette* begged its readers in 1826 to pay their subscriptions punctually because paper had to be packed in from paper mills thirty miles away "in small quantities" and lack of cash kept them from buying more.
5. Polly Moore, Hannah Briggs's sister, widow of Thomas Moore.

~

[To Isaac Briggs]
The Cabin 11th mo 10th 1826
My dear brother and all of you,

As I have some messages from Jos exclusively for thee, I will despatch that first to make sure of it as it is latish, and this must go before day tomorrow. If thou hast relinquished all prospect of visiting us shortly (oh thou of wavering mind), Jos wishes thee to send the money by mail, to procure as large notes as thee can, in United States or Baltimore notes, cut them in half, send one half and retain the other till thou hears from us, keeping a particular description of them and the half of but 1 note at a time. . . . He would write it himself but it seems almost impossible for him to write a letter now. His time is constantly taken up every day. And at night, by the time the children are out of the way, his weary frame requires the rest of his bed. I hope it will not be so always, but now is the press of business with us.

They are all striving with might and main to get part of the house habitable, which we now have a prospect of in about 2 weeks. The size of it is 36 by 24. It is beautifully situated on a considerable hill. It fronts the south. the chinking will be finished tomorrow, of the chimneys in 2 more days—we shall only finish one end of it now. There is to be a balcony above and piazza below in front of the house. The wood pile was made 2 months ago. It is close to the kitchen door, and more than we could burn before spring, all good sound seasoned wood. (Oh, for the soap. Mine still holds out that I brought.) There will be a brick oven near the kitchen.

This house is far the coldest one I ever was in. The <u>yawning</u> fireplace is so deep that it throws no heat beyond the hearth. I am at this moment sitting close to a blazing fire with Granville's pantaloons (clean ones I have been patching) round my neck for a shawl. The side next the fire is scorching, and the cold frosty wind from many crevices assailing the other and albeit which side that this letter showeth not. From compassion I have become an early riser as I have to get them breakfast (a simple one of boiled milk and bread which they prefer to anything else). They start by daylight. I always get coffee and tea for myself as I can't do without. If I attempt it, I am so overcome with stupor and drowsiness I can't get on with my work. <u>Exercise has become easy to me</u>, all but <u>washing</u>. Granville assisted me faithfully last week. He did all the hard rubbing, but nevertheless I was much outdone and, after I was done at night, had to <u>have my face rubbed with camphor to relieve a faintness.</u>

Maria is very helpful to me. Thomas and Hannah grow very fast, have uninterrupted health. Hannah is fatter, if anything, than ever she was, and certainly looks like Mother. Her eyes are becoming black. She is good-natured and the least trouble of any. She is a darling with her father, and her happy station of an evening is hanging on his knee and looking up in his face. She shows more of that talkative forwardness that from her infancy gave trouble in Maria. She still lisps and talks as comical as when she left you. She went to set Guard after a ground squirrel. She called, "Here, Good, tick um, tick um, tick um." It sounded so funny. Thomas laughed immoderately and teases her about it.

And dear little Deborah—I know <u>you</u> would think her sweet and interesting. She is not in the least shy or unsociable as Hannah was. She runs all about and tries to say almost anything. She is very fond of Henry and calls him "Ninny." She has very dark hazel eyes, <u>light brown</u> hair (becoming darker), rosy cheeks, tolerably fair. Her teeth are exactly like little Isaac [Bond]'s when I left you.[1] I don't know whether she is pretty or not. Everyone calls her a sweet and good and many call her "a pretty child," but I mostly take that as a thing of course. Thomas, I think, grows handsomer, the rest of <u>us</u>, I believe, are about as <u>pretty</u> as we used to be. My neighbours and Henry tell me I look "twenty percent better than when I came," and the first chance I got I clambered up and got down a broken looking glass from off the drawers, and after wiping off the dust and looking, could see but little to brag of. . . .

Levi's Ann gave me 2 hens and a rooster and Sarah Holland a pair of fowls to begin housekeeping with in the forrest. Poor Sarah has been ill for 3 weeks with erisypelas in her leg. She is able to sit up a little now. I spent yesterday there. She is such a dear, kind friend, so much dignity, such winning, affectionate manners. And she don't "my dear" a body all to pieces neither. I think her daughters most amiable, interesting girls, and I love them dearly. Susan is spinning 3 lb of stockings for me.

I go out sometimes among my neighbours and spend an afternoon, and a great many come to see me. I spent one afternoon at James Shore's. I was speaking of you all and the tears ran down the old woman's cheeks in a stream. She has been one of my kindest neighbours, though we have not visited before. We get a gallon of milk every other day, and many a pint of cream has she sent me.

We have had a long wet spell of weather and some (to me) dreadful gales of wind. 1st day was a week in the evening it blew so I expected nothing else but the roof would go. We could hear the old trees crashing in the forrest, and I counted five in a few minutes. It is a customary thing here. It takes much less wind to overturn a tree than with you. Here they are so large and the tops so heavy and the roots very shallow. A few evenings since we had quite a thunderstorm.

I do wish you would take the trouble to look over and answer some few of the questions I have asked in some of my last letters. I cannot say of your letters that "they are just the sort to give satisfaction" in this dreadful separation, for I confess they are not particular enough. There is too much room taken up in apologies for not doing better. Try the way I mostly do, begin sometime beforehand and add when you can. In your two last my dear sister's name was not mentioned. How is her health? Why does she not write to me? I do almost think hard. And Sister Sarah takes no notice of my request. If she does comply, I will try my best to answer it, though I have never been able to frame a tolerable rhyme since I came here.

This is 6th day night. Tomorrow is a laborrious day for me. It is after 12. I would not ask any of you to do this much for my satisfaction, yet when I think how glad I am to get long letters from you, I am willing to sacrifice my own ease. I was sorry our certificates did not come. Maybe when they are ready Cousin James P Stabler would write a little and enclose them. I received his shorthand letter and have been tantalized too much. Granville has been so employed that he has never read more than half of it. Yet I wish I had learned to read it.[2] I will answer it if we should

<u>live to get through it</u>. Oh, don't direct to Grizell's post office. We have nine chances to Lisbon to one from there, though it is nearer.

And now, Bro Isaac, I am concerned about thee, for fear thee will act as the poor dog crossing the stream with the piece of beef. Don't lose the substance in grasping the shaddow. I cannot say in regard to thy long-talked-of visit that my expectations were ever as strong as my wishes, for I know my brother's <u>wavering turn of mind</u>. . . . Jos says please see Samuel Banks and tell him 2 of the axes proved good for nothing. In that case he promised to return the money. Henry sends his love and says he is looking out a <u>fortune</u>, has one in view, and is going to look out one for thee. . . .

Well, I must bid you all farewell. With endeared love, Anna Bentley
What about Uncle Sammy's coming?

1. Anna's nephew—the son of her sister, Deborah, and Joseph Bond—who was raised by the family at Sharon after Deborah died in childbirth in 1825.
2. Some members of the family wrote in shorthand, but obviously Anna couldn't read or write it.

~

The Cabin 11th mo [1826]
First day afternoon
My dear, dear friends,

I have just been looking around me and concluded everything about our cabin wore a look of neatness and comfort and calculated to inspire cheerfulness in a mind usually of a contented turn. The yard is swept clean; pots, kettles, ovens, &c occupy one end of the porch, a large high box the other end, on which one arranged milk pans and pail, &c. My dressers are white and neatly fixed, the house and hearth clean (buckwheat cakes rising). I wish some of you could just pop in.

6th day. Well, I began this 1st day thinking to write a good, long, <u>very interesting bit</u> to you, was interrupted by company and have been too busy since, and now I fear my moody mind may infect my letter unless, as is mostly the case, writing to you may pass it off. You know my mind partakes of the nature of some kind of an ——ometer; I forget which—not thermometer, though (but it rises and sinks with the wind), and when I tell you the wind is now moaning tremendously through the forrests, it may account to you for dulness.

I spent part of [1st] day at our (clearing, as they call it here) last week. Oh, it looks so beautiful. The situation is one of the handsomest I ever saw. I begin to feel an attachment for the place. I went alone 1 1/2 miles through a continued forrest—not alone; Guard was my companion. The squirrels, black and grey, barked at me and were so saucy as to pretend to come part way down the trees <u>to attack</u> me. We expect to move the last of next week or beginning of the week after.

3rd day night. My night cap on, just ready for bed. I began this 2 weeks ago and have not had time to finish it. . . .

We expect to move the last of this week. On 1st day morning it began to snow and blow, and Oh—! the snow came through a hundred crevices in our most wretched cabin, covering beds, clothing, and everything. <u>Unfortunately we could not muster wood</u> enough to make the house <u>warm</u> enough to melt it any. We cast some rueful looks at one another as we crowded nearer and nearer round the scanty fire in our deep yawning fireplace and dodged as once in a while the snow would fall through on the back of our necks as we had them <u>streched forth</u> toward the fire, till at last Henry manfully sallied out and in the meadow scrabled up 2 or three tremendous logs. He soon made a cheerful blaze, and as the chill subsided my face contracted to its <u>usual moderate</u> length. And felt glad you could not see us just then. Henry and the boys had to strech them on the carpet and had a <u>good night's</u> sleep. We have a severe spell of winter weather but are cheerful under a hope of being more comfortably fixed so soon.

Sarah Miller, a smart, good, affectionate girl aged 16, daughter of Levi, is going with us to spend the winter. Her compensation is that I should pay some attention to her learning, correct any impropriety of speech, &c. She washed here today. She said, "I know Maria and I shall be able to do all the housework, and thee can get all thy sewing and knitting done up. I can knit a stocking for myself in a day with no other hindrance, and then long evenings we can do a great deal." Maria is a very smart girl for work and does a great deal.

Little Deborah grows handsomer. Her rosy cheeks, red lips, and dark eyes and her sweet, engaging ways attract a good deal of attention. She has a sweet-toned voice. She comes to me sometimes and says, "Take a, Mamma, <u>take a</u>." When she sees anything that pleases her, she says, "Oh, my doody." She is very fond of kissing any female but will never kiss even her father. . . .

3rd day night. They returned from the woods with news we can't move till the first of next week; the weather is unfavourable to getting the stable up this week. My mind is all afloat. A neighbour of ours has just returned from Pittsburgh. He says on his return 3 days' journey from here he met 2 men travellers that said they were acquainted with us, made particular inquiries about us, said they had bussiness in other parts of the state but were coming to see us. One was an elderly man, both very <u>nice men</u>. Who can they be?

There is a <u>runaway black girl exactly</u> like Harriet Ross at Levi's. Her mistress is a great lady named Wilson from New Orleans. About 2 years since, her husband died and she took to travelling, has been to Philadelphia, New York, &c. The girl heard she was to be sold and made off with herself. I will relate a conversation I had with her.

"Did thee know a person in N.O. named Briggs?"

"Yes, Ma'am. Mr Samuel Briggs.[1] He lived in the next square to us, boarded at Stull's Tavern."

"Well, how is he making out?"

"Oh, very well. He is very rich. He and Col Winter has a great steam Grist and Saw mill, and he owns half a large warehouse and has a great many 'prentices."

"Does he drink now?"

"Very seldom. He did drink very hard once, but he left it off, and once in a while, only when he dines out, he sometimes takes a little too much. But he is very well off."

Who knows what may be? Shall I write to him and beg a few lbs of sugar?

I spent this afternoon with my dear old afflicted friend Sarah Holland. It is now 6 weeks since she has walked a step. She has the St Anthony fire in her leg extending from the ancle 8 inches above the knee. It has been lanced 7 times. There are now 4 lints in it. Her sufferings have been and still are extreme. She wept much when I bid her farewell and said, "When thee writes to thy dear mother, give my love to her." She gave me yarn enough to knit Granville and Franklin each a pair of mittens and said, "Tell the boys to put up a henhouse and come to me. They shall have half a dozen fowls." She whispered to Susan, and when I went out at the room Susan stood there with a cloth containing a nice roasting piece of pork.

Now, what do you think of these many instances of affectionate kindness? What ought I to <u>feel</u>, is there not something remarkable in it? I can't convey to you the manner that accompanies it, it seems to spring from pure genuine benevolence and affection, without a shaddow of ostentation, and they feel like favours from thee, Mother. . . .

The people are killing numbers of deer and foxes near here. A fox came in open daylight to our woodpile 2nd day. Game is very abundant now. Oh, I have nearly closed this for the night without informing all <u>whom</u> it may concern, that I have now on my back a warm comfortable linsey gown. I have added a neat body to my petticoat and shall wear it to meeting with a <u>clean check apron</u>. Who of you would DARE do such a thing? Here the <u>poor, simple</u> folks know no better than to sacrifice show and pride to comfort and usefulness.

1st day afternoon. 4 kind, agreeable neighbor <u>men</u> are here, and I expect Levi Miller and wife, Morris and his wife and 2 children to drink coffee and stay till bedtime. Dear, precious, kind people, they come to spend the last afternoon with us in our cabin. Tomorrow we expect to leave it forever. I spent 6th day at Levi Miller's. Ann requested her love to be given to Mother and all the family, "For I feel as if I knew them and loved them."

4th day night, 13th. Well, my dear friends, we have left the Cabin and are now dwelling in our <u>own</u> habitation. We came here last 2nd day was a week and have had a busy time of it, have had 2 raisings since at a barn and a stables—it is 24 by 20. We had 12 hands to breakfast, dinner, and supper the first day and the same number to supper tonight. We have 11 constantly in family. Sarah Miller came with us and will stay the winter. Joseph commenced his school 2nd day with 17 scholars and expects upwards of 30. After school they go to burning brush, and Oh, how often I think of Elizabeth when I see their high blazing fires. . . .

Brother Isaac, Jos is at this minute abusing thee from his bed and says he never will look for thee till he sees thee. This letter has been so long on hand it feels a task to finish it. It is now first day night the 17th. I rode Kit to meeting today and dined at Morris's. She is as gentle as old Bet and more so. She has never been known to start or show any tricks. Oh, if you were near us how happy we should be. We have 2 warm comfortable rooms and room in the unfinished part for a great many things. When it is all finished, we shall have a large, convenient, strong house beautifully situated. . . .

Conclude, your own affectionate A

1. Anna's uncle, the brother of Isaac Briggs. He was known in the family as a heavy drinker.

~

2nd mo [1827]
My dear friends,

There has never been so long an interval between my letters as the present, and I hope you have not suffered yourselves to become uneasy. Since the weather has been so that the children cannot play out, I find a poor chance to write, and as Henry and the boys sleep in the room where the fire is, I can't take <u>my usual time</u> when all are asleep.

I expect you have passed many an anxious moment on dear Brother Isaac's account. I cannot find words to express my joyful surprise at his unexpected arrival. I was stooping at the fire putting down a jonnycake when I heard a rap at the front door. Jos went out. I looked out of the window and saw a man with a knapsack, his shoulders drawn up, & talking in a foreign accent. (It was in the dusk of the evening.) Sally says, "Oh, it looks like a beggar man."

He accosted J with, "Do you vant any puttons or pin or neetles or any such ting?"

"No, we do not."

"Maype te madame of te aus would like some."

"No, she does not want any."

"Well, coot I get a night's lodging?"

He was refused, and after more conversation directed to a neighbour's house. Then suddenly extending his hand, he said, "Well, it's hard, after travelling so far, if I can't stay all night."

I had left the window. The children called to me, "Mother, Father is shaking hands with that man." Still, I did not suspect, till he came in. Jos said, "Here is a stranger that wants a night's lodging." One single glance was enough for me. I will leave for him to tell all that has passed since his arrival. I look with dread to the parting.[1]

He seems more and more <u>delighted</u> with this <u>delightful</u> country. He also thinks (and we join him in the belief) that you have formed very erroneous ideas of our getting along here. I don't know any that have to work harder than Uncle James Brooke's family, indeed not so hard, for there is not so much occasion. And that is not one in 20 that have such difficulties to encounter as I had last summer, having to provide for the men, and their work at such a distance, no oven, little kitchen furniture, small house, children, &c. And what great disadvantage has it been to me? I never enjoyed such good health since I was a child & never since my recollection as even a flow of cheerfulness.

Since our removal here I have an easy time, our dear Sarah taking the most of the domestic concerns, all of the washing, &c off my hands. She is a kind, affectionate girl and feels like a sister. I never knew such a healthy neighborhood. We hear of no sickness except the "<u>ailment</u>" some of you Marylanders are so subject to, which as yet I have escaped.

The news contained in your last letters affected me strongly, but not with apprehension of evil. I wish you had been more particular as to <u>date</u>.[2]

Brother Isaac can tell you so much of our concerns and situation that it will not be worth while for me to write very particular this time. The neighbours here have solicited me to undertake teaching a school through the summer. I should have upwards of 30 schollars. They would build a schoolhouse where we please. Hannah Miller, for a moderate compensation, would come and take charge of all domestic concerns. She is for industry and management such another as Cousin Margaret Brooke.[3] To commence as soon as matters can be arranged, perhaps in the 4th month, for $1.50 per quarter, which is more than equal to $3.00 with you. What do you think of it? Joseph's school is larger, and he is highly thought of as a teacher.

My dear friend Sarah Holland is going about again. 3 weeks ago Joseph went home with them from meeting. She directly sent her son John, a handsome young man, with the sleigh for me. We spent a pleasant afternoon, and at 9 o'clock he brought us home. I have not written but once since we moved here, and I think Sister Sarah is mistaken in thinking we have not received all your letters. Some perhaps I have received and not acknowledged. I have mislaid thy last letter, Sister Sarah, and forget if there was anything to answer in it, but I know it deserved my thanks and I tender them sincerely.

I must tell you how much pleased I am with my new flannel dress. I do wonder that such is not worn with you. I think if Mother was only to try it once she would never want bombazet in winter again. And when it is dressed properly it looks as nice and is so much more comfortable, and it would outlast 2 at least. I do think I feel it something like a duty to tell thee a little about it. If thee would get some of your finest wool, have it washed in 3 parts warm water and 1 chamberlye,[4] then it will card smoother and free from lumps. Then if it could not be done at home, get Becky Ghue to spin it 20 cuts to the lb and have it wove white, then send it to the fulling mill, have it slightly fulled, coloured, and pressed. Thou would not believe how nice it looks.* Brother can tell thee. Then, when it is washed, have it damp and iron it with a heavy iron as hot as it will bear. Iron it all one way. How glad I would be to hear thee had a dress of it. Then you would feel the good of your wool. One flannel dress lasts 4 or 5 winters.

Levi's wife, Ann, Maurice's wife, Ann, and Sarah Holland all send thier love to Mother, and all seem gratified when I give her love to them. They all seem to share in my joy in Brother's arrival. Sally sends her love to you all.

6th day night, 16th of the 2nd mo. Bro Isaac is now at Levi Miller's, where he went yesterday morning and arrived, Thomas on his back. They want the latter to stay a week or two. I expect they are making sugar. I tapped 5 times today and have collected 5 gallons of water. I have it on boiling now to see what I can do with it.

I leave it for Brother Isaac to tell you how we have passed our time since he has been here, of the extraordinary weather, &c., of the dear kind people amongst whom my lot in this life is cast, who strive all they can to make me forget that I am in a strange land. Shall I own to you that I am letting in a great dread of letter writing—I feel as if I <u>cannot accomplish</u> it to any but you. As I have no place to retire to out of hearing of the noise of the children, it makes it more of a task to write. . . . Give my love to all my friends. I expect Sally will leave me next week. They require her at home. They have 4 boarders in addition to thier own large family. I am in hopes Joseph will take time to write. If he don't, I know he loves you.

And I am your own affectionate Anna Bentley

*The peice of mine I send is not a sample of the nicest. It is only 18 cuts to the lb.

1. Describing the same scene in a letter to James P. Stabler, Isaac wrote, "As sister A looked at me from the window she thought I was so ill looking that she tryed to persuade Henry to go out for fear I might do some harm to Jos."
2. Apparently referring to the pregnancy of her sister, Mary Brooke.
3. Possibly Margaret E. Brooke, born 1798, the daughter of Richard and Deborah (Thomas) Brooke of Sandy Spring.
4. Urine, once used as a water softener.

~

5th mo 30th 1827
My dear friends,

I will make a <u>beginning</u>, at least, of a letter, though I have just roused up from a nodding spell by the fire. I have had to cook for 5 hearty men today and feel tired. "What had thee for dinner?" Why boil'd ham, potatoes, stewed fruit, currant pies, apple pies, bread and butter, pudding. "And for supper?" the same with the addition of a <u>gallon</u> of coffee and for good neighborship and that each came with a grubbing hoe and worked faithfully all day grubbing. Last 6th day we had another set that did a great day's work. The people plead so hard I could not get off from the school. The logs are all ready and the subscribers are to meet and erect it on 7th day.

1st day 3rd of the 6th mo. A cold rainy day and the children as cross
and noisy as feels comfortable. I received (2 weeks after date) your letter
containing the joyful tidings of my beloved sister's safety and the arrival
of that dear little stranger that with his mother I could so gladly press to
my bosom this moment. The tears both of joy and sorrow flowed so fast
when I read it that for a long time I was unable to read further than the
passage that announced the birth of the little Henry.[1] Oh then I felt
more keenly than I ever did before the bitterness of separation from you.
For awhile it was almost overwhelming, till I felt reproved for indulging
selfish feelings instead of thankfulness to the gracious power that brought
her through & that has so often brought me through trials and
difficulties.

I do most earnestly wish that you would be more particular in
writing to me of your little everyday concerns. Nothing is a trifle or
uninteresting to me that concerns you. You that are dwelling on your
native sod, amongst the friends of your infancy, must not forget that I
love that sod & those friends and am separated from them perhaps
forever.

Please tell me something of Uncle Sammy's family. Levi Miller is
anxious (and so are we) to know their expectations. I could not describe
my disappointment at receiving no letters by the Higgins. Such a good
opportunity. And I [was] also in hopes Brother would have remembered
the pr of shoes I once requested him to have made for me. It is a difficult
thing to get good leather just in this neighborhood. And Jos set himself
up with the thoughts of a good chew of tobacco once more, and the boys
took it for granted Uncle Isaac would send the books he was talking of.
We were all disapointed. I cried a little, and then joined the rest in
abusing you.

Do tell me more concerning the Higgins. They are extremely
dissatisfied here. Brother knows what a poor place they have gone to near
Ben's on the burnt hills. He has acted so as to get in great discredit as a
man that speaks not the truth, and the people have an idea he would
cheat if he could. He is considerably in debt, and some talk strongly of
suing him. He is a poor simple fellow to manage. The ladies of the family
have been accustomed to move in such a circle that the dear homespun
hospitality of our kind-hearted females who are so rough and low that
they think nothing of carrying to them a pound or 2 of butter, a dozen
or 2 eggs, a quart of cream, &c (this is fact) that it is a shock to them to
think of spending their days among such an unpolished set.

I do say it for them I never met with any people like them. They don't make a long face and in fine language express their sympathy for me or sorrow for any little difficulty, but they suit their actions to their words and apply every assistance in their power. Alice Jackson, though in a humble situation, has proved one of my kindest, most useful neighbours. She has never suffered me to do a washing since Isaac was here. Often sends me a plate of butter, a baking of currants; and every logrolling or grubbing we have she hastens over and does all the cooking (and she is an excellent cook), taking all the care off of me. I could not enumerate her many kindnesses. You know my disposition enough to suppose I would not be willing to lie under obligations. . . .

I must now tell you some news: We have an addition to our family—a still, quiet old lady, a first-rate seamstress. She patches and contrives just like Mother. She would gladly do all the sewing and knitting in my family for her board. She is too old and weakly to attend to domestic concerns. She is remarkably nice, in dress and person is like Aunt Polly Moore. Her name is Nancy Hoopes, wife to Seth.

The schoolhouse is raised, and in 2 or 3 weeks I shall have to commence. I expect to get a girl, a very good one, and Mary Ann McLaughlin at 50 cents per week. She will spin for me, too. I can get wool clean at 20 cents and flax at 6 1/4; then I can have a piece of fulled linsey for Jos and the boys. Franklin, Thomas, and Henry will go to school, and the township pays 1 bushel and 1/2 of wheat for every child that is sent to school, so I shall have 4 1/2 bushels for teaching my own, besides the advantage to them.

How beautiful our home in the woods looks now: On one hand a field of excellent wheat, and on the other flourishing corn in which watermelons, cantelopes, cimbuns,[2] pumkins, beans, and cucumbers are growing in abundance. Our fruit trees—that is, apple, peach, cherry, damson, and plum trees—all thriving. A great number of grape vines, choice kinds (by the bye), that is becoming a matter of speculation and is thought will be more profitable than farming. We have an exellent spot for a vineyard and intend planting one sometime. My chickens hatch finely. I have 4 hens with 32 chickens, 2 setting and 3 laying every day as hard as they can. The woodpile will last all summer. The cow gives more than a gallon of milk, and I have not had the tootheache.

5th day, 7th. Samuel Holland spent the morning and dined here, & Levi Miller, his wife, and little daughter Debby spent the afternoon here. I have had 6 men to cook for besides, as we had a little logrolling. Samuel and Levi could not say enough in praise of the beauty of our situation or of the wonderful progress Jos has made in his improvements.

I only wish Bro Isaac could have seen it in its present beauty. I wish my
love to be given to all my friends, my coloured ones included. Does
Dorcas live at the factory yet? Deborah has been quite poorly for some
days cutting her eye teeth.

I am your affectionate AB

1. Henry Briggs Brooke, son of Mary and Richard Brooke.
2. Probably a simlin or simnel, a squash with a scalloped edge. She later spells it "cimbler"
and "cimblin."

~

7th mo 14th 1827
My dear sister Sarah, Elizabeth, and Margaret,

Though I have written 7 pages since last night, I will commence one to
you if it was only to set you a good example and express my tender
affection. And who knows but it may put it in your hearts to write me
each a separate letter by the bearer of this. I want to try an experiment.
Each of you write without looking at what the other has written. Don't
fear a repetition, but just give daily concerns, the affairs of the
neighbourhood, the sayings and doings of the children, how little Henry
looks, your garden, your cows, horses, chickens, and pigs, and even Ajax.
Tell me who of the young folks are swerving from simplicity in dress, and
try to delineate the people and things of my old neighbourhood so that
as I am journeying on through time in my distant habitation I may keep
up a kind of accquaintance and not feel like a stranger in my own dear
native land, if ever I should visit it again. . . .

Does Dorcas live at Triadelphia yet?[1] How is she doing, and how is
S Gilpin making out? Is there any talk of wedding or any <u>symptoms
indicative thereof</u> amongst you? How is Cousin Deborah Stabler?
Where does she spend most of her time? . . . I have discovered
something in the woods which is common here but I never heard of
before: A kind of curly knot grows on the bark of an old decayed
hickory, beech, and white oak which smells like a delicious pineapple
or a handful of sweet-scented shrubs. It scents the woods for more than
a hundred yards round. It is about as large as my fist and in its sweetest
state has a number of little black bugs in it. When pulled off it does
not retain its scent more than 2 weeks. They call them sweet knots. One
will scent a whole house. The children have found several, but they are
too old to send you.

Can you tell me where Isaac Ashton's widow lives and in what circumstances?[2] Nancy Hoopes wishes to know as she was acquainted with her. I really feel so fatigued with writing I must draw to a conclusion. My dear Sister Sarah, wilt thou not try to write me a little rhyme? Surely an absent sister might claim a favour that was granted to an <u>unknown friend</u>.

How does my dear brother, William Henry, do? Does he improve in his learning? Is he a good, obedient boy? Does he grow fast? And how is his lameness? Give my dear love to my poor Aunt Polly Moore. My warmest feelings of sympathy for her and the dear family she is with. I love too many of my friends to name them all. Dispense it to all you think would care about me or us. <u>To all my coloured friends give my remembrance, but you need not tell them how glad I am that there is so few of their colour here. I have never seen but 3. There is something so sweet in the state of perfect security we live in. Here no dread of dishonesty, no door or window ever to fasten.</u> Do you ever hear anything of Lady Hamilton or her offspring?

Well, my little housekeeper has made 3 ovens full of biscuit, and tea is almost ready. I have hid myself from the children in a bunch of high weeds behind the house. Oh, this beautiful place. I wish you were here now to enjoy looking at it with me. What <u>must</u> it be named—"Woodly" or "Oakly" or "Dulce Dormum" or "Bentley's Forrest" or &c or &c or &c?[3] I must now say no more than that I am your sincerely affectionate sister, Anna Bentley

Tell Bro Richard he must have made a mistake in the date of his letter. It was dated 6th mo 2nd and postmarked 6th mo 30th. Oh, I forgot to tell you, Joseph has some hopes of his brother (who has lately married a second wife) will come out here. Also his brother-in-law, Ezeckle Hall, the husband of his favourite sister, Allice, who, he says, in disposition, manners, and everything was more like Sister Deborah than any others. She will be a great comfort to me if they settle so near us as we expect.

1. Triadelphia, the town laid out and developed by the brothers-in-law Isaac Briggs, Thomas Moore, and Caleb Bentley, was a prosperous little community with a cotton factory, which possibly was where Dorcas Pumphrey worked at this time.
2. Related through Isaac Briggs's mother, born Mary Ashton.
3. They named it Green Hill. The name came to apply also to the post office, of which Joseph was the first postmaster.

～

One of Anna's biggest daily challenges was keeping her family healthy and nursing them when they were sick. Besides the inevitability of accidents on the farm, the settlers were plagued by a host of ailments, some of which we know today only from history books. Antibiotics and other medical break-throughs have nearly wiped out some illnesses that killed contemporaries of Anna Bentley in the prime of their lives. Outbreaks of scarlet fever and diphtheria (putrid sore throat) carried off children with great regularity. Relatively minor farmyard accidents often led to infections and blood poi-soning. Flies and poor sanitation brought typhoid fever (called typhus), cholera, dysentery, and other bacterial ailments, which could be fatal. Child-hood diseases such as chicken pox, measles, and whooping cough had to be taken seriously. In the summertime, mosquitoes carried what was called "ague" or "intermittent fever," now identified as malaria. Daily life threw up many obstacles to achieving a healthy old age.

When illness struck, Anna frequently turned to old home remedies, such as cayenne pepper for toothache or poultices for bellyache. For more serious cases, the Bentleys had to put themselves in the hands of the local doctors, like Dr. James Robertson of Hanover, a practitioner of traditional medicine. When Joseph and Anna first went to Ohio, American medicine was dominated by the belief that disease was caused by disruption of the arterial system. Doctors therefore tended to identify the liver as the source of difficulty and took steps to eliminate poisons from the system. As re-spected as he was in his time, Dr. Robertson would not have hesitated to bleed, purge, vomit, blister, sweat, and salivate his patients, at the same time administering large doses of powerful minerals such as mercury. Such heroic measures sanctioned by the medical establishment often nearly (or actually) killed patients.

One of the commonest medicines of the day was calomel, or mercu-rous chloride. Mothers and doctors used it on children and adults alike, in large doses, for a variety of ailments from tetanus to yellow fever. In large enough quantities it caused increased flow of saliva, or salivation, which was considered part of the purge. Salivation also made the patient's mouth extremely sore. We now know that the administration of large quantities of calomel was a form of poisoning, from which some patients never recov-ered. Over time, calomel also led to the loss of teeth. Nevertheless, children were dosed with it regularly.

Other common practices were blistering and bloodletting. Again, even the smallest children would be lanced for blood to relieve their ailment, no matter how weak they were from disease. Purging was done by using Epsom salts, calomel and rhubarb, tartar emetic, or castor oil, sometimes followed by some bloodletting to relieve a fever. The dry skin of a fever might be relieved by causing a sweat with spirit of nitre or antimonial wine (tartar emetic in wine). Visits by the doctor must have been frightening, especially for children, for the cures were often as terrible as the diseases. Home remedies, however inefficacious, at least were more likely benign. Given the medical practices in Anna Bentley's day, the resilience of those who survived was admirable.

∼

Columbiana 9th mo 6th [1827]
My beloved friends,

My last letter was written on a sick bed. I gained strength very slowly till last 6th day night Thomas was taken with the croup and I had to be up all night (Mary McLaughlin had to leave me in 10 days to attend Yearly Meeting[1]), and finding some difficulty in getting a suitable girl, Jos concluded he and Maria could do all. 3 or 4 times, though, in the course of the week, I had fainted from the least exertion.

Enough of myself. On 7th day my darling babe was taken ill. . . . On 7th day night and 1st day she had a raging fever, laid in a stupor with very difficult respiration. We sent to the Dr for advise, and he thought as we did that it was worms and sent medicine for her. She has never been quite well since her fit, and her belly swelled so that all observed it, but her appetite was uncommonly good, the medicine not operating (calomel and rhubarb), and she becoming worse so that we had to set up and watch her constantly.

On 3rd day we sent for the Dr. He came and pronounced her very ill with a remitting fever. Her medicine would not act according to expectation. The symptoms have become more alarming. The Dr was here early this morning. He pronounced her in great danger, her liver much affected, but still has some hope if the medicine he has left has good effect, which has not yet been the case. She is very billious, has taken no nourishment since 7th day, has fallen away very much indeed. Nothing has power to amuse or attract her attention. She lays mostly in a stupor and her moans peirce my heart with anguish.

My feelings I cannot attempt to describe. Her sweet, engaging manners, her most animated playful ways and innocent prattle attracted the attention of all that saw her. I have often been told by those who noticed her, "She is too sensible. She is too lovely. Such children seldom live long." I have often thought my affections were more wrapped up in her than they have ever been in any of the rest.

As yet I cannot feel the least resignation of my will, and my ardent breathing of soul is that this dear treasure may not be torn from me, though she is in the hand of the Lord; and I know that in times past when he has bruised me with his rod he has not withheld his staff. But oh, my child, my sweet, innocent babe! How <u>can</u> I give her up?

We had set up with her ourselves till yesterday when they heard of it at Levi Miller's and Hannah came over in the afternoon, made pies and baked them, got supper. Susan Holland hailed Franklin when he returned from the Dr. When she was informed how Deborah was, she had her saddle put on [her horse], mounted her, and came here prepared to stay till a change takes place. Dear, kind girl. My heart owns her as a sister. She is a most experienced and tender nurse. She has gone over the whole house, cleaned and put all to rights, and is now bending over the washtub after setting up all night. And she staid away from a wedding, too, today to come. . . .

Hannah had to go home last night, for she left Sally sick in bed and the rest gone to Yearly Meeting. She took Thomas and started by moonlight. They keep Thomas half his time, and he is the darling of the family.

The neighbourhood is more sickly than it has been for 7 years, the intermittent sinking into Typhus. We have had several deaths in the neighbourhood.

3rd day night. <u>My dear babe is now convalescent.</u> On 6th day last she appeared so alarmingly ill that the Dr had very little hopes of her. I looked among her clothing to select some to bury her in. On 7th day morning the disease took a turn. (She was not so stupid, took a spoonful of milk, the first nourishment since that day week.) The Dr pronounced her decidedly better, left elixir of vitriol with two other medicines for her. Her mouth was very much affected with the calomel and fever together. She has since continued to mend, has a craving appetite, though her mouth is so sore she is affraid to venture on some things she would like. She sat up today in the bed without propping a little, while she is much reduced in flesh—though she was so fat before that a stranger would not take so much notice of it. Her delicate complexion (the colour has returned slightly to her cheeks), her large dark sparkling eyes, and her pensive countenance look very interesting, if not beautiful.

Her imminent danger has occupied my mind so that I have not yet mentioned the great sufferings of our dear Granville. He has been confined to the house for 2 weeks. For a week he suffered with constant headache, then was taken with most violent earache which terminated in gatherings[2] the worst I ever saw—one ear discharging 2 or 3 tablespoonfulls in 24 hours, also discharging through one nostril. Both ears have been affected, but one more than the other. I put a blister on behind his ear. I hope it will do good. It drew pretty well for 3 days. He eat nothing and eats very little now.

Susan staid till first day. They expected the carpenters this week to tear down and rebuild their house. She is going to be married next month to R[obert] Miller. . . .

Tell Cousin Elizabeth Thomas from me that she little knows how very much our necessities call for the prompt payment of our little accounts. Our late afflictions have added 4 Drs visits, medicine, and advise to our debts here. We have no way of paying him. I am very weak and miserable but cannot keep a girl for a few weeks till I can see some way to pay her. . . .

We have a piazza with a nice large pantry at the end at the southwest end of our house. Jos has laid off a beautiful yard in front like Brother Richard's, with a fall. The garden is to be in front of the house laid off in falls. One fall is made; he intends laying it off, hauling <u>all</u> the manure from the barn, digging it in, and paling it this fall.

You did not tell me where the snuff came from. Does Brother Isaac still talk of coming out here this fall?* Seth Hoopes wishes to know by the first opportunity if you are willing to part with the spectacles that were Father's and at what price. If they do not exceed $10, Brother Isaac can bring them along—and please don't forget a thimble, if you can get a steel one for me. If Bro Isaac does come, just tell Uncle Caleb [Bentley] if he has an old rusty one in the stove and will give it to me, I'll be bound I can polish it in making up tow linnen trouwsers for Joseph and the boys.

Jos just gives his love to you all and a message to Bro Isaac: If he has <u>really</u> determined to leave Sharon, he wishes him to come here as soon as he can and join Seth and him in erecting a sawmill, which they intend doing this fall, if Jos can get seeding done in time.

9th mo 12th. Deborah is still mending; she cannot walk yet, though. Granville is better, though very hard of hearing, not yet so as to leave the house or do any good in it. . . .

We expect to have a logrolling tomorrow and I must be up early, so with love to all I am, your affectionate A

*It is not because we are not prepared to receive thee with open arms that

I say nothing to urge it, for while I consider my own feelings and believe it would be to thy advantage, I cannot help thinking of Mother and feel a delicacy in giving my own real sentiments; but don't play any trick with me this time.

1. The annual assembly of the Ohio Quakers was held in Mt. Pleasant, Jefferson County, in those years.
2. Abscesses.

~

To James P. Stabler
12th mo 20th 1827
Dear Cousin,

The family are all quiet in bed. I am seated before a warm hickory fire, I have two eggs roasting in the embers, and I feel pretty comfortable. And (as is always the case under such feelings) my thoughts recur to former times and dear distant friends. Ah, my dear cousin, it is a hard thing to bear, this separation from those we love while yet on earth. Those that have passed away from all the cares and sorrows of life, however dear they were, we know they cannot return. They are blest and we give them up. But for those that are still subjected to all the vicissitudes of this ever-changing scene, how many anxious fears will arise, with the faint hopes of meeting once again.

Independent of the convenience a correspondence with thee affords, it is very gratifying to us, as I scarcely ever finish a letter at one sitting. I will commence writing to the Sharonites, and if I should have anything farther on my mind for thee, I will put it down at the conclusion.

Thy affectionate cousin, AB

My dear friends,
I think you will find me now a frequent correspondent as Cousin James's kindness will remove the greatest barrier (the postage) to my writing very often[1]; and as that is the only medium of intercourse now left us, oh, do not let it be neglected, for there will now be no reasonable excuse some of you might write every week. . . . When I am writing to you I always think that which will place us the most immediately before your eyes, will be the most entertaining to you, and I have no fears of being charged with egoism by you. I write to you as I would be written to. I want to know what you are doing, how clothed, how provided for in eatables,

how many horses, cows, sheep, and pigs, and even <u>cats</u>. Elizabeth, you don't say enough about Sister and Brother Brooke and their little son, as they <u>will</u> not say anything for themselves. (Do they ever enquire after us?) And dear little Isaac [Bond], I love to hear his little speeches. I will not enquire of you, for Bro Joseph [Bond], dear <u>generous</u> brother, he speaks for himself, he writes frequently. I want all the news of my dear old native land, though unless affection for you would tempt me to place myself in an unpleasant situation, no other consideration could ever induce me to wish to exchange my present home to become a resident there. These are the honest sentiments of my heart. My health is improving. I can now assume my domestic labours moderately without innconvenience.

Last week we got through with <u>our</u> butchering: a fine fat beef and nine hogs. My kind neighbour Alice came over and assisted in everything that <u>Flora</u> could have done. The men, when we had done with the entrails, took them to the spring run, opened, and mashed them for soap fat. I have them all in strong lye. Hannah and Benjamin chopped the sausage that night (a bushel and an half after it was chopped). We have it <u>all</u> stuffed in the entrails. <u>We</u> did, and <u>Benjamin did</u> it in 3 hours with a machine called a sausage stuffer. Alice took all the tallow home with her, rendered it, spun candle wick, and dipped 26 dozen candles for 40 candles, and I footed <u>one</u> coarse stocking for her. I had 2 dozen candles before, so I am well supplied, and I have 6 or 7 lb of tallow left.

We find <u>Benjamin</u> is an excellent hand. <u>When it is too wet to work</u> out, he helps in the house about anything I set <u>him about, is very handy</u> and as obliging as he can be, seems to take an interest in everything as if it was his own. Hannah had to go home last week to stay 3 weeks. She is a fine girl. I have the head and neck of the beef chopped for mince pies. Benjamin and Granville cleaned the tripe ellegantly, and I have had it in salt and water changed daily for 10 days, shall boil it tomorrow.

For 11 dollars worth of coal—70 bushels—we have got a 3-year-old bull, a 2- and 6-months-old steer, and a ton of good clover hay. They are, as to color and shade, an exact match, though the steer is rather the smallest. We only wait for a remittance from Bro Isaac to encrease our stock with a cow; ours is quite dry, and when we do get any milk to go in coffee and tea, we have to send a mile and a half for it, except once in a while Reeders can spare a teacup full. Jos and Seth talk of beggining the sawmill shortly, and the coal bank seems to be opening a source of great proffit to us, as it is in great demand as being the best in the country and appears to be inexhaustible.

12th mo 23rd. Tomorrow I shall have an opportunity to [send to] Lisbon, and though I am so fatigued I can scarcely set up, I must finish this tonight. I walked with Jos to B Higgins and everything there looked so desolate and neglected compared with our own comfortable house, it made my heart ache. The old people coming out here has been the ruin of them. They spent most of their time there neglecting all at home: let an excellent cow go dry for want of milking, got another and contracted debts imprudently, promising cash when they knew there was none coming, have quarreled with all their neighbors, many of whom had confered great obligation on them but, wearied with their ingratitude and their riddiculing them behind their backs, are now only anxious to have them removed from their neighbourhood. They have sold their home at a great sacrifice, and when their debts are paid will have little left and will move tomorrow in a small house with Nicholas [Thomas], who is even more out of credit with the neighbors than them. He won't work and what will become of them? This night, it is probable, will add another to his family, as his wife sent out this afternoon. And what might have been our situation if we had followed the same course? We had more difficulties to encounter than they, but we did bear privations rather than go in debt beyond our means and did not endeavour to enforce respect by haughtiness but [won] it by gratitude and affection, and I feel we have succeeded. . . .

What a strange weather we have had here for the last 3 months, not 2 days at a time without rain and sometimes more than a week without a glimpse of sunshine. Such weather has never occured within the memory of the oldest people here. The roads are almost impassible. Sloane's waggon has not yet returned from Baltimore. How has it been with you? It has been fair here for the last 2 days.

My dear little Deborah Bond Bentley is the sweetest little prattler, as healthy and easy as we can wish. Yesterday I told her not to follow me. She did not mind, but came after me in the pantry. I spoke sharply, and said, "Begone out of here." She looked up in my face with the most innocent expression and said, "Mamma, I ain't a dog. I not a dog, Momma." Well, farewell, all dear friends.

Most affectionately, Anna Bently. . . .

1. James P. Stabler was the Sandy Spring postmaster for many years, and, like other postmasters, he took advantage of his franking privileges for himself and his relatives.

∼

Among the family papers is Hannah Briggs's reply to this letter. She empathized with the money problems, as she herself was unable to pay off a debt for bacon and other items she owed Joseph Bentley. She wrote, "I feel now under the necessity of proposing that Joseph will let it stand as a part against that <u>debt of honor</u> (as his Father used to call it[)] to the Estate of Isaac Briggs." She was happy, she said, that they had an increase in their livestock, for "a good fresh cow is no small comfort in a family." In tribute to Anna's descriptive powers, she added, "I seem to see Joseph enjoying his bowl and helping the children and Maria churning the butter."

Hannah Briggs also wrote to Sarah Briggs in December that she had received two letters from Anna, dated November 19 and December 7. In one Anna had given a "clever" account of her friend Susan Miller's wedding, and the sad news of the death of Ann Miller's son, Isaac. As Hannah Briggs put it, "He was subject to holding his breath when he cried—and at one of these times not all they could do would make him breath[e] again."

TWO

1828–1830

~

In 1828, the Society of Friends, whose governance was based on unity and consensus, split wide open. Polite differences of opinion grew into open hostility. The rift had both religious and social components. In cities like Philadelphia, urban Quakers who had become prosperous and influential eventually wanted to be a little less "different" from the rest of the Christian world. The religious revivals of the period, such as Methodism, popularized enthusiastic styles of worship. Some Friends wanted their religion to be on a firmer doctrinal footing than the concept of the mystical, personal Inner Light and sought religious revelation from more concrete and traditional sources, such as the Bible. Arguments arose among Quakers about the proper amount of simplicity in daily life, the need for a professional ministry, the introduction of organized prayer, even the divinity of Christ. Rural Quakers like the Briggses and Bentleys, on the whole, clung to classic dress, manners and forms of worship. Inevitably, factions formed in the monthly meetings, and common ground became harder and harder to find.

The situation was complicated by politics, especially the politics of race. On one side fell the activists who followed Quaker social teachings about pacifism, equal rights, and abolition of slavery. Merely being on the right side of the question wasn't enough for some. By the 1820s, Quakers were in the vanguard of the new abolition movement, but not all Quakers felt comfortable so far out in front of the country's social norms. Some didn't like that Quaker abolitionists mixed with non-Quakers or allowed the meetinghouses to be used for political activism. It was one more thing to argue about.

Quakers who leaned toward modernizing their religious practices, organization, and doctrines—in effect making Quakerism more like other forms of Christianity—were called Orthodox. The social activists, on the other hand, were the doctrinal conservatives, who wanted to return Quakerism to what they felt were its roots. Their spokesman was a fiery reformer named Elias Hicks. He was a friend of several of Anna's relations, including Edward Garrigues of Philadelphia. Like many Quaker ministers, he traveled widely and tirelessly. The Quaker historian Howard Brinton describes him as a "genuine mystic" who disapproved of outward manifestations of religious devotion and freely questioned the divinity of Jesus. A fundamentalist in matters of Quaker practice, he had resisted paying military taxes, supported separate schools for Quaker children, and preached against authority, even within the church, where the true authority should be consensus or Inner Light.

Hicks incurred the wrath of Orthodox Friends especially for this last position, as well as his hard line against slavery. (He even opposed the purchase of goods produced by slavery.) But the charismatic old preacher attracted a large following, especially among rural Quakers.

In 1828, the eighty-year-old Hicks traveled to Ohio, where he packed the meetinghouses and imported the divisions that had already led to schism back East. He attended the Salem quarterly meeting, then the New Garden meeting. By the time the old preacher got to Marlborough in Stark County, he was attracting large crowds. If Anna and Joseph didn't go to hear him, they at least heard about the sensation he caused everywhere he appeared.

Like most of her relatives in Maryland, Anna was firmly in the Hicks camp. She must have expressed her views in letters back home, for her brother-in-law, Richard Brooke, had written her in February 1827, "I see by thy letter that some friend had condemned E. Hicks on account of his doctrines. I do wonder whether he really knows what he does preach—he is often misunderstood and often [thought] to say, what he never did say, dear old man (my eyes are filled at the expression) they cannot hurt him. There must be a shaking, a sifting in our society. . . ."

Brinton concludes about the schism that "both parties were to blame for their behavior: the Orthodox party for their belligerent attack on persons holding what they considered unchristian opinions, and for their disowning of all members of the Hicksite party; and the Hicksites for their impatience and unwillingness to wait, in the time-honored Quaker manner, for greater unity." A further split some twenty-five years later divided the Orthodox party, while the Hicksites themselves slowly dwindled in numbers. It wasn't until the twentieth century that old antagonisms were finally laid to rest.

By 1828, Anna and Joseph Bentley had become less dependent on the kindness of neighbors for their staples, but financially they were far from well off. Like a lot of other pioneers they were well fed but cash poor. Without ready cash they were hard-pressed to acquire anything they couldn't actually produce on the farm. Anna often wrote begging letters that hinted broadly at her family's needs. One such solicitation led to embarrassment. In January 1828 her mother chided her gently for asking a favor of Aunt Dorothy Hopkins. Unbeknownst to Anna, Gerard and Dorothy Hopkins had fallen on hard times and had had to sell their house in Baltimore and move into smaller quarters. Aunt Dorothy regretfully couldn't send Anna the cotton she had requested. Hannah Briggs wrote, "If she comes up on a visit as has been talked of I can make further enquiry and let her know thou wert ignorant of her tried situation."

～

3rd mo 2nd 1828
My dear friends,

I expect this will be delivered into your hands by our much-esteemed neighbor, Morris Miller, who expects to start for Washington next 4th day and intends paying you a visit. His wife's brother (a fine young man) will accompany him. His name is Daniel Votaw. For my sake treat them royally and write vollumes by them. Morris says he will with pleasure carry anything either to you or from you. I would that I had something pretty to send you, but we have not been here long enough to raise anything that could be sent, though I would now gladly exchange with you, if I could, 6 dozen eggs for 2 lb of rice, which I have not seen in this country, or 3 fat hens for a lb of coffee or 3 bushels of turnips for an old check apron; all my check is worn out.

Well, what do you think of me for this long silence, and what must I think of you? . . . I will offer my excuses for not writing in the daytime. The noise of the children and many indispensable duties (as I have no

help but Maria) entirely fill up my time, and for a long time I have been
subject to such an unconquorable drowsiness and stupidity of evenings
that I cannot write as I used to. Indeed, it overcomes me sometimes in
the day so that I can fall fast asleep in my chair and the greatest noise of
the children will not raise me. Sometimes it will be so all the afternoon
that I cannot sew at all. I know many things have passed that have
slipped my memory which would have interested you much, but my
memory is now so bad I cannot recollect what I have told you already.

In the first place, I have an excellent appetite. My strength is much
recruited, though I am not yet able to do the washing. Mary Miller
comes and washes for me, and how I am to pay her is all uncertain.

A day or two after I wrote last I walked down on 7th day morning
and spent the day with Sarah Shore, from there went to Sarah Holland,
went to meeting and home with Robert and Susan [Miller]. They live in
our dear old cabin and I never was in as sweet a looking place in my life.
The [most] perfect neatness is everywhere displayed; 2 nice beds with a
very handsome bureau between occupy the east end of the room, the
north a looking glass, a bright polish cherry dining table, 2 window
chairs, the west the fireplace, a chair each side the south front. In the
corner next the fire the dressers beautifully and plentifully arranged, a
white bench with a white water bucket by the door and 2 more chairs.
Out at the door, a bench with a delicate-looking milk bucket, dish tub,
&c under it, various iron utensils. I may describe but you can't think
how sweet it looks.

And dear Susan—I am constantly reminded of Sister Deborah when
with her. Catharine also reminds me of Sister Sarah, and Robert is as
amiable. Oh, he is worthy of Susan. She looks forward to the 7th month
with painful anxiety. I hope her resemblance to my dear sister may not
extend to a similar fate. Robert lived 10 months with his former wife, a
lovely woman by all accounts. She left a female infant who lived but 6
weeks.[1]

After spending a delightful afternoon (it felt just as if I was at an own
sister's), we started at 9 o'clock back to Green Hill—that is, Catharine
and William with a blazing clapboard and myself. The more I am with
that family the more I love them. They not only express it but all their
actions bespeak that they also feel a sympathy and nearness of affection
for me. Sarah is one of the most agreeable women I ever met, with a
refinement of manners, a gentle charity of feeling that extends to all. She
is beloved by old and young, applied to for comfort in affliction, counsel

in difficulties, and aid in sickness and distress. She seems like a mother to me. As Catharine was sitting by me she said, "What is it, Anna Bentley, that makes me feel so towards thee? Why, thee feels to me exactly like Susan, and it always feels as if I had parted with an own sister when I bid thee farewell."

On 2nd day morning they had an exellent break[fast]. One article that I had for sometime past felt a great desire to have, that was real boughten coffee, exellent good. I only drank 4 large cups. (How much I have wasted in my time, and Oh, how glad I would be now to have the grounds that so many in your parts throw out, for in part I attribute my stupidity and drowsiness to doing without it often, having always been accustomed to it. I have not used quite all the tea cousin Thomas sent me—but I have digressed.)

2nd day morning I bade them farewell and went across by Robert's. Susan accompanied me over to Levi's where I was most affectionately welcomed. They were very pressing for me to stay all night, but I thought I had left my young housekeeper long enough. I drank 4 cups more of good coffee—they are dear kind affectionate people. I returned home much benefitted by my visit. The next first day Jos and I had a very pressing invitation to dine on roast turkey at John Battin's, but I was not well enough to go, having over-fatigued myself in prepairing for a chopping frolic and sewing party we expected to make on 2nd day. I had finished the quilt Sally Stabler[2] gave me a beginning for and fixed it to cover an old one. Seth made me a nice pr of frames and I got it ready and 2nd day we had 22 women and 20 men. (On 1st day night Ann Battin came and kindly offered her services to help cook.) Allice Jackson helped with the baking and house cleaning 6th and 7th day. For dinner we had a turkey, 3 fowls, 3 quarters of a small fat veal, a nice peice of corned beef, potatoes, turnips, cold slaw, parsnips, pickled cucumbers and beets for supper and exellent green apple pies, peach and green apple sauce, real coffee, tea, rolls, light bread, pickles, fruits stewed, and relishes of the cold meat left at dinner, pie, &c.

After tea Maria let the tea board fall and broke every china saucer but one that I had—that is 10—and 3 china cups and 3 glass tumblers, a very heavy loss to me indeed as all such articles are higher here than with you. Well, we got the quilt out and some sewing done but I never will make another sewing party, though they are very common here. I was almost overcome with fatigue. It will be cheaper to hire a woman by the week though the price is a dollar for sewing.

The 7th day previous to the sewing poor old Nancy Hoopes was burried. She had only been confined to her bed 3 or 4 days, appeared to have made her peace with heaven. The erysipelas had attacked her stomach inwardly. On 6th day morning she said she felt much better and desired Ann Miller to lie down, which she did for a little while; but feeling uneasy, got up and went to her bedside just after daybreak. She seemed to be sleeping so sweetly that she stood and watched how easy she breathed to what she had done. She sat down by the fire for about 5 minutes and returned. The breathing had ceased. Without a sigh she past from sleep into eternity!

The cleaning and chopping that has been done is for an orchard. It is on the hill above the meat house, Isaac, and extends a good peice upon the chestnut ridge. The nice little cow we bought turns out very well, is as gentle as ever a cow was. She is only 2 years old. Our other cow, Muly, will certainly have a calf in a day or two. This is her 3rd. She has now a monstrous bag. She is an excellent cow. Granville still does the milking. He is a faithful, industrious child. His father has oftener to check him for doing too much than to urge him forward. Jos went to meeting one fourth day. On his return Granville met him half way with the waggon drawing a load of coal to a blacksmith. He got back safe, and since that has slipped off with another load. And Franklin don't care who works, so he can get clear.

It does not appear probable there will be much sugar made this season. I have made about 10 lb. We have had the most memorable winter ever known in these parts. We have had but 2 or three snows and they did not cover the ground nor last 24 hours. We have not since the 11th had more than 3 clear days at a time, and very seldom more than 2 mo very cold weather. It has been very sickly in the neighbourhood of Hanover ever since last summer. Poor old Ann Reeder (Brother Isaac heard her read at Hollands') is dead, 4 or 5 are ill in and about Hanover. The Dr says it is a Billious Typhus fever.

3rd mo 4th, 10 o'clock at night: Well, I filled all the other sheet after the family had gone to bed and will have to charge you with a drawing of tea or coffee as it was a cup or two of strong tea that enabled me to do it.

I have had many friendly visits from my neighbors and have paid many since I wrote last. One first day Jos, Seth, and I went to Augusta Meeting[3] and spent the afternoon at George McNeely's. I have spent 1 afternoon at John Battin's, the one succeeding him to us. I spent 2nd day afternoon (Jos joined me in the evening) and till bedtime at Nathan Townsend's, a near neighbor not 1/4 mile. His young wife is a grandneice of Levi Miller's. She has a person and dresses gay like Cousin

E Pleasants and bears a <u>more</u> striking resemblance in features and expression of face to dear Sister Deborah. I <u>fear</u> I shall be <u>sent for</u> there before morning as I have had warning given, and hear she is very poorly this evening. She has been 15 months a wife. They do live as nice as can be. They live in a cabin in which is an elegant walnut cupboard, mahogany bureau, table, and worktable, beautiful walnut [?], windsor chairs, 2 nice beds, delicate white curtains to the 12–light windows, elegant-looking glass.

I just mention these things to shew the comforts of life are here abundantly enjoyed even in the lowly cabin. And if you could only see the plentiful table spread and enjoy as I do the warm simple welcome unchecked by cold ceremony. Well, yesterday afternoon Alice [Jackson] sent over for me to come and spend the afternoon with her. Jos joined me in the evening, and we staid till 10. She gave us for supper teas, muffins, rolls, fresh light bread, fried ham, stewed dried beef, cream gravy, pickles, peach and apple sauce. I spent 1 afternoon last week at J[acob] Reeder's, our nearest neighbors, and Jos and myself expect to spend 6th day evening at Owen Stackhouse's and 1st day to Augusta Meeting and by special invitation the afternoon at George Monahun's.

I will close this and take up the thread again in one to the girls.

Your Anna Bentley

1. Like Anna's sister Deborah Bond, Robert Miller's first wife, Catharine Hole, had died in childbirth.
2. The granddaughter of Deborah Pleasants Stabler, daughter of Thomas P. and Elizabeth Stabler, and niece of James P. and Sarah Stabler, Sally Stabler (1816–1904) married her cousin, Augustus Jordan, in about 1841 and moved to Norfolk, Virginia, then to Washington, D.C. Her brother, John, eventually married Anna's daughter, Aliceanna.
3. They were officially members of Sandy Spring Meeting until they transferred to the New Garden Meeting in August. But Augusta Meeting, on the Carroll County line, was nearby.

~

Green Hill
4th mo 28 1828

I have 1/2 an hour before school to write to you, and now I shall have a chance to judge of the wish of some of my dear friends to afford me a greatly valued comfort by writing often. Yet every week some of you could if it was only 20 lines on a scrap of paper. And if my time here should be limited (as my present situation often suggests to a mind deeply impressed with dread of former dangers), then I know it will be a consolation to you all to reflect how much you had added to my enjoyment in the only way now left for an exchange of intercourse. . . .

Morris Miller & co returned with strong expressions of esteem and gratitude for attentions received from the kind friends in your parts. I went to see him the day after he returned. They insisted on my staying all night, and he brought me home next morning on the same beast that had so lately been sheltered and fed at Sharon, Morris trudging on foot through the mud. I have not time to express to each individual my thanks for what was sent but do thou to each express what thou supposes I feel for things that had five-fold the value to me here that they would have had there.

The scholars are going by to school now and I must hurry with might and main. A few weeks since, Granville gave his foot another bad cut with an axe, cutting a leader.[1] After hobbling a few weeks on crutches, he has got about again. When he had been lame 1 day, Guard got his hip broke by a falling tree. . . . Jos got his lame knee strained again as it was once before. We had then use for 2 pair of crutches. He laid them by last week and limped off to his work fencing, is much better though still lame. We have had 3 or four log-rollings, a great deal of trouble. I overheated myself baking about 10 days ago and have suffered much pain and something like dysentery ever since. I have been keeping school 6 or 8 weeks. Hannah Temple has returned and expects to stay with me mostly this summer. We are all well. I wish I could tell you of the neighbors' kindness when they were all lame.

What are Isaac's present prospects? I cannot tell you all I feel for you. Tell Cousin James P Stabler if he takes any newspapers or could procure any from those who do and would forward some to Jos once in a while he would thank him much, any except the *National Intelligencer*.[2] I was so disappointed about cellery and hoping, Brother, I would have procured a little in town.

Hannah Miller has laid her intentions of marriage before the meeting last week.[3] the Orthodox party left the meeting house at New Garden in possession of the Liberal party monthly meeting. Oh, what scenes of confusion and downright quarrelling. The spirit of persecution is great. I cannot say more but that I love you very dearly and don't disappoint me of the enjoyment I promise myself in a week or two.

Your affectionate Anna

1. Tendon.
2. A pro-slavery newspaper in Washington, D.C.
3. Born on Sept. 25, 1805, Hannah Miller married a fellow Quaker, Jacob Reeder, on June 27, 1828. Hannah's love life is the subject of a local folk tale. She was earlier engaged to be married to a young Quaker named Jesse Farringdon, so the story goes. When the Hicksite

controversy in the Society of Friends began, however, she and Jesse found themselves on opposite sides. Eventually, she broke off the engagement. In his anguish at being spurned, Jesse nervously twisted two hickory saplings together, telling her that their love might have united them like the two small trees. While Hannah moved on with her life, the two saplings grew entwined together, and were still a local attraction decades later, after Hannah and Jesse were both dead. Hannah and Jacob Reeder settled on his father's farm for a time. Eventually they moved to Iowa.

~

Two thousand people attended the quarterly meeting in Salem while Elias Hicks was there. A couple of days later he was at the New Garden quarterly meeting. In Hicks's own words, "Here Friends had a trying time, as those called Orthodox, although they were but a small part of the meeting, had undertaken to disown a number of Friends; but Friends did not acknowledge their authority, nor consider their disownments of any effect, and they all came together as usual in the quarterly meeting. The Orthodox strove hard to get Friends to withdraw, but they refused, and proceeded with the business of the meeting, which those called Orthodox interrupted for a time, but finding that Friends would not give way, they finally left the meeting, and retired to a school-house, and Friends had a comfortable season together, and conducted their business in much harmony and condescension, and were evidently owned by the Head of the Church."

On August 18, he attended Marlborough Meeting, noting it to be "very large, notice having been previously given of our intention to be there." Again, though, the Orthodox members of the meeting "made great opposition, which greatly offended the people." Hicks zigzagged around the countryside, appearing twice at New Garden before showing up at Sandy Spring Monthly Meeting, where "a precious solemnity pervaded the assembly." Later, at Mt. Pleasant, the site of the Ohio Yearly Meeting in Jefferson County, the assembly almost came to blows.

~

10th mo 19th 1828
My dear friends,
    1st night 11 o'clock. As 2 mails have gone from here without our writing, I feared you would feel uneasy and will no longer wait for <u>brighter prospects</u>. I (or we) have received letters from you every week but not having any of them downstairs cannot tell what dates they bear. The last was from Sister Margaret. I thank her for it but must charge her

with a great omission in not ever mentioning Sister Mary and little ones. At this time I particularly want to hear from them, and still continue to give all the information you can of Brother Isaac. We still continue to enjoy good health (except my head, which continues to ache 2 hours from 10 to 12 every day, sometimes most violently). Please describe it to Dr Howard and ask his advise. Tell him I have nothing left to pay him with but thankfulness, if he can release me from it, for besides the suffering I can ill afford the time it makes me lose.

We are in no better fix about provisions than when I last wrote, have been for a week at a time without a mouthful of bread in the house of any kind, and no meat either; our cows both dry, but we get 3 pints a day from our exellent neighbour Polly Smith (a neice of Levi Miller). We have now a little butter in the house and expect buckwheat flour tomorrow, enough to last a week. It will do no good to tell you the worst. There is no danger of our starving; we have potatoes and half a barrel of salt yet and Contentment still, that great blessing. When I think how many dollars I have spent that need not have been and what a small sum would now make us so much more comfortable, I feel certain I should never abuse prosperity as I have done.

I went this day week to see Susan, staid all night, went to Morris's 2nd day and staid there all night. Morris desired his love to be given you. 3rd day went to Sarah Holland and returned home 4th day evening. I was received and entertained at each place as a near and dear relative. How soothing it was to me! I fear my dear motherly friend Holland is not long for this world.[1] She has had a violent attack of erisypelas again. Her tongue swelled and turned black with great ulcerous holes in it. She is now better so as to set up and knit. She gave me yarn enough to knit Granville and Franklin each a pr of stockings. (Neither Granville or one of the children have a pair to begin with; they finished those I footed for them last winter.) . . . I know not yet how the children are to be clothed this winter. Such good linsey is to be had for 40 cents and 37 1/2 in Hanover, if we only had the means to get it. As for myself, I have but 1 flannel dress. I brought a pattern of calico with me, which I intended to change for bombazet, but I had to sell it for necessaries. Oh, that the wool my dear mother talked of sending would come.

Samuel Kempton wrote to me last week and said [Delia] intended leaving some things for me at Uncle Gerard T Hopkins's store for the first conveyance. I wrote to them and told them of Joseph E Bentley being PM [postmaster] and requested them to write. He sends us newspapers.[2]

I have with Jos's hearty concurrence went abroad almost <u>every other</u> day for <u>3 weeks</u> past for my head <u>or something</u> prevented my gaining strength and I seemed likely not to have milk enough for my babe. I have a strengthening plaister on my back and one on my forehead. We have a good crop of corn and Seth is building a nice corncrib and we have some rye. The waters are so low there is great difficulty in getting a little grinding done, and we are not alone in our straitened circumstances. Wheat is very dear and rising. It is from 62 1/2 to 75 per bushel. There are several hundred Germans come into this neighbourhood. They are trying to buy Hanover and 10 miles round it, offering cash, and 500 more are on the way. They talk German but I believe they are Swiss.

The neighbourhood is very sickly yet. Some families all down, a good many deaths. I heard Nicholas Thomas had run off from Pittsburg for your neighbourhood taking with him upwards of 30 dollars belonging to a man he had hired. That story is currant here. I parted with Hannah Temple 3 weeks ago, and Maria insists on doing the washing herself and has done it twice. My dear little Aliceanna[3] grows very fast. (We never call her Alice alone.) She has a round face, a very placid countenance. The first exclamation of all who see her is "how much she is like Deborah," and <u>she</u> is a little, hearty, fat, short chunk of a girl with light brown curly hair, rosy cheeks, very lively large dark hazel eyes and a most <u>comical tongue</u> and is called by some a beauty. She catches a tune very quick and goes singing about as happy as can be with an apron full of <u>roast potatoes</u>.

2nd day. Well, I left off last night because I was sleepy, and now my head is too bad to add much more. Only one thing: As this is a newly established post office and very little business done, Joseph feels some scruple about so many free letters yet awhile; for there is seldom anything goes or comes but to and from us, and he fears it will appear altogether a matter of self-interest in soliciting for the office. . . . If the dear children write, it will have to be in our letters. . . .

Your own Anna

My dear aunt, I had a right smart letter written.

1. Actually, Sarah Holland was still alive for the 1850 census, age seventy-six.
2. Samuel and Delia Kempton proved to be good friends to the Bentleys in Ohio, frequently sending not only newspapers, but also cloth, needles, old clothing, and other staples.
3. Born in mid-1828, she was named for Joseph Bentley's mother and sister.

As Margaret Briggs wrote to Isaac on January 19, 1829, the family at Sharon had been sitting around the table, the snow outside falling thick and fast, when suddenly someone heard a horse and rider approaching. Margaret teased Brother Isaac that he would never guess who it was. She passed the letter off to her mother without telling him. Hannah Briggs went on that the visitor was "dear Granville S. Bentley who had been so anxious to pay us a visit that by working hard he says he had got leave of his Parents to start with a couple of waggons bound for Alexandria and according to his estimation 100 and 10 miles he has <u>walked</u>."

Granville went by horseback from Washington to Waterford, Maryland, and stayed a day or two with Uncle Joseph Bond, who gave him a map to Sharon. But Granville had trouble finding his way in the snow, got lost, and ended up at Brooke Grove, where Uncle Richard lent him a horse. That horse soon fell down and ran away. At last, after much trouble, Granville arrived at Sharon.

"We did not know him untill he pronounced 'Grandmother,'" Margaret wrote. He and his young uncle, William Henry, hugged and kissed "repeatedly." As his Aunt Margaret later asked James P. Stabler, "Dost thou not think it was an extraordinary undertaking for one so young? he is only a few months over fifteen."

∼

2nd mo 1829
My dear friends,

For fear of meeting with the interruptions that prevented my writting the 2 last mails, I concluded I would make a beginning tonight, though it is half past 12 on 6th day night. For two mails previous to the last your letters came a week too late, which, as my anxiety was so great to hear particularly from my dear son, was a very great trial. His father and I regret we desired his return with the Reeders, as Harmon Brown,[1] who is expected back tomorrow, is going immediately back to Baltimore and will be at his uncle, Abel Davis. But it can't be helped now. We did it for the best, and I don't know either if the poor boy's clothes would have lasted him so long.

Dearest Mother, I read thy letter stating the things thee had sent with many tears. I am afraid thou hast robbed thyself, or yourselves, of what you need for our sakes, and from this time forward I want thee to know it is not with the expectation of relief from you that I have mentioned our situation. Your sympathy is so soothing that perhaps to obtain it I have acted wrong, perhaps I ought to have kept it from you, but then I could not have written at all, for it would come out. To dear cousin Deborah Stabler[2] express my thanks for her contribution towards our comfort. Tell her it is hard <u>scuffling</u> but I have not given out yet, and cornbread seems quite <u>natural</u> now; the children thrive on it. Our cows both have calves, one 3 and the other 2 weeks old. We shall kill both and then, Oh, how glad we shall be of the milk and butter.

This week has been most severely cold. My poor boy—I have not heard half enough to satisfy the anxious mother of such a child as <u>I think</u> him. What do you think of him, all of you from Mother down to Billy? What has become of Mary Ann? And now, Sister Mary, if thee loved to give me pleasure half as well as I do thee, and if thy <u>babies</u> were half as sweet and as much worth talking about as mine, I don't see how thee could have helped writting to me. It is a downright shame, and to tell the real truth I do think so. Why, there is thy old man as good as any old woman, I expect, in the writing line, Cousin MMB, <u>Anna</u>, and a girl in the kitchen, and <u>Tom</u> and <u>Kirk</u>. Well, if thou cannot find time to write to a sister <u>situated as I have been</u>, why, how does thee think I can? I have but one room to cook, eat, sleep, scold, and grunt in, and waiting till the children are asleep is out of the question. <u>My mornings till 12 are spent in nursing, sewing, and scolding; from 12 till sundown grunting with the headache, then till 10 working, sometimes all their stockings</u> (they have all, Jos too, but 1 pr a piece) <u>to wash, dry, and darn them. I think no hardship to even sit up till 1 rather than miss writing.</u> I never get to bed till after 12 and very often 2—and Lizzy don't care a fig for me.

We sold Lawyer for 2 fine ewes which we are to have before shearing, and, Oh, if I could get 3 dollars I would soon have a spinning wheel. My fire is too low to write more tonight.

7th day night, 15th. 12 o'clock and all asleep but me. Deborah is not well. She has a bad cold and pain in her side. I heard today that Ben Higgins had rented a farm 1 mile from here and would come the first of April. I am going to copy a piece of poetry, and I want your opinion of it. [Here she inserted the verses of "Broken Ties," the "dissevered chain" of family connections that now "in sparkling ruin lies."]

I wish dear Sarah would write a piece once more for me. Oh, ain't it hard that I cannot shew you my sweet little blossom of the wilderness?

Her sweet good-humoured smile attracts much admiration. Deborah looks like Margaret used to when her age, and Franklin strikingly like Brother Isaac. Joseph has taken such a dislike to letter writing that I have to do all for him, but he loves you all. He be grown thin as an ould sixpence. . . .

E Bates is in the neighbourhood preaching away, they say <u>very mildly</u>. . . .[3]

I must conclude.

Your very affectionate A Bentley

D is better, my head very bad.

1. Harmon Brown, whose father had been an early member of the Ohio Legislature, was "reputed to be the most skillful teamster in the township, and performed many extended and remarkable journeys," according to a Columbiana County history.

2. Deborah Pleasants Stabler, the mother of James P. Stabler, taught for many years at the Friends school at Fair Hill.

3. Quaker historian Rufus Jones described Elisha Bates of Ohio as "one of the most famous of the American Ministers and Quaker leaders of the time." He later became an evangelical Quaker, then left the Society of Friends altogether.

~

3d mo 1st 1829

My dear Mother and all, . . .

I suppose our dear Granville is on the road now. How anxious I am to see him and how many fears <u>will</u> beset my mind on his account. I fear his clothing is not sufficient for this severe season—but I know it is useless to give way to fear. I wish I could be with you to unburthen my heart, for writing, though a great comfort, is an inadequate means when there is so much to say as I wish to now. I have felt so much of thankfulness, of brightened hope, and I know not what all for 2 or 3 weeks past—but more particularly since this day week—that I seem a new creature. I wish I could arrange my ideas a little. The letter, dear Mother, that informed me of the prospect of such great relief was the first circumstance that cheered me up, though I wept often to think perhaps it was curtailing your comforts to alleviate our distresses. But it gave me fresh heart to patch and darn many a night till after 1 o'clock to alter my cotton dresses for Maria, as her linsey would hang together no longer, to wash and darn their stockings when all were asleep but me.

The next week, dear Mother, also brought a great and unexpected relief in a present of 20 dollars by mail to me from a stranger to me* [*but not so to Jos] but whose name I am not at liberty to tell. (I would rather you would not allude to it in your letters to me.) I immediately gave it to Jos with the feeling generous letter accompanying it. What we both felt I cannot describe. He got on Tom and went to the stores where we had accounts, divided it among them, got me 2 cents worth of snuff and a quarter of tea and himself a lb of tobacco and returned without a cent but with a lightened heart. We have debts to the amount of more than that, but they will wait awhile, I hope.

The 5th day after, we killed Rose's calf with feelings of heartfelt gratitude. I poured out for all as much good milk as we could drink, and though we had nothing else than coarse cornbread warm, I could not set at the table but went off a piece with my brown mug of rich milk and cake and really shed tears of joy as I looked at their happy faces and heard their rejoicing over it. They will now no longer have to eat their cornbread alone, which they often did without a murmur. . . .

2nd day. . . . My babe has for some days been suffering with a very bad cold which has affected her breast, eyes, and ears, and she was so poorly yesterday evening I could not write. She had the earache and I gave her laudanum. She is now sleeping under the effects of it. She has sat alone for some time, and though I do not suppose she means to apply the name to me, she has a way of calling "Mumma, oh Mumma," when she is begging for me to take her. I weighed her the day she was 6 months old; she weighs 18 lb. I want Sister Mary to weigh Hannah then and let me know that I may judge of her size by comparison. . . .

On 2nd day Harmon Brown arrived and brought me fresh cause of thankfulness and joy. I had written to dear Cousin William and FSB[1] stating some of our difficulties and to know if it would be entirely convenient for them to send me some articles and receive pay in produce, such as flax, butter, linnen, when we could have time to raise it. I told them our prospects. Dear, kind, generous friends. . . . They sent all I sent for and a great deal more. Cousins A and W both wrote to me. . . . Cousin A, often expressing her sympathy and telling about the goods, says, "I shall probably enclose the bill as thou requested, but not with the prospect of making thee uneasy about payment, but as thou requested it. I thought it would be best, and if thou should never find it convenient to pay, it need not cause thee any uneasiness. I have some books left of my late occupation as teacher which I thought might be acceptable to thee among the children. If so, I shall be pleased they may be accepted for my good will and not their real value."

Cousin Thomas S Stabler took from here to sell for Jos a breast pin worth 10 dollars or more, which we said he might take 5 rather than miss. I told them that might go towards paying. I will just draw off the bill that you may see what was sent. The cow was for Jos and the cloth for Seth. Dear old man, he seems to consider us his nearest friends and says he never will call on us for the work he has done for us. He is making me a churn. [Here she itemized what had been sent—among which were shirting, calico, plates, a mended brown teapot, six pounds of coffee, two pounds of tea, oil of lavender and mint, two each English and New York readers, two spelling books, a quire of paper, and four lead pencils.]

I know not whether to attribute it to the <u>excellent coffee</u> or to the effect of the mind on the body, but since the day after it came my long-suffering head has been easy and an abundant flow of nourishment for my poor babe. Well, this is not all. By Harmon came SAT Kempton's little package containing the following articles—the cellery seed is all I ever asked for of them, but they have kept up a very friendly correspondence with us since we came out here, and S sends us 5 or 6 newspapers weekly. Though he don't take them himself, yet he takes the trouble to collect them of his friends, seall them up, and send them every week. . . . [The Kemptons sent fabric, ribbon, pins and needles, and other notions in addition to an ounce of "cellery" seed.]

I write particularly that your minds may be cheered on our accounts. Some of our trials are lessened, and those that remain we feel resigned to bear patiently. I know trials are good for us; it teaches [us] to feel gratitude for favours bestowed. My babe prevents my adding any more now than endeared love to all.

Your Anna Bentley

1. I have been unable to identify Cousin William, Cousin A, and FSB.

⤳

3rd mo 15th 1829
Dear Mother and all—

Last night just at dark we were all delighted by the return of our dear Son safe and well. Elizabeth, I suppose it is two weeks this day since he left you. He had considerable fatigue till he joined the waggons 19 miles from Waterford.[1] From having to walk too fast to keep up with his company his leg became so sore and stiff he could not get on as fast but staid all night at G Gore's, a rich old bachelor's. It is an old maid keeps

house for him. Started at 8 AM, got to Union about 1/2 past 11, was
accosted by a man [in] the street who enquired where he was from,
where [he was] going, and his name, which, when he heard, he
[announced] himself no less a personage than Seth ——th!!! [obliterated
by sealing wax] He made him go in and eat dinner and asked him so
many questions that his wife laughed and told him she expected
Granville's mother was someone he had been in love with. He told her it
was a fact.

A mile and a half from there he joined the waggons and came on
very comfortably, stinting himself, though, in his eating but without
much fatigue. He is now seated opposite me amusing himself with
snapping a pistol at me which he found on the road, and his father and
he keep such a talking I can scarcely write. How shall I thank you all for
your most acceptable presents? The cape still retains a smell of Mother. I
have got it on and am delighted with it. Everything else is beautiful and
doubly dear, coming from you. Brother Richard's and Sister Mary's
presents I thank them for and admire them more than I can tell. You
cannot judge how valuable they all are to me. Aunt Peggy's present to me
and the kindnesses of that dear family to our dear son tell them we feel
sincerely grateful for. And what shall I say to my dear Cousin Caleb,[2] for
I do love him. . . .

We had a visit from Benjamin & Mary Higgins and children 2 weeks
ago. She seemed rejoiced to see us, pled with me to come and see her,
looks better than ever I saw her, and their neighbours say they are
gaining credit and striving to do the best they can; and I hope they will
get on now they have rented a farm to the shares on good terms and are
industrious.

My head is much better, but I have had a bad cold, sore throat, and
pain in my face for a week, caught in attending to my sugar. Then we
had 2 days a good run of water and I turned out through mud over shoe
with my spiles, augur, and brush to clear troughs and tap trees, then,
with a bucket on each arm, to collect water. We boiled it down in the
woods till after 12 at night on the 2nd day (Jos assisting and making new
troughs). I stirred off at the house 13 lb of beautiful lively sugar with my
one kettle and pot when many with 3 times as many trees and 6 kettles
did not make more than 6 lb. Snow and cold weather stopped me, and
we are waiting a fresh run to get fresh colds, fresh aches for good sweet
sugar. But I will try to let no comfort slip for the want of all the exertion
my "poor frail tenement" can make. If we can make more than with great
economy is enough for our own use, why, it will help to extricate us from

debt. I sent 2 1/2 lb of nice butter to the store last week. It is only 8 cents per lb, but "every little helps."

There has been 7 to see Granville today, and 4 neighbours eat supper here, among whom was our dear friend Morris. He enquired after you all as one who felt an interest for you, seemed gratified to hear you enquired for him, and sent his respects to you all. And now, Mother, dost thou know what a conquest thou hast made of the old widower Samuel Reeder so that he joked with Granville often of going back sometime to persuade thee to come out, said, "Stranger things had happened than that he might have to call him grandfather." He is a worthy man, much respected, wealthy, & lives in a nice brick house. Will thee come?

Oh, dear Sister Sarah, Seth is going to make nice frames for Mother's and thy profiles. How glad I am to have them. It is a good likeness. My babe and Deborah have very bad colds yet. Aliceanna has been quite poorly. You can't think what a sweet lovely <u>babe she</u> is. (Remember the Owl.) Everybody says she is beautiful, and I can't help listening. There must be <u>some</u> truth in it when she appears so <u>even</u> in my eyes. Granville thinks she is much larger than your dear little Hannah. Was that Isaac Bond's hair in the letter? Aliceanna's is very light-coloured now but will grow darker as it was dark at first. All send love to all.

I am your own, Anna Bentley

1. Waterford, Loudoun County, Virginia, an old Quaker town and the home of Granville's uncle by marriage, Joseph Bond.
2. Probably Caleb Moore, son of Thomas and Mary (Brooke) Moore.

～

4th mo 5th 1829
Dear friends,

Two mails and no letter. Fie upon you. The mail previous 2 came, one written before Granville left you and one enclosing sister Sarah's very pretty poetry for which I thank her. She was certainly correct in her judgement that the poetry I sent was not mine, for if I could have written as good I should be too proud of it not to have avowed myself its author. I got it from a newspaper SA Kempton sent. . . .

It has been either 2 or 3 weeks since I have written to you. I have been closely engaged in the laborious <u>work of sugar making, Granville</u> and Thomas my only assistants. Our trees are scattering so that it is a great round to collect the water, more than 1/2 a mile. We have to carry it all in buckets, for they are mostly where the brush and timber cut down in clearing will not admit of hauling on a little sledge as is most common. We had not time to get half troughs enough for all our trees. We have but 1 10-gallon kettle and a 4-gallon pot to boil and stir off in. It takes a barrel of water for 5 lbs, and we have had but 4 good sugar days. It is great trouble to make spiles, tap trees, &c. I have set up all night several times and often till 2, and what have I gained by it? Why, 60 lbs of beautiful sugar. Ain't you glad for us? And my head so long afflicted is now well.

Jos was so engaged with getting his ground cleaned ready for corn he could not help with the sugar. He is a good deal uneasy on account of having no way to plough his ground. He has been trying to get a yoke of oxen. There is an excellent yoke of well-broke ones for 35 dollars, but the man must have cash. He has been trying to sell his watch, offering it for 20 dollars less than cost, but it is still too high-priced for this country. Now, ain't it a pity? If he had the oxen he could haul coal enough already bespoke to pay for them very shortly, and now, though he could find immediately sale for hundreds of bushels, he can't haul any. But so it is.

Our wheat looks beautiful and green. We have made an arrangement with Nathan Townsend to plough our flax ground and sow it (an excellent spot) for the liberty of a peice to sow some for himself. And now the very first $2.50 I can come honestly by I intend getting a wheel to learn to spin on. It is high time Maria was put to it.

What are we to do with RHG and family till they can get a home, for I expect they will come here?[1] They will think it rough times, I fear, and crowded, too. We have but 1 spare room finished. Granville began a letter to Sister Margaret last week but could not get it finished. He loves you twice as much as he did before his visit.

Last 7th day, the 28th, I took Granville and Thomas to help me along to Sarah Holland's, was received as I used to be at Sharon. Susan got sight of me from her door (it is just across a meadow), and soon came over with her little Holland, just such a lovely dispositioned, good child as Isaac Bond was at his age (8 months old). Oh, they are such good people. No fear of deceit there, for they have that which is the best foundation for true friendship—religion. The next morning before I went over to Susan's Sarah gave me a large hank of beautiful fine dark sewing thread and said she hoped when the walking was better I would come oftener as she had nothing suitable to ride and could not walk to see me. I spent the day delightfully at Susan's—Catharine, young Sarah, and Hannah with us in the evening.

Sally Miller came in and was very pressing for me to go home with her. I told her I had before intended to do so. Her mother was here 2 weeks ago and pressed me to come, assuring me they had no wish to hold me at a distance but that I had always felt very near to them. To tell the truth, she was one of the overseers and watched from her house here. My reply was, "I looked for thee day after day when I was sick and thou visited me not among strangers, and thou came not to comfort me." And I turned to her, smiling, and said, "And yet thee could even walk over this long road to help turn me out of meeting." It seemed to affect her, so I changed the subject.

They seemed not to know what to say to me, for I treated them as kindly as I could, got the best dinner I was able, &c. They seemed as if they were at a loss and not willing to condemn me for anything. I thought I would help them out and told them they were at liberty to proceed with regard to disowning me as they thought proper, though I did not consider myself as a member amongst them, having joined New Garden Monthly Meeting. I thought they tried to entrap me to acknowledge I had "left the Society of Friends and joined the followers of Elias Hicks." It was all a very peaceable opportunity. I was candid and so shall be excommunicated.

Well, to go back to when I digressed from, Susan and Robert went with me to Levi's. On first going in I thought there seemed a little restraint, that all did not seem as it used to be there, but it soon wore off. They were very kind. I staid till after dinner 2nd day. They pled that Thomas might come and stay there as he used to when I was coming away. Ann loaded me with onions, beans, cakes for the children, and sent Beckey and Debby all the way home with me to carry Aliceanna.

4th mo 12th. Well, I had got thus far last mail day when, it being a good sugar day, I was obliged to go out with my auger, Thomas, and buckets to freshen the trees, collect water, and begin boiling. The camp is some distance in the woods. Before I had near done freshening, I was sent for to the house for Co[mpany]! the Orthodox committee were there. I came up and after speaking kindly sat down awhile. They seeming to feel some backwardness. I told them I did not wish to be rude but would be glad they would relieve their minds as soon as they could and not deter me from work I considered of importance. They hemmed and haughed, called Elias [Hicks] and Thomas Wetherald deists, &c. I told them I was convinced they were not so and felt unity with their views as far as I knew them; and they were at liberty to proceed with me after this avowal as they thought proper; that I had never held any other belief than that I now held, and it was in accordance with what I believed the early Friends held. They shook their heads and lamented my <u>delusion</u> and departed, pressing my hand and expressing a hope I might be favoured to see the error of my way and return to them. There were none on the committee I had any personal acquaintance. One that I knew who was appointed would not come; 2 of those who did I have often watched <u>sleeping comfortably</u> in Sandy meeting.

Well, when they were gone it was too late to finish my letter. I went back to my work, carried water, and tended the kettle till night; went down in the morning with Thomas and boiled down till noon. The water having ceased running and it raining on me, I stirred off 7 1/2 lb of beautiful sugar and a quart of molasses, but have paid dear for it in taking cold in my face. My jaw pains me so of nights on my <u>weak</u> side I cannot sleep. It was dreadful last night, and this evening I have had a most excruciating spell about 2 hours till I was near fainting. A cup or two of good coffee (which I am too <u>stingy</u> of to use often) has relieved me for an hour past, and I must hurry before another spell comes on. Sugar making is all over for this season.

I received dear Mother's letter dated the 24 of the 3rd mo last 3rd day. I wish she had mentioned when RHG is expected to start. We have got a cabin 1/2 a mile from here for them to go into till they can get fixed, which I expect they will for the present year be in a farm 3/4 of a mile from us. I intend cleaning and putting in comfortable order the house they will occupy at first, for we are too poor to entertain them many days; and if they will profit by the counsel our experience here will enable us to give them, perhaps it will be of advantage to them. If not, they will never be satisfied here.

A man who passed Harmon Brown in the mountains informs us we may look for him in 2 days. He will bring thy box, dear Mother. I received a letter from dear Isaac last week. He expected to leave there shortly, was uncertain where he should bend his course in search of employment, said perhaps he might try the city of "Gotham" again, and we need not write till we heard from him; he was well and in good spirits. Dear <u>boy</u>, how I long to see him. Ah, how I long to see again all. Almost 3 years since I left you. The fatigue of the long, long road would be no consideration as an obstacle if I could have a good opportunity to pay you a visit. The expence would not be great if provision was cooked to take along. Oh, that one of my dear, dear sisters could pay me a visit. I even look forward to the hope of seeing my mother here sometime.

Our grain and grass begins to look green, and Green Hill will soon be an appropriate name for this place. Tomorrow and the next day will be toilsome days for me, tomorrow in baking, pickling, and preparing for a log rolling the day after. We do not expect more than 12 or 13 hands, but they for 3 meals, which must be as good as we can get; will occasion a good deal of trouble. Polly Smith offered to help me but was sent for to see her son who has cut the cap of his knee with a drawing knife.

Jos bought 4 bushels of wheat and a beautiful China sow and 7 stout pigs at a sale last week on a credit of 11 months. He paid, or is to pay, 6 dollars for them. We have all grown very fond of cornbread and thrive on it, even the sweet rosy Aliceanna. You would smile to see her with a chunk of pone in her hand eating as happy as any of us. I think she certainly is the prettiest babe I ever had, a better one no one ever had. To judge from her actions when at play, she will be as wild and mischievous as will be convenient. If anyone nods their head at her, she will immitate them in a comical manner just with the motion of a hominy beater. But Deborah is the smart one. She has a most expressive pair of large, full, dark hazel (darker than Granville's) eyes, the brightest colour in her cheeks, her face an oval. Her hair never was cut; it parts on the top of her head as soft and glossy brown. She is very fat and the picture of health and happiness. She substitutes the letter "t" always for "s," is very quick at learning poetry. Thomas and Hannah were getting a peice called "Old Casper, or The Victory," and by hearing them she learnt it as quick as they did, though it is a long one. I wish you could hear her repeat it and many others. She is a darling with Seth, who has made and presented her an elegant curled maple crib to sleep in. It is a beautiful peice of furniture, and would cost 8 or 10 dollars in Baltimore, I expect.

I wonder how often I have described these children to you. But you can't see them to judge for yourselves. Oh, if my naughty Sister Mary would do so by me, what a pleasure she would give me. If she don't write I will think she is serving me as she did before, but I charge you all not to do so.

I want to know what thee dresses little Hannah [Brooke] in. Please enclose small patterns of some of her dresses in a letter which thee must write me. Sister Margaret sent patterns of all the dresses they have got since I left you. Among Sister Sarah's was a calico, the handsomest I ever saw, which I would rather have than my crape, which I never wore but once.

Granville did wish much to write this week, but it will be out of his power, and Maria had a long letter to her Aunt Margaret written on the slate, but having the headache couldn't copy it tonight. Franklin loves you all, too. I fear he will always be weakly. Much hard exercise, such as sawing with the crosscut saw (at which he is an excellent hand) and chopping, gives him a violent pain in his back and breast. His back is very weak and subject to pain. He grows strikingly like his Uncle Isaac.

I examined the cherrystones I planted last summer and expected to find them decayed as they never came up. But to my great joy they are sprouting. I hope Robert will bring the Mangel Wurtzel[2] I have so often been disappointed in getting. My face is beggining to pain me again. Jos, Granville, Franklin, and Maria send love to you all, Cousin Margaret always included.

Your affectionate Anna Bentley

Past 3 o'clock. I am just going to bed a little relieved from pain after suffering severely 2 1/2 hours. I have put to my face scorched tow with pepper and whisky in it and the smarting is pleasant compared with the pain. It is not <u>my old sort of tootheache</u> but the <u>same old tormentor</u> that <u>lived</u> in my head so long.

1. Robert H. Garrigues and his family. He was the son of William Garrigues and his wife, Hannah, the sister of Isaac Briggs. Robert married Margaret E. Thomas on May 22, 1816. He was about thirty-five when they came to Ohio with their three oldest children: Deborah, age about ten, Sarah or Sally Ann, about five, and William, about one. Robert was half-brother to Sarah Garrigues Brooke, wife of the elder Samuel Brooke, so his nephews were the Brooke boys Abraham, Samuel, Edward, William, and James, several of whom became well-known Ohio abolitionists. Robert's brother, William Garrigues, whose children later married into the Bentley family, moved to Marlborough in Stark County about this time.
2. Sugar beet, for cattle feed.

~

5th mo 10 1829
My dear friends,

I intended to write you a long letter this week as I have not written for 2 or 3, but it is now 1 o'clock and I have a considerable washing to do tomorrow, and last week was a toilsome one to me—indeed to us all. Last 5th day Granville came running for the rake, said Jacksons had sent word the <u>woods was on fire</u> and had got on our quarter. The thick black smoke rose fearfully. I sent to Reeders' and 3 men came. The wind fell and, with great exertion, by making a circle and firing the leaves as they went, they stopped its progress after it had run over 10 or 12 acres of our woods and 1/2 of a mile the other side. Before it got to ours the fire had got into one tall tree, which we feared would scatter fire again when it fell. The [men] raked a very wide circle round it and pronounced all safe, but I could sleep very little that night.

Jos had concluded to have a log rolling 7th day, so on 6th day he had to ask hands. I got up, set rising, and started at sunrise with Franklin and a wallet, a jug, and tin bucket to John Battin's. I got a peck of dried peaches, a quart of strong vinegar, 4 lb of lard, 3 fowls to be paid for when we could. We eat a good breakfast and returned home tired—it is a mile and 1/2. I did up my pickles, stewed my peaches, begun to make my bread. . . . I sent Maria to Reeders' for some milk for custard and to ask Ellen if she could come and assist me. When I put the bread in the pans at 2 o'clock I went out to kindle a fire in the oven. The wind was blowing hard. I looked up the hill towards the woods and found the fire had got out again. I left the babe in care of Thomas and run to Jackson's. He was not at home. I sent on to Owen [Stackhouse], who was plowing, and then I ran all the way home. As soon as all came in sight from Reeders' I sent her back. Three men soon came from there and I hailed another that was going by. Maria started off for her father, Ellen came, and though in terror as the cry of fire came nearer and nearer toward the back fence, I was obliged to go on with my work, for the hands were engaged. Poor Jos came running, his waistcoat and waistband unbuttoned. As soon as he joined them a precious shower of rain relieved them from their hard duty. It burned over 20 or 30 acres but has as yet done no injury.

Well, yesterday we had 9 men and Morris 2 yoke of oxen, and I made a potpie and boiled a ham, &c and waited on them. I had another race to the fire with Granville. We succeeded in stopping it just as it began to spread. They got all the logs together. We have had 1 other rolling before. Since I wrote you have got 1 field of corn planted and one of oats. Granville is plowman. We get Nathan Townsend's mare and he gets Tom in return when he needs him. Our flax is up and looks well. Our wheat, grass, and flax look beautiful, the finest in the neighbourhood. We have our field planted in corn and two more nearly ready.

It is after 3 o'clock. I must go to bed after saying I received Mother's letter last week.

2nd day morning. Oh, dear, the ground is covered with snow and it is falling as fast as possible. The fruit, the fruit! But we must leave all to providence. I have a great many young chickens: 7 hens and 3 ducks setting. I am compelled to conclude for want of time. They have appointed Jos clerk of the preparative meeting.[1]

I am, affectionately, your Anna

Dear Brother Isaac, I am glad thou art returned.

1. A sort of committee meeting that prepares items of business to be brought up at the monthly meeting.

6th mo 29th 1829
Beloved friends,

Several weeks have elapsed since I have written to you, and just as I was preparing to write you a long letter this morning, company came to spend the day. I must now be brief. We are all well and are cheered with the hope of a near approaching <u>plentiful harvest</u>. Jos has commenced his hay harvest. Granville has written 2 letters to his Aunt Mary and torn them up, and indeed he has so much hard work to do that it unfits him for letter writing. He has done all the ploughing and that in new ground. Our corn is far the best in the neighbourhood—about 8 acres; one field is far higher than my head—<u>abundance</u> of broom corn, pumkins, cimblins, cucumbers, cantelopes, beans, potatoes, flax, &c and 100 chickens. The hens and <u>me</u> have hatched 12 this morning.

And now just a little glimpse of the other side of the picture. <u>The children are absolutely in rags.</u> I have shirting sufficient for us, but I will now tell you I have never received the box my dear mother sent, and for some weeks was under the disheartening impression it was lost—as I received a letter from Cousin D Hopkins informing me it had been sent on with an addition from her dear mother—but I have since heard the man who took it was disappointed in getting a waggon and returned it in safety to Uncle Gerard T Hopkins. I have now a prospect, a pretty certain prospect. Hannah and Deborah have each one old calico and one very ragged cotton absolutely <u>all</u> their dependance till Cousin MEG gave Deborah a new very light gingham, too light to wear every day if I could help it—I am so happy that releif is at hand that I don't feel the least cast down, and you need not <u>for</u> me. Indeed, it's good for us to be humbled. It prepares the heart to receive with thankfulness the favours bestowed on us.

I said we were all well but forgot <u>Franklin's accident. He cut his foot badly with the axe.</u> It was fortunately cut aslant and thus escaped the tendons, though he has not walked on it for 10 days. It is not painful and is healing fast. [Here Anna drew an ovoid shape about 8 inches long; she wrote inside it, "This is the size of it. The axe slanted an inch further under the shin."]

You will want to hear of Cousin RHG and family. They arrived here safe and well 3 weeks wanting 1 day after they left Brookeville. The house we had rented for them (about a mile from here) wanted a good deal of fixing. We invited them to remain a week here to recover from fatigue. . . . They seemed so uneasy at the large addition they made to our <u>small</u> family and seem inclined to <u>doubly</u> compensate for all favours received. They appear to feel in a strange <u>land</u>. Cousin Margaret will not be satisfied if I am not there every few days. She is sick of Sally Waters who has too many airs for this country. She expects to get rid of her tomorrow.

Cousin Robert and Margaret, Joseph, and myself spent yesterday afternoon at Nathan Townsend's all mutually pleased with <u>OURSELVES</u>. Cousin Margaret slipped to a drawer while she was here and poured 3 or 4 lb of coffee and 2 cakes of chocolate in it. R got meat, butter, and wheat flour and would have <u>their</u> coffee <u>used</u> (not that she gave me). Little did they think the rough fare they got here was so much better than we are used to. I was there last week. Cousin Robert brought out a most exellent pair of Wilmington striped pantaloons rather too small for him, which he gave me for Granville and cut off 5 yds of wide stripe cotton for me—a dress, which last article I am to pay for in eggs, chickens, soap, &c when it suits me.

I am not <u>led away</u> but I still do retain my <u>opinion</u> that her naturally resserved disposition and misfortunes were in a great measure the cause of what her friends mistook for a dislike of their company. I still think it was the place of some of her near relations to have taken a little more notice of her. She was talking to me while here with the tears rolling down her cheeks. "No one on earth knows how neglected and desolate I often felt. I have had sufferings that none knew of and with the feelings that few would care for me if they did." She shed tears and looked pale. She expressed much affection for "dear Aunt Hannah," made no <u>reflections</u> on anyone. . . .

I am your own affectionate Anna

∽

7th 26th 1829
My dear friends,

. . . I don't want you ever to suffer any uneasiness if a longer interval than usual should occur between my letters, for I now promise you that if any misfortune or affliction befalls us you shall not be kept in ignorance, and you need never attribute it to that cousin. I will try for the future to write once every 3 weeks and plead with you to write longer letters every 2. And why has not my brother, my dear brother, sent me one line or even one little message of love? Does he ever think of coming again to see how we come on here? How rejoiced we would all be to see him.

I believe I told you in my last of Franklin's wound. I have had a great deal of trouble with it. He is still confined principally to the house and unable to do anything but sew (which he can do very well). It partly healed up about 2 weeks since, when he walked too much on it and it swelled, inflamed, and opened again, throwing him into a fever. Proud flesh appeared in it. I am now trying to erradicate that with burnt alum. He is very thin and looks badly. It is not all laziness that makes him complain of laborious work, for he really is not able to undergo it.

I believe I never told you of the grand new cupboard Seth made me. It is of walnut. It is very large, 5 foot wide, 4 shelves in the upper part, which is a foot deep; the lower part projects another foot with 3 drawers at top of the middle one with a division for knives and spoons and 2 shelves under. It is a very handsome and very useful peice of furniture. Seth said it might go towards paying his board.

Last 4th day was a week, Cousin Robert took Cousin Margaret, Nathan and Sally Townsend, and myself to Hanover in his waggon to see an elephant, a Brazillian tiger, a lynx, 2 ichneumins,[1] 8 monkeys, and the beautifullest little teeny horse that I ever beheld, being the first wild animals I ever saw. My delight and astonishment was great, such wonderful obedience to thier keeper, it left me no ears for the music, the drum, clarinet, violin, bagpipes, Jewish cymbal, triangle, &c, and I would think it utterly impossible for anyone to keep from laughing at the feats of these little caricatures of man, the monkeys, and the poney.

Cousin Robert assisted Jos in cutting his wheat (an exellent crop) and will be here soon in the morning to assist in hauling it in and then to finish a field of grass, half of which is now in the barn. The children and I must finish pulling the flax tomorrow, and I have dinner to get: chickens, beans, potatoes, cucumbers, &c, and 10 loaves of rye bread to bake, just the last of our bread stuff. What a blessing it held out! We can have wheat now as soon as they can get time to thrash it. We have had one field hauled in 2 weeks ago. We have borrowed here and there till we owe 150 lb. Now we can soon pay it. How glad I am. We shall have abundance of hay if we have success in curing it, a prospect of more winter provender than our present stock can consume. Oh, that some fortunate occurrence would enable us to get a yoke of oxen—35 dollars —and the great demand for our coal would enable us to get clear from debt, for we have now no way to draw it—but I digress. . . .

Seth had 2 hives of bees and as he was at work some distance from home this summer left them in charge of Granville and me. (Jos is affraid to go near them.) They swarmed 4 times. We <u>hived</u> them all. He gave Granville and me each one hive, and none for the honey. If they swarm again I am to have another hive. We have 2 larger sows and 16 shoats and about a hundred chickens, which we have been killing this 2 weeks, for Alas we have no meat.

Mother, if thee wants to have some idea of Aliceanna's looks, call to mind Cousin Peggy's little William, for they are as much alike as it is common to see twins, except Aliceanna is very fair and <u>wilder looking</u>. They are thought to be the prettiest babes in the country. <u>He</u> is a lovely child indeed, and I know you would think Aliceanna so. She stands alone and will walk, I think, as soon as I shorten her clothes a little. . . . I leave her sometimes all day with Maria and Franklin.

Cousin P[eg] was very sick last week and sent for me. We gave her a puke and it helped her. She is still not well, <u>poor thing. I am truly sorry she is</u> <u>ailing</u> so soon after coming here. Her babe is much disordered, and Eliza seems threatened with dysentery. She does her own washing and all her work seems well-satisfied, and if she does not regard us with the affection of a sister there is no truth in <u>my feelings</u>. The more I become accquainted with her, the more I feel convinced that many of her friends in Maryland, judging from false rumors, formed a wrong estimate of her character, made too little allowance for her, and did not take that notice of her or regard her as I am sure I ever should the offspring of a sister or brother of mine. Not from her account do I judge, for she has made <u>no</u> complaints to me. She is very kind to me. I shall go there 3rd day morning and stay till 4th day evening as Robert expects 7 or 8 mowers and she is a stranger to the ways here. They do not seem satisfied unless I am there at least every week.

Benjamin Higgins is really doing well. He will have a <u>great deal</u> of wheat, rye, oats, and corn <u>to sell</u>, a large crop of buckwheat, potatoes, and soup beans, a most ellegant garden and everything that the united labour of his wife and self can raise on a very rich farm, which he has leased for I don't know how long. They are gaining esteem everywhere. As soon as harvest is over, Cousin Robert is going to take Cousin Margaret and me to Cousin James Brooke's. If any of your news carriers are in want of a subject, tell them I have taken an old coat is Thomas's, turned it hind part before, and set onto it a petticoat of the same kind of Maria's and made Hannah a right decent frock, and out of three old ones made Deborah another. And it's nobody's business if they have none to change with, for who knows but they may have by the time they give out?

Harmon Brown is expected from Baltimore tomorrow. I have seen people many a time pining and discontented, surrounded by blessings they did not feel grateful for, and would I be willing to exchange lots with them? No, not I. "Dear me," says Mother. "How <u>big</u> poor Anna talks in <u>harvest time</u>. She's forgot the <u>potatoes</u>."

The chickens are crowing. I must run to bed. Farewell, dear, dear people. Now, if you don't answer this with a longer one, I will think hard. Dear, faithful Margaret, all of you, farewell.

Your Anna Bentley

1. Related to mongooses.

~

8th mo [1829]
1st day night, 12 o'clock
My dear friends,

I gave you my promise in my last to inform you always if any mischance befel us, little thinking I should so soon have to perform it. But before I begin—as you know, I always detail any such events circumstantially, just in the course they occurred. I will try to prevent unnecessary alarm by informing you that the Dr who has just left here pronounces my dear child <u>not</u> in <u>danger</u>, though he must undergo severe suffering, and Dr Roberts[on] has never been known to flatter.

After dinner today Polly Smith came by for me to go with her to Robert's. I accompanied her. Just before we came away I felt an unaccountable feeling of <u>dread</u> come over me. When we were half a mile from home we heard in the direction of this house a report much louder than any gun. A sickness seized me as I sprang forward and exclaimed, "Oh, Polly, I feel sure from my impressions that is some accident that has happened to Granville with the gun." I listened and heard someone call many times. I could not answer, but made Franklin, who was with us. My tottering limbs could scarcely bear me along, though the others seemed certain it was not in the direction of Green Hill.

Jos met us some distance from the house and told me Granville had met with an accident. How bad he could not tell, as it was nearly dark, the fire had gone out, and he could not get a light. (Maria had run to Reeders' for fire and some of them to come.) Hannah and Deborah were weeping bitterly, and on the step of the front door sat our darling, his face enveloped in a bloody cloth, his shirt and waistcoat also, and a quantity on the steps and floor and one sleeve much burnt. For an instant, I gave way and uttered a cry that I hushed instantly on seeing its effect on him—Jos and he assuring me it was not so bad as I might suppose. Polly, after hearing how it happened, ran home to send Nathan and some candles.

The fire had gone out, and Granville got the gun to strike fire. There was one spark in the tow. He laid down the gun and took the flask (a strong copper one, with about 8 loads of powder in it) to put a little more powder on it. It communicated to the flask, burnt it all to peices, knocked him down, a piece of it cutting a terrible gash in his cheek. It also knocked Maria down, stunning both her and the child for an instant, but they are not hurt. He got up directly and met Jos at the door. His sleeve was in a blaze, which his father put out, and staunched the bleeding with sugar and tied it up before I got home.

Four of the Reeders (that is, all the men) with a candle and fire came running in, and Nathan Townsend and his apprentice soon after. We lit a candle and scraped lint, got laudanum before we opened it, but the moment we saw it we bound it up, and each one offered to go for the Dr. Nathan was the most active, and mounting Tom, went as fast as he could. Granville bore it like a man without the least complaint. He expressed a wish to see Cousin Robert, and 2 of them went over for him. He soon came. We sent all the children to bed, who sobbed themselves to sleep, not one could eat any supper. I mastered all my weakness for his dear sake. The Dr came very quick. When he washed off the clotted blood, he told us that the jawbone was not broken—though from his cheek being much bruised it would leave a considerable scar that would disfigure his face some—that it had cut a small artery, which we could see beating, from which he apprehended no danger and would not take up. He said it was a most hairbreadth escape, as it barely escaped a large artery in one part and his temple in another. He sewed it up, applied a great number of adhesive plaisters, and bandaged it up. One strip goes across his nose, round his head, to keep it in its place. He says he apprehends it will swell very much tomorrow (it has already) and that his head will be much affected with considerable fever, for which I must give salts. He has left particular directives: He must live very low and not talk or use exertion, and the more we can allay inflamation in it, the greater chance for preventing a large scar, which, and the soreness, is all the danger he apprehends from it.

Several of them offered to stay all night, but I prefered sitting up with him myself, and as his nose keeps bleeding, I am affraid to leave him, though he sleeps quietly. And my babe has not been well today. She has now a very high fever, I think from teething.

The explosion broke 4 panes of glass and blew the ashes all over the room. It was heard more than a mile off, I know, at RHG's, and I doubt not could have been more than 3. The wound is, I think, about 3 inches long and reaches from near the corner of his mouth to the top of his cheekbone near the temple, where it makes a little zigzag turn. Oh, dearest friends, how I have suffered for the dear patient boy, my precious, noble-hearted child.

Another hairbreadth escape Thomas had lately. He was in the mow, and Jos pitching in hay with a very sharp polished spring fork. He did not know Thomas was so near, and pushed with force, the prong entering and slightly wounding his neck, so as to [cause] the blood to run down exactly over the jugular vein. And poor Franklin, I beleive I told you of his foot being worse again. Well, the day week it seemed healed up, and he was taken with a violent pain, or stitch, in his side, so that he could hardly breathe and could not lie down. He remained very poorly all the week, his side much affected like pleurisy, hacking cough at night. He is much better now, is up and about but looks miserable. His foot is well. He is a great help to me in sewing, which he does quick and neatly and never gets tired of it.

If it was not for Cousin Robert I don't know what poor Jos would do, now his right hand man is disabled. He is not near done his hay, and his oats ready to cut, but Robert seems as much interested in helping Jos with everything here as he did in getting his own hay in. A noble crop he has, all secure in barn and stock, about 8 tons. We had roasting ears the last of July. I never saw such pumkins, nor so many of them, fit now— one field of them—to make pies and stew; abundance of beans, cucumbers, peas, most grand potatoes, two long rows across the cornfield of the finest broom corn. Poor Granville has a good prospect of watermelon, and Samuel Kempton sent me some cantelope seed in a letter. I shall have a great many. They are not ripe yet.

I have a great many chickens. Something disturbed them night before last. Granville and I went out and set Guard on. He soon caught—Oh, the <u>stinkenest polecat,</u> and killed it not more than 20 yds from the door. We were almost suffocated. As soon as he had killed it, the <u>sensible</u> dog took it in his mouth and ran scampering over the fences to the far corner of the back field, where he decently buried it. We shut all the doors and burnt tar over the house, but the polecat was still strongest, and is still.

It is now 3 o'clock. Granville rests well, except talking in his sleep. We have had a complete thrashing floor made of the old stable and have had 2 grits of our new wheat ground. It is the most beautiful floor, and we have such elegant nice bread. . . .

Please, dear friends, write to dear Aunt Dolly, Cousin Benjamin and Mary Moore[1] and tell them we received safely and from the bottom of our hearts most thankfully thier acceptable and valuable presents of clothing, and I would write to them to acknowledge thier kindness but at present my mind is so harassed, and so much for my hands to do, I cannot do it. Tell them they cannot judge of the extent or full value of their kindnesses unless they could know how bare for clothing we all were. And thy box, dear Mother, too, came at last. I need not repeat my thanks to thee. I wish I could tell thee all the things they sent. There was a large box full of thier children's clothing &c. There was an exellent black coat that looks like silk, a pr of cinnamon-colored trousers, ditto a very handsome buff waistcoat for Granville, a pair of nice silk stripe drilling, 1 of linnen drilling, and one of light stripe pantaloons for Franklin, a waistcoat, 8 shirts, and a nice blue cloth coat with J Kempton's name in the lining (I don't know how it came there) for Franklin, 2 pr drilling trousers and 8 coats and great coat and hat for Thomas, an exellent most new furred hat for Granville, a leghorn for Franklin, a pretty little leghorn which I have trimmed for Aliceanna, a calico frock for Maria, one for Hannah, a gingham for Deborah. Oh, dear, this ain't near all, but the poor sick babe is awake and Granville restless.

Farewell. It is near daylight. I won't call Jos and lay down as I sat up last night till 2 tucking Aliceanna's frock. She has walked since she was 11 months and says many words.

I am your own distressed Anna Bentley

1. Dorothy Hopkins and her daughter and son-in-law, Mary and Benjamin Moore.

10th mo 26 1829
My dear friends,

Nothing but a fear you might feel uneasiness at my long silence could induce me under my present severe suffering to attempt writing a letter. For the last 4 days my <u>same old</u> pain round the left eye has returned with violence. It gets worse every day, lasts all day, and seems to settle in the jaw and teeth at night. Oh, my work, what will become of it? If I stoop down it feels as if my head would come open. It has gathered, I am sure, and will break soon—So much for my old goodfornothing head. Let the rest come from my heart and it will be more pleasing. I have often found in writing to you when under the pressure of suffering, either of body or mind, a soothing something that actually does mitigate it. Why is it so? When I began this I was <u>really</u> in an <u>agony</u> of pain, and already it has greatly subsided.

I intended to have written you a long letter this week, but you must excuse me now. I have run out of paper, for one thing, and have not one cent to buy a sheet, so have to tare leaves out of the boys' book. I repeat it to you once more: Never be uneasy if a long interval like the present occurs between my letters, for I renew my promise of never keeping back any accidents or misfortune—and still let me entreat you to write often without waiting my regular answers.

I have been exceedingly gratified with dear Elizabeth's awakened energy. She no longer is contented to leave it to others to tell me she still loves me but now seems willing to do her part towards lightening this painful separation. My dear sister Mary seems inclined to verify in her own case a sentiment she and I used to contend about, that a married woman's affections become contracted. She may have a good sort of an old man and <u>right clever sort</u> of children, but if they were <u>anything like as nice as mine</u> how can she resist the temptation of writing to me about them and delighting my heart (as I cannot see them myself) in describing from time to time their unfolding charms and endearing actions? This is the last time I will ever urge thee on this score.

Hast thou weaned thy darling? (No equivocating.) I have not weaned mine, nor do I expect to before warm weather, if I do not get too weak and miserable. I am very thin but hope to pick up a little when we get a little better living. We got out of meat in <u>HARVEST</u>, have had <u>none</u> since till this morning Cousin Robert jumped in at the door, throwing 7 lb of fresh beef on the table, which set the dog to whining and all the cats in the house to <u>mewing</u>. We have had a great many fowls, but I soon tire on them. We get very little butter and rather [scarce] of milk. But my dear Jos and children never were heartier. We have sold 6 dollars worth of pumkins and still have more than ourselves and stock <u>can</u> consume, the best and largest crops of potatoes and turnips we have ever raised—have not dug them yet.

The weather has been so wet we have not done seeding yet, expect to finish this week. Have five acres in and five to put in new ground. Granville does all the plowing and hauling. He says, "Tell them I love them all dearly but can get no time yet to write to them; I dream of them every night and would be willing to start alone on foot to see them again." He has never been in a neighbor's house to spend an hour but once since he came home, and has not one associate though he seems to be a favorite with all who know him. He is nearly as tall as his father. Franklin and Maria send thier love. Franklin often complains of pain in his side, is very thin. Maria does a <u>great deal</u> of work and gives me a <u>great deal</u> of trouble with her tongue. Aliceanna is a <u>pretty</u> little blue-eyed, rosy-cheeked girl, as full of life and mischief as a kitten, continually in action, begins to talk, &c.

Our colt, Jewel, seems very gentle, allows the boys to saddle, bridle, and ride it about very quietly, but we fear it also is <u>diseased</u> from its mother, something of the glanders,[1] I expect. It had the distemper when it was a week old, and its mother trod on its nose and broke one part of one side that, when it healed, stopped that side up, which makes it blow after running or exercise. There are 2 kernels swelled a little under its jaws, but it is lively and heavy and in good order. . . .

Jos and I went to meeting yesterday and dined at Morris's. Poor Ann. I had not seen her since her murdered sister was buried. She was much overcome. Morris wanted to get on his mare and come here for Aliceanna that I might spend some days, but I felt too miserable to stay from home. Ann's father and mother seem to be entirely overcome with sorrow which admits no ray of consolation. The universal opinion here is that she was first deluded and then murdered by the villian Courtenay.[2]

Company has just come in. . . . We were rejoiced to hear the good news from Sister Betsey.

I am your own, Anna

---

1. A contagious disease of horses, the symptoms of which include swellings under the jaw.
2. Ann Votaw Miller was the daughter of Moses and Mary Votaw, who had emigrated from Pennsylvania with six more Miller brothers and their families. The sister in question probably was Ann's younger sister, Mary. Their first cousin, Phoebe Votaw, had married Edward Courtney, from a nearby Quaker family, in 1823. Edward can't have been the "villian," for

he and Phoebe continued to live in the neighborhood and produce children regularly until 1840. But one of his family may have "deluded" and murdered Mary. In July 1831, Ann Miller gave birth to a daughter. She named her Mary.

~

1st mo 16th 1830
My dear friends,

I had intended writing last week, but the mail did not come, being prevented by high waters, and it has been so long since I have written that I forget what I have told you and what remains to be told. If I should give you stale news, please excuse me. Oh, how my thoughts have dwelt with you in the past week. On 4th day as I sat with the children (Jos from home) at the table, it being then 1/2 past 1 o'clock, I thought what a different table was then perhaps spread at Sharon. We had a little bit (but enough) of fat pork and fried cabbage. Had you anything better? Did not you? I know you did, the very happiest of you, wish that poor I was among you then. And I durce like cried because I could not be. I shall certainly expect a letter forthwith from somebody expressing the great pleasure and satisfaction he feels in possessing the priviledge of calling ME SISTER.

I was surprised when J Howard's family came out to hear them speak of your intentions when I had been keeping the secret.[1] They spoke confidently but would not tell how they heard it and laughed at my pretended ignorance. J and Mary Thornton expect to return to your neighbourhood in a few weeks. We think it a wild plan for her in the midst of winter a lone female, in delicate health, too, to set off such a journey in company with 8 waggons. But he has received letters from home advising and entreating him to return; though if he would apply himself to industry he has several chances here to do well. I do not know what the family of Howard will do. There seems no situation to suit them in this neighbourhood, though thier present one will support them till spring. Their expectations were raised too high. They do not think the society polished enough for them, and I fear they will not be satisfied.

Sally Ann Howard spends the most of her time here and is a great help to me in sewing, knitting, &c. It was at the request of her parents and her own choice her being here, though when it was proposed, I stated as an objection my utter inability to compensate her. They said they did not wish it in the least, but thier house was small, and if she would only pay for her board it was all they wished. I borrowed a wheel, and she has spun all the stocking yarn Jos got on credit, linsey enough for Maria 1 frock and Thomas a pair of trousers, which I must make this week. Thomas is a <u>bundle</u> of patches and Maria in striped cotton. I sold a <u>bedspread</u> for flannel enough to make Deborah and Aliceanna each a frock. Aliceanna has enough for the winter. I have just made Deborah's. She and Hannah are in cotton yet, and what to do for Hannah I know not without I make her a <u>patchwork one</u>. I have patched and turned inside out my old flannel, and it <u>comforts my rheumaty</u> pains so I dread to see it getting threadbare.

Jos and Granville have been toiling almost beyond their strength in getting a barn, or rather a large stable, built. It is now up and the rafters up. If the weather is fit Seth will shingle it this week. It is on a line with the west end of the house. (Bro Isaac, the lane runs by the meat house.) It is two stories and will contain more than room sufficient for all our stock, and when we move the others to it, it will be a roomy barn. Morris Miller came last week and worked 2 days faithfully on it (and he is allowed to do the work of 2 men in one day). He would make no charge, said he had often wanted to assist us—the pleasure of doing so was sufficient pay. . . .

I wish I could give you a better account of my health than I can at present. Last 5th day night was a week, I was attacked with one of my dreadful spells of colic. I laid moaning on the hearth for 2 hours before I woke up Jos. I had taken oil of mint and laudanum without effect. He gave me a large dose of castor oil, but I continued in great pain. Ann and Fanny Battin came to spend the day. They both bathed my feet, gave me rheumatic drops (a pattent medicine), applied hot salt, &c, which relieved me a little, but the soreness was so great I could not move without great suffering till 1st day evening. I have had a great deal of the toothache since I wrote last, which follows the least exposure to cold or damp feet and lasts for some days past. My head has begun to ache often, its old problem again, and I am affraid to try Dr. Howard's medicine till the questions in my last are answered. I am obliged to drink that hateful rye coffee, which I do believe makes it worse.

I am very thin and weak, the children have all had something like influenza attended with very sore throats, and Aliceanna has an eruption which we believe is the chicken pox. She has, I expect, 2 hundred on her body and head. Many children have it in the neighbourhood, though she must have taken it naturaly as she has not been exposed to the infection. The whooping cough is prevailing also and within a 1/4 of a mile of us. I hope the children may escape. The 4 youngest are to have it—or rather have not had it.

I have not weaned my babe, which I should be very sorry to do (though she is old enough) if she takes the whooping cough. She is cutting her jaw teeth, too. I wish you could see her and hear her sweet prattle. Sally Ann says there never was so sweet a child in the world or one she loved half as well. She is in constant action from daybreak till night, singing, talking, and in all kinds of mischief. Nothing escapes her quick eye. If I have rising set by the fire, she will go to it a dozen times a day, raise the cover and look in, then cover it and walk away as she has seen me do. I was going to fry meat a few days since. I put it in the pan on the hearth and went to the dresser for salt. She snatched the pepperbox from the table and before I could get to her had the top off and poured all in the pan.

Has Sister Mary weaned Hannah yet? I cannot help thinking hard of her, surrounded as she is by the comforts of life and having it in her power to afford so much pleasure by writing to her poor absent sister, that she persists in such neglect.

Well, I must draw to a conclusion now, for my fire is so low I shall pay for getting so cold. We have 3 hogs to kill tomorrow. I shall have no time to fill the rest of this paper. There are several waggons going from here to Alexandria and Baltimore in 2 or 3 weeks. Oh, how I wish I could go in one of them. Give my love to all that care for me and write me a long particular letter immediately.
Most affectionately,
Anna Bentley
Cousin MEG sends love.

1. Probably the engagement of Sarah Briggs to her cousin, James Pleasants Stabler.

~

2nd mo 14 1830
My dear friends,

We received Sister Sarah's acceptable letter last week. Now, darling, thou wilt no longer be inclined to ridicule anyone telling how dearly they love a dear kind husband and delighting to dwell on his perfections. I am glad thou hast such a one and hope thou wilt love him enough but not too much.[1]

About 2 weeks since, one bitter cold evening, we were seated round the fire waiting supper for Joseph, who had gone to Hanover, when he opened the door shewing 2 strangers, saying, "My dear, here are 2 travellers who want a night's lodging." I looked up with a feeling of dismay at a powerful athletic-looking man with a glittering rifle and knapsack. The other a very handsome, tall, genteel-looking young man, which I stood wondering that Joseph should have consented to admit them and thinking I should not sleep a wink for fear. He, smiling, led the largest one forward, saying, "Aaron, this is thy aunt. My dear, these are Brother Jeffrey's sons, Aaron and Ellis." You may imagine my surprise. The poor lads had walked all the way this bitter cold weather, and Joseph accidently met with them in Hanover. They did not know him and enquired if he could inform them where Joseph Bentley lived. Jos made himself known to them.

Ellis is about 20 and the image of Granville, only handsomer. He is a paper maker, and after staying a few days left us to get employment in a paper mill 15 miles from Lisbon. Aaron has a tract of land in Jefferson County 70 miles from here containing 750 acres which he expects to visit in the spring, but in the meantime told his uncle if he could find employment enough here for him to pay for his board till then, he would stay here till then. He is a mason by trade, and if the weather opens he will put up our other chimney, which want of means to pay for it has heretofore prevented us from having put up—and now a way seems to open to have it done free of expense! He is a twin; his brother Caleb is, they say, exactly like him. He is very still and diffident, and we all love him much.

My friend Catharine Holland is married to Jehu Coulson,[2] Alice Jackson's natural son, a lad of 18, and Gulielma Whitacre, aged 24, ran away and were married last week.[3] Her worthy parents are almost broken-hearted, for he is as worthless a chap as can be found. Joshua Hanna, son of Benjamin, has made himself the 3rd husband to a beautiful rich widow aged 24!![4] There have been 5 or 6 more weddings among the people of this neighbourhood this year and are very remarkable. One took place last week 3 miles from here, a child of 12 years old to a man of 27!! This is a positive fact.

The measles and whooping cough are all through the neighbourhood. I expect you will shortly have the company of Morris Miller. His present prospect is to leave home this day week. All of you be sure to write by him and please send some more cherrystones and some little pretty things. That miserable Sister Mary and Brother Isaac—will you please tell something of his employment prospects and destination?

My affectionate feelings are <u>deeply</u> hurt to think he has never since his return <u>ever</u> so much as sent me <u>one</u> message of love or remembrance. . . .

Sally Howard was here last 2nd day and would take yarn to knit Franklin a pair of stockings, saying Elizabeth had nothing to do and she did not like her to be idle and she felt for me with so large a family and no help with my knitting and sewing. They have knit Jos a pair, Aaron 2 pr, Granville a pr of gloves. Sally Ann Howard will not come while Aaron is here. She says it would be thought imprudent.

Jos and I spent yesterday afternoon at RHG's. They were well and sent love to you. Let us hear all you know of Mary Thornton's arrival &c. I wanted to have filled this paper but was interrupted last night and am too much hurried with my work to take longer time now—all send love and wish to hear from the three-footed pig. I wish you could this moment hear the sweet prattling of my lively little girl. Does Hannah Brooke talk?

I am, very affectionately, your Anna Bentley

1. In 1830, Sarah married her cousin, a nephew of Hannah Briggs. James P. Stabler was a widower with a son, Pleasants. JPS, as he's often referred to in Anna's letters, resembled his brother-in-law Isaac in being intelligent and clever but seemingly unable to stick with a career or make a good living. He variously worked in watch repair, silkworm farming, and Thomsonian medicine. He eventually had jobs with the burgeoning railroad lines in the 1830s, but his health became increasingly poor.
2. Jehu Coulson (1801–1865) was the oldest of a large family of sons and one daughter. He and Catharine Holland (1808–1883) had four children. Her younger sister, Hannah, married Jehu's younger brother Saul.
3. Gulielma Whitacre married Abia Stackhouse on February 2, 1830.
4. Joshua Hanna, uncle of the famous Ohio politician, Marcus Hanna, married Susan McFarland Richardson Lathrop in Paris, Stark County, in February 1830. Born Susan McFarland, she had first married Jason Richardson in 1824, but he died six months later. In 1826, she married James Lathrop.

~

[March 1830]
Dear Sharon folks,

I have received several letters from you since I have written but have been so taken up sugar making and patching, &c that I could not take time. I am glad Sloane called on you and that you were pleased with him. Joseph thinks highly of him. I am not acquainted with him. He is much esteemed. His wife, Jessie, is Dr. Robertson's sister.[1] And Morris, dear Morris, though he is not handsome (one of Sister Elizabeth's reasons for liking S), he is our valued friend. I had intended going to stay all night with his lovely wife tomorrow night but fear I shall have to prepare for another log-rolling on 2nd day.

I wish thee had sent me a <u>stinking old pipe</u>. I know not whether I shall not become a smoker at last, for I have the tootheache always after eating, and a whif or two of one of Aaron's cigars always relieves it without making me sick. I could slide into the practice right easy. Must I? Joseph has found his nephew a very great help to him. He is a dear fellow. I love him like a son. He is good-natured, obliging, affectionate, modest, and very diffident when strangers are present. He seems interested in our affairs, and I think it would be a great trial for him to leave us. I am sure it would be so to us to part with him. . . .

Aaron and Granville geared up Jewel when they went for the apple trees. For the first time and to our great satisfaction she performed as quietly and well as Tom. She went to the waggon 14 miles. She is no trouble in breaking. P and Sally Miller paid me a visit last week, and my dear friend Susan Miller also. I spent last 4th day with Hannah Reeder, Levi's daughter, that lives 1/2 a mile from us.

Oh, Sally Ann Howard has not made her home here since Mary left here. They are going to mow week after next 10 miles from here near Cousin James Brooke's. I have—to my full <u>satisfaction</u>, I was going to say, but not quite so either—<u>experienced</u> the truth of your confidential letters some time since. I want you to write me word of how J and Mary [Thornton] are coming on and all you hear of them.

Oh, if I had a good opportunity and money enough to bear my expenses how gladly would I pay you a visit this spring or summer. Everything would suit so well for me to travel: Aliceanna old enough to wean, Maria old enough to take care (under her father's directions) of affairs at home. But it is all a vision and cannot be. The fatigues would not be a drop in the bucket to prevent me.

I hope Aaron will put up the other chimney soon, and then we can have the other half of the house finished. Well, I must go to getting supper for my large family—21 in number. I have patching to do tonight that will keep me up after midnight. It was 2 last night and 1/2 1 the night before when I went to bed. But I have got used to it. . . . [letter stops short]

1. George Sloan (or Sloane, as Anna spelled it) was an early settler of Hanover who ran a store and also acted as a teamster transporting goods back east. His house still stands in the village.

∽

5th mo 2nd 1830
My dear friends,

I would fain take a whole sheet after my long silence did I not feel so dull and stupid that I doubt my ability even to fill this with interesting matter. I have felt considerably indisposed since 3rd day, though not to lay by on that day I worked very hard all day in the garden and overheated myself. The next day I could not raise my hands to my head and scarcely bend my knees, accompanied with general soreness, fever, and great lassitude, which feeling (except the pain in my shoulders is exchanged for one in my back) still attends me more often, making my doleful complaints. I will try to get on to something else.

I am not so <u>dangerous</u> but that slowly and wearisomely I hobbled down this morning to see how poor Cousin MEG's children were coming on in the measles. They have all got over it but Charles, Sally Ann, and William,[1] who are speckled enough that I think the worst is over with them. And they have all had it very favourably.

Cousin Margaret has had a fatiguing time but is as usual patient as a lamb. She and Cousin Robert appear as affectionate to us as an own brother and sister, although that little artful mischief-making Sally Ann Howard was very near making a coolness between us—for what cause except it was an innate love of malicious mischief we none of us can find out. For the few weeks she was here she felt like a burden <u>imposed</u> on us, and when Aaron came I made that an excuse for not inviting her back. She made mischief in every family she became acquainted in here and has left a name not very creditable for Marylanders. I shall write to her parents this night to inform of her duplicity. Cousin Margaret has done. So they have gone out of the neighbourhood and taken a large farm with a fine house and a large mill much out of repair. They have leased it for 15 years at a high rent, have bespoke a <u>sideboard</u>, cherry dining table (Seth made them a poplar one for which he cannot get pay), a bureau. They have got 18 Windsor chairs (they had 6 splint-bottom ones before)—all this on credit.

They live near Cousin J Brooke's—would that their unsuspecting natures could be put on their guard. I want you to write and tell me all you hear of Mary Thornton. Oh, I had like to have forgot. Cousin James Brooke's son, Gerard, came to Robert's yesterday. Robert brought him here this morning, and Jos, Granville and I went down with them. He returned at 3 this evening.

My dear Sister Mary, I must here thank thee for thy handsome, serviceable, and acceptable present. It is dearer to me because thou hast worn it; and though I have worn it many times, it does indeed still retain thy <u>very</u> smell, which brings thee oftener and more tenderly near me in thought than any present I ever received. And it sends a comical, watery kind of something from my heart to my eyes every time I put it on. . . .

Aaron feels like a son to us. He will remain here till fall. His brother Ellis, just 20, settled at a paper mill 30 miles from here. (He is a paper maker—gets 6 dollars per week, but being offered much higher wages in Steubenville intends leaving there in a week or two, paying us a visit [before] going to S.) Aaron, who is well used to the management of horses, said the other morning he would put Jewel to the plough with Tom and break her. He did so, and with much anxiety we went out to look, expecting to see some capers. To our pleasure and surprise, the quiet, docile animal went to it as steadily and gently as an experienced horse and does so to the waggon, plow, or under the saddel. She is 3 years old. . . .

I am, with near and tender love, your Anna Bentley

1. The Garrigues children born up to this time were Helen, Deborah, Charles, Edward, Sally Ann, Richard, William, and Eliza.

~

7th mo 5 1830
[addressed to James P. Stabler]
My dear sister [Sarah],

It will not do, it must be done, another week <u>must</u> not pass without writing to my dear brother and sister even though the poor mind partaking of the infirmities of the body should only paint the drowsy dullness that encompasses it. About 3 weeks since I had a most violent attack of billious colic which confined me to my bed several days and left me so weak that I concluded it was a folly to part with my strength still further in keeping Aliceanna at the breast as she is a healthy babe, and on 5th day morning I commenced the painful task of weaning her. She takes it very hard. I sat up with her all 6th day night and all last night, was much disturbed on 7th day night and slept more in the day to make up for it. She pleads so pitifully I was nigh giving way the first night. She would clasp her little arms round my neck and kissing me repeatedly would say, "Pese, mumma, darly mumma, let poor Alitanna tuck leetle titty."

I cannot make you sensible with what feelings of grateful affection I received your last letter. The day before it came Jos said to me, "I really am ashamed to see Harmon Brown. He has never been paid for bringing them boxes from Baltimore. He only charges $1.00, and he asked me for it today for the first time." On the next morning before the mail came, I had taken a <u>pile</u> of ragged shirts and seated myself out of Aliceanna's sight on the stair steps, saying to Jos, "What shall we do? I cannot make these shirts hold out much longer."

"But maybe some way will turn up yet," added I (seeing the melancholy expression of his countenance), "for us to get some of Sloane's exellent elevenpenny shirting."

He replied with a sigh, "I don't know how that will be. I can see no way without going in debt. And here is Joe Curry downstairs come after the dollar 30 cents I owe him for beef we got last winter. He is in distress for the money, and he will be warranted this afternoon because I have it not for him."

"Well," said I, "don't be discouraged."

He shook his head. "There is the post boy's horn."

Well, it brought your dear letter. The instant I opened it and the enclosed dropped out, I could not restrain my tears. Harmon and Curry were paid and the shirting got that afternoon. I finished my patching with a lighter heart than I began it, breathing many a wish that it might be multiplied tenfold to you.

If health and ability are given me, I will try to make some <u>very nice</u> sugar for you next spring but know not yet if it will be in my power to supply you with as large a quantity as was requested; but hope, as 2 years were allowed me, I may perhaps be able in that time to meet the demand. And I do really expect it will <u>be sweeter to you</u> than any sugar you can get. What I made this season has lasted till now. I used the last yesterday.

We have about 2 1/2 acres of very fine rye now ready for the sickle, better than 3 good oats, 5 acres of the best corn in the neighbourhood, plenty of pumkins and cimblers, 8 acres of exellent wheat, 7 of fine grass, 8 of woodland pasture fenced, in part grubbed and clear'd; and he will finish today grubbing a field of 6 acres for wheat, at which for the last 2 weeks he has worked like a slave.

Granville eat some cherries 7th day, which made him sick, and he was in bed yesterday and the most of this morning, now (12 o'clock) is better. Now Jos has Thomas, Hannah, and Deborah picking brush. We have our last grist ground. We parted with 15 bushels of wheat to get linsey last winter. We can easily borrow wheat. We shall have nearly double the quantity this year. One blessing among many, <u>our bread seems</u> sure. We have but 3 pieces of meat but a great many chickens and shall kill a fat lamb in harvest.

Our beloved Aaron has been for some weeks employed on a building at Lisbon. (He is a mason.) He comes home every 7th day and stays till 2nd day. No rain or storms prevents his coming. He seems to cling to us with the affection of a son, and his <u>great</u> reserve and diffidence among strangers seems to increase his affection for us. We do his sewing and washing. As he brought no summer clothing, I have had all to make. He will come 7th day to stay 2 weeks and assist through harvest. He will also put up our chimny, springhouse, and plaister our house this fall.

I have 4 pair of trowsers and 8 shirts to make, my wool to pick to have spun and linsy made, besides a great deal more sewing. It is almost too much for me. I lost 3 swarm of bees last week though I succeeded in hiving them, and some staid 2 days and went to work.

Well, Jos is hurrying me. He bids me assure you he participates in my feelings of gratitude and affection towards you, but his leisure moments are so few and those his weary frame requires the exclusive privilege of appropriating to rest, added to an increasing aversion to writing, he begs you will excuse him from communicating with you only through me.

And in his name I now trouble my dear brother James with a request for his assistance: The last time Cousin Asa Moore paid us a visit he borrowed 10 dollars from Jos, promising to pay him the next week. The week before we came away he saw Jos, and, recurring to it himself, made many apologies, said it had from time to time slipped his memory, that he had it not then but would get and send it to him before he started or immediately afterward. It never came, and when cousin Caleb Moore was spoken to about it, he said he thought he recollected hearing Cousin Asa say that Jos had borrowed the same sum of him at Roan Ash. Jos says that is entirely a mistake, for he never had occasion to borrow one cent of him there, but Cousin Asa many while there, which he punctually returned. Jos wrote a plain statement of these facts to Thos L Reese and requested his attention to it, telling him the great difficulty we were in, also entreating him to make some inquiry for a man to whom Jos had sold a pr of elegant pistols for 15 dollars who promised payment when called on. TLR never deigned to take the least notice of it or make any reply. Will thou, dear brother, speak to thy brother Caleb or to TLR? Jos' patience is exhausted.[1]

I must conclude with love in which the children and Jos join me. Your very affectionate sister, A

[Sarah Stabler, who received this letter, wrote two notes in the margin, as follows:] 1. JPS spoke to TLR on this subject, and he never received the letter mentioned or heard a word on the subject. SBS

2. Beginning—You will not understand all sister Anna says without an explanation. The night before I wrote to her, I dreamed Isaac and I went to Ohio on a visit to them, and just when we arrived they seemed quite in distress for a small sum—with which we furnished them and had the happiness of seeing them relieved. In the morning my dream weighed heavily on my mind, though I did not mention it even to James. I wrote to her and twice had my hand on a 5 dollar note to enclose, but after something of reflection about poor James's life of slavery to earn it—his privations, expenses, &c &c, I concluded I had no right to it. I put it away with a heavy heart, sealed the letter, and when James came from the office, without mentioning a word of my dream or any of these circumstances, I handed it to him and asked him to put it in the P.O. He took it immediately, broke the seal, and enclosed a five dollar note in it and handed it to me to seal again without reading a word in it—He wrote a line in pencil requesting sister A to send him a pound of her own make of sugar in the course of two years for it.

The circumstance seemed remarkable to me, and with tears of pleasure I added a postscript telling her it was my dear James's own deed, and that I had not mentioned my dream to him. When he read her letter, his heart and eyes were full to think so small a gift could do so much good and cause such gratitude. SBS

1. Asa and Caleb Moore were the sons of Anna's Uncle Thomas and Aunt Mary (Brooke) Moore. The confusion about the money appears to have been exacerbated by the death of Asa in 1828.

∽

12th mo 12th 1830
My dear friends,

When I wrote last I was confined to my bed in great suffering where I remained 4 days longer and for a week was unable to stand straight or walk without pain—3 large doses of castor oil and several of laudanum, which at last seemed to remove the excruciating pains which at times tormented me. It was the worst spell of colic I ever had and left me very weak. Last 5th day week we killed our hogs (8 of them) and the beef. I managed with the help of Helen and Maria (who neither had ever assisted in the like business before and could not do much) to get the entrails cleaned and the fat rendered that night. The next day they took 2 hogs to Sloane weighing 305 lb and got a barrel of salt. 6th day cut up and salted the meat—760 lb of pork and 330 beef. I rendered all the lard (2 firkins[1] like my old one) and the tallow. Franklin and I opened and cleaned the tripe. I then scalded and scraped it and put it to soak. After night, had Granville and Franklin to help. We cleaned the feet and chopped and seasoned the sausage (about <u>3 pecks</u>), went to bed weary at 1/2 past 1. Got up late, washed up the greasy things, M scoured the floor, I combed, washed, and dressed the children and sat down to rest, when company came: Robert Battin,[2] son of John, his wife, a very fine woman, and Massey Reeder.[3] R Battin has bought I Leeke's land joining us and is going to build 1/2 a mile from us, a great acquisition. They left us at sundown, would not let us get supper.

2nd day. I boiled the feet and 3 heads and made souse—which is too <u>good</u> to <u>keep</u> long—and stuffed 60 links of sausage and put away the rest in jars with melted lard over them. Half the links I have put in brine and half packed in lard.

3rd day. Jos, Aaron, and I went to Cousin Robert's to help them butcher. With Helen's help I cleaned and rendered the gut fat of thier 3 hogs. The next day the other chopped and seasoned the sausage, cleaned the feet, and came home <u>sick of the grease</u>. I did not think it was suitable for Cousin Margaret to do it; she never had done such work.

5th day. Maria washed.

6th day. I knit Granville a stocking.

7th day. Boiled the tripe, having changed the water every day and cut it in small peices. When done, seasoned and put in vinegar, and it is a delicacy. Got my patch box and set down after supper, darned 4 trousers and patched 4 very <u>holy</u> shirts. Slipped into bed 1/2 past 3. Out again at <u>8</u>, eat my breakfast, and hid myself upstairs at my patching—another shirt, which took 3 hours' faithful work. I could not eat dinner, but dressed and came down soon after. Nathan and Sally Townsend with thier sweet little Emmeline came soon after.

Hannah Reeder, she came to tell me our flannel was ready to go to the fulling mill and to know what color I wished mine. Early in the spring she offered to spin my wool that Mother sent (4 lbs of rolls, 18 cuts to the lb), if I would pay for the weaving of hers. She don't expect more than 4 yds at 8 cents per yd. Mine will be 5 or 6. The weaver was very glad to take the bonnet, which was Susan Stabler's, for pay. It was done up very nicely and looked like a new one. Hannah told me that her brother Levi, who has just built a fulling mill, had told them all that this year he intended to do all thier coloring and pressing for nothing, but afterwards they should pay for it and that for my kindness to her she intended sending the whole peice as her own, for she had done 5 times as much for him; and so it will come <u>easy</u> to me all round.

Indeed, <u>I have worked like a slave since I was sick</u>. There has not been but 2 nights since I could sit up that I have been in bed before 12 and many nights after 1. I do not wish to abuse my health, for so far, except that colic and toothache, I never was so favoured with good spirits and strength to rub through difficulties as at present. . . .

I am afraid you have all sent me too much, though I long to see what, as it comes from you. Anything that you <u>have used</u> will be <u>dearer</u> for <u>that</u> cause. When I made the request I did not expect or desire <u>much</u>. I thought a trifle to you would help me out and I would try to make a little do. Sister Margaret's present was very acceptable and her message to Cousin MEG gave great pleasure. It brought the tears from her eyes. She says, "Always give my love to them when thee writes. I am awkward at expressing what I feel, but they can't tell how gratifying their expressions of kindness are to me." Poor thing, her time is out tomorrow.[4]

The hail is now pattering on the window. I would not like to <u>turn out</u> tonight. Hannah is much better but there are many sores of the same kind hers were on Deborah and Aliceanna's heads, some larger than a 12 1/2 cent peice. They are all taking the same medicine. They are all hearty enough. Granville is an inch or 2 taller than his father. He has never shaved yet.[5] Tell William Henry Franklin has grown much this last summer. The clothes Granville wore over the mountains just fit Franklin now. Granville could not squeeze them on.

2nd day morning. Franklin is still thin and not able to do <u>hard</u> work. Thomas is a very hearty, fresh-looking lad, grows fast, very affectionate; his disposition naturally so mild and gentle shows some of the ill effects of <u>teasing</u> and bad example, but when from home he is generally thought one of the finest boys that ever was. He looks something like Elizabeth. His new teeth are very handsome, and the dimples in his cheeks shew plainer than they used to. Hannah is bashful, a little stubborn at times, which is increased by the disposition some of the others have to tyranise over the younger ones, grows tall and slender. Deborah is a fat, short-necked broad-shouldered, Irish-looking girl with large dark hazel eyes almost black and very dark brown hair. Hannah's hair and eyes are beautiful. Aliceanna is a pretty little lively prattler with the sweetest disposition, a darling with all the family. Her father puts her to bed every night and sleeps next to her, which none of the rest ever would do, and he is much set up with it. She calls him "pawa" and me "mumma," Granville "gamen," Franklin "Fankin," all the rest plainly.

Sally Townsend told me yesterday if I would come there tomorrow and bring some milk and eggs, which she has not, she will make an oven full of pumkin pies and divide with me. Now, it happens just so that pumkin pies has been an object of my most earnest desire for <u>better than sometime</u>, which she did not know, so <u>I asked her yes</u> and intend going.

I have the neck and head of Muly boiling now for mince pies, if I can get sugar, apples, and cider to make them. Oh, what a blessing to have plenty to eat. Our grain looks beautiful indeed. We have about 16 acres.

I shall be thrown out of making sugar this year as I shall have other fish to fry about the middle of the 4th month.[6] Granville says he intends to do great things at it if it is a good season, but I never found any of them would have the patience with it I have. Jos is from home, and if he don't come in time to divert this, I will direct it to brother James,[7] Sandy Spring, to save you postage. I must go to my work. Farewell, says your affectionate A Bentley

1. Casks.
2. Robert and Abigail Battin. They had a son, Josiah (1827–1833).
3. Born Massey Campbell, she married Abraham Reeder on December 18, 1828.
4. Her daughter Hannah was born in December.
5. Granville is seventeen.
6. She was pregnant with her ninth child, Edmunds.
7. Brother-in-law James Pleasants Stabler, postmaster of Sandy Spring, Maryland.

THREE

1831–1835

~

A chronic problem for farmers in many areas of Ohio was how to get their goods to a market. The lack of transportation meant a shortage of ready money and capital. Even in the late 1840s, William Lloyd Garrison noted as he traveled around Ohio trying to raise money to fight slavery, "Money here is not usually plenty, although they have every thing else in abundance." Joseph Bentley seemed to be forever in debt or seeking to raise cash to pay taxes.

Canals linking the Ohio and Mississippi rivers to the Great Lakes had great potential for bringing Midwest products to market. The success of the Erie Canal, which Isaac Briggs had worked on, inspired many imitators. In 1829, when the Sandy & Beaver Canal Co. was incorporated to build a canal from Pittsburgh to the Muskingum River at Bolivar, Ohio, farmers along its route saw prosperity just around the corner.

But the Sandy & Beaver struggled from the beginning. It was seven years before work began. Then the financial panic of 1837 set back its progress until 1845. The canal wasn't open its entire length until 1849, although it provided a route east from Hanover to Lisbon for some years.

The canal was built in stages by contract. Canal work involved backbreaking labor by gangs of men with picks and shovels. East of Hanover, where some 150 workers were employed digging a tunnel, one man was killed during blasting.

To keep its charter the canal company had to run a boat the length of the route by January 1848, even though the canal wasn't quite finished.

According to a history of the town of Hanover, this was the scene the day
the first boat floated through:

> The boat came from the east and had reached a point on West Fork
> creek near the site of the Frost mill the night previous. A number of
> Hanover people, headed by the band, went to meet it. At the point
> mentioned the boat was grounded, there being a raise of three feet
> necessary in getting again to water in the channel. Morris Miller
> with seven yokes of oxen came to the rescue and with all lending a
> hand the boat was lifted over the barrier. From here all went well
> until after entering the Big Tunnel. The band was playing and all
> were happy, but when near the east shaft a huge stone rolled down in
> front of the boat. Here again was turmoil and delay but finally the
> boat was got past and amid great eclat it reached Hanover, anchoring
> at the lower warehouse.
>
> It was said to be the only boat ever to ply the entire length of the
> canal.

For a time the canal shipped grain and the local coal east to Pittsburgh.
Then the Cleveland & Pittsburgh railroad, built in 1852, took much of the
canal's business. On the whole, the canal was a bust. According to Henry
Howe's history of Ohio, "The aggregate loss to the stockholders was nearly
two millions of dollars."

~

2nd mo 6th 1831
My dear friends,

I cannot make you sensible of the anxiety I feel to hear from you all, as
the letter last week did not bring the tidings I expected. If they should be
evil, I fear my mind is not strong enough at present to bear it right,
though from my inmost soul I could rejoice at the contrary.[1]

Aaron, Jos, and Granville have each thier schools to attend to. I have
been qualified to open the mail. They have each about 25 schollars, and
since the day they commenced that, if they had been at home they could
have done nothing, and Aaron attends to everything here. Franklin,
Thomas, and Hannah go to Granville, and Thomas reads and writes
quite smart, but poor Jos—my heart aches for him. This extreme cold
weather he has to start before sunrise, walks more than 3 miles over a

hilly road, has to break it after each fresh snow—it is more than a foot deep—often gets there and finds not a spark of fire, and returns after sundown. Oh, that an easier way could be found to procure the necessaries of life and extricate ourselves from debts.[2]

On thrashing our grain, we had the disapointment to find it would not turn out as much as we expected by a great many bushels, so that we have had to lay an embargo on wheat flour and confine ourselves to corn and rye. And it does not agree with me. It creates an acid on my stomach that distresses me much, and I have a very poor appitite. Our cows give very little milk, not enough to do without tea or coffee.

Our little sow presented us with 4 fine china pigs, and 3 of our ewes each a lamb (one spotted with brown) 4 weeks ago. Our flock is now 9 in number. The foxes have become so abundant and mischevious Jos has taken 2 beautiful hound puppies to raise—our old Lawyer's grandchildren. They are exactly alike: Ringwood and Marlowe. We had never seen him for more than 2 years till about 3 weeks ago. One night as I opened the door I met the poor old fellow, who seemed overjoyed to see us all. He is here yet—is, or has been, the most noted foxhound in this part of the world. He was shot through the knee some time ago and lamed but still keeps foremost for a while. Our chickens—5 or 6 frozen to death. No encrease amongst the cats yet, but expecting (a poor young inexperienced thing, too).

Last New Year's Day an impudent fox took 2 of them away. Aaron went out and bought a *hen turkey [*which has since turned out to be a gobler]. We fed it with an intention of killing it when fat, but the day before we intended doing so, Aaron went out with his rifle and shot a very large fat wild turkey, young and tender. This day 2 weeks I roasted it and a nice duck on a string before the fire. Cousin Robert had brought Cousin Margaret here the day before; we feasted and talked and enjoyed ourselves till 2nd day evening, when Cousin Robert proposed sending Aaron to take Cousin Margaret home, for me to accompany her in the sledge [between lines: "I forgot how to spell"], and he to take my place behind Jos for the night. We did so.

Aaron came for me 3rd day evening, since when I have had a fatiguing time. Something like influenza has gone through the family. Aliceanna was taken 2 week's since, suddenly, with the first attack of croup she ever had. It was before we had gone to bed. Its progress seemed so rapid we were much alarmed. We immediately put her feet and legs in warm water, greased her breast. Granville and I dug from under the snow in the garden some garlic, which I bruised, mixed with sweet oil, and rubbed her back, breast, and feet with very good effect in a short time. I found the antimonial wine[3] from being unstopped had evaporated, so I was fearful to give it, but ventured 5 drops. It puked her eleven times and entirely conquered the terrible disease. I sat up all night with [her] in my arms.

She has been very poorly with influenza for 10 days and Deborah also. Indeed, Deborah's cough resembles whooping cough. So I should think it was, if she had stood any chance of taking it. I also have a deep cold and gathering in my head. I hear the putrid sore throat and scarlet fever is very prevalent and fatal in New Lisbon and its vicinity. From one family last week 3 children were buried in one grave! . . .

Last 6th day the box &c from Baltimore came. The waggon was detained by sickness and deep snow in the mountains 3 weeks longer than he expected. I had become very uneasy about it. How shall I thank you all sufficiently for your kindness? It has made me feel rich. With the little I had it is more than <u>sufficient</u>. There was a great deal more than I expected.

With the rest came a bundle from Delia Kempton and a letter. (We receive letters from them very often (and newspaper every week for nearly 3 years.) D's letter made many apologies and begged me not to be dissapointed or offended when I opened the bundle to find a parcel of old clothes, which they feared was not worth sending; expressed the warmest sympathy and affection. (She would not have known our difficulties had I not answered one of SA Kempton's letters at a time when difficulties and almost starvation had sunk my spirits so that I was tempted to tell them a little of how we fared as they have expressed such an interest for us and a wish to know how we were situated.) Well, the envelope of the bundle was 4 yds of coarse, very strong domestic cotton, 4 pr of good drilling and jeans trowsers for Thomas, 3 other pr to mend the first with, 2 coats of the same, and 2 beautiful fine twilled bombazet coats for Thomas—they are bright blue lined with olive cambric, almost new and fit him exactly—2 most beautiful gingham frocks of Henrietta's to be cut up for little frocks, a paper of pins—4 rows large ones—2 yd pale blue ribband, 2 pink, 2 yellow, 4 yds different patterns lace, 1 piece of broad twilled tape, 1 plain, ditto ditto, 4 other peices of different sizes, 2 peices cord, 1 narrow braid or bobbin, a silk thread case well-supplied with needles, 3 capes muffled all round. . . .

Aliceanna came to my elbow just now. I told her to go away, I was writing to Grandmother. She said, "Well, tell my granmumma her mut tend Aliceanna nunga frock. I loves she."

Sloane sent us word today he was going to Baltimore with a waggon next week. Perhaps he will give you a call. Granville says be sure and give my dear love to them all, Aunt Meg specially. Dear Sister Mary's letter I read with great interest and pleasure. They come so seldom I must mention hers in particular. Oh [torn paper] do you as great a kindness as you have me—each article worn by you feels dearer to me for that cause even [torn] smell is still in them they all laugh at me so for my [torn] things I waited till they were gone to bed and spread them [torn] gazing on them gave vent to my feelings. . . . Your own affectionate Anna

There was so much bother taken of my last long letter I could not forbear writing again, tho I am very much pressed for time.
Not quite as usual,
JE Bentley

1. Anna probably was referring to the expected birth of her sister Sarah's first child.
2. Interestingly, Hannah Holland Coulson and her husband, Saul, named their son Granville Bentley Coulson (born 1848) after a schoolteacher, according to the Coulson family Web site.
3. Tartar emetic, dissolved in wine.

~

The harshness and uncertainty of contemporary "traditional" medical practice in those days encouraged the rise of alternative schools of medicine and a good deal of quackery. One theory that fell somewhere between science and chicanery was Thomsonianism, named for Samuel Thomson, who advocated the use of steam baths and herbs, especially lobelia root. The influence of Thomsonianism was short-lived, but while it lasted the "steam doctors" practiced widely, especially in the South and Ohio. They set up their own herbal pharmacies and held national conventions. The abolitionist William Lloyd Garrison periodically took a daylong Thomsonian treatment that consisted of a purge of coffee laced with lobelia or cayenne, which caused him to sweat and vomit, followed by a steam bath, a nap, another drink, and so on. By 1850 or so, the Thomsonian craze had passed. At its height, however, it drew in Isaac Briggs, who became a devotee and then a practitioner. His sister Anna begged to differ.

~

3rd mo 13th 1831
My dear friends,

I know you think too long a time has elapsed since I have written to you.
And even now if what I write takes its coloring from my gloomy feelings,
perhaps I had better not write. But I have sometimes found it to disperse
the clouds and have a soothing effect when I got fairly into a letter to
you. Your 2 last letters each came to hand a week later than they should
have done. I was kept in much anxiety by the delay of the expected
intelligence from dear Sister Sarah.

Some weeks previous I had a dream that, in spite of all my reasoning,
would make me forbode some evil tidings. And the event only fulfilled
the fears I had already entertained. I thought I had been called in haste
to Sharon on that occasion, that I travelled in a carriage till near there,
when the horses took fright at an object that crossed the road and stood
on one side pointing its finger towards Sharon. I got out of the carriage
and was wading on foot through a deep snow, when I came near the
object. It was Father. He went on before, but I could not overtake him
till we arrived. The family seemed to be passing to and fro in agitation at
Sister Sarah's room door (the little back room). Sister Deborah met me
looking like and dressed as a corpse. I expressed great surprise at seeing
her and concern for Sister Sarah. Her reply was, "I came to attend on her.
She (with emphasis) is likely to do very well, but"—I then awoke in
much agitation, and after spoke of my dream to Joseph and Cousin
MEG.

How deeply I sympathise with her in the trying bereavement, this
extinction of her tender maternal hopes. I cannot express by word, but I
trust and believe that e'er this thou hast been favoured to experience that
"feast of reason," that "Sabbath of the mind" that flows from a perfect
resignation of heart to him who gave and who has taken away. Oh, my
sister, I have felt it fully and entirely, even while the clods were falling on
my little Edward's coffin. . . .[1]

I am very "crippling," as Mother used to say, with my hip and back,
sometimes can scarcely walk at all and am getting to be almost good for
nothing. Oh, that the 18th of next month was safely over. . . . My
precious Sister Mary, thou knowest how to sympathise with me in the
weakness, fears, and depression of spirits incident to my situation.[2] So
often, too, I have had it to undergo. Then withhold not thy mite from
me. No subject can be more interesting to me than thy darling children.
The others don't say enough to satisfy me of them. Brother Isaac, have all

his feelings of brotherly love cooled towards me that he has never by the slightest expression of it noticed me? Tell him my feelings are deeply wounded by his neglect.

Cousin Robert's family are well. He has purchased the farm he lives on, and the ensuing season a canal is to be commenced from the Ohio at Geo[rge]Town heading (Oh, I forget where), but it will come through Hanover and Cousin Robert's farm not 2 hundred yds from his house. It was located last summer, and the subscriptions are nearly completed: $500,000. There are rapidly improving times in prospect for the farmer now for this particular section of country. Wheat in Massillon 23 miles from here brings 73 cents per bushel, and constant demand for it. Our crops look beautiful since the long deep snow left them. Our winter has been pretty much as it has been with you. Jos has had a trying time indeed attending his school but never left it 1 day on account of weather, often wading through water half-leg deep, his drawers and pantaloons frozen stiff when he got home. . . .

Dear Sister Margaret has twice asked what we thought of the Thomsonian system and I blame myself for not speaking candidly before now; though from the love I bear those who are exercizing it, with at present such apparent success with you, I should feel great reluctance were I not so fearful (from the tenour of your letters) some that are dearer may fall its victims. About 3 years since it was introduced here, some chance cases of great cures performed by it created a great reliance on it by many as it seemed something simpler and cheaper, and withal was something NEW. But fatal indeed was that relliance to many. We have heard the widow, and she a stranger here, as with her nine children she followed the remains of her husband to the grave, exclaiming, "Oh, if it had not have been for the ignorant steam Dr, he would have been with us yet. He was not dangerous till he was called in, and grew worse from that time. Oh, that I had never sent for him, for he has made me a widow and my children fatherless in a strange land." Many other cases of death occured under its administration caused by it, I have not the smallest doubt, and many others that would have ended so, I do believe, if Dr Robertson had not been timely called in. . . . It is now held in such detestation (except amongst a few who bought pattents), the steam Dr had to decamp in a great hurry as he could not ride out without being insulted. His wife, who, till he commenced the cooking process with her, was a stout hearty woman, is far gone in a decline, his 7 children the most pale sickly looking set I ever saw out here. Jos's opinion and mine are the same on this subject.

The Lobelia grows out here in great abundance and luxuriance. Will you find sale for it if I come in with a waggon load of it and red pepper? For I shall never use one leaf of it.

The tetter[3] is breaking out again on Hannah, poor child. I wish you could hear Aliceanna talk. She is very amusing, she is so lively and affectionate. Last week in the afternoon there came up a severe storm of thunder and wind. It became so dark I could not see to sew but was looking in terror out of the window at the falling trees and limbs, which were broken off in abundance. I exclaimed several times, "Oh, my dear Joseph, if he should be coming home, what will become of him?" The little creature took hold of my hand with both hers, pressed her cheek against it, and looking so innocently in my face said, "Sweet Mumma, de needen't care for Daddy. He's to skule."

Well, it is very late and my eyes smart, so I must conclude. With love to each precious one,
Anna Bentley

1. It seems that Sarah's baby had died, just as Anna's fourth child had died in 1824.
2. Mary, too, was pregnant; her son Charles was born in July.
3. A skin eruption, probably from impetigo or ringworm.

~

4th mo 3rd 1831
My dear friends,

We received a letter from Sister Mary last week. From some carelessness in the post offices, we have received your 4 last each a week later than we should have done. We have always before received them in 10 days after date. I will proceed immediately to answer part of the letter which relates to a bundle sent by Cousin M Bentley. Of such a one I had never heard. Cousin Robert coming in while I was reading it, I read that part aloud to him. He appeared much concerned, said it had never been committed to his care; neither had he ever heard of it, but supposes Abraham must have had it if it was sent, and that it either shared the same fate with the other or a worse one, if lost. If it was so, I think he would have been more thoughtful of us (even if he was under suffering himself) if he could have known the privations we were then daily undergoing, and that we even had to borrow the coffee, sugar, butter, meat, and flour that we set before him while here, though he partook more sparingly of them than we wished and would gladly have made him welcome to better. He

saw nothing but the fair appearance of <u>future</u> good or plenty, which I
<u>hope</u> is in store for us, and saw not the dark side now. I wish some of you
to see Cousin M <u>as soon as possible</u> and know of her what it contained
and assure her that though her kind intention failed in its benefit to
whom it was designed, yet the good deed was hers, and gratitude as
much her due and as warmly felt (be it little or much) as if I had <u>received</u>
it. And give my love to all that family. Who knows but in the
unsearchable will of Providence it may not be the last time I shall be
allowed to express it—but stop! I may not venture further there.

Then I wish you to see Aunt Sally [Garrigues?] and know of her to
whom she committed it. Please attend to it as <u>soon as possible</u> and let me
know all you can learn, for I am very anxious to hear on several accounts.
Cousin Robert is very uneasy about it also. He went up to Cousin James
Brooke's yesterday. Last 3rd day Cousin Margaret received a letter from
Howard which ought to have come 2 weeks ago stating that young James
Brooke and Cousin Hester were both ill. Cousin Hester had been
mending but from alarm at James's increased illness was then worse; that
the Dr had called there that evening on his way from Cousin James's,
said James's disease had turned to typhus, he was sinking very fast, and
could not live; that Paulina was also very sick and several in Isaiah's and
Basil's families. We feel very anxious to hear from them.[1]

Henrietta is married!!! Her husband's name is McKenzie—a very
clever young man of good family—her friends all pleased. J Howard has
a very bad cough and other symptoms of decline. They have taken a
house and I expect moved near Salem. Cousin MEG's Eliza has been
there ever since Cousin Robert went over the mountains. Cousin
Margaret's little Hannah is one of the loveliest and best babes I ever saw.
She would have all my particular washing brought there which she did
and ironed all nice. She has invariably acted like an own sister since she
came here, and Cousin Robert seems to be as affectionate and kind as a
brother, and the dear children, I do believe, love us as well as our own
uncle and aunt. Helen is a fine, industrious girl—milks, washes, bakes,
and indeed does all the housework. She is larger than her mother.

Franklin and Granville finished their schools yesterday and are
rejoiced to be at liberty. Thomas has learned to read and write very
smart, Hannah to read. Deborah did not go to Granville quite 3 weeks
and in that time learnt first her letters and to spell in 4 syllables and
began to read. She is a fat, awkward chunk of a girl and I do believe is
going to be a little crosseyed. The titter still shews in Hannah's face but
don't run any. Aliceanna grows handsomer, her <u>flaxen</u> hair curls in the

richest glossy ringlets over her head, her pure red-and-white complexion, her laughing blue eyes, very red lips, beautiful white teeth make her look like a little cherub. She is as straight as an arrow, round and plump but not very fat. She is full of animation, quick in all her motions, and so affectionate and sweet in her temper. Don't shew this to anyone who would not remember that it is to a mother and sisters who have not seen my little blossom of the wilderness brought forth and nourished through many a difficulty and with its expanding loveliness soothing me with hopes for the future.

Yesterday Maria was very busy ironing and Aliceanna in a very mischevious mood would get in the tub of clothes just to plague her. She took her out several times and at last got out of patience and said, "Aliceanna, if thee don't behave, I really will slap thee and put thee out of doors. I don't love thee."

She looked up and said, "Why, Maria, I love dee. I love dy eyes, and dy teeks, and dy mouf, and I love all of dee."

Maria's anger was all gone, and she kissed her, saying, "It's no use to scold thee." She looks more like Thomas than the others.

About 2 weeks ago I got my flannel and made a dress for myself. It is rather coarse but soft, a kind of London brown color.[2] I had worn my old one till from its shrinking &c &c, its <u>age</u>, and mustiness it was not decent; but I was obliged to wear another over it for I take cold so easily I could not leave it off.

Poor Maria has got entirely through her linsey, is compelled to wear her only calico that her Cousin A gave her. She has some ginghams made out of that light one of mine. She has no other change. I won't make the one her dear Aunt Mary sent till we can get something rougher for her for fear she will be obliged to wear it too much. Hannah has one good linsey and one old one, no other change in the world, Deborah one good linsey and an old thin, tender gingham, the cotton thou and Cousin Deborah Stabler sent. . . .

Poor Thomas met with an accident to his clothing this week. He had 2 pr of linsey trowsers that I hoped with faithful patching would last till the weather was warm enough to change. One pair that I had just patched with new all over the seat and front of the legs got burnt up. While Maria was washing at the spring, a storm of wind coming up and the fire blew among the clothes. It burnt a hole 1/4 of a yd in that new striped bed quilt we made, Mother, an old check apron of Maria's not worth much, and the trowsers. She had come up for something and not down in time to prevent more loss.

Franklin has worn all this winter without a change the trowsers
Uncle Roger gave Granville, which he wore all last winter. I would patch
them after he went to bed till 2 weeks ago I made him a pr of corduroy
got on credit. Jos has worn this whole winter a pr made of the linsey dear
Bro Richard sent for Thomas. I have patched them with some a good
deal like it and they are likely to last till warm weather yet. Granville got
cassinet from Cousin R ditto.

You think me too trifling for anything. You never write to me about
such trifles, but there is nothing comes so near conversation as to sit
down and forget all cares in trying to present ourselves to your view even
in our old rags. When I began this I thought I could scarce fill the half
sheet, but as I went on I found I could not make it do. Shall I tell you
now of our herds, of our flocks, our crops, &c? Well, our herd he's lousy;
our new cows have been dry for 2 weeks, and I fear it will be several
weeks before they will have calves. Rose, our only dependence, gives a
pint and a 1/2, has not had a calf for more than 2 years, is not with calf.
Our heifer Cherry is a fine gentle thing a year and a half old. We have
not had an ounce of butter in the house since New Year's.

We have 5 ewes and a buck. The ewes have each a fine lamb, the
youngest 2 weeks old, the others 3 months. Our grain looks as beautiful
as the brightest green can make it. We have a very favourable season for
it. We have 6 or 7 hens sitting and the noise of 30 or 40 others cackling
from morning till night. Our horses under Cousin Aaron's care are as fat
as moles. He plaistered my room upstairs, laid the hearth, and fixed the
oven, which has long been useless. We made very little sugar, about 40
lb, and owe 10 lb of that. The winter broke too suddenly and the sap
rose. I have soap to make tomorrow—or to begin, rather.

I know not how I shall get through, for I have been so helpless and
miserable for 2 or 3 weeks I have scarcely been able to get about. My
back and hips have given out so sometimes I cannot walk at all and often
have to hollow out in attempting to rise, which is mortifying. Before
Aliceanna I think I was held like I was before Thomas was born, and that
has a depressing effect on my spirits, which I strive to reason away.
Another thing: I know not how in the world I shall be able to pay a nurse
($1.75 for 2 weeks), and I have not yet engaged one though there are 2
fine girls either of whom I could if I had the means. The Dr has not yet
been engaged. The next letter I write will be after that event, if it should
terminate favourably for me.

Dear Sister Sarah, I thank thee or brother JPS for the touching lines enclosed signed JPS but I think composed by thee. I can enter into the feelings that drew them forth. I have written a piece since, though not on that subject, which I will send, if I live, another time, for Granville and Maria send their love and mine. Receive your share and distribute a share to any what may value it.

Your affectionate A

PS: Where does Aunt Deborah Stabler stay, and how is she? Give my love to her.

1. Paulina Brooke lived, but James and Hester's sons, James and Basil, died. Basil left a pregnant widow, Rachel.
2. "London" was a fancy adjective describing several colors of cloth, as in London blue, London black, London russet, London scarlet etc., even something called "London smoke," a shade of gray.

~

7th mo 18th 1831
My dear friends,

It goes against my conscience to take half a sheet to write on, but I have a considerable headache and fear I shall not ever fill this. I think I overeat myself yesterday at Cousin R's. She [Margaret] had stewed chickens, peas, beans, bread, butter, milk, and an elegant rice pudding for dinner. She makes the best rice puddings I ever eat, and it is such a rarity to us here. . . .

What a cold, wet season we have. Many fear the grain is much injured by it. We have not got through with our harvest yet; rain today has stopped them. They have had no help but expect to do all themselves. Jos, Franklin, and Thomas reap; Granville binds and shocks. We have 100 dozen of rye and I don't know how much wheat done and about 5 acres to do yet. Granville's feet are poisened so badly he can scarcely get on. Our corn looks fine but the squirrals, cut worms, and ground squirrels destroyed a great deal. Some have had theirs taken up so that they ploughed the fields over and sewed buckwheat. About 2 weeks ago they were hoeing the corn, the dew was on it, and they all were barefooted with their pantaloons rolled up. Jos had his hoe raised when immediately under it, close to his naked foot, he saw curled up a terrible rattlesnake. He sprang from it, calling Thomas up, got out of its reach. Franklin ran and with one stroke of his hoe took its head off. It had nine rattles. There has been 4 killed since we came here and all in the same place, which makes us think there is a den somewhere of them. They are never known to travel far from their dens.

We have built a large nice springhouse and find it a great convenience. We are raising both calves (one of each <u>sort</u>).

The pain in my head, which I think is rheumatism, has shifted its position and takes possession of my teeth, where it has sorely tormented me at times for 6 weeks past. I had a spell that lasted a week night and day, defying the power of mustard plaisters, laudanum, and of mint, <u>smoking, chewing tobacco</u>, and everything else. I have just now been smoking till I am too drunk to walk straight.

My boy[1] is getting to be pretty good and grows amazingly. He is a very fat, large child, at 3 months weighs 17 lbs and is now laughing, cooing, and kicking with all his might in the cradle. Thomas, Deborah, and Aliceanna had a very sick spell last week with headaches, sore throats, pains in the bowels and breast, and violent fevers. Deborah seemed quite ill for 2 days and nights. I rubbed their throats with camphire, sweet oil, and salt (a thing I never heard of before but tried it with complete success in giving them speedy relief), bathed their feet, to Deborah's breast and stomach put a flannel bag with bruised rue, wormwood, and garlic. It broke the fever, and I never saw children that seemed as ill recover as quickly. They were all about and well the next day. I think it was cold from the sudden change in the weather. Some days have it excessively warm, and a change will take place in the night; the next day we cannot be comfortable without the doors shut and a fire.

We have pretty good luck with our bees this summer. We had 2 hives in the spring. The first swarm went off after Granville and I got them safe (as we thought) in the hive, but we have hived 3 other swarms that work well and the first warm clear day another will swarm. No one here will venture near but Granville and me. I wish you could see our onion bed. It is about the size of a square in your garden, and such monstrous large onions. We eat them in various ways at every meal. Think how we must <u>SMELL</u>. We have had cucumbers once, a fine prospect for more. Granville says tell William Henry he has a noble prospect for <u>watermillions</u> and mushmelons and cantelopes, beautiful vines in a patch he cleared in the woods as large as your garden. . . .

I feel more anxiety now than usual to hear often on my dear Sister Mary's account. Poor Mother, did thee get thy potatoes planted at last? Granville often says, "Poor Grandmother, I know if I was there I could make her a good living off the 2 farms." If my aching teeth will let me, I intend to write a letter to Bro Isaac and see if that will make him notice his poor sister. And as I don't know how to direct to him, I shall send it to you to forward, if you please. I am, most affectionately, your Anna Bentley

1. Edmunds, born in April, was named for Joseph Bentley's mother, Alice Edmunds Bentley.

12th mo 10th 1831
My dear friends,

A letter from dear Sister Mary arrived 3 weeks since and one from Sister Meg 2 weeks, relieved me from the most painful anxiety that had taken possession of my mind on your accounts from the long, <u>long</u> interval since hearing from you. . . .

I believe I will first begin with our distresses, at present a too fruitful theme. We scuffled along without meat so long that we felt as if we could bear it no longer, and having very scant provender for our stock to winter on, we killed our nice little heifer, Cherry, 4 weeks ago. (We did not know she would have <u>been in use</u> next summer.) She was very fat.

Two weeks since, our beloved Granville left us. He is gone to learn the waggon-making business 2 miles from Cousin James Brooke's. Oh, how we miss the dear boy, for he is a precious, noble-minded youth. Aaron had been poorly for some days with a pain or stitch in his side, but went with him and led the horse back. As there had been a great many applications to Jos for coal, so that it would be likely to cover many little debts, he got new houns[1]—I don't know how to spell it—put to the waggon and went to <u>work digging coal.</u> Aaron assisted him in digging a deep ditch to carry off the water. The weather was excessively cold. Aaron got fresh cold in his side and suffered much for some days, but I made him a flannel shirt and he applied British oil and got well. They hauled about 50 bushels.

Last 7th day Franklin was sent to a neighbor's. He took the gun, and in looking for game had a very long walk, got his feet very wet. He has been very weakly all this fall, often pains in his back, breast, and limbs. On first day he looked bad and complained a good deal of pains and weariness. 2nd day he was up at the fire. By 2 o'clock he could not sleep for pains in his hips and thighs. By night his ankle joints were much swelled and inflamed. Poor fellow, he is suffering with the inflamatory rheumatism in both knees and feet and can only move with help and extensive pain. I have this night applied Judkins ointment and give him red pepper and pennyroyal tea, which has stopped the chilliness he has constantly complained of. He is now asleep. For the 2 last nights he has slept none after 11 and none in the daytime.

I must now go back a little. On first day my throat became very sore, on 2nd day much ulcerated, attended with fever and chilly spells. I too was taking a deep cold. I slept but little 2nd day night. 3rd day Jos not able to be up—soreness in his breast and limbs and headache. I tried to feel well enough to wait on Franklin and him. 4th day, Jos rather better so as to be about, Deborah was taken very poorly with pain in her breast, headache, and cough. I gave her coltsfoot tea, bathed her feet, rubbed her breast with camphor, laudanum, and sweet oil, and she was much better in the morning. But 4th day I had observed my little one look paler than usual, his eyes watery and heavy. I put him to sleep. He slept long and heavy. I took him up; he had a burning fever. He did not fret or cry, but seemed stupid. His upper gums have long been swelled, so I took resolution and cut them through with my thimble. He has 4. It seemed to relieve him. In 5 minutes his fever was very high. 4th and 5th day nights and he has been sick and fretful, but better today.

Jos concluded it would be best to kill the hogs yesterday as they were in pretty good order and we should need all the corn (our wheat being very light). So Cousin Robert came to help, and the very first hog they butchered Aaron came in to me holding his wrist and the blood running from a wound in it. He had made his knife nearly as sharp as a razor and somehow or other had cut all across his wrist just over the artery, wounding a leader. His skin is remarkably thick and the cut is not deep. Well, I got my needle and silk ready and attempted to sew it up, but the skin being so tough, my sight began to fail, and Jos took a stitch. I bandaged it up, and he would go out to work again. And he stuck at it till all was done.

Cousin Margaret sent Helen to help Maria. We were sitting at dinner, Helen and Maria at the other end of the room taking the fat off the last bowels, when who should walk in but our cousins W and A Brooke.[2] We were glad to see them, and now you must tell me in good earnest if there is any truth in Mother's getting Kersey[3] to wear winter and summer.

Aaron suffered very much last night and today with his wrist. Hannah eat no supper, complained of sore throat, headache, and soreness in her flesh. Aliceanna is complaining much in her sleep, and Jos is quite poorly again this evening; the cold seems to have got into his bowels like dysentery. It is something like influenza we have. I could fill another whole sheet with little grievances and discouragements but will not now. I must thank dear Sister Mary for her letter and wish I had time to write her a great long one for her owny-dony. I long to see the little cherubs she writes so fondly of. Her descriptions are the only ones that have ever seemed to bring them before my mind's eye. I wish you would write more particularly of little Isaac Bond.

Abbey Preston had her 15th child last week.[4] They are all living and but 1 married and studying medicine. They join places with Cousin Robert 1st day. The red pepper and Judkins put Franklin in a profuse perspiration. He rested better than he has for a week but is now complaining of a thickening in his right shoulder. Jos complained of great pain in his bowels and chilliness in the night. I gave him some red pepper and it made him easy and sweat like a horse. Cousin Robert and Aaron came early this morning and staid till 3. Judkins ointment has relieved Aaron's wrist. I hope we are all better. I never knew such severe cold weather this early in the winter as we have had for 10 days. It has disappointed us with our linsey, which is at the fulling mill and was to have been done a week ago, but the mill can't work till a thaw. There is 47 1/2 yds more than a yd wide and exellently woven. We shall suffer if we don't get it soon.

A sleigh has just gone from here. Sarah Holland and Massy Reeder just called to see how we were. Jos, Cousin Robert, and Robt Battin (son of John) stirred about and obtained a district school—RHG clerk, R Battin treasurer, JEB teacher—at $12.50 per month. I don't know when they will commence.

We got about 17 acres of grain in. I found a peice of poetry in an Ohio paper which I admire, and I want to know what you think of it. 'Tis by Mrs Sigourney.[5] I think she must be the author of that beautiful peice, "The Father's Lament." There is a similitude between them.

> There shone a beam within my bower,
> Affection's diamond spark.
> The spoiler came with fearful power
> That beam is quenched and dark.
> There was a shout of childhood's joy
> A laugh of infant glee.
> The earth closed o'er my glorious boy
> My nurslin—Where is he?
> There seemed a sound like rushing wings

So thick my sorrows came.
A blight destroyed my precious things,
My treasures fed the flame;
An ocean of unfathomed greif [woe]
Swept o'er me with its waves [swept on with all its waves].
And here, all desolate I stand
<u>Alone</u>, amid my graves.
<u>Alone!</u> there flows no kindred tear
No sympathising sigh.
The feet of curious crowds [throngs] are near,
Yet [But] every cheek is dry.
And there is nought but curtaining turf,
And cold earth loosely thrown,
To shut me from those cherished forms
My beautiful, my own?
Yet who this fearful charge [deed] hath wrought
Who thus hath laid me low?
Was it a hand with vengeance fraught,
The malice of a foe?
No!—He who called my being forth
From mute, unconscious clay;
He who with more than parent's care [love]
Hath led me night and day;
Who erreth not, who changeth not,
Who woundeth but to heal,
Who darkeneth not man's sunny lot
Save for his spirit's weal;
Therefore I bow me to his sway.
I mourn, but not repine,
And chastened, yet confiding say,
"Lord, not my will, but thine."

The three last verses I think are particularly beautiful.
1st day night. Franklin is better but Deborah more poorly. I wish
you would all join and write me a great long letter. Sister Elizabeth is
"<u>unnatural</u>-like," and Mother, if thee don't write I will think sure
enough—I won't tell thee what. . . . <u>Ain't</u> you looking for me in West's

waggon? I ain't there indeed. Oh, if all had suited how glad would I have gone.

2nd day morning. I believe all are better this morning, but dear little Aliceanna has a hoarseness and cough that is much like a commencement of croup, poor little thing. <u>She has not had shoes</u> on yet. Her measure was taken in time. The shoemaker disappointed us week after week, and when they did come they were an inch-and-a-half too long. Jos is gone to bring home another pr. I have Edmunds' very nicely fixed for the winter. The lining of Maria's plaid cloak is as good as new. It is very fine, a bright deep blue pelisse flannel. I have made him 2 handsome frocks of it. He has 4 nice petticoats of flannel. I brought with me 2 new ones and 2 that were Aliceanna's.

Jos has just come without the shoes, and I must quit. I shall not have time to fill the envelope as I intended. Give my love to everybody.

I am your affectionate A

1. The hound was the part of the buggy that connected the axle to the shaft and took the main load of the forward pulling motion.
2. Probably the brothers William and Abraham (or Abram) Brooke, who had moved to Ohio with Uncle Sammy Brooke and the rest of his family, settling in the neighborhood of Marlborough (now Marlboro), Stark County.
3. A coarse woolen cloth.
4. Abbey (usually spelled Abi) Hole married Peter Preston in 1808. Both are buried in the Quaker Ridge Cemetery, once the site of the Augusta Friends meeting house. Their stones say he died in September 1854, age sixty-eight, and Abi died in March 1859, age sixty-six. Descendants live in the brick house Peter built above the canal.
5. Lydia Huntley Sigourney (1791–1865), a popular writer of her day, who was often compared to the flowery English poet Felicia Hemans. This poem appeared in Sigourney's 1834 collection, *Poems,* under the title "Thou Hast Made Desolate All My Company." Bracketed words are variations that appeared in the later version.

~

1st mo 22nd 1832

I do not feel at all satisfied at the way we have got into about writing. Yet I think I am more excusable than you. I find so little leisure in my large family that it leaves my mind with too little energy to make a beginning, which is the worst part of the <u>difficulty</u>. Thy fears, dear Mother, were too true with regard to our not getting our linsey in time. It was taken to the fulling mill the week before the freezing cold weather began and there it staid till last 2nd day. We got the 20 yds fulled for the <u>he</u> part of the family. I cut out a pair of pantaloons for Jos 2nd day night and finished them, a <u>monstrous</u> pair for our <u>monstrous</u> Aaron, and a pair for Franklin

I finished after midnight last night. Though "I say it that should not say it," they are very neatly and very strongly made.

First day Maria washed and I had all the housework to do, and the child has been troublesome all the week, so I think I was smart. The 7th day before, it (the linsey) came, Susan Miller came and brought me 3 cuts of exellent sewing thread coulored to suit it. Said she had been spinning for herself and sister Catharine and remembered "I was a worthless thing and could not spin." It is now scarcely worthwhile to tell how I have had to patch and patch since we are so well off now, i.e. the linsey. It is very good. The other 29 yds for the she folks will be done tomorrow week. Poor Maria has had to do all winter with one old cotton frock, which, when she washed, she had to put on one of mine. She has the calico Sister Mary sent for first days. Those 2 are all she has in the world. She wants but 1 inch of being as tall as I am. The 3 little girls had each an old linsey frock which are going very fast, and week before last dear Cousin Margaret sent Aliceanna an exellent linsey frock that Eliza had outgrown.

They are all comfortably clad having had the good fortune last winter to be disappointed in getting thier linsey soon enough to make up. Thier house, though small for thier large family and the number of visitors that resort there, is kept very comfortable by a stove and fireplace. They have a set of fine good children. Helen is an amiable affectionate girl, very modest and diffident. She does all the work of the family and is growing quite pretty. Little Hannah is a dellicate pretty little creature, very smart and interesting. And Cousin M takes snuff and I smoke like forty.

About New Year's 2 of our ewes presented us with twins and today 2 more is added, several more expected. We have 15 SHEEP. Our sow managed badly last year somehow, for we had not a pig left for next year except a little one Cousin Robert gave Maria last August.[1] We shall have 2 more tomorrow about 10 weeks old, remarkably fine ones, which I bought for 25 cents apeice. We did not weigh our hogs—but hope our meat will last till it is gone.

The day before Christmas our dear Granville came to see us. He is pleased with his situation in every respect. Cousin A took him home on 4th day in the sled. It is 15 miles and 2 from Cousin James Brooke's. Granville went there one 7th day and staid till 1st day. They pressed him to come often, "to come as to a father's house, every 7th day if he could." (It was a place recommended by Cousin Jemmy for Granville.)

Two weeks ago yesterday Jos, Thomas, Edmund, and I went up in

Cousin Robert's sleigh to see Granville. Oh, what a satisfaction it is to have this dear good boy so agreeably fixed. His master we did not see as he was from home. We had told Granville to expect us that day. We got there a little before 12. A dear old motherly woman—his mistress, Helen Snode—met and welcomed us <u>expected friends</u>. Her 2 sons—Benjamin, 22 years old, and William, 19—had with Jos assisted us out of the sleigh and seemed as glad to see us as Granville did. An only daughter, Mary, aged 17, a fine, amiable girl, is all of this worthy family.[2] It was not like strangers meeting for the first time, but there seemed on both sides a something that I don't know how to explain, but we felt as if we had long known and esteemed each other. We found that Granville was a great favourite. He says there could not be kinder or cleverer people than they all are. Their house is small. They intend building next summer. Everything about the house is kept as sweet and nice as could possibly be. There is plenty of everything. He says they keep an exellent table. Dinner was soon set before us. It consisted of a fine, fat roasted goose, sausages, soused cheese, pickles, grand apple butter, stewed apples, green and dried, potatoes, butter, bread, and exellent mince pies.

We passed a delightful afternoon till after 4. They entreated us to stay all night, but as we intended [going] home the next day, thought we must go to Cousin James Brooke's. Granville went with us. It was near dusk when we drove up to the door. Gerrard was going in the house with a log of wood. He looked back and as he recognized us shouted out, "Holoa, holoa, jump out, jump out." He run in with the wood and was instantly followed by the dear old man, who met us with his warm welcome. I have never yet seen him as well as he appeared to be. They all appeared truly glad to see us. Poor Cousin Hespy has miserable health, is not able to do anything but knit or sew. It was a heartstroke to her the loss of her sons last summer. She was speaking of poor Basil's widow[3], the mother of 3 helpless children, and hourly expecting another and none but her children with her. Paulina Brooke was nursing her sister in Salem, and Ann was all <u>thier</u> dependence. She said, "Poor Basil would have his youngest child named after Sister Debby.[4] I have thought sometimes if she had a chance and could send it some little thing that she could easily spare and that can't be got as easy here, how it would please his poor distressed widow. It seems as if as yet she could not be comforted. We want her to give up her 2 youngest children <u>entirely</u> to us, but she cannot consent to part with them yet."

We sat up talking till near midnight and staid till one and left next day. They both desired their love to be given to Mother and the rest of you. We got home safe and . . . [here the letter stops short].

1. One of the few times Anna uses the common term for the month of the year instead of the Quaker numbering system.
2. Joseph Snode had arrived in Columbiana County, Smith Township in 1824 with his wife and three children. Benjamin, who moved to Lexington Township, Stark County, died in 1876; Mary, who married Richard Haines, died in 1873; and William died sometime after 1879. The crossroads where their farms were located is still called Snodes Station, or just Snodes.
3. Rachel Morris Brooke had married Basil Brooke in 1826 when she was twenty and he was twenty-three.
4. Probably sister-in-law Deborah Brooke, wife of Basil's older brother, Isaiah Boone Brooke.

~

4th mo 8th [1832]
My dear friends,

After so long an interval of silence, I would gladly endeavour to fill a whole sheet but doubt my ability to fill even this. We have had a most trying anxious time here since last 4th day week in nursing poor Seth with a violent [spell] of pleurisy. None that saw him (till day before yesterday) had the least expectation of his recovery. He was bled and 3 blisters successively applied to his head and breast. I applied and dressed them all—different kind of medicine every hour and sometime 1/2 hour, every dose of which Jos or I administered night and day. I had not my clothes off for 10 days. I sat up 2 nights hand warming half the night previous and from 1 the night after and all the next night and more than half of every other night till the 2 last, which 2 Edmunds has been so sick with fever and vomiting from cold and teething that I got but little sleep. The Dr had no hopes but told us if we could keep him alive through the 9th day and night he would hope he might recover. It was indeed an awful time. Life seemed, as it were, to hang on a balance. I sat by him with my fingers on his feeble fluttering pulse almost constantly through the night.

All thought him dying. Sometimes his pulse would cease, he had the rattles. Jos and I went to his chest and laid out clothes to lay him out in. At sunrise he began to revive, and he has been getting better since. Yet still we have to sit up with him. He has an obstinate dihoreaa and dreadful sore mouth, tongue, and throat. The neighbours have come in crowds, 25 a day sometimes. A great many would sit up, but we could not trust them to give the medicine. We wrote down the time for giving each dose and gave it punctually. He is so patient, takes everything given him so good. All that is done for him is "very good," "very comfortable." He looks so like Father, and every groan—his breathing, voice, and all—brought the last sad scene so plain before me.

I feel very stupid and sleepy. Jos was up last night, and there has no one come to sit up tonight, so we will have to. There has been a great many here today. Edmunds has been as troublesome and cross all the time as ever he was, so that I am nearly <u>kilt up</u>.

2nd day morning. Seth seems better. Edmunds very cross, high fever last night. I feel miserable. Granville came to see us 2 weeks ago, is well and happy. I am <u>very anxious</u> to hear from you. Received a letter from Bro James P Stabler last week. Thank'um. I have lately drawn likenesses by Mother and Sister Sarah's profiles and painted them. They are striking likenesses and sometimes I cry at 'em. Maria has a box of paints Cousin Anna gave her. I have for amusement drawn and painted miniature likenesses, which are pronounced <u>beautiful</u>. I never knew I <u>had</u> such a turn for it as I never had the least instruction or practise till lately. I have tried to draw likenesses of my children but cannot succeed, yet it never occupies any other time than a noisy first day.

I wish you could procure me some Bene seed and send in a letter as soon as possible. . . . I am your own stupid, weary, good-for-little, A

∼

4th mo 15th 1832
To Frances Stabler[1]
[from Maria B. Bentley]
My dear little cousin,

We received the inteligence of thy birth with delight, and I thought it would be an act of impoliteness if I did not write to thee. As thee is a stranger to me I hardly knew how to adress thee, but first I will congratulate thee on having such a tender nurse as our mutual Aunt Elizabeth: so tender and affectionate even as much so to thee as to a <u>kitten</u>. Indeed, if I was thee or in thy place I would not have a rival in a cat if I could help it. She says in her letter that thee does not look stupid and dull like my mother's children all did. Now, as I am one of them I must tell thee that appearances are often decietful, though I do hope not in thee. I do wish I could see thee before thee gets ugly and dull like us, but I don't much expect I will.

Thee must be a good little girl and never cry, only when thee is
hungry or when Aunt Elizabeth sticks pins in thee. Thee must try to curb
thy temper if thee has a fiery one, for I know by sad experience how hard
it is to conquer our evil propensities if we do not begin soon as we are
capable of it. It pleased My Maker to give <u>me</u> a very great deal to war
with, more I sometimes think (though wrong I know), than I can
manage. . . .

Thee must forgive me, my dear little cousin, for my giveing thee
advice when there is so many around thee so much better calculated to
give counsel than I, but thee must beg thy Mother and <u>our</u> aunts and
Grandmother to write a few lines to me some time or other to give me a
little good advice, for every little helps, as the saying is. Give my love to
thy dear Father and Mother and tell them I love them <u>dearly</u>.

<u>I have a dear little brother, his name is Edmund Brooke Bentley</u>. He
is nothing but skin and bone hardly. Oh, yes, he is too; but he has had a
very severe spell of sickness, but he is getting better now but is very cross.
We sent for the Dr last 7th day afternoon, and he said it would have
been attended with danger if we had not sent for him. He thought it was
teething and a deep cold that had settled in his breast. Father and
Mother are most worn down. We have had a sick family of it this five
weeks past.

Old Uncle Seth Hoopes came here some weeks ago, very bad indeed.
We sent for the Dr, who attended him a week but gave him out entirely,
and we had to set up with him for about 10 nights. He is getting better
now but is very weak yet. It was the Plurisy that ailed him, and Mother
thinks that he is sinking into a decline. I hope not. He is a very old man.
He has a short, hard cough that hurts him very much. He seems so
thankful for everything that we do for him. I have had to wait on him
altogether now, as Father & Mother's minds and time are taken up with a
far dearer and nearer interest. Poor little Edmund, he has had a suffering
time of it. Franklin has been very poorly too. We expected him to have
an attack of the Plurisy, but it is gone off now. Aliceanna has been quite
ill, but she too has got better again. Father is now out in the clearing at
work & Thomas too. Franklin is hauling wood, and I just done
[shooing] the children on out at play.

Cousin MEG has been here all day, and her & Mother are chattering
in the next room so that I cannot think of what to say. Do, Aunt E, let
me hunt thee a young man out here that would go there and bring thee
out here. Then we could fit up a part of our house for you to live in. Oh,

how happy we would be, and then I could go back with you when you want to pay a visit. . . .

7th day evening: I've got the house all sweet and it has just begun to rain and looks as if it would not stop very soon. I feel as tired and stif as I supose an old plough horse must feel after a hard day's work. I have churned and cooked and scoured all manner of things, & Cousin Margaret fully expects Cousin Robert and Cousin Betsey*² the last of next week. Helen spent the afternoon here yesterday. I do love her very much. She will be 15 next 7th day. I tapped a few sugar trees this year and made 7 lbs and three quarters, want 8 more + (and roasted coffee). Oh, how I do wish I could just pop in at the back room window some of these nights and skare you all. I remember one night I slept with Grandmother. How she made me cry because she and Mother said that she put her big toe in my mouth. And the time I got under her rocking chair after her snuf box.

MBB

*R[obert] & E[lizabeth] P Thomas

1. Born on March 31, 1832.
2. Betsy Thomas was MEG's sister. She is mentioned frequently in the letters.

~

7th mo 22nd 1832
My dear friends,

Don't you begin to think I am growing very remiss in writing? I had thought there was nothing in the way this afternoon to prevent my writing a long letter to you, but just as I was going to begin was attacked with my old tormentor the tootheache, which so far obstinately refuses to yield to the pipe which has heretofore never failed. I have been so thronged with work this summer that it has seemed as if I never could find time to write, and several weeks when I would have done so I had no paper. I really forget how long it has been since I wrote last, and think it likely I shall tell you over again somethings or leave others, thinking I have told you.

Franklin has been nearly 3 months at a trade—carpenter and cabinetmaker—is likely to make a workman. Well and happy, is as tall as his father, slim and well-shaped, full of mischief. Granville, well and happy, steady as a grandfather now (first day afternoon). Stocking a plough for his father in the smoke house. His good old master gave him 2 weeks time in harvest, and though he was offered 50 cents cash for every day, he came down to help his father. We are about 1/2 through both grass and grain, have all that is done safe in the barn without a drop of rain on it, Aaron and Granville our only assistants. We have a plentiful harvest and the greatest crop of early potatoes now as large as <u>my fist</u>, 3/4 of an acre, and more than an acre of flourishing ones for winter use. Our corn among the best in the neighbourhood, very fine, more than 8 acres.

Our mare, Jewel, has a fine, beautifully formed colt foaled the 15th of May. It is very fat, grows rapidly, its color a dark dappled grey. It is a darling with us all. Thomas carries it every day. It is as playful and gentle as a lamb. And we have upwards of 200 chickens and 5 young half-grown turkeys. Poor Thomas has had the misfortune to lose one of his old ducks with nine young ones half grown. I expect a mink or fox took them. His other duck hatched 11 yesterday. Our meat is all gone, and we have eat a sheep besides.

Oh dear, my tooth.

I hope you dried my cherries &c. Poor Cousin Margaret has weaned little H[1] and ought to have done so 4 or 5 months sooner. I have been trying 2 or 3 hours to obtain a little ease and set my mouth on fire almost with red pepper and whiskey but <u>fear</u> it will have its own time at last. So I will dash away and you must not wonder if it is all unconnected (a thing not unusual in my letters). . . .

Poor Jos has worked very hard this spring and summer. He misses his boys. Aaron has worked most of the time at his trade. Poor old Seth's sickness threw us back with everything. Aaron ploughed the ground and Maria had to turn out to help her father plant all the corn, to hoe it also when Jos ploughed it. Jos ploughed the potatoe ground, Maria and I dropped them, Jos and Thomas covered them.

I never saw any person work so constantly and take so little time to rest as JEB does, and he begins to feel the effects of it too, for he is not so stout as he used to be and looks very thin and broken. He has a large clearing on hand which he expects to get ready for wheat.

Cousin Robert and Elizabeth P Thomas arrived here safe and well in 8 days after starting. She has spent 2 days here, is now in Salem at J Howard's, where she expects to spend 2 or 3 weeks. She looks very thin and miserable, but her appetite is better and she looks better than when she came.

Seth is exactly in the same situation father was a few months previous to his death. I think he will not stand it long, poor old man. He is a great pull back to us, but he has no one to take care of him and seems to cling to us with all the grateful affection of a natturally ardent disposition. He requested me the other day if he died in this neighbourhood that he might be burried in our orchard in a beautiful spot where we intend to have our family laid to rest. Oh! who of us may be laid there first?!

What do you all think of this Cholera? I want you to tell me how Brother Isaac is coming on.[2] Is he laying by anything for himself? Is he a good boy, &c &c? And why did you never tell me anything of Uncle GT Hopkins's illness?

How are my dear sisters Mary and Sarah coming on and thier little ones? Cousin Robert says, "Tell Cousin S her little Frances may do for a Maryland production but is nothing to compare to what is produced in Ohio, as both thee and I could produce evidences to the truth of." He says Charles Howard is like Edmund, and Cousin E says Aliceanna is like Hannah.[3]

I think Maria will have to finish this. My toothe or rather teethe ache too bad for me to say more than love to every dear one among you.

Your Anna

2nd day morning.

My teeth got easy last night at midnight after steaming it over wormwood and southern wood and bathing my face with red pepper. But I feel very weak this morning, indeed I do every morning for some weeks past. And Edmunds has something that I am almost affraid will end in dysenterey. I dread weaning him, he is such a fracsious fellow, but believe it would be best to do so. Oh, dear, dear, I am discouraged and sad. I was at 2 quiltings last week, 4th and 7th day afternoon, just across our meadow at Wm and old Jacob Reeder's.[4] I have not been from home before this summer except to RHG's. Susan Miller, my dear unchanging friend, came to see me last week with a basket on her arm containing a very fine fat lake fish larger than a shad, a tin of lard, 2 lb of cheese, and 3 cuts of beautiful sewing thread. She went to picking wool for me and picked faithful till 12. We eat dinner and she joined me in making a shirt at which she worked till sundown. You would love her for she has been always as a true sister to me. She has but 1 child the age of Aliceanna— Holland, his name is. Granville says, "Tell them I love them dearly but don't get time to write, but if William Henry will write me a long letter I will answer it. I am determined to come and see them some day, if I live."

Mary Higgins spent a day here a few weeks ago. She is as lively as a wren but looks very thin and has to work very hard. She has a scuffling time to get along. Benjamin works as hard as any man can. Please write very often; it is a comfort to me. Well, I have a shirt and pr of trousers that must be made by the day after tomorrow for Aaron as he expects to go 60 miles to work at his trade, to be gone all summer. I made him 4 pr and a shirt after 4th day last and have some mending for him to do. I am your most affectionate Anna Bently.

I always include Brother and Sister Bond when writing to you—if you can collect me a little dried fruit of any kind to make preserves of in the spring please do, to send by Uncle Sammy's folks, but don't shew this, I do not like that way. Maria sends love and will write soon. She is now as tall as I am.

1. Hannah Garrigues was born in December 1830.
2. At this point in the letter Anna's handwriting has become a scrawl, presumably because of the amount of whiskey she has consumed for the toothache.
3. In 1832, Maria described Edmunds to her cousin Sally Stabler as having "jet black" eyes that everyone admired and a very fair complexion.
4. Jacob Reeder had married Elizabeth Byers in 1813. His son, William, married Lydia Battin in 1820.

∼

10th mo 21st 1832
My dear friends,

I began a letter last week but was prevented from finishing it by the indisposition of my little Edmunds. Both Cousin Aaron and he were taken with something like Cholera morbus and were very sick for 2 or 3 days. They are now quite well. We have all, with those exceptions, enjoyed good health in spite of our diet, which has been almost entirely vegetable and fruits and chickens for 2 months past. We have no meat and cannot get it in this neighbourhood, and we do not get plenty of milk or butter but we are mostly happy and contented. We have 8 acres of wheat seeded and expect to keep on seeding as long as the weather is favourable, which is the case at present. We have the greatest and best crop of corn (all cut) that we ever raised, the same of pumpkins, a noble crop of potatoes, about 40 bushels of buckwheat; our stock (to which are added a fine quiet yoke of oxen) are all in good order, with plenty of winter provender laid up for them. The oxen are not paid for, but we hope that they will pay for themselves in drawing coal, for which there was so much greater demand than we could meet for want of a way to haul it, and they save so much labour in a clearing and farm, are so gentle Thomas can yoke and manage them. They are 5 years old. Cousin Aaron has bought a fine colt, 7 months old. Our Mohegan is a very fine handsome animal.

Our dear boys Granville and Franklin came to see us yesterday. Franklin is well and happy. He went home this afternoon. Granville is still here but is suffering very much with a violent headache which came on this afternoon accompanied with a sickness of the stomach and soreness of the flesh all over him. I have been trying some simples[1] for his relief and he has gone to bed. I feel uneasy about him. He is a dear good boy as any mother need wish for a son. He brought with him 2 very handsome clocks valued at 6 dollars apiece which Jos Snode gave him for his services out of the line of his trade. He never pretends to employ him without paying him, has given him a nice black mixed caponet coat and cloth pantaloons. They clothe him well, knit him long ribbed stockings finer than he would get at home. As I looked at my precious boys last night looking so like men and their happy-looking father, my thoughts turned to you (as they always do in feelings of heart). I wished my mother could see him and my offspring and share in our feelings of happiness and the tears would fill in my eyes. Oh, the inward yearnings of a mother's heart, thou knowest them all.

Poor old Seth Hoopes is no more. He died 3 weeks ago, his disease dyspepsia. He loved us as a father, I do believe, and we loved him. He had lived so long in our family rejoicing with us in our seasons of prosperity and sharing our adversity. He left me among many other little proofs of his affection a large armed rocking chair which he bespoke for himself. It is not quite finished yet but will be in a few days. Poor old Seth, how we shall miss his cheerful lively conversation.

This neighbourhood has become healthy again. The dysentery has entirely ceased. Cousin MEG feels very anxious to hear from her sister. She never has since she left here. They are all well there. I was there 2 days last week drying apples on a kiln Cousin Aaron made there. Cousin Robert was in Lisbon at Court as jury man. She [Cousin MEG] has so far conducted herself towards me in all respects like a sister and I believe feels me like one to her, poor thing. I wish her <u>trying time</u> was safe over—the 1st of the 12th mo.

I come on but slowly with my spinning. The rolls are very nappy and I am spinning it 18 cuts to the lb. I have done the stocking yarn. I cannot yet spin more than 6 cuts a day of the fine yarn but hope to become more expeditious. I wish you had told us when our relatives expected to start. . . . Oh, that some of you were with them, if it was only on a visit.

Sister M mentioned she expected our rich country produced plenty of apples and quinces. It does apples, but I have never seen but one quince since I came here and that was brought from Brownsville and shown as a kind of curiosity. Ah, Molly, Molly, thee bees a good-for-nothing little thing or thou would try to write a time or two now and then, if it was only to tell me of thy husband and children. I want to hear of them again from thee. What good it does me to hear Sister Sarah that used to be so unmerciful upon folks that spoke of the perfections and interesting traits of thier "brats." I say, how I love to hear what she says of hers. Does thee beleive it is any nicer nor ours or that her <u>old man</u> is any cleverer than we think ours? Don't tell her that.

I wish you could prevail on Brother Isaac to write to me. Tell him to get Fanny to help him and between them write me a long letter on a medium sheet. Well, I must draw to a conclusion for tonight. If I get time, I will add some in the morning. If not, give my love to all my dear friends. I am your own, AB

P.S. I have only time to say Granville is releived from pain this morning. I bound beet leaves to it last night, which is an exellent thing, gave him a dose of magnesia as his stomach was <u>sour</u>. I intend to wean Edmunds the beginning of next month, for he is too bad about sucking at night. I get up in the morning so weak I am goodfornothing. He is a fracshious fellow. Now only hear Granville. Maria and Hannah are gone to milk, and I hear him clearing off the table. He has swept the room and gathered up the dishes, put the table away. I just called to him to give me a message for you. He says, "Tell 'em I hate '<u>nastiness</u>' and am clearing away the dirt."

1. Medicinal plants or herbs used alone, without being mixed with other agents.

1st mo 24th 1833
[The first part of the letter is from Maria.]
My dear friends,

. . . Mother generally spends first days at Cousin Robt Garrigues's and
she started down there this morning to spend the day, and the <u>children</u>
<u>are kicking up</u> <u>a great dust around</u> me. They are <u>whooping and</u>
<u>hollowing and ripping and tearing</u> at a great rate, so if I make many
mistakes &c, you will have to lay it all on them. Cousin Robert received
a letter from Aunt B Luken week before last.[1] They were all well and
happy. She had set up a boarding school for girls. She sent down to know
if he knew of any coarse wool and feathers (for beds and mattresses) for
sale. They have not been down to see us yet owing they say to the
dreadful state of the roads. We would be delighted to see them.

My beloved brother Franklin paid us a visit of two days week before
last. Dear fellow, how he improves: How proud I would be to show him
to you. He looks more and more like dear Uncle Isaac. Why don't <u>he</u>
write to us sometimes? Nothing in the world would delight <u>me</u> more
than to recieve <u>even</u> a short letter from him, and I often think how
supprised and delighted we would be if he and our dear Uncle William
Henry would take a notion to pay us a visit some of these days and pop
in upon us unawares. I expect it would set some of us almost crazy.

Do, dear Aunts Elizabeth & Margaret, get married and come and
settle out here somewhere. If Aunt Elizabeth is like she used to be, this
country would suit her exactly. Here instead of old fields covered with
stones and briars, she could ramble through the wild forest and sweet
valleys hunting <u>curiositys</u> from morning till night, though she would
have to get a man that could do her work while she was so engaged, for
there is work to do here as well as anywhere. But if you will take my
advice, you will let me send a couple of Ohio beaus to bring you out, for
they know better how to work than most of the Maryland ones.

Now, you must remember that my part of this letter is to all of you,
from Grandmother down to Frances, and as such I expect it to be
answered. Thou asked me in thy letter, Aunt Elizabeth, where I got them
flower seed I sent thee and if the name was one of my invention. Firstly,
from Eloisa Maria Preston, a young girl in this neighbourhood. I am not
much acquainted with her only having spent two afternoons in her
company. . . . Now remember, I expect a great, great, great long letter in
return for this uninteresting scrap. I spent a part of last 1st day in reading
the correspondence between Aunt Sarah and Cousin Abraham Brooke

and could not help laughing to think how nice she fixed him. How I
wish she would write me a piece of poetry. Give my love to everybody,
not forgetting dear Dorcas. Do tell us how she comes on.
Affectionately,
MBB
[from Anna]

～

Dear friends,

I keep promising to do better and [?] again by letting such long intervals
occur between my letters. And all things considered you are no better
than I, so many of you that can write! And poor me, often bowed down
with cares and sorrows, so many to clothe, to make, mind, knit, patch,
and darn for, and my Edmunds still a very troublesome child and not
weaned yet. He has had a severe cold for a week past, eats nothing and
hangs upon me constantly almost. Hannah, Deborah, and Aliceanna also
have very bad colds. I never knew so many sudden changes in the
weather. The scarlet fever and putrid sore throat has taken off many
children within a few miles of us—4 in a family I have heard of. It is still
prevailing, though of a milder nature.

I had written this far when I was alarmed by Aliceanna's waking
suddenly with the croup. I waked her father and as soon as I could heat
water, bathed her feet. I fortunately had (that best of all remedies for a
cold) colt's foot syrup prepared.[2] I gave her that and onion syrup with a
few drops of antimonial wine, and she was quickly releived and now
sleeps and breathes easy; but I fear to go to bed yet.

A grievious accident happened to me last week. I had but 2 table
cloths in the world. One was nearly new, a cotton diaper; I bought it
with rags. The other I have had more than 20 years; it is almost gone.
Well, the beast of a colt tore the new one all to peices, and in a few days
after, Deborah overset the breakfast table and broke 5 plates, a bowl, 2
saucers, 4 cups. I have now 2 cups and 4 saucers to put on my 1
tablecloth; and if any company was to come here to lodge, I should be
compeled to borrow a pr of sheets, for I have 1 sheet for each bed in use
(that is 4) in the world. Only think what I have come to. But I don't fret
about it, and I am sure you need not. I always had such plenty of
bedclothes that I never thought how it would feel to be fixed so. My
straw bed ticks too are all giving way, and poor Jos was sued for 20
dollars* and had to sell all the grain we could spare to make it up. We
will have to live a great deal on corn, but ain't it a blessing that we have

that and plenty of exellent potatoes and many other blessings? We get very little milk from 1 cow but expect to have 1 fresh cow in a few weeks and 3 others in succession between now and harvest. I have not tasted butter for <u>months</u>, but won't we have it this summer?

We lost a fine ewe last week. She got hurt somehow between the logs of the barn. We have 5 nice lambs, and I expect there will be 2 or 3 more in the morning.

I think Sister Elizabeth is a right scaly thing for taking no notice of my repeated requests for violet seed or roots. Don't be surprised if George Sloane should pop in upon you in a few weeks. He starts for Baltimore tomorrow week and expects to go through Montgomery.

I told Cousin MEG I should write this evening. She said, "Well, give my love to dear Aunt Hannah and all of them." Helen and Deborah also sent thiers. Little Wm,[3] hearing the rest, said, "Tozin Anny, dive mine too," and little Hannah said, "Mine, too." She is a beautiful child and a very smart one. Helen, too, is a very fine good girl. They are all uncommonly good, affectionate children.

2nd day morning. Well, I did not go to bed till after 3 o'clock. After that Aliceanna slept well. I feel dull enough this morning. I just says Geo Sloane expects to call on you. Now do have a great long letter written to come by him all of . . . [Here the letter ends.]

*between 20 and 30, I don't know exactly.

1. Elizabeth Luken (or Lukens), Isaac Briggs's sister, had married Samuel Luken. Along with the Brooke brothers, Abraham, Samuel, and Edward, her son Joseph Luken became an active abolitionist in the Salem area. Elizabeth came to Ohio in 1832 with her daughters Mary, Susan, and Hannah, the last of whom married Edward Brooke in 1834.
2. The herb colt's foot was commonly used as a cough syrup ingredient, as well as a remedy for asthma and a soothing bath for hemorrhoids.
3. Born in 1826.

❧

5th mo [1833]
My dear friends,

Week after week I have been prevented writing for want of paper. I borrowed this half sheet of Cousin MEG, and it is now past 12 and we all have orders to breakfast before sunrise and all hands but the 2 youngest and me to go to planting corn. We have 6 acres to plant; have 8 of oats in and 3 of barley. I am going just to huddle all our concerns in as it comes in my mind and leave the <u>pretty part</u> of my letter for the last.

We have 2 young calves, expect another soon; going to raise them all. Counting them, we have 10 head of cattle. One is 2 weeks, the other 6 weeks old. We have 15 sheep and 8 hogs. We have 5 acres of most beautiful clover and a prospect of great plenty of hay. We made another fruitless attempt to procure a little orchard grass seed this spring. I wrote to Uncle G¹ promising him clover seed to pay for it. He took no notice of it though 2 waggoners have called on him since. If it was only a gallon it would have been a great accomodation. There are always many opportunitys every season to get it from there.

I have worked faithfully in the garden this spring, but the weather is so dry the things will not grow. The scarlet fever and putrid sore throat has been very prevalent here, sweeping off 5 and 6 children in a family. It has been and is now very near us. Robert Battin, who corners East with us a 1/4 of a mile off, buried a son 5 years old a day or 2 ago, and his other 4 children all have it. The three eldest better, the babe very ill. They used Thomson's medicine. Altogether our family and Cousin Robert's have escaped as yet, though it has been within a hundred and 50 yards of Cousin R's at Reeder's—no fatal case there, though Franklin had a slight attack of it and his master lost 2 children.

The dear boys some weeks ago one moonlight night got here after midnight, slipped upstairs to bed (as we never have fastened a door since we came here) and surprised us by coming downstairs in the morning. They look like men. Granville has made Cousin Robert a complete waggon.

We had quite an alarming time here last week with the fire getting out in the woods. The wind was very high. It got out from Battin neighbors the same day, surrounding us on the east, south, and west, though it was stopped before it got to our land, for old J[acob] Reeder that joins us on the south. And all in sight and hearing it burnt between 3 and 4000 rails! For hours his house and barn was in immanent danger. They had holes burnt in their shirts while throwing water on some of the cowsheds which were thatch. The straw kindled in many places round the straw stacks in the barnyard. It was a grand and terrible sight from here after night to see from a high hill back of his barn more than a hundred old dead trees all in a flame, sometimes the living limbs breaking and throwing thousands of sparks as they fell. We were in much danger from the fire on the west as the wind blew from that quarter, but it lulled at 2 o'clock AM and they got it under. The fire was out in a great many places that day.

I witnessed a trying scene a few weeks ago. I was at Owen Stackhouse's.

A little girl came running, said Tacy[2] and I must go as quick as possible to Eli Wickersham's, 1 of the children had just died in a fit and one of James Charlson's children that lived a few yds off was dying in a fit, both taken at once. It struck me instantly they had eat something poison. We were there in 20 minutes. We found they had been eating wild parsnip. The fathers were both from home, the children all playing together at Wickershams', when Lydia Wickersham[3] observed little Bonner fall at the door and struggle. She ran to him and found him in strong convulsion. She screamed for Margaret C, who ran in. Her own child, a beautiful boy 4 years old (Cousin Margaret says much like Henry Brooke), was lying on the floor in a fit, but the other was almost gone. She left her own and took the other from his mother who was fainting. Charlson then got home. He collected some neighbors, his own child in fits all that time.

The first died in less than an hour. The other we drenched with melted lard in place of sweet oil, new milk, and molasses camphor, till the Dr came. It vomited him. The Dr instantly gave a vomit that operated in less than a minute and repeated it till we supposed he had thrown all up. The fits left him. He seemed delirious for many days, but is well now.

I went and staid there the next day. I never saw such a scene. They are newcomers from Chester Co., old neighbors of Joseph's friends. The old woman Wickersham, Eli's mother, is in her looks, dress, and manners more like my mother than any lady I have seen. We have visited several times.

I began weaning Edmunds 3 weeks ago, the day he was 2 years old. He is not half the plague he was to me. He talks very sweet . . . .[Here the letter ends.]

What is the reason Sister Sarah never writes more?

1. This may have been Gerard Hopkins or one of her Garrigues relatives.
2. Tacy Stackhouse, born Heston, was Owen Stackhouse's wife. They married in 1817.
3. Lydia Wickersham, age about twenty-three, was Eli's wife.

~

10th mo 19th 1833
[The first part of the letter is from Maria.]
My dear friends,

I have seated myself for the purpose of writing a few of my _ideas_ to you all, although they are not in very good order and I hardly know how to dispose of them exactly right, so I will just relate whatever comes first. Father started this morning to see our dear Granville. We were sadly disapointed yesterday, for we all expected both of the dear boys to see us. They have not been down for a long time, and they promised to come when chesnuts were ripe, and they are ripe and gone now. There are very few this year and what there are the pigs manage to destroy, so that we have a poor chance of gathering any for you to eat when you come to see us this Winter.

I have never written a letter since I wrote to you except one to Franklin. The answer to it I recieved last week. He was well and very busy. He had been working out of town for 4 weeks. They are very much thronged with work this fall, and I expect that is the reason he did not come yesterday.

I was at a apple cutting last night at Cousin RHG's, and we had a merry time of it. When the boys come down they are going to have another. There is a very interesting family that lives close to Cousin Robert's. I expect we have mentioned them before. Their names are Preston. They have a family of 15 children. There are 2 lovely girls there, Mary and Eloisa, very handsome and well-educated and of refined manners. Yes, we can have refined manners even here in this Western world, this loveliest of all other countrys (that ever I knew anything about).

1st day evening. Well, I have spent a dull day. For many reasons it has been a Dull one to me, for it has been just such weather today as always depresses my spirits—that is, cold and wet, not actualy raining but drizling and foggy. To me all nature wears an interesting though mournful aspect at present. To see our beautiful forests stripped of their green leaves and our meadows all seared which so lately wore such a vivid and lovely appearance. Oh, Winter, cold frigid winter, is coming, but spring will come again and then we will be more sensible of its beauties after a cold winter. Autumn was always my favorite season, though I fear the lesson it teaches makes but a temporary impression upon my heart.

I think I am as bad a girl as ever and have not profited much by the good advice dear little Fanny gave me in her letter. I am going to make a great skip now and begin about family affairs. Well, tomorrow I am going to do one of the greatest day's work you ever heared tell of— digging potatoes. I shall not finish my letter tonight, and I will tell you how many bushels I dig.

Mother has a letter to write to our kind friend Samuel Kempton tonight, and as she cannot write when any person is in the room I will have to <u>potter</u> off to bed. Edmund has just recovered from a very severe attack of worms. We were quite uneasy about him for a time, but he is well now but as cross as a hornet.

[Anna's handwriting follows]

11th mo 4th. I have just returned from Temples' where I went to sit up with the corpse of poor Hannah Temple who formerly lived with me. Consumption laid its blighting hand upon her and she is gone. The poor mother. Oh, how my heart aches for her.

Harmon Brown will be in Baltimore in 3 or 4 weeks. He has business at Uncle GTH's[1], and if Mother has dried any quinces or cherries more than she wants and there should be an opportunity to Baltimore, how glad I would be of a few. I have made no preparation for a certain event, shall make but very little except flannel which is enormously high here and so coarse and rough. I fully expected to have had a bag of clover seed to send by Harmon, but Jos has been too busy to get it out.

Oh, dear, I have to go to a weaver's a mile off. I have been disappointed in getting it wove by the one I expected. It will be 50 yds and a pr of blankets. We shall need it before we get it. Well, I must say farewell and be off. Your own A

1. Gerard Hopkins.

～

1st mo 5th 1834
[from Maria]
My dear friends,

We recieved your letter last week, but not before we had began to feel quite anxious from not recieving one for so long a time. And we found that our fears for your health and well-doing were not without foundation. I hope the injury dear Grandmother sustained will not be attended with evil consequences, only for a few weeks. . . .

We have bitter cold weather now and it is uncomfortable to be anywhere else but in the chimney corner. You need not expect either a bright or very entertaining letter from me, for all the children are playing and talking around me with an occasional "howl" from Aliceanna or Edmund, which discomposes me dreadfully. Mother is upstairs fixing some little nameless articles, and my authority over the young ones is very limited and our children are seldom ever still. If you have any idea of perpetual motion or would like to see a thing which has been discussed by many, you should see Aliceanna and Edmund—in the daytime, I mean. They are not of the dull, still kind that will sit in the corner and suck their thumbs and <u>never say</u> a word. But theses, <u>our smart little dears</u>, are always running from one room to the other clambering in the Garret hunting among the <u>carpet strips</u> for <u>doll rags or quilt pieces</u> or playing fox chase, some barking like dogs and others shouting like hunters. Oh! dear, it nearly stuns me. When father makes his appearance they fly to their seats looking as demure as if they had been making no . . . Why, what in the world am I about, just describing the children's play? I will try to think of something more interesting.

In your last letter Grandmother said she hoped we had our linsey at home—Yes, we are all comfortable clothed with the fruits of our <u>industry</u>. Our own sheep provided us with wool, and we spun everry thread ourselves, which <u>I</u> think right smart considering many obstacles in our way. We have not got our blankets at hand yet. We have Edmund in coat and trowsers and he often has a cry at night when they are taken off. He carries something less than a <u>bushel</u> of "<u>pretty things</u>" in his pockets. A few weeks ago we recieved a Bundle from our kind friend SA Kempton (by Harmon Brown) containing many valuable articles, among the number a very handsome dark calico dress for me (already made) and three blue broadcloth roundabouts for Thomas and a large comb (for Mother) of a very superior quality, a pink cambric frock which exactly fits Deborah, and a Gingham one to cut and make a smaller one with a great many cap ribbands and several caps, one ready made and so "<u>bedaubed</u>" with ribbands (having no less than six bows on it besides many bands) that mother took it to pieces. And a good many balls of coloured cotton and bolts of tape, and too many things for me to tell. They are kind friends indeed and may Heaven bless them. His 2nd son is married, his oldest is at sea. He writes to us frequently, and one might suppose by his affectionate style that he was a near relation.

When you write, do for my satisfaction tell me how Dorcas comes on, how many children she has and what are their names. Give my love to her and tell her she would hardly believe what a great strapping wench the poor sickly Maria has grown to be. Only to think nearly 9 years has elapsed since we last met. What in the name of wonder has be[come] of Uncle Isaac? He never even sends his [love]. I wonder if he ever calls to mind the visit [he paid] us so long ago. Oh, I wish he would take time to write even a few lines to us. Tell him I am afraid he is going to be an old Bachelor. Now, if he will come out here he can find a wife whenever he wants one, and if he only will speak the word I will bespeak one for him.

I wish the 3 or 4 coming weeks were over and all of us enjoying good health. Do you not join in my wish?

Mother told me to thank Aunt Sarah for the beautiful affair she sent in her letter. Give my love to Uncle James, Uncle Joseph Bond, and Uncle Richard and Aunt Mary.

Affectionately Yours, MB Bentley

❧

In January 1834, people in New Garden, Ohio, formed an auxiliary of the American Anti-Slavery Society. Other local groups sprang up in the months following. The Ohio Anti-Slavery Society was founded in 1835. Anna and Joseph had come from a strongly activist background. Cousin Edward Garrigues in Pennsylvania had been involved in anti-slavery activity since early in the century. As other relatives arrived in Ohio, several of them took an active role in the abolition movement in Salem and the vicinity.

Anna, however, had more immediate concerns at Green Hill. Her daughter, Caroline Elizabeth, was born in February, only ten months after her son, Edmunds.

❧

2nd mo 24th 1834
My dear friends,

I have defferred writing till mail day again and shall be hurried. Must acknowledge the receipt of Sister Mag's of last week (in which I think I smelt a Rat) and the still more wonderful phenomenon, the one from Sister Elizabeth to whom from this time I give freely the occupation and title you once bestowed on me with full grant to practise anywhere but in my own family. Oh, appropos, what has become of Jenny Sulivan? Jos says our nearest neighbor lost a fine boy 4 months since, I veryly believe through the application of the steaming process in Scarlet fever. And they have now another 10 years old, if he still lives, at the point of death, with some disease they know not what to name, slight in its first appearance but assuming great violence on the first application of the steam and horrid red pepper. They are intelligent people and well-acquainted with the Thomsonian practise—which I never wish to be, having less than no faith in it and moreover having in our family more need of a cook than a doctor of any kind.

Well, to go back where I left off so abruptly in my last. After writing the letter I felt fatigued and my head ached some, so I went to bed again.

Two neighbors spent the afternoon. One of them washed, <u>fixed</u>, and dressed Caroline. In the morning (is this 5th day) I got up and dressed without assistance, washed and dressed the babe, went to scouring. Two more neighbors spent the afternoon. Laid down an hour or 2 next day. The 7th sat up nearly all day. Two more neighbors and 2 cross children set my head to aching. Better in the morning, more company. Never have laid down in the day since she was a week old. Went downstairs to tea on the 9th day and ever since to my meals. Eat meat, cheese, butter, eggs, and anything and as much as I pleased since she was 2 days old without any bad effect, being regular every day in my bowels. I took a dose of castor oil the next day after her birth, which prevented any fever at the coming of my milk. I have done a heap of work since, have made Caroline a beautiful feather cap. My spirits have been good and I never have fared half as well. Ought I not to be thankful?

The weather too has been so favourable to me since a week before her birth. It has been like May weather. On 7th day we had a considerable thunderstorm. This morning it looks more wintry as a sleet covers the trees. It is still raining.

I have not, I believe, given you a description of my babe, and I don't know how to go about as I cannot get rid of a notion that I have made myself ridiculous to you in time past by describing my children so often, so particularly, and with a mother's pen to you. Anyhow there is an awkward feeling now that used not to be in such attempts, and yet if I judge of your feelings by my own there should not be, for it yeilds me great pleasure to hear of those dear little precious ones, my sisters' children, more when thier mothers speak of them than any others.

Well, she weighed 9 1/2 lb, very plump and fat with dimpled <u>elbows</u> and shoulders, a round face and head thickly <u>kivered</u> with sitch truck as I send enclosed. Black eyebrows, blue eyes, a beautiful mouth with <u>some sort</u> of a nose above it. She looks pretty to me, and every body else says she is an uncommon pretty young baby, and she is healthy and very good. But Edmunds is the fine-looking fellow that attracts the most admiration, his soft flaxen hair curls in close glossy ringllets all over his head. Cutting it don't in the least stop its tendency to curl as it did Aliceanna's. He has a high, finely formed forehead, as fair and <u>spotless</u> as can be, dark eyebrows and large, full, beautiful dark eyes as sparkling and bright as—as a spider's. His black eyelashes are so long and thick that they give a softness to the expression of them. His cheeks are dimpled, his skin delicately fair. He talks very <u>funny</u> and sweet. He is called a beauty by all that visit here. I sometimes do think as I look at Aliceanna and him that <u>even you</u> would think them right sharp-looking for Ohio children.[1]

I must tell you, Aliceanna is becoming strikingly like sister Elizabeth, her hair and complexion the same. Aliceanna has more red—rather, the eyes, eyebrows, and expression of countenance remind me of her every day. She is a mild, gentle, affectionate little girl. I wish from my heart some of you had her for her own sake. I think she would make a lovely something or other if she was from under the influence of bad example and teasing, that baneful evil that I cannot prevent here.

Mother, I really do think if you knew the many acts of affectionate kindness of Samuel and Delia Kempton to me you would for my sake visit them when in Baltimore. I have <u>no</u> relation in Baltimore except Aunt P[olly] Moore that <u>I</u> prize <u>more</u> highly. Samuel has sent Jos 5 or 6 newspapers every week for 6 years, folding, sealing, and directing them. He does not take them himself but gets them from others. He writes often like an affectionate brother. He never meets with a waggon from this neighbourhood without sending something valuable. Some months ago he accidently met with our neighbor Harmon Brown in Baltimore. Well, Delia packed up a dark calico frock of Henrietta's for Maria, a pink gingham that fits Deborah, another like the peice enclosed that I made Caroline a frock, and 2 long-sleeved aprons; 4 coats for Thomas like the peice enclosed—not a break in them—a yd of book muslin, a yd of crosband muslin, a large new cambric cape for me, a cross-barred one with lace edging for Maria, a large elegant comb for me, 2 little caps, lace for 4 borders, and muslin for half a dozen spotted Swiss, more than a dozen yds of different colored ribbands, a lb of raisins, 1 of pearl barley, nutmegs, 3 peices of tape, 3 of cord, paper of pins, 2 large spools white cotton and 20 of different coloured, &c, with many appologies for not sending more as the man could not wait and requesting me always to let them know when any waggon went from here.

Sister Peg, thy name would have been the choice of Jos and me, but as Granville wanted to name her we could not refuse. Never mind, J says. The next.

Your Anna

1. "Everybody admires his eyes," Maria wrote in 1832.

~

Anna Briggs Bentley, 1796–1890. Photo courtesy Anna Chavelle.

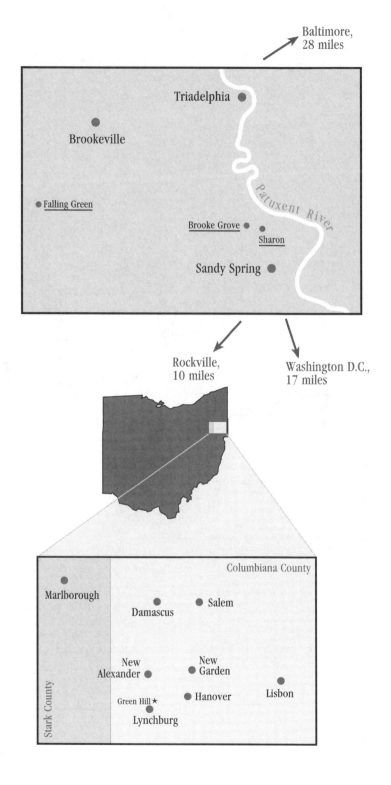

"Thy letters are so refreshing to me, a real comfort." Sarah (Briggs) Stabler. Photo from the Maryland Historical Society, Baltimore, Maryland.

"Peradventure, he may make us to laugh in our old age." Isaac Briggs Jr. Photo made available courtesy Sandy Spring Museum, Sandy Spring, Maryland.

"And dear little Aunt Margaret that used to get me to help make [the] garden, and give such good advice that I could never be bro't to follow." Margaret (Briggs) and William Henry Farquhar. Photo made available courtesy Sandy Spring Museum, Sandy Spring, Maryland.

"Hannah is bashful, a little stubborn at times, which is increased by the disposition some of the others have to tyranise over the younger ones." Hannah (Bentley) Preston. Photo courtesy Joan Blosser.

"Maria never complains now except when she gets lazy and wants an excuse to get hold of a book." Maria (Bentley) Garrigues(?). Photo courtesy Charles N. Heston.

"He is growing more and more squire-like, yet will not restrict his appetite for good things all that I can say." Richard Garrigues. Photo courtesy Charles N. Heston.

"It goes harder with Thomas than any of them. He wants to 'go back to live at Uncle Richard's,' and his modesty is an affliction to him." Thomas Moore Bentley. Photo courtesy Charles N. Heston.

"Thomas brought her here on a visit and we all love her." Ruth Anna (McMillan) Bentley. Photo courtesy Charles N. Heston.

"I am affraid, tell her, she is rayther too fond of company for a portionless girl situated as she is." John Stabler and Aliceanna (Bentley) Stabler. Photo courtesy Bill Sprague.

"Alban is just a matter-of-fact child, was intended for a very good one if bad example and bad management do not sow evil in his guileless affectionate heart." Amelia (Walton) and Alban Edmunds Bentley. Photo courtesy Charles N. Heston.

6th mo 15 1834

My dear Mother & my dear sisters,

As I cannot send this free, I would gladly take a whole sheet and make it
better worth the postage, but this is every scrap of paper I can find. How
I long to know particularly how you are all coming on. Dear Sister Sarah
is, I hope e'er this, past her state of painful suspense and doing well.[1] My
health is very poor: no appetite, great debility, and nervous excitement.
Did I tell you that when I was at Snodes on a visit Aunt Hetty and I
concluded to go home with Mary [Snode] Haines? In going I met with a
severe fright from a large unruly horse that was tyed to the waggon
behind. It began rearing and pulling back, and the bed of the waggon
seemed to be coming off. Well, we had the horse taken away and put in
the gears[2] and hitched one of the others in the fence corner till William
went back. We were all much alarmed, but the effects were not so
apparent till, about the same time the next day, I was suddenly taken
with nervous tremour and faintness; loss of strength, appetite, and spirits
succeeded for 3 or 4 days. I was held so I did not know what to take but
at a venture had a bowl of strong red pepper tea with plenty of ginger in
it, of which I took freely.

Oh, how glad I was to get home, though when I got in the waggon
to come I had no idea of reaching it or more than reaching it safely. But I
got a great deal better. I began taking composition and nerve powder and
poplar tea immediately and got quite smart so as to work in the garden,
make soap, put in and quilt 3 quilts (2 for Maria). Well, one night we
had the most awful thunderstorm any person here ever remembers,
which lasted 5 or 6 hours. I thought I was more calm than usual for me
to be, but the same nervous symptoms returned next day and followed
me up for a week. I got better and as Cousin MEG had been here twice
lately I was prevailed on to walk there 8 or 10 days since. Well, the walk
home in the evening fatigued me very much (over such hills). The next
day the tremor, faintness, and loss of appetite, strength, and spirits
returned.

I cannot coax my appetite back, and my strength is wasting for that.
I am affraid to take the nerve powder—I gathered a quantity of nerve
root and took to eating it till I got so fond of it I believe it hurt me.
(Would it [threaten?] you?) I feel a constant craving for something.
When Bro Isaac was here, he spoke highly in praise of the virtues of a
medicine called Woman's Friend. He gave me a receipt and the materials
for making it. I have done so. Now please tell me particularly of when,

and how, and for what, it is taken, its effects, &c. And any other advice will be acceptable. Situated as I am, I shall be compelled to employ Dr Robertson.

Oh, dear, I have such piles of work to do, and I cannot get on with the speed I could when I felt better. How I miss Maria's company. Though she comes up often, it is not like having her all the time. Deborah and Cary go to school, and poor Hannah is little comfort to me. Love to . . . every one of you tenderly from your tried, A

1. Her daughter, Elizabeth (Lizzie), had been born on May 11.
2. Harness.

~

12th mo 14th 1834
My dear friends,

Do please forgive me for my naughtiness in omitting to write to you for so long a period. My only excuse is want of time and want of paper. The latter excuse has often stood in my way when my heart was full and running over toward you. I really do not recollect when I wrote last. Maria has written 2 long letters (one to Brother William H Farquhar[1]) which never went. Our dear Granville came home the 1st of the 11th mo[th]. They were very anxious for him to remain there this winter. It seemed almost too great a trial for them to part with him and it was so to him also. It seems as if they could not say enough in his praise. His freedom suit[2] is a beautiful olive brown coat, very dark (almost black), vest and pantaloons of the finest, best quality satinett, fine shirt, an elegant silk pocket handkerchief, fine long doubleribbed stockings, &c, &c, &c, and plenty of very good clothes besides. And he is with us, a stay-a-comfort, a companion, and, may I add, the pride of our hearts. He has been applied to to teach School 3 miles from here, which he declined for he is likely to get more employment than he can get through with at his trade.

The Canal is begun. A great change is taking place in our neighbourhood. Little Hanover is rapidly improving, buildings going up; lots that sold for $80 last summer sold 2 weeks ago for $280, and last week there was a town laid off and a great many lots sold at a high price a mile from here on Amos Preston's land. The canal commences a little below Hanover. Morris Miller has contracted for 1 mile. It comes close by the Cabin we used to live in (Robert Miller's) by S Holland's, along by Shaw's place (Bro Isaac) through cousin RHG's meadow close to the house. It is to join the Ohio canal somewhere or other. The next 1/2 mile to Morris's contract is taken by Thomas Judge, a brother of Margaret's, and he has applied to Granville to make him 30 wheellbarrows and expects to want more after a while and many other little jobs, and it is supposed Granville can get a great deal of work. His master says he is a rapid and exellent workman. This will enable him to pay the 22 dollars he still owes for his lot in Benton, which is improving rapidly.

Oh, dear Isaac, if thou could only come here and find employment for a while. They are rushing on with this canal tearing up the trees by the roots, &c.

Franklin spent 2 weeks with us the last week in the 10th and 1st in the 11th mo. He is a dear fellow too and gives great satisfaction to his employer and us. He will be a good workman at his trade and he is, I hope and trust, a good boy too. He has precious feelings and the advantage of a worthy religious man for a master, though not a member of our society. They clothe him very genteely.

Maria made a quilting, had 7 girls, and the boys had a log rolling with as many young men, and they spent a happy evening together. Us old folks and the children staid upstairs. (Well, it does seem comical to be the mother of young men and a young woman.) As to G's having a notion of getting married, William Henry, I doubt whether he has as much a notion of it as Frank. And dear Elizabeth, don't think of such a thing among even the possibilities as Maria paying you a visit, for even if a way offered and all else suited, we could not raise the means. Money is as scarce as ever with us, though our comforts seem to be encreasing. Joseph has hauled and sold 60 dollars worth of coal since harvest. Thomas digs it. He could sell it as fast as he could haul it in Hanover, but the roads are too rough and frozen now for the oxen to travel. He can haul 2 loads a day, 16 bushels a day (mostly) at 6 1/2 per bushel. This all goes toward paying our debts, and many a bushel more it will take. When the oxen can travel, no weather stops Jos.

I would not mind this so much, only I am constantly uneasy for fear of its caving in on them. Several times during the night enough has fallen to have crushed them if they had been under; but they have made another excavation, and they tell me it is propped securely.

We have killed a 3–year-old bull, an exellent beef though small. He was fat and tender, his weight 304 lb. Also 8 of our hogs, thier weight between 8 and 9 hundred. We have 7 more to kill besides a turkey and Thomas's 6 ducks for Christmas and 9 shoats left for next year. A fine large cow we intended for a beef was killed by a dead tree falling on her, and a valuable buck sheep worth 5 dollars about the same time got injured so in fighting that he died.

I forget if I told you this before: I made souse cheese of the hogsheads. It is elegant. My sausage is exellent also, upwards of 80 links besides 2 jars for present use. Within the last 2 weeks we have (or Maria has) made 70 pies, and they are all gone but 11; 30 were pumkin, the rest mince. Our flannel is very pretty and good. We have 12 of flannel that is a dress for Maria, Caroline, and myself; 18 of fulled cloth; 10 of colored and pressed linsey for the 3 little girls; and 15 of fulled linsey. The flannel is dark snuff brown (Macabou[3] snuff). Now, is not this comfortable? But Oh dear, such a parcel of ragged patched shirts, male and female.

We have about 14 acres of wheat, should have had 5 more if the weather had been favourable a week longer. We have all had something of the influenza but are getting over it. Edmund and Caroline both had the croup, which yielded to colt's foot syrrup and antimonial wine and greasing thier breast and feet. Caroline has 6 teeth, says a good many words but does not walk. She is a sweet little pet.

Why don't you say more of your little pets? I wish Bro James would undertake another description, and dear sister Mary, I do wish she could be prevailed on to write. Tell her if she has got an old cap past wear she may enclose a border in a letter one week and the rest in another, and if she will come and see me I will pay her 5 times the worth of it. Hannah says give her dear love to Grandma and tell her please be saving calico peices for her for she is making a quilt and we never get calico here.

They are well at Cousin RHG's. What has become of Cousin Betsey [Thomas]? They think quite hard of her for not writing. Cousin MEG and Helen send thier love. Maria went down there today and has not returned. She intended writing to you this week. Granville sends his love to you all and to William Henry says, "Why he no come see a body? If he lib as near him as he do, he came see him ebery day." Thomas sends his love also and to dear Uncle Richard and Aunt Mary. Indeed, they all bothered me with thier messages of love before they went to bed.

Benjamin Higgins has just recovered from a severe spell of illness, inflamation of the tongue and throat. Cousin Mary's health has been delicate since her illness last summer was a year. It is peculiarly so now. How hard it is she cannot hear from her friends. Was it Amelia who is married? They have been hard run lately to settle some of thier necessary debts, and in her present situation how acceptable a trifle of money would be if any of her friends would be good enough to send a little. I think they would if they could only know how difficult it was here to procure the little articles and comforts she will soon need. Benjamin was sued last week for 16 dollars. They both work very hard and are very economical. She has no dresses but of her own [spinning] and 1 or 2 old silk dresses. I do pity her. They have plenty that is good and comfortable to eat.

Well, I love every one of you as dearly as I can, and Jos does too. He will write some day and tell you so. I am your own, A

[On the side of a page: "Sister E, darling, please send me some chrysanthemum seed when they ripen."]

1. Margaret Briggs married William Henry Farquhar in 1834.
2. Indicating that he was free of his apprenticeship.
3. A rose-scented snuff.

$\sim$

Anticipating a boom from the construction of the Sandy & Beaver Canal, local entrepreneurs bought and built. Amos Preston and Eli Wickersham platted the village of Lynchburgh in 1834, locating it at a canal lock. In 1835, George Sloan bought twenty acres near the canal and laid out another town, now called Dungannon. Others contracted to dig portions of the canal bed, or, like Granville Bentley, to supply those who did.

Sometime around early 1835, for reasons never made completely clear, Anna and Joseph sent Aliceanna, only five or six years old, to live with the Snode family between Salem and Marlborough, the same kindly people who employed Granville. The only hint Anna gives in the letters as to why she and Joseph took such a radical step is that Aliceanna was especially affected by the teasing of her older brothers and sisters.

$\sim$

4th mo 5th 1835
My dear friends,

I intended to have written last week, but my little Caroline was quite ill for a week. I believe a severe cold and teething occasioned it. She had very high fever. I cut one jaw toothe through, which relieved her very soon. She cuts teeth hard, has 3 foreteeth, 1 jaw tooth, and 3 more nearly through. She is now pretty well again. She takes constant watching to keep her out of mischief. Shall I describe her? Yes—well, she has a <u>head</u>

that everybody that ever notices her says is a <u>beautifully shaped head</u>, and it is thickly covered with <u>very</u> glossy hair about 4 inches long. (I will send a sample if I think of it again.) She has a high forhead, finely formed, dark eyebrows and lashes that make her bright, saucy-looking blue eyes look darker than they are. To examine them closely, they are a shade darker than Thomas's. <u>I think</u> she has a very pretty mouth and chin. She is very fair, her cheeks rosy, her lips so red and sweet. She is thought to resemble our dear little Aliceanna, and I say she is the image of her father, more like him than any of the rest ever were. Everybody sees the likeness. She is as plump as a partridge, not very tall. She says a good many words very sweetly, has walked ever since she was 10 months old.

It was a trial <u>to part with our lovely gentle Aliceanna, but we think</u> it <u>will be greatly to her advant</u>age. She is a great darling with them. She is very happy and they say very good. They are sending her to school close by. Granville says she learns rappidly. I hope they won't spoil her. <u>Oh, it</u> did greeve me to see her mild temper warped and ruined by <u>bad example</u> <u>and teasing, &c.</u> There she is free from it all, and Granville says, from an intimate knowledge of them, he would not hesitate a moment in trusting to thier fostering care this the loveliest lamb in our flock, though it goes hard with the <u>old ewe</u> to part with it. Jos has been twice to see her. He was there this day week, says she is getting as fat and her cheeks as rosy. Her little heart was full at parting.

Granville has been there at work for 4 weeks. We expect him at home the last of this week. Benjamin Snode and our dear Frank will come with him. Granville has made 2 waggons there. He gets half. We have not seen Franklin since New Year's day.

Oh, we forgot to send the Bro William Henry's letter to Granville, which must be an excuse for his not receiving an answer. We could recognize the pictures, Willy dear, but <u>I</u> have a livelier and more <u>correct</u> one, only I can't get at it to spred it out for the inspection of others. But I fancy Green Hill on paper drawn by Granville will cut a poor figure, though it is a lovely picture—our noble forrests, verdant hills, fertile fields, green meadows, winding streams, which can be seen from our door sparkling in the sunshine.

Oh, how I long, yes, with an aching longing, for some of you to come out this summer and see us and our home. 9 years. Oh, it is so long. Mother, do try to come.

They have made considerable progress with the Canal between Hanover and Cousin Robert's. The Commissioners were examining it over last week. Contracts are to be sold out next month. I dare say Bro Isaac could find some situation here in our fine healthy country, for a while anyhow.

Poor Cousin Margaret looks badly this spring, is in poor health. I pity her from my heart. Maria went there last evening, and I fancy she will not get home tonight for it is snowing and raining like fun. Helen mostly spends a night here every week. We have lived in uninterrupted harmony and affection. There is a great change in Cousin Robert. You knew of his joining meeting? He has not for more than a year made <u>any</u> use of spiritous liquors. This is not saying that he <u>was ever</u> in the habit of using to excess. I love them all. Benjamin Higgins also has entirely quit the use of it in any way for more than a year past.

Poor Cousin Mary looks anxiously to the 20th of this month. Oh, that just puts me in mind of what I heard of Aunt Henny's saying about my writing for help. I was at Cousin Robert's when I got the letter. Mary Higgins was there. Well, I just read it to her and Cuz M. Mary said, "Oh, Aunt H needn't have got in a passion with you because she didn't choose to send me anything. And as to my feelings being hurt by your writing <u>for me</u>, they never were. Now, I never said they were to any human being. But they were hurt that <u>no notice</u> should have been taken of it. Why would it hurt my feelings, when what you told me you had written was just what I had told you I wished you would write to her? But she did not want to help me. You know well enough how bad off I was for many things, though it's true we don't want for plenty to eat nor ever have."

Cousin Margaret thought if Aunt Henny ever had heard Mary's feelings were hurt it must be from some misconstruction of a letter she had written to Cousin E which I saw before she sent it. She did not know that Mary <u>had got me</u> to write, which was the fact. Though she did not see the letter, she told me what she wanted written and I told her every word I had put in it, which she approved of and long watched the post office, expecting an answer.

Cousin Margaret has been and still is a kind friend to her, and she still needs it, and I am almost vexed enough to say what I have done. When she was taken sick I ran every step of the way. It was on 2nd day I staid with her and nursed her and did all the work of the family till 6th day, sent for Maria 4th day and did her washing. Cousin Margaret staid there 3 days and nights, but having a very cross baby had it not in her power to stay as I had. We both did all we could, I had my curtains round her bed. Well, I wish she was safe over this. She wrote to her Aunt

Betsey this summer and got an answer by the bearer with a small bundle of little articles ready made and never used by <u>her</u>.

Well, we have had poor luck with our sheep. Lost all our lambs but three and today a grown sheep died. We have 17 in all. We do not get a drop of milk and shall not till the last of May, when we expect 3 calves. Our dear neighbors are very kind. I send a pint flask alternately to [Battins] one day and Taylors the next and they will send cream. The Taylors I am much pleased with. She is a lady.

Why, what shall I say to Sister Mary? She has forgotten to care for me. Now, thou used to dispute with me and say marriage and its ties contracted the affections. I said nay. Now, if thee does not write to me soon, I will think it has thine. Only to think how long since thou hast written. Even the event has past that by promise was always to entitle me to a letter, and it comes not. I want to hear of the young 'uns and that animal (I won't call him bro till he sends his love to me), thier daddy. I wish Mother and sisters would each send me a lock of your hair and I would care if Mother would spit in the next letter that I might look at it. And I wished I had some little of mother's and your dresses. There is one thing—would be much obliged to some of you, for I cannot get any good needles at any of the stores nor never could since I came out. My stock has given out except the numbers 9 and 10; I have plenty of them. Now, if Mother and each of you would stick 3 needles, No. 6, 7, and 8, in your next letter, why it would make a dozen—and it would accommodate me much.

. . . The quarter of land east of us is owned by Benjamin Farquhar, son of David of Brownsville. Is he a relation? He talks of coming to live on it. Your own affectionate A

Please give my love to everybody.

~

5th mo 9th 1835
My dear friends,

Joseph told me just now he wished me to write to you tonight and enclose the few lines he has written and entreat that it may be attended to as soon as possible for fear the chance of having our meeting near may again fail and the privilege of holding one may be taken from us. The place where it has been held is so unhandy for most of the members that it is very thinly attended. For my own part, I can very seldom get there, and indeed we cannot hold it there much longer for the property is sold

and the building to be removed. Then the advantage of a school for our
poor neglected children is a great consideration. It will be undertaken
immediately when they can obtain the deed.

Well, now, Brother Jim and Sister Sarah, I've a mind to jaw you like
the nation. When I begin my letters "Dear friends," you know you are
included. Mother's share is the biggest and all the rest equal. . . . When I
write I put you all as it were in a bundle and the cord that binds it is
love. . . .

I have not your last letter by me, so I can't answer it regularly. The
needles were thankfully received. I cannot give Bro James any
encouragement that there would be any sale for his MACHINES. We are
all such a hearty set here, and children or nurses that can preform that
office are always handy.[1]

Oh, how glad I was to see dear Mother's writing, and I did cry at it
till the children were scared and thought something was the matter.
Cousin Robert was here, and I read it to him. He said, "Tell her I say if
she would only undertake the journey she would soon complain of
feeling better. Two of them might very comfortably come out for 15
dollars." Oh, Mother, my dear Mother, do try to come. . . .

Granville returned the 18th of 4th mo, left Aliceanna well and very
happy going to school; learns very fast and is a great darling with them.
We have not seen our dear Frank since New Year's, but expect him this
week.

And then, dear Margaret, it felt pleasant to see thy writing again. I
hope as thou hast laid a nest egg thou wilt continue, same as the speckled
hen that laid two every day and a Sunday 3.

We are going to have a neighbour of your name. John Farquhar owns
the quarter cornering East with us, a young man. Think it would be
practicable for you to pay us a visit this summer or fall. Oh, how joyfully
would we welcome you. If you visit, the cares and clogs of the world will
be gathering faster and faster arround you and you will not get off.

1st 7th day, 2 weeks. A little after daybreak a messenger came for me
to go to Cousin Mary Higgins. I got there before 6, just as the Dr
arrived. Cousin Margaret and 2 other women made our company. At 1/2
past 7 she was safely delivered of a daughter. Cousin MEG had strained
her ankle that morning and was quite poorly besides, but we prevailed on
her to stay till the next day as her company was a comfort. I remained till
2nd day morning as nurse, cook, chambermaid, and friend. She was
smarter than common. Maria came 2nd day morning and will stay till
next 7th day, making 3 weeks.

I have had a slavish time without her as Caroline is teething and fretful. Poor thing, I have not milk enough to feed her with and she depends too much on me. Hannah and I have done the washing, and it does go hard. The blood would run to my finger ends. We have Aaron's washing to do. Hannah pleaded to do the scouring for the first time, and she did do it as nice as boards could be scoured. We do look sweet and clean.

Jos and I went to Cousin Robert's today: I in the morning, Jos with Cousin R from meeting. Cousin Margaret is in rather better health than she was, but there will be <u>no end to her Ailment</u> before the 10th mo. Poor thing, how like a sister she feels to me, and I believe she feels me as one to her. The most uninterrupted affection subsists between our children. Helen seems to consider Granville as a brother (not <u>nearer</u>). Cousin Robert attends meeting regularly with his family, is altered much for the better. Cousin Margaret says, "Give my love to Aunt Hannah. What does make me love her now better than I used to, and I always loved her better than any of my aunts."

Our clock has just struck 12, and Jos wants breakfast by daylight for he is going to Salem and back, 30 miles.

[Granville adds a note] My dear Aunt Elizabeth, I wish thee would take a notice and write me a letter. I think it would do me as much good as a dose of <u>Red pepper</u> or <u>Lobelia</u>. I don't recollect that thee has written to me since I left you, and if thee has I am quite sure didn't answer it. But never mind. Don't be discouraged. Try it again, and if I don't answer it, tell me of it. Thy nephew GSBently

[On the outside of the letter Anna wrote: "I left this last night intending to finish it this morning. Jos thought it was done and sealed it. [Harmon Brown] had breakfast over, and he was gone before I waked. I love you all. Your A"]

1. Like others in his extended family, James P. Stabler was a sometime inventor.

〜

Aug 30th 1835
[The first part of the letter is from Granville.]
My Dear Aunt Lizzy,

I received thy very acceptable letter some <u>3 or 4 or 5</u> weeks ago and should most certainly have answered it sooner, but indeed we have been so very busy with our harvesting that we have not even taken time to rest on 1st day when the weather would permit us to work at it. This has been a very unusually backward and wet harvest with us. There are a great many that have not finished yet, and we amongst the number. We have the best crop of wheat we have ever rais'd before and double the quantity of hay. Our corn looks very promising, and provided the frost don't come on very early, I think we will have twice as much of that as we ever raised before. Such is our present prospect, and I hope by careful industry and perseverence we may after awhile get things fixed pretty comfortably about us. And I assure thee there shall be nothing wanting on my part to make the latter days of my parents smoother than a great many of the former have been. Father has had to toil and work very hard since we came out here, and Franklin and I going to our trades made it come still harder on him, so I think it's no more than right for us to turn in and help him now.

Thy letter was a great satisfaction to me. I was when I recieved it very poorly in bed (which is very unusual for me) with something like the cholera morbus.[1] I was taken very severely with it, and your plaguy Thomsonian medicine would'nt have any effect without it was to make me worse; but I took 2 large doses of Casteroil and was soon up again.

There is another of our family gone to live from home. Sarah Holland was anxious to have Deborah, and as they are such very clever people, they concluded to let her go. I have no doubt but she will be taken good care of there and be learned to work, too. Maria went with her yesterday and has not returned yet. She expects to go tomorrow to spin for Mary Higgins and will be gone for 2 or 3 weeks, so that our family circle will be lessened as well as yours.

We recieved a letter from Frank last week. He had met with a slight accident at a raising by a rafter falling on his foot, but he expected to be able to go to work in a few days. Oh! how I wish it was so that him and I could pay you a visit. I would like you to see him and me too. We are both very clever fellows. But I have'nt much hopes of our coming very soon. I shall never forget the happy hours I spent with you several winters ago. . . .

I have some notion of putting up a shop here this fall, one large enough for Franklin to work in too when his time is up, and then we will be here together again and likely continue so for awhile without we give into a notion to take a wife or two and begin to get too much crowded here; then we will have to 'sperse about elsewhere. What is thy opinion of

these <u>matters</u>? Does thee think it's right for a young man that has to
<u>scratch</u> hard to get along decently himself to take a wife, or not? Some
will argue that two will <u>scratch</u> best together, but for my part I don't
pretend to know much about it. I should like to have Uncle William
Henry's opinion about it. . . . Give my love to all, and if I have been
<u>bad</u> about not writing, believe me thy very affectionate nephew, GL
Bentley

8th month 31st
Dear friends,

I do not like so much blank paper to go, and I feel in a poor fix to say
anything interesting, for I have felt quite poorly for several days. 5th day
I had something like the colic and have felt great soreness and debility
since and considerable pain after eating. It is so unusual for me to be sick
I get <u>down in the mouth</u>. I think I must wean Caroline, for I have but
little for her and she eats hearty enough when I am from home.

I spent yesterday at Cousin Robert's. Cousin Margaret looks badly,
expects in 5 weeks &c.

There, I have just swallowed a monstrous dose of salts, and it wants
to come up mightily.

Last 7th day week I received a message from my dear friend Holland
that she was sick with the Erysipelas and wanted to see me. 1st day
morning I took Thomas and went. (I had not been there since the burial
of poor Louis.) I passed by Susan's, my sister-friend. I found a change in
the looks of the place. The dear old Cabin that sheltered us was removed
some rods. In the former place the foundation of a large brick house was
dug. The canal passed by within 50 yds. of the front door. They now live
in a sweet little brick cottage with its back and front piazzas shaded with
thick clustering Nasturtiums and morning glorys, cypress vine and scarlet
runners. And Susan with her warm, open-hearted welcome as I caught
her half-dressed. "Oh, Anna Bentley I am glad to see thee. Indeed,
Mother will be pleased. I know she has wanted thee to come."

She was going to meeting. I did not stay long there. My heart
warmed within me as I came near. The whole front of the house is
<u>entirely</u> concealed with the wild cucumber vine. They tie them back
from the windows and door. The dear old woman wept as she expressed
her satisfaction to see me. She looks badly but was better than she had

been. Oh, they are the dearest friends. It is like being at Sharon to be there.

Well. I am so sick with my medicine I can't write. Love to all of you. . . . Farewell.

Yours,

A

1. Bacterial infection of the intestines was a common summer affliction from poor sanitation.

FOUR

1836–1842

In the 1830s, the Bentleys were joined in Ohio by more relatives. Among them were "Uncle Sammy" Brooke, Hannah Briggs's older brother, and his family. They were ardently anti-slavery. His four sons—William, Abraham, Samuel and Edward—threw themselves into the cause, both in the village of Marlborough, Stark County, where Samuel Jr. settled, and in Clinton County, where Abraham and Edward lived for a number of years.

In 1837, Ohio was the second most active abolition state in the Union, after Massachusetts. It had 213 anti-slavery societies with more than 17,000 members. There were 90 members of the Ohio Anti-Slavery Society in Marlborough in 1836; William Garrigues was president, and Abraham Brooke was secretary.

~

8th mo 14 1836
[Addressed to James P. Stabler, near Elkton, Maryland.]
My beloved sister,

This is 7th day morning. I have just collected a large pile of tattered garments to undergo thier weekly repair and came upstairs, when the sight of the inkstand and a sheet of paper reminded me that the mail will go Eastward from this place today and revived the strong desire that I have often of late felt that it might bear to thee, my dear sister, some expression of the unabated love, the tender, heartfelt sympathy of thy poor weak sister. I have wished to write ever since I heard of the trying dispensation which it has been thy lot to pass through for thy good, for

thy purification, though it was the dregs of the bitter cup. And I have
earnestly craved that the same merciful arm might be stretched forth for
thy support and that thou might lean upon it in humble submission as I
was enabled to do on this day 12 years since, when the precious blossom
I had reared in my bosom was transplanted to bloom forever in its native
soil.[1]

I think my dear sister would feel compassion for me if she could only
know the tried state of my feelings, both of mind and body, for some
months past. (Now, I must write with freedom even if Bro James should
see it. He need never let on.) I suppose it was not a reasonable
expectation, but somehow or other after the birth of Caroline[2] I had
encouraged a belief, with such confidence, that I never should have that
trial to undergo again, that the conviction to the contrary has been a trial
almost too hard for me to bear with any degree of resignation. Harassing
fears, gloomy forbodings, and greater weakness of body than I ever
experienced before at times envelope me with feelings of such sadness
that I at times almost fear I shall not be permitted to feel the support I
have heretofore experienced. The 12 of the 11 mo is the time I look
forward to.

It seemed to be such a good time to stop, for Caroline had worn out
all my stock of small apparel except a few little caps, 3 white frocks of
little account in winter. Not a single shirt, frock, or flannel petticoat
left—and nothing old that I can spare to cut up (for I have cut 3 dresses
and one of them is patched). It takes all we can sell to pay former debts.
We are considerably behindhand yet and shall not have near as much to
sell this year as last, the grain crops being lighter. So all these little things
seem to harass and distress my mind. I have made no preparation.

What a change there is in the dress of the people here since we came.
Then 1 decent calico and plenty of homemade was sufficient; now there
is scarcely an old woman of my accquaintance that could not count 3
nice dresses to my 1. They have thier silks, pongees, bombazets, merinos,
while poor me is as contented as any of them when I can put on a clean,
whole (ragged and dirty I will not go) calico dress with cape of the same.
My children that are at home have 2 dresses apiece—Caroline has 3—
besides old linseys for cool days so they can keep decent. I never suffer
any to go ragged. Deborah and Aliceanna have plenty of nice clothing
and are both going to school and learning rapidly. Poor Deborah is just
recovering from the whooping cough. She has had it lightly, they say. I
expect both her and Aliceanna to see us today—have not seen A since the
2nd mo.

Though Maria has fewer dresses than any of her associates, she
generally looks as well and as neat as any of them. She works hard and
keeps as sweet and clean a house as I wish. She expects to take in what
spinning she can at the rate of $1.00 per 6 dozen to help get her a cloak
this winter.

We have had a visit this week of several days from Cousin William
Garrigues's daughter, Elizabeth,[3] one of the most lovely, unassuming girls
I ever saw. She is polished in her manners without affectation in pride.
She is artless and affectionate, a fine understanding which has been
cultivated. She is beloved by all that know her. She and her sister work
like everything—all thier own housework, spinning, &c. She
corresponds with Maria. I think her a very profitable associate.

We expect dear old Uncle Samuel Brooke[4] down 3rd day next. He
has good health this summer.

Maria just calls out, "Give my dear love to them." She is a-scrubbing
and splashing at a great rate. Shall I tell tales on her? She expects a young
gentleman here with her bro Franklin from Salem this evening. He was
introduced to her while she was there on a visit 5 or 6 weeks since,
gallanted her home and wished to come again. He is from Philadelphia,
his name Charles Weaver,[5] very accomplished. Now, don't be uneasy. I
ain't.

They are getting in the last of the hay harvest, a fine crop. Have cut
and secured all the grain and hay without any rain upon it. We have a
very large crop of oats not ripe enough to cut yet. We have had a long
dry spell. Rain is much wanting for the potatoes, corn, and mills. Our
young apple trees are so loaded with fruit that they have to be propped.
We have also a good many peaches, and I have a plumb tree in the
garden that is full of the most delicious blue gage plumbs, as large as a
good-sized peach. I have got 1/2 a gallon of molasses, and as soon as I
finish this am going to preserve some. I can't afford sugar, and folks
couldn't make a frolic here without some kind of preserves.

Oh, I wish you could see the bower in the garden. It is entirely
covered with the most beautiful grape vine. When foliage is so luxuriant
not a ray of sunshine can penetrate. Thick clusters of fruit hang on it. It
is the wine grape, almost as large as a fox grape. Maria spends a good deal
of her time there sewing &c and building air castles.

I fancy I did think when I began this that I would inclose a few lines
to dear Bro Isaac just to spur him up to write to me as I don't know how
to direct to him, but I don't know now whether I shall have time and I

can't write a <u>pretty letter</u> any more. I am sure I love you and your little darling. Do write very soon and comfort your affectionate sister, Anna Bentley.

Please send the enclosed to Bro Isaac:

Perhaps you recollect Elizabeth Gillingham, John's daughter. She is an amiable woman married to a Joseph Hillerman,[6] a hatter in good business living at Hanover. We visit her sometimes, and she has been here. Poor thing, my heart aches for her. She had a little daughter who always had very delicate health. When 16 months old, 2 days after the birth of a lovely boy, it died in her arms. In her weak state it was nearly too much for her. Her little boy, Francis, grew to be a lovely interesting child of 10 months old. It seemed as if the parents' hearts were bound up in him. I never saw parents seem to doat on a child with more fondness. But alas, 6 weeks since he took the whooping cough. Nothing could be found for his relief. And a week since he was laid beside his sister. This was a bereavement indeed, and her parents and sisters at a distance, too. I wish I could get to see them.

I am your most affectionate sister, A

1. While it seems clear from the letter that Sarah Stabler had lost a child, I was not able to determine what child had died.
2. Anna's tenth child.
3. Her father, William Garrigues, was Robert's brother. She was second cousin to the Bentley children.
4. Samuel Brooke was Hannah Briggs's brother. His wife was the former Sarah Garrigues.
5. Charles Weaver became a doctor under the tutelage of Dr. Benjamin Stanton of Salem, a noted local physician and Quaker (and a relative of Abraham Lincoln's Secretary of War, Edwin Stanton). In 1839, Weaver married Dr. Stanton's daughter, Rebecca.
6. Elizabeth Gillingham and Joseph Hillerman had been married in October 1833.

∼

11th mo 22nd 1836
My dear Mother,

I am seated with numbed fingers in my chamber upstairs to preform a task too long delayed of answering my dear mother's letter. It has even become a task to write a letter to thee. The aversion to letter writing has grown upon me lately. . . . But forgive me, all of you, for a little while longer, and if life is spared me I will do better. . . . It is right down selfishness that I cannot now withdraw my thoughts from myself enough to think or write about any other subject than <u>my</u> feelings, <u>my</u> cares, <u>my</u> anxious troubled fears and weary burdened helplessness—but I trust I may now in a measure speak of something more like a feeling of resignation and trusting in the merciful arm that has hitherto been my support.

As to my health, I am more helpless and less able to use exercise than I ever was before, though my appetite is good and after 12 I rest well at night. I think when I get through with some piles of sewing I shall feel more at ease in my mind, but I have so much of that to do that it scares me to think of it, and I have kept putting off the <u>small</u> work to patch, knit, and fix up for the winter that I am getting very uneasy when I feel much amiss, as I often do.

I had a 40-yd peice of fine linsey taken to the weavers in the 7th month. She has disapointed me so about it. It is not half done yet and has to be colored and pressed at the fulling mill; yet I had enough for Caroline, 2 dresses beautifuly colored and striped woven at first, and had that and a petticoat for myself cut off, which I coloured <u>bright yellow</u>, that is all made up and very comfortable. Our wool is very fine and it is as soft and pleasant wear as need be, but here is another greivance: The coarse linsey rolls, our only dependence for Thomas' and Edmunds' winter wear, <u>are still at the machine</u>. And now there is ice round our door, the ground frozen, and it looks and feels wintry indeed. We sent it in good time, but the man was taken sick.

Poor Jos began his ploughing early and was getting on so well with it he intended putting in more grain than ever we did, but when he had got 14 or 15 acres done had the misfortune to break his plow all to peices and was not able to get another. And from some cause or other our last crop of wheat has a little smut in it so that he was not willing to sow of his own and found such difficulty in getting seed wheat that it put him back very much and it is not near done yet. But Benjamin Higgins is here today stirring the fallow, and Jos is sowing, so I hope he will get it all in yet.

The boys are butchering a nice young steer this morning. Oh, ain't you glad, for we have been out of meat this 3 weeks, except chickens. We have killed <u>53</u> of them, as fat as need be, and have as many more, but I soon get tired of them. You know I always had a gross <u>mannish</u> appetite for meat. Oh, how often would I gladly have helped dear Mother to my chicken for some scraps out of your under cupboard. I have 2 shoats in the pen fattening and a fine fat goose when the beef gives out.

Our corn is excellent. We shall have but little wheat to sell, not half as much as last year. We have 15 bushels buckwheat, our potatoes most of them still in the ground. I have plenty of beets and cabbage and our dear little orchard bore finely. We dried 3 bushels of peaches and better than 1 of apples. I don't know how many the boys gathered. I dried 1/2 a gallon of my larger grapes in the garden and they taste like raisins. We had some of the largest peaches and the best I ever saw. Some would not go in a big tin.

We have our dear Franklin at home. He is a dear, lively, affectionate, openhearted young man. They say handsome. How tenderly attached and united the two brothers are and always have been. His freedom suit is really ellegant.

Don't let the old folks scold me that I allow the 2 brothers and Maria to sing Caroline to sleep sometimes.[1] I am very sure Mother and Aunt Polly would be tempted to sit down and listen and would say they had seldom heard more melodious sounds. Franklin's voice is full, rich, and full of melody, and Maria's—but I am affraid she will want to see this and will only say its tones are music in her mother's ear. Granville also sings very well.

Poor Cousin MEG has had a trying time this summer, 5 or 6 contractors on the Canal boarding there all summer, in addition to her large family. Poor little Susan had a most violent convulsion fit that lasted more than 3 hours 3 or 4 weeks since, and since large sores broke out all over her. Several of the other children had the erruption. The Dr thought it the chicken pox but the largest he ever saw. She is not well yet. And Cousin Margaret has not been here since April, but as I know it is not for want of inclination, I don't think hard, though I miss her sisterly sympathy.

And Cousin Mary Higgins: As a tender sister my heart feels for her. Her study seems to be to bow meekly in submission to the will of her God. She is a dear lovely sufferer now confined to her house, a violent chill and fever every day and cough all night. They had the misfortune last week to lose thier three finest hogs, the cause unknown.

I cannot express my thanks to dear Mother and Sister for thier assistance, and I ardently hope you may none of you ever feel inconvenience from the want of it till it is in my power to replace it. . . . Maria is sending so many messages of love. I could tell a tale on her if I chose, and not about a <u>weaver</u> either, but mum for a while. . . .
Most affectionately, your Anna Bentley

1. Music and singing were discouraged by the Quakers as worldly.

∾

On December 13, Anna gave birth to her 11th child, Alban.

❧

12th mo 31st [1836]
My dear Mother,

Week after week has gone by and we have not written, and now I have
commenced I find my hand trembles so I can hardly write. As thee
knows my tedious egotistic style of writing, I will prepare this by saying
we are all up and about now and our number all complete. Death has
not visited us, blessed by the protecting arm of mercy.[1] Well, to go back
six weeks: Cousin MEG's dear little Susan was so poorly she had to leave
me the next day after Alban was born, with tears of sisterly affection. The
weather set in so rough that for the first week the neighbours (dear kind
neighbours) could not get to see me, and my dear child and her father
took all the care of us they could. I had a suffering time with the worst
sore nipples I ever had, and the piles,[2] which last I had 6 weeks previous
to my confinement, but still my mind and spirits were supported and
partook not of the body's weakness, and the babe was very good.

I had a visit from Dr Robinson's wife and sister (Geo Sloane's wife).
They are real ladies. From some cause [or] another the blood don't
circulate in one of the fingers of my right hand, and that wrist is so weak
I can't lift anything with it. At first I attributed it to the violent <u>pressure</u>,
as my neighbor said I had nearly crippled her, but it gets no better. I have
never been out yet and am very weak and thin, though I have a good
appetite. It seems as if my nourishment all went to milk, of which I have
a great flow. And such a fat, hearty, strong babe. Almost everyone that
sees him says he looks like a child of 4 months old. He holds up his head
and stands on his feet, strongly laughs and crows. I never saw any child
grow as fast. His head is shaped like his dear grandfather's (my father),
his hair light, his dove eyes large, full, and clear—a dark blue—a sizeable
snout, beautiful mouth and double chin, a dimple in one cheek, most
delicately fair skin, the prettiest hand and arm full of dimples. His father
looks at him with a mighty satisfied air, and Maria devours him with
kisses, and she and the other girls, Hannah and Deborah, say he is the
prettiest and smartest of all the other babies. My back is so weak and
painful I cannot turn in bed without help.

This is quite enough about myself. I have kept my room now 8
weeks. Well, yesterday was 5 weeks Franklin returned through the rain

from where he had been at work 12 miles from here. The next day he complained of great soreness and stiffness of his flesh and joints, which got worse. He attempted to work it off, and on 2nd day went to help Benjamin Higgins butcher. He could scarcely get home, was delirious all night, 3rd day morning hobbled in my room. He was in great suffering all day, first on the bed, then on the floor, where we found by his joints swelling and other symptoms that the poor fellow was attacked with <u>inflamatory rheumatism.</u> Granville and Maria had to carry him downstairs at night. He was again delirious. It affected all his joints. He was entirely helpless and in great suffering. I was then unable to walk down to see him from that painful disorder I told thee of.

He had been sick a week when I got a note from dear Cousin Margaret informing me that she had been sitting for several days with her poor little babe on her lap extremely ill. They were in constant dread of convulsions, one side of it useless, the Dr said from palsy, its brain threatened with inflamation. He had but little hopes of its recovery. She said not one neighbour had been in. She had sat up alone the night before and expected to that night. Granville said he would do all for Franklin, and Maria sent for Asenath Taylor, our precious kind neighbor, and they went down.

Well, the dear little sufferer lingered on for another week, was held exactly as Mary Higgins' child, and convulsions closed the scene. Poor Cousin Margaret held her patient, unwearied watch by its cradle. The Dr said he could but admire her "quiet, devoted attention." Cousin Robert sat with his Bible, from which he seemed to derive great comfort. Joseph went down every day. Once or twice Maria staid several nights and days. They were continually in my thoughts. I tried to write words of comfort to Cousin Margaret often. She said they were so. But she had a better comforter, and she sought and found its support. Oh, she is a dear and precious woman. She feels like an own sister to me. Cousin Robert brought her here last first day. She looks very pale and bad. Susan was 14 months old and was a beautiful babe.

Well, the Dr visited Franklin, thought him in a critical situation. He did not tell us so, but told others that he must be very careful or it might settle on his lungs. He left medicine that slowly helped him so that he is now able to walk about.

Well, 2 weeks ago last 5th day Jos was helping Thomas load the sled with wood and just felt his back hurt a little in the old place. Did not mind but walked to the shoemaker's, 12 miles of a walk. That night he slept but little but did not tell, untill the next day some of the children said, "Mother, something is the matter with Father. He has made a bed on the floor and has been laying down, and he groans every now and then."

I went down and sure enough found him unable to turn. Granville had started that morning to Marlborough to pay his first visit. I did not know what to do or how he was to be got upstairs to his bed. Franklin was as weak as a little child, and I could do but little. When who should step in but our dear Aaron, as strong as 2 men? He lives at Lisbon and had not been here for 2 months. He carried him up here where he has been confined better than 2 weeks, as patient as a lamb till within a few days past. He can walk about again but complains more today again, says it seems to be fixing now in his hip. We have had to assist each other in turning. Poor dear fellow, he has been so patient and gentle.

This is not all. It seemed all summer as if I had so much to feel and dread for myself that I was affraid I was growing selfish, but before I passed through my time I was enabled to give up all and feel resigned quietly to endure all I brought through and supported wonderfully, and it seems to be my lot since to have to sympathise and feel deeply for my dear friends.

Poor dear Cousin Mary Higgins is going fast. She has wasted away to a skeleton, has a dreadful cough, shortness of breath, a chill every day succeeded by cold, clammy sweats, has to keep her bed a great deal, her husband often from home at work all day. No kind neighbor comes in to comfort and assist, none to do the work of the family but thier poor little faithful Caroline, who, though 12 years old, is no larger than Aliceanna. Maria and Helen went over this week and washed for her. They found her at 10 o'clock in bed and her [house] that used to be kept so nice so out of order. She wept, but quickly wiped her tears away, said she had thought during the night she was ready and would be thankful to be taken away but hoped she might be preserved in perfect submission of heart to wait the Lord's time. She wept as she spoke of the children, said their father had to be so much out at his work and she was too weak to enforce obedience [that] they were getting very unruly.

She is destitute of so many comforts in dress, beds, and bedding, and the children, too; and she has near relatives, rich, too proud to help her. Well, I intend fixing up some clothing next week for Caroline. My heart aches for her. As soon as I am able I intend to take all and go over. Maria will clean the house and put things to rights, and Maria and Hannah will go every week to wash for her. If she should last till spring, George Sloane is going to Baltimore for goods. Oh, if Aunt Henny would send her something for herself or children.

Cousin Robert and Margaret and Helen all desired thier love to be given you when I wrote. Granville and Maria send thiers. The others all love you but did not know of my writing. Sister Elizabeth, Maria was right much vexed at that part of thy letter that alluded to her. She says as thee must blab the first hint (among strangers, too) she won't allow thee to hear any more. The very chap is here now, but don't hint I told you. I may have something <u>every way agreeable</u> to tell you at some future period, but mind this is not to be spoken of nor hinted at in your letters to me. This must come to an end, Alban says so. Farewell.

Most affectionately, Anna Bentley

1. Back in Maryland, however, on December 31, Lizzie wrote to her sister Sarah, who was away on a visit, "Cousin Betsy Thomas sent us a message this week by Polly Humfree, giving us some mournful news from bro. Joseph Bentley's family that 'cousin Anna Bentley had lost her youngest daughter.' Polly seemed quite certain she told her it was the <u>youngest daughter</u>, that is Caroline Elizabeth. But we cannot help thinking perhaps it was the baby, and we were disappointed not to get a letter from them by the mail we got your last." A week later the family was still in suspense, and remained so until Anna's reassuring letter arrived.

2. Hemorrhoids.

~

3rd mo 17th 1837[1]

My dear friends,

I wish I would write oftener for I can't remember when I did or what I have told you. My first going out from home was when Alban was 2 months old. Cousin RHG came in a sleigh to take me to see poor dear Mary Higgins. Cousin MEG was there. Oh, she did suffer. She seemed to feel it such a comfort to have us near—would look so piteously in our faces during her agonized struggles for breath and call us her dear sisters. Talked with the greatest composure, even about what would be wanting washed for the children to wear to her burying. Had her own things got out. We found the shroud cut out and pinned together by herself. When the messenger was sent for the winding sheet and muslin for cap and handkerchief, <u>she</u> gave directions and told us she wished us to make them plain and simple.

Seeing her look at Matilda and say, "Poor, ragged dirty children. What is to become of you?" I said, "Do not let thy mind be troubled. They will be cared for. If it will be any relief to thy mind, I will tell thee I sent word this morning by Granville to Maria to alter a good linsey frock that Hannah has outgrown for Matilda, and it will be done tonight."

Oh, such a look she gave me as she clasped my hand in hers and said, "My dear sister—bless you."

I cannot describe the parting scene. With heavenly composure she called first her husband and children, kissed them, then beckoned to us and kissed us, then fixed her eyes earnestly for a while on each of her children, then Cousin Margaret and I, then turned them calmly on her beloved companion, and her suffering spirit was soon quietly released from its wasted tenement to find "beauty for ashes and the oil of joy for mourning."

Poor Benjamin. He sat with his arms round the 2 youngest, whose plaintive cries wrung my heart. I went to him, stood by his chair. He looked in my face and said, "Cousin Anna, is she gone?" I replied, "Yes, the dear creature is at rest."

His pent feelings then gushed forth. "Oh, my dear Cousin Anna, what is to become of me and these poor, poor motherless children? Oh, Mary, my dear Mary." I held his throbbing temples as he leaned his head against me. He had no sister or relation near. The children crowded round and hung on me; they always loved me.[2]

The day she died Alban was taken very ill. I could not get home till after the burying. He remained very ill for a week. I expected convulsions every minute, when he began to mend and soon got well. Then Cousin Robert came for me in his sleigh and I spent 2 or 3 days there very pleasantly and he brought me home again. Well, about 5 weeks ago I awoke in the morning feeling very unwell with a bad cold—headache, fever, a hard, inflamed breast. I was right ill for 3 or 4 days and expected nothing else but to have a gathered breast, but we <u>fout</u> it manfully with hop poultices, goose oil, &c, and I got better, but still a bad cough, very unusual for me. Two weeks ago yesterday in the morning, a shooting pain seized me in the forhead and eyes. Cousin Margaret came and I tried my best to overcome it, but it continued to get worse. I had to keep my bed, could eat nothing, could scarce forbear screaming with the anguish.

On 2nd day Cousin Margaret came and Jos went for the Dr. He pronounced me in danger of inflammation of the brain and said there was a general debility of the system he could scarcely account for, put a blister on my forhead and another the back of my neck. I had to take Quinine, valerian, soda powders, cathartic powders, and I don't know what. Dear Cousin Margaret, like a sister, staid till 6th day night. After the blisters drew, the violence of the pain abated and it would be easy at night. I kept my bed entirely for 10 days and still have to be down part of the day.

While it was at the worst, my face and forhead swelled so as quite to close my eye. It is not the same side that used to be affected. I fear I am going to be afflicted with one of my old spells—have fallen away much, have a very troublesome cough, and am very weak. My back has been dreadfull weak since Alban was born. He is a fine, fat, good boy. His complexion is like the monthly rose[3]; his beautifully short, fat, dimpled arm and hand looks like pure waxwork, a kinder transparent-like. He has large, full, very blue eyes, pretty spunky-looking, pretty mouth, double chin, dimpled cheeks, and snotty nose, for he has a considerable cold.

Evening: My head and face has been very bad this afternoon. I am something easier now. I applied another blister to my temple; it is drawing like fire but feels good to what the pain does. My hand trembles so I can scarcely write, and I have a great deal I want to say. Tomorrow morning we shall part with our dear Maria for 6 months, I expect. Cousin M B Grove (Brooke that was)[4] made her a kind offer that if she would only come and be to her as a sister she would board her and she should go to school all the time to Cousin Anna Stroud.[5] And it should cost her nothing, and what little turns she might choose to do mornings and evenings, and she would assist her all she could in her studies. She will keep a hired girl, expects to be confined in the summer. She took a great fancy to Maria during a visit she paid there in the winter, seemed to feel a great interest for her and wants her as a companion and comforter.

Though we shall miss the dear child, we could not but approve of her going. Her young friends here, particularly Cousin Robert's family, seem to lament her going from them. If she is my own, I must say she is beloved and admired. Helen is here now helping her and looks so sorrowful. She said to me just now, "I shall feel lost till Cousin Maria's return. There is no one can fill her place to me."

I am not at liberty yet to satisfy Sister Elizabeth's curiosity on a certain point. My letters have rather too wide circulation for me to write on all subjects with the same freedom I would if only your particular family saw them. I can assure you there is no prospect of any speedy important change in her situation; farder I mout not say.

I have taken a notion in my head that I dwell on with delight, and that is that Brother Isaac is going to come and see us. For I saw a man, that saw another man, that saw Bro Isaac and said he talked of coming to Ohio. And now whenever Trusty barks I hobble to the window and think maybe I shall see my darling brother. Poor Maria has fretted and scolded at his neglect in not answering her letter to him, a very long one it was. But we had the mystery explained in the form of a reprimand from the PM general to JEB for abuse of his franking privilege. The letter was opened at the general PO. I think it is likely that letter will cost us 10 dollars—ain't it provoking?

We have 9 pretty lambs, and we have only just got the fulled linsey from the fuller's. Well, it is good and beautiful and we have got along right well without it, though it comes in good time now. Hannah and Deborah are fully capable of doing the housework, and we shall sell the most of the wool this summer as it bears a high price and it is cheaper to buy. The dear boys are both at home. Granville is just finishing a first-rate waggon, Franklin is making bedsteads. I look at them and their sister sometimes and wish you could see them. And Thomas—Oh, what a laugh he and the rest of us had at Sister Elizabeth's fancy of his whiskers &c. Let me draw his picture from the life: 15, not 17; 5 feet 2 inches high, rather chunky built; light brown hair, high fair forehead, eyes like his grandfather's; very rosy, dimpled cheeks, white teeth, and no more beard than a peach has.

7th day, 18th. Maria has gone and I feel sad, for a furious equinoxal gale is blowing. She rode our colt, the first time any woman ever did. Had a cloak on without any arm hole. The roads are too bad for a carryall.[6] It is 29 miles. Franklin went with her. Bully is very gentle, though.

My blister drew well, but I feel the pain is coming on again. I weighed Alban yesterday as he was just 4 months old. He is short and very small-boned and weighs 19 1/2 lb. He has fallen away very much since he had this bad cold, but he is getting better. There has never been so much sickness or as many deaths since we came to Ohio as there has this fall: the Smallpox or variloid[7] within less than a 1/4 mile of Cousin Robert's; influenza, whooping cough, and a great many cases of inflamation of the brain. And mad dogs have become fashionable here, too.

Maria sent much love to you all, so do Hannah and Deborah. Cousin MEG says always give hers when I write. If any of you know where Nicholas Thomas is, Benjamin Higgins wishes to write to him, if he knew where to direct. I must stop and be down.

Your own, Anna

Well, now, what must I do? Jos is gone from home, and if this letter goes it will cost you more than it is worth. Maybe you will think I wish I did know what you had rather I should do.[8]

1. This letter sat in the post office in Rockville, Maryland, until the family at Sharon picked it up in May.
2. Benjamin Higgins married Mary Albright on April 1, 1838.
3. The Indian or China rose, which was supposed to bloom once a month.
4. Mary Brooke, daughter of Samuel and Sarah Brooke, married Robert Grove (or Graves) in 1835. They lived in Marlborough.
5. Another daughter of Samuel and Sarah Brooke, she was married to Jacob Stroud.
6. A four-wheeled, one-horse carriage.
7. Varioloid, or variola, is another term for smallpox, or the precursor to smallpox.

∾

In April, her sister Sarah Stabler gave birth to a child, Henrietta (later Frances), and was sick afterward with a malady of her breast that made her unable to breast feed. Her husband was also in declining health at this time and undergoing a course of Thomsonian treatment, including lobelia and steam baths.

∾

4th mo 30th 1837
My dear Mother,

This day thine came to hand, and I felt so sorry to think thou wert feeling uneasy about us. My last to you was dated the 18th of the 3rd mo, and I wrote with a blister drawing on my forehead and it is well maybe thee did not get it, as I expect it was filled with a doleful particular account of a spell of illness—inflamation of the brain I was just getting the better of. I was 10 days confined to my bed entirely, 3 and 4 weeks had to lay down part of the day. That last blister relieved my head. I had 2 before, 1 on the back of my neck and one on my forhead. Dear Cousin Margaret came like a sister and sat up night after night, gave medicine every hour and staid till the Dr pronounced me out of danger. The neighbors were all very kind in coming to see me. My sufferings were severe—indeed, I have been very good for nothing since Alban was born. My back is so weak and painful that at times I can't walk straight or turn myself in bed, and I am very thin. And Hannah is stronger than I am, though I have a good appetite.

And my babe is very fat. His weight the day he was 5 months old was 21 3/4 lbs. He has 2 teeth through and 2 more nearly so. I'll be bound he is as good looking as thy tother new grandchildren. How should they have prettier children than I that am so used to it!! Well, he has large, full, clear, laughing blue eyes, and he looks up so mild and gentle as if he loved a body and was glad of it, with an even ready smile to show his dimples. He is too <u>fair</u> for my idea of beauty, but it is the clearest, delicate hue, not a sickly paleness.

He is very good, but Caroline is the little loving puss that would soon win her way to your hearts. She is short, very fat, rosy, a most expressive countenance, quiet in temper but easily subdued, the most affectionate disposition and the sweetest tongue—she does talk so funny we think her uncommonly smart. She looks more like her father than any of them. We had a visit from Uncle Joseph Snode and Aliceanna last week. Dear little girl. Uncle Josy says they never were more attached to one of thier own than they are to her.

5th, 5th, 10 o'clock. Though I am weary enough to go to bed, I must add a little to this as I shall have too much to do tomorrow to fill this if I don't. Joseph called all hands out today except Caroline, Alban, and me, to help plant corn. They finished 6 acres and just had time to get in at the door when the first drops of rain began to fall of a violent storm attended with much wind, hail, and thunder, the prospect of which had made them rush ahead till they were all tired enough. Two quarts of beans and 3 of pumkin seed also were planted, and I had the housework and a very large ironing to do, and Alban not well and very fretful for him to be.

Perhaps you will wonder that I have to work hard. I forget, it was in the missing letter I informed you of our <u>dear Maria's leaving us</u>. She left us the 18th of 3rd mo to spend the summer with Cousin Mary Grove (Brooke that was). Maria with her brothers went to Marlborough on a visit in the winter. Cousin Mary took a great fancy to Maria and very kindly solicited us to spare her to come and be to her as a sister and friend this summer (she expects to be confined soon), and she would board her and send her to school and assist her in her studies all she was able. Now, was it not a kind and generous offer? We thought so, approved of it, and she is very happy. She writes every week, and we expect her on a visit tomorrow week with Cousin William Garrigues's son, Edward, and daughter, Hannah. It feels hard to part with her, and we all miss her, but we shall have to give her up <u>sometime, I expect</u>, and must try to get used to it.

Since she went, a nice young woman commenced teaching school near here, and as poor Hannah has had a poor chance, I thought she must be spared, so she and Edmunds have been going a month. Hannah stays at home 2nd days and washes. She can get done a larger washing (it must be large, you may suppose, for us all; Granville and Franklin are included) in less time and do it as well as Maria. Deborah does the housework, makes as good light bread and pies as you would wish to eat. She is a great, fat strong Irish-looking girl. She is to go to school half the time, and Granville has made a nice building in the garden and has nearly finished paling in a large front yard, which is a great improvement. He has also planted out above 50 plum trees (the blue gage). We have 2 bearing trees. Their fruit is delicious; the taste resembles an apricot. They are as large as moderate-size peach trees.

He has been working at his trade some at home this spring, made 1 waggon, a pr of cart wheels, a waggon wheel. Last week he came from the store and handed me a parcel, saying, "Mother, is this pretty?" It was a beautiful neat calico dress pattern for me—precious child. And Thomas had been very busy all the spare time he could get, and that is but little, making axe handles, which he could get 12 1/2 cents apeice [for] at the store in trade. He took them there and on his return handed me nice calico for an apron and 2 papers of tobacco. And dear Franklin has made me a nice pr of bedsteads, 2 washboards, a chair for Alban, &c. He works at his trade in Hanover but seems bent on going down the river to Louisville, expects to start in 2 weeks. We all feel opposed to it.

I have felt too much disapointed—I heard in several different ways that Brother Isaac expected to come to see us. At one time I heard that he was going to Indianna and would come by here to visit us and that I might expect him daily. And I did and still do watch the road and [pine] away sadly.

What does Sister Sarah call her babe?[1] Dear Sister Sarah and Margaret, I ought to write to them, but it is such a task to me to write, and since Jos was hauled on the coals by the Postmaster General for franking a letter from Maria and me to Brother Isaac which went to the general post office, I feel scary about writing many free letters.[2] Maria complains heavy if she don't get them very often.

Oh, I keep going to sleep. Today I brought a stick in and laid it in by me, saying to Caroline, who would make a noise while Alban slept, "Does thee see this? Don't let me have to tell thee about making that noise."

She came close, and looking so comical said, "Momma, tood <u>de</u> wip a body wid dat stick?"

"Yes indeed."

"Would de huyt dood deal?"

"I rekon I would."

"Oh no I dess not. De needent bodder dysef."

[Joseph finished the letter] Seventh day morning—Anna was sent for

in a hurry this morning to see a sick neighbor and had to leave her letter
unfinished. We had pretty considerable of a storm last night.
Affectionately,
JE Bentley

1. Although in May, Sarah referred to this child as Henrietta, her daughter was ever after
known as Frances, born on April 9.
2. Nevertheless, this letter was sent free like the other.

∼

The high-spirited Maria and a friend had a little fun with Anna and her
correspondence in the following letter. The first paragraph is in a large,
flowery handwriting that is not Anna's.

∼

July 2nd 1837
first day morning
[addressed to William Henry Briggs]
My dear friends one and all,

My heart overflowed with joyfull emotions on recieving your affectionate
epistle, and as our esteemed friend Sarah Miller once said, "My affection
for you is like unto the laurel of the mountain, which remaineth green
through the scorching rays of the meridian sun, that glorious luminary
which sheds its benign influence on the sons and daughters of men (Flah!
Shallow!), dazzles the eyes of popularity and guides the floating battery
over the Atlantic Ocean."
    [Then Anna takes up her pen and continues.]
Dear friends,

If this ain't a shame, I don't know. This is the only sheet of paper I have,
and I had brought it and laid it on my work table to begin a letter to you
when Maria and her mischevious particular friend for thier fun made this
ridiculous beginning—to help Mother out, they said. I promised to
match Maria for her part, and I now hint it to you: Ten to one if you
don't some day see the same handwriting subscribed, "Your affectionate
Grandson & Nephew." He is every way worthy—a finished education,
polished manners, amiable, affectionate heart, industrious, handsome,
&c &c. The quotation they have made except the last 2 lines was
absolutely taken from a letter to me from SM.

2nd day. My mind is so filled with you I can scarcely attend to my business. Oh, if I dared hope Mother would come. There is an elegant, well-improved farm, 80 acres for sale, with plenty of good fruit, convenient building, brick, dry house for fruit, springhouse 6 yds from the back door, &c, 2 miles from here, but the price is $2,000. . . .

[Now Maria takes a turn.]

Mother stops. If this is not almost insufferable. I know nothing about it. To think she should write that about me when I am as innocent of any such thing as a lamb. The chap who kindly helped Mother in the commencement of this letter has some notion of <u>Hannah</u>, I guess, but she not being at home last 1st day I had to try to entertain him—quite a difficult undertaking, too, I can tell you. He's a <u>little</u>, ugly fellow who has managed to ingraciate himself into Mother's good graces, and I firmly believe has succeeded effectually in so doing; but for pity's sake never say or think he will ever do the same with her <u>eldest</u> daughter. And you may believe me, for Hannah is in her teens and quite a smart-looking gal.

"My particular friend" indeed. Never mind. You will see for yourselves, I hope, and if he ever subscribes himself as Mother told you it was likely he would, it will doubtless be as <u>my</u> brother-in-law. Indeed, I have been most horribly mortified at some little things Mother has written to you just to plague me, which you have taken for good earnest and told it for a fact that I was to be married soon; which I can most positively assure you is not the case. Any thing Sally Howard gets hold of of the kind goes to cousin Betsey Thomas, then it comes right out here. And you do not know what trouble and vexation it has occasioned me. Please do not circulate anything she may write just for mischief about me among our friends. Just suppose Hannah's beau was to get to hear of it. He would think we were so certain of him for a relation that we had even written on for Grandmother's consent. For my poor sister's sake I would entreat you to consider this well.

I should write more but have a great parcel of work to do yet, and it is getting late. I dearly love you and all and long much to see you to welcome you to our Western home and then, dear Aunt Henrietta, may I make a bosom friend of thee? Oh, thy neice will love thee so dearly. I have not one intimate friend nearer than Marlboro, and my heart feels very lonely sometimes.

Come, come and let us all be so happy.

Your affectionate, Maria

[Then Granville inserts a note.]

Dear Uncle,

Mother & Maria have scratched over nearly a page & a half and said not much to the purpose after all, but you may believe what Mother says and only part of Maria's. We handed thy letter to Cousin Robert and he had, I believe, answered all the questions better than we could have done, and we will send the answers just as he has written them without much comment, believing that you will find it as he had represented. The Wheat crops now look very promising, but there is so much wet weather we are afraid they will be injured considerably. . . . This land, if properly managed, will produce well. There are some very good farmers here, and they will raise nearly double as much as others who are too careless and do not understand it. I don't think it is worthwhile to tell thee everything. We will leave something for thee to find out when thee gets here. I wish thee to write immediately and let us know when thee expects to start that we may look out a place for thee. And don't put it off too long. My love to all, and believe me,
Thy affectionate nephew, G S Bentley

[Then Anna's handwriting again.]

7th mo 7th. Well, I'll begin again. And first I do request of you not to speak out of the family that Maria <u>has a particular friend</u> or else I won't tell who it is. Cousin EPT [Betsy Thomas] wrote to Cousin Margaret enquiring about it, said Sally Howard told her "She heard from <u>Maria's friends</u> that she was to be married shortly <u>very well</u>." How it did hurt the poor child, for she had guarded her secrets in this neighborhood, and there is no such prospect for maybe a long time to come. Perhaps circumstances might occur to prevent, and then it is mortifying to have such things talked of. I am sorry my letters <u>cannot</u> be more confidential.

There is an exellent farm adjoining us on the east for sale. Cousin Robert says he has no doubt but mother could sell Sharon for enough to purchace it and put on it as good buildings as she left—and secure a home on which an excellent living might be made. The canal company owns it; we do not know thier price. I fear there will be several applicants for it. Aunt Elizabeth Lukens says she thinks mother would be more comfortably fixed here. Oh, if it could be. And Elizabeth, what for will she no come? Can't she fetch <u>him</u> along? Does Bro William Henry Farquhar still talk of coming out? If Mother don't come, please bring me one of her old pipes.

[And Maria finishes the letter.]

Here I am again. Have read what [Mother] has written. Worse and worse. I'll not say anything more on the subject but leave you to find out who is to be believed another time. How glad I was to hear from my fondly loved and kind Uncle Richard's family. Please give my love to them particularly. I never shall cease to feel grateful affection for them. Should I but meet them now, they would not recognize me, I know. It seems to me that I recollect their features perfectly well, can call to mind dear Uncle's laugh and Aunty's kind smile of approval if by <u>chance</u> I done right while with them. If I could only be with them 3 or 4 months now, I would try hard to make them love me and wipe off the remembrance of their little bad girl's conduct some 11 years ago. Can it be! 11 years! It seems as yesterday to me. I was miserable when a child. Disease had soured a temper naturally—I will not say <u>bad</u> because I don't believe it was <u>naturally</u> so, but red pepperish like and therefore was never a favorite with my friends 'cepting my Father and Brothers. I believe no sister was ever more loving or beloved than my own self. . . .

When you see my Uncle WH Farquhar, please give my love to him & his wife. I wonder if they have received a long letter from me written while I was at Marlboro. I would be so <u>gratified</u> to receive a letter once more from one to whom I am sincerely attached. And I have good reason to love him, he was such a dear correspondent. He always felt like a Brother to me since I became acquainted with him. Are they not coming to Ohio too? I am sure they said so not a great while ago. Two uncles out here! Oh, dear me—It almost sets me crazy to think of such an occurrence.

Your dear little pet I will love and assist in <u>training</u>, and if they were not first cousins our little Alban might stand a chance of getting a Maryland wife someday maybe.[1] I am so afraid you have set your hearts on seeing a right good-looking girl when you see me. Please don't let your expectations be raised <u>too</u> high, for you may <u>possibly</u> be disappointed.

Aunt Elizabeth, it's a real shame, thee almost promised me some years ago thee would come out here and let <u>me</u> choose thee a <u>help</u> meet, and thee would'nt depend upon my young judgment. Very well, all I have to say is, <u>fetch</u> him along.[2] We will love him and uncle him up like everything, but don't say thee won't come, for I remember thee with so much affection I can scarcely bear to hear tell of thee not coming along with Grandmother. . . . Do, do, do, do, do. Yours sincerely, Maria

1. William Henry and Henrietta Briggs had a daughter, Mary, born about 1837.
2. Elizabeth Briggs never married.

❧

Aunt Elizabeth didn't come at this time, but Anna's younger brother William Henry and his wife Henrietta took the two-week trip over the mountains in July, and settled down to make their fortune, counting on the Sandy & Beaver Canal to stimulate commerce. "Success attend them! is our ardent wish," wrote Sarah Stabler. By December, they had bought a house and lot in Lynchburgh just a mile and a half from Joseph and Anna, and William Henry set about the shoe repair business. Sarah's husband James wrote, "Their prospects are good to get a living comfortably—more so they think than they could rapidly have been to have remained <u>here</u>." He also mentioned he had heard the most complimentary things about Anna and her "intelligent, well-educated" brood, "as <u>good</u> as any bodys children."

William Henry and Henrietta Briggs didn't remain for long in Ohio, and it is not clear why they left. However, the financial panic of 1837 and the ensuing depression delayed work on the canal, and the new village of Lynchburgh didn't flourish as everyone had anticipated. By 1845, the court allowed Owen Stackhouse's petition to vacate forty-five lots in the village. It never was much more than a hamlet along the abandoned canal after that. So William Henry's prospects may have faded.

Anna's sister Margaret (Meg) Farquhar, who had married William Henry Farquhar and gone to live at The Cedars, gave birth to Ellen in 1837 and Arthur in 1838. Hannah Briggs's crippled sister, the widow of Thomas Moore, had been living at Sharon for three years. In 1838, Aunt Polly Moore fell and fractured her wrist, adding to the burdens of the household there.

To Anna's delight Brother Isaac paid another visit to the family at Green Hill.

❧

1st mo 7th 1839

My dear Mother, Aunt P., Sisters Mary, Sarah, Henrietta, Elizabeth, and Meg, <u>exclusively</u>,

Oh, the great undertaking of collecting my ideas together and putting them down on paper in form of a letter. All my difficulty used to be the want of leisure. I cannot so often now plead that as an excuse, but I beleive want of practice is worse. And noise and confusion distracts my attention so it seems impossible for me to write till they all go to bed, and then it is so late.

I had intended to write separate letters to several of you but never felt as if I could while dear Brother Isaac was talking so interestingly, and to tell the truth the tenor of my thoughts and spirits has for some time past been almost desponding. Is it not disheartening at my age (after so many times passing through the fears and disquietudes, the dreadful and dreaded pangs, the anxious care and solicitude of nursing, when I had hoped so confidently that it would never again be my lot) to find the same dreaded trial before me again? Ever since Bro William and Sister Henrietta left here these fears have weighed heavy upon me. I have sometimes felt as if I should sink under it, and at others I strive earnestly to be resigned & trust. Now, this is only for you females.

Well, the noise of the little ones is at last hushed in sleep. The dear ones have just formed a large circle round the fire, Brother Isaac in the center, all talking away. I'll try to see if I can write a bit. I will begin first and tell dear Sis Henrietta of events and things that have occurr'd in this neighbourhood since she left it. As far as I know, though, I have not been off the place since, except once to Cousin Robert's and once to Lynchburgh to open the mail. Your deserted dwelling called up mournful feelings. I missed your affectionate wellcome and little Mary's gladsome laugh. Granville's old house is tenanted by Fifer that married Barrack's young daughter, Hetty.[1]

It has been several weeks since I spent a day at Cousin Robert's. H was there. They appeared as affectionate as ever they were. We very quietly talked over all Old matters. Us old folks shed tears together and mutually concluded to love each other. Cousin Margaret's babe was in a suffering condition. All its nails had come off its feet, and hands all gathered. She has never been from home since you left. Helen seems to do right well—minds and makes for Edwin very neatly, has done a great deal of spinning; they say keeps her house neatly.[2] They begged me to stay all night. Helen says, "Do stay. Send home for more work and I will help, for I have no work to do. I have done all I can find of my own." I had promised to go home and I went.

There has been some theivery going on at Rochester and at Lynchburgh—2 shirts of Jos Wickersham late 7th day night; and we beleive he was prowling about here, for Trusty was most outrageous and chased someone from the shop accross the field. There was snow and we saw tracks. That Vanhorn is suspected.[3]

William Cooper is going to the wall. I fear his creditors push him unmercifully—several executions. He talks of selling out and going to Chester County.[4]

Only think how the fullers served me about my 16 yds of fine linsey. It came home a beautiful color, ellegantly pressed, but fulled up for cloth 3/4 wide, so I had to take it to the store, changed it for a nice merino dress and cassinet[5] for Thomas's coatee, which Nathan Ball made. I do look so grand in my merino.

We have had a terrible time about grinding, the water so low. Our calves thrive and look well. We only milk Storm and Lizzie, expect to have 3 fresh ones in a month or 2. And we have a very fine bay colt named Janet will be a year old in the spring. Jos has been thrashing his clover seed preparatory to running it through a machine. . . . Poor Jos mashed his finger very badly this afternoon. We have been doctoring it with No 6.

Oh, how my heart yearns towards you all. My dear Mother, shall we ever meet again? Sister Mary, thou hast not preformed thy promise yet. I was to have a letter from thee after the birth of each child![6] Maria complains heavily that hers to thee has never even been noticed. She would have accompanied her dear uncle if we could have supplied the means. And as a woman now, I know thou wouldst love her who, when a child, thou felt a tender interest for. Sister Henrietta has made me feel acquainted with thy dear little flock. Tell them sometimes of me.

My beloved Aunt Polly, dost thou ever think of me with affection? I know thou dost. I have deeply sympathised with thee in thy afflictions and rejoiced at hearing of thy amendment. Oh, how often I think over the many happy hours I have passed with thee and my own beloved bosom friend who is now in Heaven!! Ain't it almost time dear Sister Sarah was begining to think of writing one of her dear long letters to her poor sister? I should gratefully receive it. And I've a great mind to treat Sister [Elizabeth] with silent neglect. Because I am old and grey-headed and out of her sight she never thinks it wuff while to take no notice of me.

Honey, don't let Sister Henrietta forget to put thee in mind to try to send me some violet seed in a letter as soon as thee can procure them and I will forgive thee. Sister Maggie, too, precious child, I love to see thy cheerful letters that pictures as a staid matron the light-hearted girl whom I left more than 12 years ago swinging on the gate that then closed forever, I fear, between me and my native home.

Owing to the many pauses I have had to make to listen, 12 o'clock has come and I must put this by till tomorrow.

6th day evening, 11th. Well, on 4th day I felt much amiss with a severe cold and have for some time past been subject to a distressing sensation of fullness in the head. So, as Brother Isaac recommended my taking a course of medicine, I did and was much relieved.

They talk something of starting in the morning if the weather is not too unfavourable.[7] Alban has a bad cold, is very hoarse. He is a little darling. His cheeks when in health are rosy, he is very fair, his hair <u>at last</u> begins to grow fast, is becoming darker, very glossy, and curls over his head. He talks a great deal. Whenever the dog barks he looks delighted and says, "Oh, Mary comin', Aunt comin'." Has often cried at his disapointment. When he wants any of them to do anything for him, he is irresistable in his pleading. He will say, "Pease, Sissy, poor felly onts it, good boy onts it, pease dive Ammy some." Never child loved a father better. He calls himself "papa's dood boy." No need ever to use harsh means with him. He is easier managed than any of the others were. A cross word from his father or Granville almost breaks his heart. He has very seldom been tried with it. But Caroline exceeds anything I ever was tried with—the most troublesome, meddlesome, restless, fidgetty peice of perpetual motion. She has heard the words "Don't, Caroline" so often that she pays little regard to them.

I have never seen our darling Aliceanna since last 6th month. Sister Henrietta, Mary Haines has a daughter 5 or 6 weeks old. She calls it Hester Ann. Aliceanna has been going to school. They say she grows very fast and improves. My precious little girl. <u>She is</u> lovely, ask Brother Isaac if she ain't.

Tell me what you all think of our Frank. I wish you would tell how you all felt to meet him. Would that I could see the meeting. He won't tell half to satisfy us. Please, do you. I am afraid the poor fellows will have a slavish tramp, and it is raining now. I don't believe they will get off tomorrow.

I wish when you write you would let us hear how Cousin EPT [Elizabeth Thomas] is. . . . Jos says I may stick his love in somewhere. You all know that I love you, and I bid you affectionately farewell, A.

I make so many blunders nowadays I am afraid to look over my letters. Oh, Sister Henrietta, Matilda Higgins has been living at S Holland's since a day or two after you left. She is very happy and they say as good a child as they would wish. They have given her a great many new clothes, is to stay till she is of age. Maria says I must find room to tell Aunt Sarah she found it impossible to get Bro Isaac's clothes to any

decent color. They were almost black, and Frank's, too, are miserable—
the limestone water at Salem.

1. John Fifer had married Esther Barrick on August 30, 1838.
2. Helen Garrigues had married Edwin Hall in July 1838 at the New Garden Monthly
Meeting, among the Hicksites, which caused her to be dismissed from the Orthodox Sandy
Spring Monthly Meeting.
3. Several Van Horns lived in West Township.
4. Cooper, a shoemaker, apparently stayed afloat, for he was still living in West Township in
1850 with his wife, Jane, and eight children.
5. A wool-cotton or wool-silk blend fabric.
6. Margaret Brooke had been born on January 27, 1838.
7. This letter was hand-carried back to Maryland by Isaac Briggs and his nephew, Frank
Bentley.

~

Maria Bentley, age twenty-two, married her cousin, Richard Humphrey
Garrigues, twenty-three, the son of William and Hannah Garrigues, at
Green Hill on September 5. They were dismissed from the Sandy Spring
Monthly Meeting for marrying "contrary to discipline." The same month
Anna gave birth to her next to last child, Margaretta.

It was the middle of October before Maria and Richard wrote to Grandmother Briggs in Maryland. Although Richard, too, was related to Hannah
Briggs, it's clear from the ingratiating tone of his letter that he wasn't acquainted with her: "I acknowledge I am poor but I am also independant
and feel as if I could trust to my own exertions which have never failed me
yet."

The letter mentioned that Franklin had accompanied his Uncle Isaac
back to Maryland for a visit, then returned to Ohio in good spirits and
ready to go live with Richard and Maria in Salem "till he can get himself a
wife." (He married Richard's sister, Hannah, in 1841.) Father, she reported,
"met with a serious loss 4 or 5 weeks since in the death of one of his noble
faithful oxen he laid down & died just in the midst of the Fall work which
was very inconvenient indeed. But Father has purchased another very fine
yoke of cattle 4 years old for $65. He has a man here with a Patent Thresh-
ing Machine getting out all the grain which will save a great deal of hard
labor."

The "black-eyed pet," Margaretta, had good health and a good disposition, and weighed 14 pounds, she added.

On February 22, 1840, the family received bad news. Isaac Briggs wrote to Granville Bentley that James P. Stabler, Sarah's husband, had died of consumption. "His heart full of the milk of human kindness, ceased to beat on the 13 inst at a quarter past 11 oclock A.M." after four months of suffering. Later Elizabeth Briggs remembered his sweet smile and tender affection and gentleness. Because his silkworm enterprise had not flourished, James left Sarah nearly destitute. She and the children soon moved to Sharon. On July 6, Mary Moore died there age eighty-one.

∽

July 7th 1840
[from Granville Bentley]
My Dear Aunt H[enrietta?],

This was sent for me to add my mite, and I can only say a very few words before the mail arrives. In answer to a letter I receiv'd from thee some time since, I expect thee has scolded and call'd me a mean fellow many times for neglecting thee so much, but I have sinn'd so often in that way and become so harden'd that scolding or reproaching has mighty little effect on me, I assure thee, so tell the real truth. I have often been on the very point of commencing a letter to thee, but something would prevent, and I would postpone it to a more convenient season. Thee knows old Bachelors all have their faults and peculiarities and that one of thy old nephew's is procrastination, at least in regard to letter writing. I don't know how far back to commence telling the news for I can't recollect when I wrote last. The most important, I believe, is the marriage of Moses Preston to Elizabeth Kuntz of this place, the shoemaker's daughter. I had the honour to be the groomsman but will not tell thee who was the bridal maid, and I am certain thee would like to know.

I entirely forget whether I have ever mention'd my having quit housekeeping. I have been boarding at Griffith Brogan's[1] for nearly 2 months at $4 per month, consider it cheaper than keeping house and less hindrance in the shop. Emma has been very ill but is now nearly well again. She was taken with a violent pain in her side. Dr. Robertson attended. Commenced with bleeding, blistering, and salivating so that she kept her bed for nearly 3 weeks. Deborah was taken precisely the same way. I attended her and she was well directly. Ruth Brogan had the same complaint (the Dr calls it inflamation of the lungs), and Philina and I took her through a course of medicine and she was ready to attend her school in a day or two

You must not get out of heart because I do not send any money. I have plenty due me to liquidate the debt, but it has seem'd impossible for me to get hold of it as yet, and if I was to push for it these hard times I might shut up shop.

Please write soon. I think you have all got to be the darnedest[?] meanest folks for letter-writing I ever saw or hear'd of. Please tell me what has become of Uncle Isaac. My best love to him if he is with you. I guess you don't care much for your affectionate nephew, <u>G.S. Bentley</u>

1. Brogan was just a couple of years older than Granville. He had married Emma Wickersham in 1834.

～

7th mo 5th 1840
My own beloved Mother and all her children and dear Aunt Polly,

I confess my error and plead your forgiveness. I should not have contented myself with knowing that I <u>did</u> feel deeply and tenderly for my precious sister, for you all. It has become a great task to me to <u>set about</u> writing a letter. It feels a great[er] enslavery to me to nurse than it used to when I was younger, though I never had a lovelier babe than the little one who allready begins to call me "mamma." She says many words very sweetly, tries to immitate every animal and bird she hears, is healthy, good, and said to be perfectly beautiful. As she is something of a stranger and the last, indulge me by listening to a description of her: She is very fat and solid, though she does not look burdened with it (soft and <u>mushy</u> like), her hair a rich brown, her forehead high and finely formed, her eyes very dark, just like Edmunds', full and large, and so gentle in thier expression, the most beautiful mouth. Her lips look like the inside of a conch shell, only redder, a beautiful complexion. And more than in feature or complexion there is such an angelish expression of gentle innocence in her looks, her voice. Richard and Maria[1] both say she is the most perfect little creature they ever beheld. She does not walk yet but gets on very fast on her hands and feet.

We had a visit from Aliceanna 2 weeks since. I had not seen the sweet child since last 9th moth. She has grown much, grows handsomer. Her person is elegant, her manners modest and graceful. Mother, she is as lovely as I could desire, amiable and affectionate, but the dear child has an ugly cough, which I am very uneasy about. She has had the advantage of a great deal more schooling than any of her other sisters. They dress her very nice and neat, which is more than any of us can do these hard times.[2] Indeed, it takes all my time to patch and contrive to keep us anyhow decent with our very scanty wardrobe. Margaretta, thanks to your kindness, is well provided for, and she is the only one. An old merino and 2 old calicos are all the dresses of any description I have in the world, and the rest according. Don't say "poor things." I just wrote it for fun, but it's true, though. I have not a pr of shoes fit to go to meeting with, but I am going to have and I must have a new dress, for I must, if I live, go to Salem on the 8th of next month to spend a week or 2 with my poor dear child.

Oh, my own Mother, a mother's anxieties last through life. Maria's health has been better and she looks well, but poor thing is among strangers and has no confidence in the Salem Drs. She is very nervous at night and gets up and rambles over the house as I used to. The nervine[3] makes her so sick she can't take it. I have never been to see them yet, and I do know there is no way for me to get there without my suffering real agony of terror—the fright I got last summer has so increased my fear of horses that it puts me in a cold chill even to think of getting into a carriage of any kind. But I will risk it all.

Helen has another son, Milton, premature by six weeks—though doubtful at first, seems likely to live, is 3 weeks old. She weaned her other 7 weeks before.

Samuel Holland is no more. His sufferings were dreadful. His disease was a general mortification. Oh, it was awful to see his limbs blackened and shrivelled for days before it seized on his vitals. I was with him the last 3 days in his agony. He would often express resignation and thankfulness that his mind was calm and at peace. He would say, "Oh, this agony is dreadful, but it is outward, of the flesh and of the bone. Lord, help me to bear it." He calmly heard the Dr say there was no hope, then took his hand and said, "And now, Dr, receive my parting admonition. Do justly, love mercy, and walk humbly with thy God." He gave particular direction about his coffin and burial clothes—wanting them plain and simple—and a great deal of exellent advise, when delirium seized him and continued for 48 hours, when death at last gently closed the scene. His children were with him all the time—2 weeks—except Catherine. At the hour when her dear father was departing she gave birth to a son. Oh, I do feel for them, my dear kind friends, but they had that support which never yet failed. . . .

Our wheat looks fine and does not appear to be as much injured with the fly as most of our neighbors'. Our corn very good. Sister Henrietta, honey, please excuse me for not noticing thy kind dear letters more particularly. I do love thee as ever, but thee does not know how many cares I have, and it is seldom I can get hold of a scrap of paper. And another thing. We are both too poor to indulge oftener than get Granville to ease off the postage, which he won't object to,[4] at reasonable intervals.

Well, does thee want to hear about the calves I was raising? Well, Alice (Madam's calf), had a calf 16 days before she was 2 years old, is as gentle as can be. Betty (Brindle's) was a year and 2 months old. She is gentle also and a noble milker. Ned is a grand large animal, Cherry's Bill tolerable, a match for Rodney (Brindle's), who is a year younger, and Lily, a yearling heifer of Star. We are raising 3 male calves this summer, have Granville's cow, who gives pretty smart and will be fresh in November. I have made 1 nice cheese and shall turn a curd tomorrow. We don't make more than 10 lb butter a week as I want to make 1 cheese a week and the pasture has got down, but they will go in better soon.

We cured Deborah of a severe attack of putrid sore throat in a very short time. And then violent inflamation of the lungs or pleurisy at another time after the Botanic system.[5] I am fully convinced of its efficacy. I love you all every one.

[signature smudged]

1. The original says "R and M"; as Anna rarely refers to Robert and Margaret Garrigues by first name alone, I read this as Anna's son-in-law, Richard, and daughter, Maria.
2. The Panic of 1837 was followed by economic recession and a shortage of money.
3. Nerve tonic.
4. Granville was now the postmaster at Lynchburgh.
5. Like Thomsonianism, the botanic system was an alternative medicine that relied heavily on herbal remedies derived in part, at least, from Native American medicine.

~

March 25th 1842
[from Granville]
My own dear Aunt [Sarah],

I have been for some time this evening trying to decide in my mind which one of my dear aunts I should write to and conclude to address this letter to thee. When I get to thinking of you all (which frequently happens) and feel a wish to write to some one of you, it takes me some time to conclude upon which shall bear the inflictions not only of reading my poor letter but of writing me one in return, for I always expect an answer and feel much disappointed if I recieve none. It has been so very long, my dear Aunt, since I have had the pleasure of seeing a letter from thee that I feel very desirous for thee to write me a long, very lengthy epistle that I may still feel certain sure I hold a place in the affections of an own aunt whom I have always lov'd. . . .

How many years have pass'd since I last saw thee and what changes have taken place in that time! Yet I know we would not be as strangers could we meet again. Is it generally the case that the affections become blunted by being separated for a long time from those we love? It has not been so with me. Time nor distance has not chang'd the affection I was taught to feel and naturally felt for my near relatives. . . .

I believe I must be a little selfish and occupy a portion of this in telling thee of my prospects. I consider it a duty incumbent on me as a grandson & nephew to acquaint you all of the intention I have of changing my situation in life, which, though it could not be to you, yet it will be to me an event of the greatest importance. And in view of taking such a step I very naturally feel a desire it should meet your approbation. I take it for granted that thee and all of you are acquainted of the fact to which I allude and also with the character of her whose interests with mine will be united.[1]

Now I should be much pleas'd to have your sentiments in the subject and that before the 8th of May next. . . .

Has the great Temperance reformation been agitated much in your parts? It is rapidly spreading with us. We have a regular meeting in our little village and 85 signers to the pledge. Tell Uncle Willie that nearly all of his acquaintance here have join'd. . . .

I suppose thee knew I had been keeping Bachelor's hall this last winter—or WH Garrigues[2] and myself. We had quite a merry time of it, done all the cooking except making light bread. And have even had some of the young ladies in the neighbourhood to take tea with us. I suppose they had some curiosity to see how we would go about getting a meal. They seem'd astonish'd to find us such adepts in the art of cooking, considering our practice. We have too much independence to be asham'd of anything so honourable. Hannah is now keeping house for us, and we don't have to lose quite so much time from our work in the shop.

The folks at Green Hill are in usual health, also the Salem folks. We are looking for them to pay us a visit. We see them but seldom. Richard is very industrious and always so much to do (like thy dear nephew) that he don't often get to see us. Their little Norman[3] is one of the finest children I ever knew. We receiv'd a letter by last mail from Uncle Willie Farquhar and Aunt Margaret on the subject of Hannah's going to live with them. It was the first I had hear'd of the project. I believe she is very anxious to go, and for my part I should not have the least objection if they feel desirous it should be so. I am well satisfied 'twould be much to her advantage, as her opportunities for improvement in many things have been too limited and I should think this as good a chance as could possibly offer—but I would wish the advantage to be mutual and have no sacrifice made on either side. The rest will have to speak for themselves. . . . With much love to all I subscribe myself thy ever affectionate nephew, Granville S Bentley

    PS Don't forget to write soon.

1. Elizabeth Garrigues, his cousin from Marlborough, and daughter of William and Hannah Garrigues. They married in 1843.
2. The younger brother of Elizabeth.
3. Born in 1840.

~

Anna's second-oldest daughter, Hannah, went to Maryland in 1842 to live with her uncle and aunt, Richard and Mary Brooke. Anna hoped she would broaden her horizons and get some of the education that was lacking in Columbiana County.

    In June, Anna's son Edmunds died, age twelve. By chance Isaac Briggs had arrived home from Georgia about this time, so Elizabeth wasn't writing to him the family news, and no letters from Anna survive relating to her son's death. A notice in the Salem newspapers does not record how he died. Was he sickly? Was he carried away by a sudden illness? Was Anna grief-stricken, or stoical? We have no way of knowing. That fall she gave birth to her last child, Joseph Garrigues Bentley. By the end of the year, her loss of Edmunds had been compounded by others.

~

[December 1842]
My own dear Mother,

How shall I tell thee? Oh, my mother, my precious darling, my lovely, beautiful Margaretta is gone from us here forever. How hard the struggle to say, "Lord thy will be done." He only can know. She had entwined herself so closely round all our hearts. And while bowed down in affliction, my heart has yearned towards my dear Hannah. How will she bear it? Oh, comfort and soothe her. Tell her that this fiery furnace may consume the dross and leave the pure gold. I cannot be as particular as I would wish, for I am worn down with anxiety and grief.

She was taken with ulcerated sore throat and oppression of the breast on 2nd day the 7th, 11th [month], was very poorly for several days. Caroline was also very ill with it. Alban was also confined to his bed for several days, though not with sore throat. Aliceanna was taken and was very bad a week. Margaretta got a great deal better so as to be up and about at play. Her appetite returned and we thought she had come off well with the dreaded Scarlet fever when no others of her age escaped. A sudden change to severely cold weather occured, and though she had not been out or exposed, on 6th day the 18th she complained of being cold and sleepy. Elizabeth laid her on the bed. She slept 2 or 3 hours and waked. Vomiting broke out thickly, high fever succeeded, dreadful sore mouth and tongue. But I cannot describe her dreadful sufferings. She died 1/2 past 10 PM 4th day night, 23rd. Little Henry was burried that morning. Let Cousin B[etsy Thomas] know it.[1]

On the 16th my little Joseph appeared languid and drowsy. He had a very bad cold that affected his breast, and he seemed choked with phlegm. The dreadful disease was stealing upon my angel babe! On 4th day WH Garrigues rode Bet up to Salem to let them know. In an hour's time Maria was on horseback, left Norman with Richard who was to take him to Evergreen the next day. Poor Maria arrived after dark. It was very cold and stormy and her horse very rough. She was much outdone, but it was a great comfort. She stood by her poor agonized father to watch the release of the loved one from her excruciating sufferings, for I could not be there. I was downstairs with my babe in my arms.

They laid her in quiet sleep at last by her brother. I could not go to [the] grave. I sat up 9 nights in succession, sometimes getting an hour or 2 sleep in the day. And Oh, my mother, I have given up my last little one. We are watching for his release. I think I can say "and thy will be done," but Oh, the breaking up of the close tender ties have laid me as in the dust.

My precious cousin Margaret has been with me for several days. Franklin and Maria were obliged to leave us this morn.

7th day morning 12 mo 11th
My dear Grandmother,

Mother had told thee mournful news indeed. I have only time now to add to the melancholy tidings. Last evening the sweet spirit of our little brother returned to the God who gave him to us for a little space. Thee will know how to communicate the sad intelligence to poor Hannah. I fear for her but trust she may by Divine help be enabled to bear it as a Christian should. Had she only known the extreme suffering from which they have been released, she would feel only sentiments of gratitude and deep thankfulness. Mother bears it wonderfully. I could hardly have hoped to see such resignation. Granville will add some adieu, my dear friends.

12 mo 23rd 1842

I wrote in such haste that the foregoing lines are scarcely intelligible and was then too late for the mail. Granville wrote, however, and I expect you have ere this received the melancholy intelligence of our sudden bereavement. Granville and I were from home last week and do not know whether you have yet heard the sad particulars, therefore will add some to this to send by tomorrow's mail. The dreaded disease seems to have subsided as we hear of no new cases among children. The family at Green Hill have entirely recovered. They have moved down to Franklin's house. It is smaller and they think will be more comfortable during the winter, besides being near the spring, which will render it more convenient.[2]

Granville and myself were on a visit at Evergreen. My dear father last week found them well. Franklin and Sister Hannah have a young son 5 weeks old; they call him Clarence.[3] Sis looks very well. Franklin is working at his trade. Uncle Robert's family have regained their usual health. Thomas and Deborah B are going to school near home. Please give my love to Hannah and our friends with a large share for thyself. I will subscribe myself thy affectionate Granddaughter,
Elizabeth G Bentley

Dear Friends,

I can only add a few words. This letter, or Mother's part of it, was sent down 2 weeks since to go by mail but did not arrive in time. Our being away will account for another week's delay. I have not had a chance yet of writing to Uncle WH B[riggs] in answer to a letter from them rec'd sometime since, and did not feel willing to give encouragement without some more certain prospect of complying than I have at present. I do not suppose that all the property I have at this time would sell for the amount of his claim in cash. And although I have 3 times the amt on Book besides, not one dollar have I been able to get. But I shall do all in my power to assist them.

In haste, GS Bentley

1. Little Henry probably was Henry Hall, Helen's son, and Cousin B therefore would have been Cousin Betsy Thomas.

2. An old foundation, overgrown by brambles and vines, still exists down near the stream on the property. This may have been Franklin's house.

3. Unfortunately, Clarence's life was brief. On April 30, 1843, Elizabeth Briggs wrote to Isaac in Georgia that there was no news from Ohio "save that thy favorite Hannah G. Bentley had lost her sweet little Clarence."

FIVE

1843–1847

In early 1843, Hannah Bentley apparently bolted from Sandy Spring. On April 8, Elizabeth Briggs wrote to her brother Isaac in Georgia, "We have not heard a word from Hannah since she left Washington, so cannot tell thee what has become of her, whether she has gone to Iowa or really to Green Hill or not."

At some point in her stay with the Brooke family Hannah had become deeply unhappy. Life there may have been harder than she expected it to be. Perhaps she was simply homesick, especially after the deaths of her brother and sister. While Anna dropped some hints much later about the nature of her daughter's dissatisfaction, it is never made perfectly clear. One can infer from Anna's letters that Hannah was a difficult girl who tried her mother's patience.

Whatever drove her away from Sandy Spring, not everyone sympathized. Certainly not her Aunt Elizabeth. Later, Hannah herself looked back on her stay in Maryland with a mixture of nostalgia and regret.

In May, she wrote from Green Hill that except for her mother and her sister Deborah, the family had all had whooping cough. She herself had been bedridden for two weeks with an inflammation of the lungs for which the doctor had bled her. And Deborah had been felled by "some kind of fits that the Dr pronounces a species of Catalepsy," as Elizabeth relayed the news to Isaac. It was the first instance of what would become years of ill health for Deborah.

More than once Hannah or Anna asked for Isaac's address, but Isaac seems to have gone into hiding from his kin at Green Hill. In July, Elizabeth wrote to him, "We got a letter from Ohio yesterday & Hannah does want to know where Uncle Isaac is but we write this week & will answer as slightly as possible giving no precise clue." With Elizabeth (and Isaac), a bad taste lingered from Hannah's visit for years.

On December 30, Elizabeth told Isaac they had gotten a letter from Anna saying they had fifteen cats and that "Deborah's health is restored she says. <u>She</u> [Deborah] has joined the Baptists & Hannah the Methodist soci-ety & she [Anna] made no comments." The New Garden Monthly Meet-ing records confirm the news. Both young women were dismissed from the meeting.

⁓

3rd mo 16th [1844]
[to Sarah Stabler]
My own dear Sister Sarah,

I begin this to thee but expect it will run into a family letter, as we write so seldom nowadays it seems as if I must not separate you. Dear Sister Henrietta used to write to me, but as I did not write particularly to her she never writes to me now, and Sister Mary—I did dare to hope she would write in my seasons of sore trial. She did not one word, and I give that up, though I do not beleive it costs her any greater effort to write than it does me.

We received a letter last week from the children at Berea [Ohio]. They speak in high terms of the school.[1] Hannah's health is much better. She keeps house for Thomas. They have 1 boarder. They rent (very low, 50 cents per week) two furnished rooms in the same house where AliceA boards and works 6 hours for her board and tuition.'I expect Aliceanna will return the last of next month and Deborah take her place. She has some symptoms of dyspepsia but looks fat and hearty, has had no return of her nervous disorder.

She has taken a notion in her head that she almost torments me with talking about and that is to go to live with her grandmother or somewhere in the neighbourhood where she could be with you all. Says she would never want to leave you as Hannah did or be a burden for she knows your circumstances and never would be ashamed to work for you. I tell her that Hannah talked so before she went and that still her aunt had to keep hired help. Her reply is, "Mother, thee knows it would not be so with me. And Hannah never would be contented long in one place, and she has a great many proud notions that I never had." She says true. So far her disposition is more amiable than her sister's. Her temper is not so violent, and she has less of selfishness, is much more cheerful and could be happy anywhere she was beloved. You never heard anyone sing sweeter. Her voice is much finer than Hannah's though she is thought to be a good singer. Her cousin Sally Ann Garrigues[2] expects to go to her aunt when she can find suitable company, and I expect that has got Deborah in this notion.

Now I have written this to get rid of her bother and not with any expectation that such a thing as her going can take place; for even if desirable to you, we are utterly unable to find means to send her by public conveyance and know you are too.[3] The money Hannah borrowed from Hastings has never been paid. Her father has had 4 suits against him this winter and property under execution for them. By hard scraping and selling produce we needed to supply us with clothing, he has just paid them off. He has one other debt, something over $20, besides the Dr's bills, and his health and strength have failed him very much this year past.

A very clever man has just taken a lease for 5 years to clean 10 or 12 acres, is building a cabin, will assist him on the farm. He has a clever wife and 2 little children—James and Clarissa Hayes. He expects to move the 1st of next month.

Our flannel is very nice. Deborah and I have each a black and brown dress made. Hannah and Aliceanna have each a black 1, Caroline a brown which she made <u>all</u> herself, except the hooks and eyes, very neatly and strong. She run the tuck and all. I basted it for her. She began it 2nd day evening and made the skirt and finished it 3rd day, beside milking, washing dishes, sweeping, &c. And yesterday she made a loaf of bread and baked it nicely in the reflector and made and baked short cakes for supper. She is a very smart, though a very troublesome, child. Her constant activity and restlessness when left at random, or without proper aim or direction, makes her so. And Alban is just a matter-of-fact child, was intended for a very good one if bad example and bad management do not sow evil in his guileless affectionate heart.

Oh, one thing I forgot when I was telling of our dresses. Jos had some nice cloth, dark mixed. Hannah spun it before she went to Maryland, and it has been much admired. Well, he got a taylor to cut out a frock coat for him, and I made it a week or two since, and I think it looks as nice as if any taylor had made it and charged 4 dollars for it. I have got to be quite an <u>expert</u> seamstress. If practice makes perfect, I ought to be.

You will no doubt be glad to hear that Richard has gained his suit and recovered his property in Salem, the expences not exceeding $30 and much anxiety of mind. I am anxiously expecting <u>tidings</u> from Franklin's precious wife.[4] I would that you could personally know these my children. They call me Mother, and my heart accords them fully a mother's love. They are altogether lovely and precious in my eyes. You have had frequent descriptions of our sweet Norman. I can hardly trust myself to speak of William,[5] he seemed to come to fill up an aching void in my heart. The same sweet, beautiful dark eyes. And when he looks up and fixes thier earnest loving gaze on mine, it is my own my precious youngest born, restored to life and beauty, that I again press to my bosom. Last 7th day he was just the age of my little one. He is just the size and strongly resembles him. There never was a babe kept sweeter and cleaner and dressed prettier than his mother keeps him.

I hope thee will write soon a great long letter, and dear Mother I love to see thy writting and always <u>cry at it</u>. Sister Elizabeth, thee art a <u>baggage</u>. Why don't thee write? If I knew where to direct to Isaac, I would write. Tell him to please write to us and give my love to him. Always tell of him when you write. My love to every individual that loves me. Thy tenderly affectionate sister, Anna.

My dear Aunt,

I think I promis'd thee a particular description of our boy, & how <u>anxiously</u> thee may have wish'd & looked for it I know not. Let it suffice for me to say he bears some resemblance to other human beings of his age, size, and colour, sits alone, has 2 teeth, laughs, squeals, crys but seldom, and gets his living in the usual way for such little folks. To say he is one of the best is no more than everyone says who knows him—& that he is very pretty no more than every parent thinks of their firstborn. Concerning ourselves, we have been bless'd with good health, contented minds, plenty of work to keep us out of mischief, & dispositions to feel thankful for the many blessings we recieve. . . .

We are making a great effort for our canal again, and there are strong hopes entertain'd now of its completion, which will make business much more lively with us. I wish Uncle William Henry Briggs to know I have not forgotten him and that I have felt griev'd not to have it in my power to assist him as yet. Some debts I unavoidably contracted since have been urged in such a manner that I was obliged to pay every cent I could raise or suffer my property to be sacrificed. This much encouragement I can give: that I contract no debts nor have not but a mere trifle for 18 months past and feel in honour bound to pay as soon as possible. . . . Thy loving Nephew, G.S. Bentley

1. Probably the school run by Alfred Holbrook, with the support of the eccentric John Baldwin, who eventually endowed several colleges, including Baldwin-Wallace in Berea and institutions in Kansas and Louisiana. Holbrook followed the educational principles of his father, Josiah Holbrook, who "sought to teach a popularized form of natural science and to combine manual labor with education," says Baldwin's biographer. Pupils could help pay for their education by working in Dwight Holbrook's shop manufacturing scientific apparatus, such as globes, or at one of Baldwin's mills. According to Holbrook's memoirs, the school in Berea soon drew students from "abroad," including Hannah and Abram Wileman of Marlborough. The Wilemans would have been the Bentleys' connection with Holbrook's school; Hannah later married Anna's cousin Samuel Brooke. Holbrook was superintendent of the Marlborough schools briefly in the 1850s.
2. The daughter of MEG and RHG, born in 1824.
3. On March 30, Elizabeth Briggs wrote to Isaac, "We got a letter from Ohio yesterday, Sister Anna enquires very particularly after thee, wishes to know <u>where</u> thee is & <u>what</u> thee is about, <u>if</u> they <u>knew</u> they wd. <u>write</u> to thee &c She mentioned too that Deborah was very anxious to come & live with her grandmother if she only had the means to bring her, <u>she</u> wd. not get dissatisfied & unhappy like Hannah, for she had not such <u>proud notions</u> & knew our circumstances & wd. not be <u>ashamed to work</u> for us &c. &c. There were several more allusions to Hannah['s] <u>'ways'</u> that candidly told of their consciousness of the strangeness & impropriety of <u>her</u> behaviour while here & a few comparisons drawn in Deborahs favor. None of us <u>have</u> the <u>means</u> & therefore as <u>they</u> are not able to furnish them, she will not have the opportunity to make the trial. What wd. thee think of it if it <u>could</u> be done? I wd. like to <u>see</u> the gal & get acquainted with her, but I fear it wd. be a very dangerous experiment. How could they or any of us foresee what circumstances might occur that wd. render <u>her</u> just as <u>unhappy</u> as <u>Hannah</u> was?"
4. Pregnant with their second child, Walter, who was born on March 9.
5. William G., oldest child of Granville and Elizabeth, born in 1843.

~

Deborah's ill health continued, inspiring a rather waspish comment from Elizabeth Briggs to Isaac in a letter of May 25, 1844: "From our Bentley relatives in Ohio we have lately received sorrowful intelligence, in an indirect way. Sister Mary dined here last first day. Said a few days before Cousin Betsy Thomas told her she had had a letter from cousin Peggy & she said in it 'she did pity poor cousin Anna, Deborah had been attacked again with those cataleptic fits & they now employed a Dr who said <u>if</u> she recovered, & that was doubtful, she wd. either be a maniac or an idiot.' . . . From the specimens thee gave of their prudence & careful habits I never had had any idea since, they <u>any</u> of them, could ever enjoy <u>tolerable</u> health. We can't <u>help</u> them, not even our <u>sympathy</u> can do anything for them it only <u>pains</u> ourselves, & we must let them go, poor misguided fools!"

∾

July 20th 1844
[from Granville]
My Dear Grandmother,

The enclosed was sent for me to add some to go by late mail, but was too late. I percieve, in glancing it over, thee has a complete catalogue of all Deborah's complaints & ailments with nothing else by way of variety. We are all, as far as my knowledge extends, enjoying good health. We hear from Salem frequently, also from Community.[1] All seem to be getting along finely. It has been a very busy time for us, for 2 or 3 weeks past, with harvesting, and if it had not been for a heavy rain we had yesterday, thee would'nt have the pleasure of hearing from thy <u>dear grandson</u> at this time. I have been assisting Father with his harvesting. We just finish'd securing the hay & got one load of wheat hauled in before the rain. Grain is tolerably good just in this neighbourhood, though but a few miles from us it has fail'd almost entirely in places. Spring crops look unusually fine. Our harvest has never been so early. We find no difficulty in getting enough to eat & wear, if we have a mind to work for it.

I intended filling this but was prevented by someone coming in, & 'tis time for the mail. Please write often & particularly. Our boy grows, laughs a good deal, crys a little, and is about as interesting as most chaps his age & <u>complexion</u>. We have a <u>most excellent</u> garden, a <u>first</u>-rate cow, a . . . calf, two fine shoats & a <u>splendid</u> pig. And better than all do we consider our own <u>precious selves</u>. With much love, I am thy loving Grandson, G.S. Bentley.
And I love thee too, dear Grandmother.
EGB

1. Several of their activist relatives, including Edward Brooke and Elizabeth Luken, had formed an experimental anti-capitalistic Christian community near Marlborough.

∾

10th mo 23rd 1844
[By way of Sally Ann Garrigues]
My own dear Mother & Sister,

You must, you can't help, loving the precious girl who will carry this letter to you. She is a most lovely, affectionate and industrious girl. We all love her tenderly. Many a night has she sat up here in sickness and

sorrow sharing and bearing a part as one of our own. Do you make some
effort to become acquainted with her that she may soon lose the feeling
that she is far from home, among strangers.

I went down to Granville's yesterday, the first time I have been there
for 2 months. I staid till this evening. Mother, my sons' wives are indeed
to me as Ruth was to Naomi. I love them as my own flesh. Oh, how I do
wish you could see my grandsons. Norman is a fine, noble-looking boy,
the picture of health—very fair and rosy. They (Richard, wife, and child)
paid us a visit of a few days 10 days ago. Franklin, his wife, and thier
beautiful little Walter were down 2 weeks ago. Walter looks very like his
father at his age, though fairer and more delicate. He has not entirely
recovered from an attack of catarh on the lungs. His dear mother always
reminds me of Sister Deborah.

But our own sweet William is with us so often we can engage his
little heart to know and love us. He is so like our angel Margaretta. His
beautiful bright eyes are hers, his soft, glossy brown hair, his loving gaze.
He came to fill a void. He is as "the apple of mine eye." His dear parents
are very judicious in thier management, always gentle but firm. Elizabeth
is a woman of deep understanding and highly cultivated mind, gentle,
free from selfishness, and truly pious. William is in constant search of
employment. I can't say he has ever walked much, for he runs.

Joseph sat up last night with an aged man who has for some months
been afflicted with dropsy. He died this morning, and J assisted in the
last sad offices. The billious fever (in many instances combined or
running into typhus) has been very prevalent in some parts of this
neighbourhood this fall.[1]

I can scarcely remember when or what I wrote last to you, but I
think Deborah was then on the mind. Poor thing. She got so that she
was able to visit about. She went with Granville and Elizabeth 25 miles
to Marlboro to Cousin William Garrigues's the last week in the 8th mo,
was caught in a shower of rain. She had had symptoms of her nervous
disorder and dyspepsia for a week previous. She returned more poorly.
For 4 weeks she did not retain 1 mouthful of anything she swallowed,
not even a spoonful of water—would be 9 days without a passage, and if
she took anything, it would run into diahorea, retention of urine, 36 and
48 hours headache, and pain in the side sometimes so violent, like a
stich, that she would scream when she moved. Sometimes she would
have chills succeeded by stupor and insensibility for hours. Twice we sent
in the night for the Dr. She seemed a good deal better last week, but for
several days past the vomiting has returned. The Dr advises flannel next

her skin, great attention to her diet, no medicine when it can be avoided, her bowels kept regular by injections, to ride on horseback as soon as she is able. Her liver is deeply affected and she has dyspepsia. Granville and Elizabeth want her to come down and stay with them, and I hope in a few days she will be able. I have never left her to visit any of my neighbors till last week I went down to Cousin R's and yesterday.

Jos has got his seeding all done. He put in 13 acres himself with his oxen, and a neighbor put in a 5-acres field for 1/2 our corn crop. Exellent. We had no peaches this year but plenty of apples. Ours was the only orchard in this neighbourhood that had any. We dried 9 bushels, sold 32 at 25 per bushel, gave away more than 12, and have a good many for winter use.

Now, Mother, I will make a request once more. Please inform us where in Georgia Bro Isaac is, how to direct a letter to him, what is he doing, what his prospects, circumstances. Remember, he is my own beloved brother and I have no means of hearing from him but through you. And the little that has been said has not been enough to satisfy me.

Sometime since, for a week or two, the power of writing rhyme came to me, and then left me as entirely as before. While the spell was on, I wrote some which maybe you would like to have. The 1st was to my mother 2nd mo 10, 1844:

Oh Mother—my Mother—that name fondly dear,
With tenderness thrills through the chords of my heart,
And a thousand fond memories call up the tear
From my eyelids is gushing emotion to start.
I have call'd on thy name in dark seasons of woe
And long'd to be press'd to thy bosom again.
I have mourn'd for the solace thy words could bestow,
When my heart has been bow'd in affliction and pain.
And, Oh, if we meet on this earth never more,
May we meet where no parting shall torture the breast;
Where grief and affliction forever are o'er,
And the careworn and weary shall sweetly find rest.
There the babes of my bosom in purity bloom,
Now safe and unscathed from the "Evils to come."
All sinless and pure they were laid in the tomb,
And thier Father to Heaven has taken them home.

Ten little children, all under 7 years of age, are the only occupants of the graveyard at our meeting house. Cousin MEG's grandson, Milton Hall,[2] was laid there one morning and her lovely little Margarettia the evening. She was a twin sister in affection and gentleness and beauty to my own lost Margaretta. As such I loved her. On visiting her grave I wrote the following, 2nd mo 14, 1844:

1st
This lovely spot is "holy ground"
To many a mother's heart;
Fair buds of promise 'neath each mound
Were crush'd by death's keen dart.
2nd
The sinless ones who here repose
Ne'er felt the withering blight
Of baleful passions, earthly woes
To dim thier spirits light.
3rd
Two little graves in one sad day
We stood beside in grief:
A fair young boy beneath the clay [In the margin: Helen's Milton]
His days on earth were brief.
4th
And here sweet Margaret we made
Thy little lowly bed.
With smitten hearts thy form here laid
The cold earth o'er thy head
5th
Lovely thou wert and fondly loved,
Soft was thy lovelit eye.
Too pure for earth thou wert remov'd
To dwell in bliss on high.
6th
Thy memory within my breast
With my sweet babes is shrined.
Your happy spirits with the blest
In blissful joy are join'd.

On viewing the locks of hair of my departed children 3rd mo 17th, 1844:

These treasured locks of shining hair
Shaded thier angel foreheads fair;
Cleft from each pale and death-cold brow,
They are all of you that's left me now.
As to my lips they're proudly prest,
They stir fond memories in my breast.
I fix on them my mournful gaze,
A mother's tears bedew my face.
Those soul-lit eyes again I see
That beam'd so lovingly on me.
Again your voices lov'd I to hear,
Your merry voices sweet and dear,
And then I see you smitten lie,
And watch each dim and closing eye.
The pallid brow, the failing breath,
When passing through the Shades of Death.
Then comes a sweet, consoling voice.
It bids me weep not, but rejoice
That you from every ill set free
Are bless'd through all Eternity.
No sorrowing sigh or sad farewell
Is heard in Heaven where you dwell.
I would not call you back again
To bind you with Earth's gathering chain.
But when life's toils with me are o'er,
Oh may we meet to part no more.

6th day morning—Deborah seems much better this morning. She has not been from the house for many weeks till this morning. She wanted to see poor Uncle Milborne[3] once more, and as it is only across 2 of our fields, with Hannah and Caroline to lean on, she has gone to take a last look at the kind old man who loved everybody and was lov'd by all.

I expect it is my time of life maybe that makes me more prone than formerly to spells of gloom and depression. Such a one has overshaddowed my mind so this morning that it is well I am near the end of my paper, for you know I can't write one way and feel another. I am subject to <u>very</u> frequent and <u>weak spells this summer</u>. Oh, if I could only raise the means to come and see thee once more, my own dear Mother, how soon I would come. But it may not be. I do not know whether Hannah has written to any of you or not, but if she has not I expect it is because she had no paper. Indeed, it is pinching times for us to get anything now we don't raise, and we live so far from the store.

They have elected our dear Dr. George Fries for Congress. (He is a Democrat.)[4] Will sister Mary never write or send me a message of love? It is as great a task to me to write as ever it was to her. I love you all with tender affection,

Anna Bentley

1. According to John Gunn in his 1837 *Domestic Medicine, or Poor Man's Friend,* to fight bilious fever, you must "divest yourself of irresolution and timidity in the commencement of the attack." He recommends large doses of calomel and jalap, a "good puke" of tartar emetic followed by chamomile tea. "When the fever comes on, <u>bleed freely</u>."
2. Second son of Helen Garrigues Hall.
3. Joseph Milbourn built a sawmill in West Township with Jacob Thomas in 1831. Decades later, after it had changed hands and been rebuilt, it was still known as Milbourn's Mill.
4. George Fries, a Hanover doctor, was a member of the 29th Congress, House of Representatives, from 1839 to 1841.

∽

Brook Meadow[1] October the 28, 1844
[from Hannah]
My Dear Grandmother,

I thought it would not be right to let so good an opportunity pass by unimproved and so will indeavor to write, if it is only a few lines to thee. I had intended writing a letter to each one of my aunts, but as I am too <u>rotten</u> <u>poor</u> to get paper whenever I want it, I had to give up the idea of filling more than one sheet. And perhaps it is well enough so, for I do not feel very interesting these <u>hard times</u>.

Sister Deborah and I came here yesterday from meeting, and as it is so wet and rainy we shall have to stay awhile. I guess Sister Deborah is quite smart again. She seems to enjoy herself very much. I feel very much in hopes that if she will be careful and not expose herself that she may yet enjoy good health. I expect Mother has told all the particulars concerning her sickness, so I will not take the time to do it over again.

Oh, my precious Grandmother, how glad I should be to recieve letters from you all. Indeed I have thought real hard of my Dear Uncle and Aunt Farquhar for not writing one line to me since I left them. Or perhaps I am too fast. I believe I did recieve a few lines from them about 12 months previous. I am well aware, my Dearly beloved Friends, that I was the cause of a great deal of trouble and anxiety whilst with [you] and that I was not worthy your love, but still I <u>believed</u> that you did love me notwithstanding the fact that I felt that I was not deserving. You all know the bitter, bitter trials through which I had to pass. I must say they were almost more than I could bear. But it is useless for me to recall the past which wrings this aching breast. When I think of you it seems as though 'twere all a <u>dream</u> that I once <u>dwelt</u> among you and felt that you <u>loved</u> me. I know, yes, I have proved by experience, that it is wrong to set the mere creature above the <u>CREATOR</u>. I wish to love <u>every</u> body throughout the wide <u>world</u>, both black and white, rich and poor. . . .

    Hannah B Bentley

1. Robert and Margaret Garrigues's farm was known as Brook Meadow.

Brook Meadow
October the 28, 1844
[from Hannah, under same cover as above]
Dear Aunt Sarah,

I have just time to say a few words to thee. . . . I am in such a <u>splutter</u> to get up in the other room to talk with Dear Sally before I have to leave. She expects to start for Maryland tomorrow morning. I know you will love her. I believe she is a good girl and intends to do her duty as nearly as she possibly can. The weather looks rather unfavourable for travelling now. It is snowing quite fast. We have had a great deal of wet weather this fall. I was surprised to hear that thy Spot had been converted into a dwelling House. I expect it is pleasant to have your Friends so near. It will not feel now as if you were alone. Oh, Dear Aunt, when I think of the happy, happy hours I have spent with you at Sharon, I cannot ref[rain] from tears. I seem to see you around the cheerful [people all] enjoying each other's society. It seems strange to think that I was once amoung that happy land. I can truly say that my happiest hours were spent with you at Sharon. There I could have the society of my precious Grand Mother and you, my kind Aunts. Please tell the dear children that their cousin Hannah loves them as tenderly as she once did. Now, my own dear Aunt Sarah, do please write to thy Neice who loves thee more than words could express. I want thee to tell Aunt Mary that I would have written to her if I had of been supplied with paper. Give my warmest love to her and all the rest of the families. Has Hannah's health improved? I feel very anxious to hear. Have you heard from <u>Dear naughty Uncle Isaac</u>? Please give my love to him when thee writes. I really must conclude as my hands are so numb that I cannot write with any degree of sattisfaction. . . . Farewell, my Dear Aunt. I remain, as ever, thine.

Hannah B Bentley

My Dear Grandmother, I wish that I had time to write more to thee. I will just ask thee to give my love to my own Dear Uncle Willie and Aunt M Farquhar. . . . They were kind to me while I was with them, and I shall never never forget it. I wrote to them while I was at Berea [Ohio], but have never received an answer. So I just concluded that they did not care enough about me to wish to keep up a correspondence. But perhaps it is all for the best, so I will not murmur about it. . . . Hannah

∾

Sally Ann Garrigues was well received by the relatives back in Maryland. Sarah Stabler wrote to Isaac in May 1845 that she had just met her for the first time and found her to be "a girl of good sense & excellent principles," but not in good health. She was in the care of a relative, Dr. Magruder.

About this time, Sarah Stabler made a point of writing to her brother, who was still in Athens, Georgia. In fact, she reassured him, "I shall not so bind myself to any others as to make me overlook or neglect my duty to thee. I have hitherto endeavored to be as punctual as circumstances wd admit of, have declined taking <u>any</u> part scarcely in the correspondence with the Ohioans, & slipped out of some others that I might be wholly devoted to thee."

In June, Elizabeth wrote to Isaac the news of <u>Hannah Bentley's</u> marriage to <u>John Preston</u>, conveyed by Granville "in two or three lines, no comment or remark any way, only the simple fact stated." Although Elizabeth noted that Henrietta Briggs had described him as "a very clever young man & in very easy circumstances," she also took the opportunity to score on Hannah, adding, "I feel sympathy for both parties. What does thee say to it?"

About the same time, Sally Ann Garrigues's health was failing. According to Elizabeth, she was suffering from dysentery and hemorrhages, and her teeth were so loose she was afraid to touch them with her tongue. It was clear she was going to be unable to work for her Aunt Betsy Thomas this summer.

In August, Maria Bentley Garrigues sent her grandmother a snuffbox containing locks of hair from their family. As Elizabeth wrote to Isaac, Maria spoke very highly of her sister Aliceanna and Aliceanna's devotion to the sick Deborah. Elizabeth also passed on Sally Ann Garrigues's opinion of Hannah's marriage: "Sally Ann told me her husband was 19, one of 15 children & a methodist preacher, & one of whom she had made much fun before she left there. I reckoned she learned better manners afterwards."

As the summer ended, Sally Ann's health was the topic of much comment. From being a help to her relatives she became a burden, spending weeks in bed with a cousin at her side as nurse.

～

[no date; Fall 1845]
My dearly beloved Mother,

Forgive me once more for my long neglect. I do believe if notice had been taken sooner of my letters by Sally Ann I should have made strong efforts to have conquered my propensity of putting off writing and to thee, at least, preformed my duty better. But I took it for granted that my exertion then would meet with a prompt return and suffered the greatest uneasiness of mind for a long time, and then got a little spunky, not considering that you could not know how my time was taken up— part of the time in anxious watching over my poor Deborah, whose agonizing sufferings for weeks left my mind and body weak and enervated, but still craving your words of sympathy.

Then Hannah's marriage called for so much exertion of mind and body. It was so little we had to give the poor child. I had to make and scratch and contrive, make bran new things out of old. I fitted up her Aunt Margaret's wedding dress for her, and they were married in Deborah's sick room, Deborah propped up with pillows, none present but our particular family, Granville and wife, the minister, and Alexander's brother. Aliceanna got a nice supper—she roasted her pet goose.

Alexander is to a day one year younger than Hannah. He was 21 the 28th of last month. His parents, Peter and Abi Preston, are highly respectable, from Lynchburg, Virginia. They had a family of 16 children. One of them died at 2 years old, a married daughter died two years ago, thier oldest son Dr Charles P (an eminent physician) died last summer.[1] All the rest are living, 9 single. One is a Dr, 3 are Methodist ministers. There are 6 as lovely, intelligent girls as I know anywhere: Mary, Eloisa Maria, Sarah Ann, Minerva, Eliza, and Charlotte. They have a farm the size of ours, a large ellegant brick house (which Peter built himself; he was a mason). He works hard like Joseph, for he has not had a great deal of help from his boys. Several of the girls have taught schools (they are well-quallified), Mary is a milliner.

Alexander is tall and slender, goodlooking, has dark auburn hair (some say <u>red</u>, but it is not exactly), black eyes, very fair skin, a sweet mouth, white teeth. He is rather reserved in his manners, serious (for one so young) among strangers, but lively and cheerfull with his friends, affectionate, and very pious. He was in delicate health when they were married and remained so through the summer till 6 or 8 weeks ago he was taken extremely ill, and for 2 or 3 weeks his friends and anxious wife were in painful suspense. He was at his father's. Hannah went to him, and I sat up many nights with him, but he has recovered his health and has put up a cabin on his father's place, which they expect to move into in a few weeks. He is going to work on the farm, to the shares. They will have to be very economical, for it is but little each of their parents can give them.

Poor Jos fails very fast. His hair is very grey, his earlocks white as silver, his face thin and furrowed, and he is very lame in his feet. He works to the utmost limits of his strength; and the crops this year failed so he was struggling to pay part to all his creditors—and had settled part with all but one, and that was the largest debt, which he expected to pay half of this winter when he got out his wheat. The man bought a farm and traded off that note with many others to a hard man, the owner of the farm. He immediately put all in the squire's hand with orders to push. Jos's is 75 dollars. He says if he can make up half of it by New Year's, he will withdraw suit, pay costs, and wait till spring. I don't know what will be done. His tax amounts to nearly 10 dollars this year, and that must be made up.

I wish I wouldn't write so.

I am glad the time has come to put on my flannel dresses, for I shall wear them all winter, and maybe by summertime I may be able to supply summer's wants. We shall have plenty to eat, plenty of wood, a good stove, good beds and beddings, that being in debt can't deprive us of. But as for poor dear Brother Willy, we cannot pay him yet. Jos has lamented often that he ever took anything at the sale.

I dread to think of next Spring, for poor Deborah. Dr Fries* says if the periodical habit could only be broken (her attacks come on at the same time every spring) he would have hopes, if she could only travel awhile previous, <u>but poverty forbids</u>. Her shoulders both slip out of place that she is not able to wash, scrub, or lift, but she is smart with her needle, an exellent knitter. She is cheerful. Oh, if you would hear her sing. Her voice is perfect melody. She has perfect command, can noise it to the highest note or sink to the lowest with ease. If she hears a tune over, she knows it. Hannah sings sweetly, but nothing to compare with her. She has been in Salem going to school (for which Thomas pays) since the 8th mo, will come home next week.

Thomas has taken a school to teach 4 months 24 miles from here, at the expiration of which he expects to locate himself at Green Hill to farm the place. And in the summer I expect he will be married to a lovely, intelligent, well-educated girl, Ruth Anna McMillan. She is 18 years of age. Her mother is a widow with 2 children: Joel, a young man older than Ruth Anna, and her. She has everything necessary for housekeeping and 8 hundred dollars, the full approbation of her friends of the choice she has made. She lives near Salem. The girls Deborah and Aliceanna are well-acquainted with her. Thomas brought her here on a visit and we all love her. You need not say much about it when you write (though they make no secret of thier intentions). She belongs to our meeting.[2]

Alice at now past 17 is the mainspring in the machinery of this family, full of life, health, and cheerfullness, a favourite wherever she is known. Oh, how you would love her. Caroline, 12, is large of her age, has dark brown hair, blue eyes, good features, fair, smoothe complexion, maybe will be the handsomest of all; uncommon quick perceptions, great perseverance ~~when her mind is fixed on anything~~, great constructiveness. She will make an exellent seamstress, an exellent writer, & she <u>can</u> be as smart a girl as I ever saw—and often is as troublesome a one. She is affectionate, will make a very smart, talented woman, and a naughty one.

4th day, 12. Well, I am the sole occupant of this house today. Poor Jos is limping through the mud away to New Garden, 7 miles, to try to collect 2 dollars that has been owing him 3 or 4 years and which he has walked there for at least 15 times. Aliceanna and Caroline have gone to Hanover to see a great Menagerie (I forget how to spell it). Four elephants hitched to a waggon bring the musicians. Seventy grey horses bring in the cages of lions, tigers, leopards, &c &c &c. They never saw anything of the kind. Alice got her admission fee with butter, and Alban had treasured up till now a shilling his Uncle Isaac gave him. I gave Caroline 2 quarts of chestnuts which she sold for hers, and Granville takes charge of them. All the rest of us have seen the wild beasts. Happy children! I enjoy thier pleasure as much as I did my own.

I officiated (for the first time) today in capacity of clerk to the preparative meeting,[3] came home and fed the hogs and myself and it seemed so quiet I thought it would be my best chance to finish this, for when the children get home I expect they will talk ever on for days. Thomas has bought the house Franklin built here last first day. He brought a waggon load of fine grafted fruit trees—50 peach and 20 apple trees—and set them out.

Jos has just got back without the money: old story, pay in 2 weeks. He met the elephants and saw 4 albinos, did not go in. Saw the children. <u>Alice had a beau</u> that was taking her and Cary to see other parts of the exhibition, not included. We know him, and <u>he is eleven</u>.

We had to sell a fine young cow and calf, the one we milked so long before she ever had a calf, <u>18 months</u>. We sold her for 10 dollars to help raise money to pay that judgment. Deborah's little heifer, Myrtle, had a calf last week and is as gentle as a cat. We milk 2 fine cows besides and make a little butter to sell every week. Poor Granville's exellent cow died from eating green corn (a storm blew the fence down). They have another good one.

It feels to me sometimes as if I would be willing to start to walk, if I had suitable company and means to bear my expences, that I might behold thee once more, my own precious Mother. Time has, I expect, wrought more change in me than it has in thee, but my feelings don't get old and withered like my face. Oh, how I wish thou couldst have a Dauguerotype likeness of thyself [letter ends]

*Our beloved <u>Dr Fries</u> starts for Washington this week. Oh, I wish some of you could see him. If you knew how he had been to us, you would love him. He has never hinted anything about payment. He is a perfect gentleman.

1. Charles Hole Preston (1809–1844).
2. The McMillans were from the Quaker community of Mt. Pleasant, Ohio, in Jefferson County. Joel became a well-known bookstore owner and abolitionist in Salem. In 1848, he married Sarah Morris, who worked with him against slavery and was prominent in the early women's rights movement.

3. The basic unit of the Quaker system of meetings, with the monthly meeting, quarterly meeting and yearly meeting.

∽

During this period, Isaac Briggs was practicing medicine in Athens, Georgia. The state had stopped fining practitioners of Thomsonian and botanic medicine in 1839, thereby opening the door for Isaac to earn a living while he tried to establish a claim on land his father had bought decades before. From there he wrote immense letters to his sister Elizabeth in a tiny, cramped hand, filling each page from edge to edge with medical case studies, theories and personal anecdotes. Even by Anna's standards of conserving paper by leaving no space unfilled Isaac's are stunning. He and Elizabeth shared a dry, sarcastic wit and a critical view of life.

The sojourn in Georgia starting in 1843 actually was a pause in Isaac's almost lifelong wanderings. In 1840, he had been at Sharon. In 1842, he had traveled to Mercer County, Ohio looking to settle there, but within months he was talking of setting up a practise in Salem or near Green Hill. Instead, he returned to Sharon before going to Georgia early the following year. His 1845 letter to Granville apparently broke a silence from him that had started after Hannah Bentley had fled Maryland more than two years earlier.

∽

Sept 9th 1845
[from Granville to Isaac Briggs]
My Own dear Uncle,

Thy truly acceptable letter came to hand by last mail, and I assure thee I was much pleas'd to see the scratch of thy pen once more and to hear particularly from thee, which had not happen'd for several years. I have never yet entirely despaired of getting a letter from thee when the right time arriv'd and the spirit urged <u>severely</u>, and I have no doubt but thee had struggled against its promptings considerably to have so long kept us, the near and loving relatives, in utter ignorance of thy prospects and whereabouts. I have always enquired particularly for thee when writing to the folks at Sandy Spring, but all the satisfaction I could get was that "Isaac was well when we hear'd from him last and is in Georgia." It was some satisfaction, to be sure, to know this much, and I sometimes thought they did'nt wish us to know any more of thee. Now, since thee has opened thy mouth and thy tongue had ceas'd to cleave to the roof thereof, I shall hope to hear from thee frequently until I see thee face to face, which I hope will be sometime this fall.

I will, as thee requested, give a short history of some of the folks since thee left and then discourse of other matters. In the first place, to begin with our <u>dear</u> selves. We still live in Lynchburgh, are right comfortably fix'd, and still work at our trade and farm a little occasionally so that "when one missed, 'tother is sure to fail." Between the two we can make a good living without going in debt. We also have a son, and his name is William. He is something more than 2 years old, is an <u>uncommon</u> child, of course, but don't know that he will ever be as <u>smart</u> as his father. Franklin & his wife live in Salem, are getting along very comfortably, have one child, Walter, about 1 year old. They lost their first when 5 months old. Franklin has become very steady & industrious, gets plenty of work and is at it constantly. His trade suits him much better than farming. Richard & Maria are getting along about as when thee saw them, no change for better or worse that I know of. Richard is very industrious and is still picking up a little. Norman is a noble little fellow. Thomas lives now in Salem & has Deborah keeping house for him, works at his trade part of the time and goes to school & travels round the balance. He went to a manual labour school at Berea near Cleveland last spring a year ago. Work'd at his trade in Cleveland during the summer & fall. Took a school near there in the winter and then commenced lecturing on Phrenology.[1] I don't know what he will undertake next. Hannah took a notion to get married last spring to J. Alexander Preston, a <u>red-headed</u> son of old <u>Peter's</u>. They talk something of going out West this fall, but I don't know that they will get off. Deborah has been much afflicted for 2 or 3 years past by spells; her health seems to be improving now. Aliceanna lives at home, is hardy as a pine knot & worth all the rest put together for business. Father, Mother, & the rest plodding along in the old way, not much change since thee saw them.

Thee enquired for Aunt Betsy?[2] I was at Marlboro a few weeks since, saw Aunt who lives there in Community with cousin Edward & 2 or 3 other families. She seem'd cheerful & happy. The community does not seem to increase much but is rather on the decline, I believe. Abraham Brooke lives in Clinton Co. O., is very much changed and has become a practical Non-resistant. Will have nothing to do with government, works very hard, charges no fees when attending the sick. His dress is of the coarsest material, and he does not shave but lets all his beard grow and,

what seems stranger than all, is respected & belov'd by all that know
him.[3] Samuel is traveling the State as agent for the A.S. Society, appointing
conventions, &c &c.[4]

Thee asks how the cause progresses? I can say there has never been as
much excitement on that subject as at the present time. The celebrated
and eloquent Abby Kelly & Jane E. Hitchcock, with Stephen S Foster &
others, have been holding a series of conventions through the Northern
part of this State. They are in favour of moral suasion for the overthrow
of slavery & utterly discard physical force or political action. Thousands
go to hear them & they have many prosolytes.

We have also had a severe drought unprecedented and shall not
make more than half a crop. The greatest difficulty will be provender for
stock as there is plenty of breadstuff. Currency is getting more plenty, &
we are calculating in having lots of it passing among us in the spring as
they have commenced operations on our canal again. They have funds
sufficient for its completion and wish to get it through as soon as possible.

I can give no information as to the progress of the Botanic cause
generally in this county—for our parts we use no other medicine. Others
around us put their faith in the MD's. I do not wonder thee should
become sick and tired of the South, but do marvel at thy staying there
this long, for I don't see how any just & honourable man could prosper
amongst so much wickedness; and I think thee had better flee as Lot did
of old ere the rotten fabric falls about thy ears. Now, if thee wishes me to
tell thee where to go, first promise to take my advice. I think thee says
"amen." Well, just pack up as fast as possible and scarcely look behind
untill thee sees Lynchburgh, Col Co., Ohio. And I'll ensure thee enough
to live upon comfortably as long as thee wishes to stay. I have quite set
my heart upon thy coming, and as thee will not be likely to get into
business this winter, thee had better spend that time with us, and perhaps
against spring something better may appear than we now think of.

Now, my dear Uncle, I feel that I have not said half that I should to
comfort thee. I know thee must often feel lonely amongst strangers,
especially in sickness and other circumstances as harassing—that thee
must need the sympathy of thy kinsfolk. I must leave some space for
Elizabeth to fill. Please write soon and tell us of thy prospects. As ever,
thy nephew, G.S. Bentley

My dear Uncle,

I too was glad to hear from thee once more as we have suffered much uneasiness on thy account, not being able to hear anything definitely concerning thee since thee left Sandy Spring. I want thee to leave Georgia and heartily second Granville's request that thou should sojourn with us this ensuing Winter; and I will do what I can to make thee forget how much thee has suffered in Athens. We live in humble style but are contented, happy, and comfortable, and if we could only know that all our fellow beings shared the same blessings, would have little to wish for here.

Granville had given thee a pretty general history of our friends hereabouts but did [not] mention that my dear Father and Mother & brother, Will Henry, are now on a visit to our friends east of the mountains. They have been absent from home rather more than three months. We are now looking for them. Charles takes charge of the farm, and Margaretta is housekeeper. Edward has been living in Cincinnati for more a year, was married about two months since. We have not seen his wife. Charles is acquainted with her, says she is a very lovely woman.[5] Thee wishes to have the Gossip of the neighbourhood. I don't believe there is much stirring and suppose it would be my province to deal it out to thee. Griffith Brogan had left the place, and we cannot <u>manufacture</u> much. Lynchburgh is growing in importance, if not much in size. We have raised a small store here, which makes rather more bustle in our quiet village. . . . Do leave Georgia. It is no place for thee. Mother desires her love to thee. Farewell till we see thee.

Affectionately, thy neice, EGB

1. A popular pseudo-science that associated intelligence and character with the shape of the skull.
2. Elizabeth Luken.
3. According to Clinton County history, Abraham Brooke—a graduate of the Medical College of Baltimore—was a local anti-slavery activist during the ten years or so he lived in Oakland. He delivered a speech to the quarterly meeting of the Clinton County Anti-Slavery Society in December 1842, and was an active member of the Underground Rail-road. Recalled Isaac Morris forty years later, "I remember at Abram Allen's and also at Dr. Brooke's the fugitive slave always found food and shelter and safety. And I think that either of these men, or either of their excellent wives, Katy Allen or Elizabeth Brooke, would have endured any hardship rather than to have betrayed the sable men and women who trusted them" (from the Wilbur Siebert collection at the Ohio Historical Society).
4. Abraham's brother Samuel, who lived in Marlborough, was also very active in the Garrisonian faction of the abolition movement, along with the nationally known figures mentioned in the next paragraph.
5. Elizabeth's parents were William and Hannah Briggs Garrigues; Charles, William Henry, Edward, and Margaretta were her younger siblings.

In June 1846, Robert Garrigues traveled to Maryland to bring Sally Ann home. While there, he told the cousins that he and Anna's son, Franklin, were interested in the latest fad of mesmerism. In fact, Robert was present when Franklin had mesmerized Deborah, "& then he told her when he wanted her to wake & took out his watch stating the precise moment & at that very moment she opened her eyes & followed him all about the room, she became sleepy every time he came near her that evening."

The year 1847 started on a much more upbeat note than the last one had. Elizabeth Briggs wrote to Isaac that she had heard from Anna that Deborah's health was much better, and "she seems now to enjoy life & sings as merrily as a bird." Granville and Elizabeth Bentley had another son, Joseph Edmunds, and Hannah and John Preston had a daughter, Laura Maria. Thomas married Ruth Anna McMillan February 22, 1846, before a justice of the peace and were dismissed from the Salem Monthly Meeting for marrying contrary to discipline.

While 1846 had brought some red letter days, the greatest joy still awaited Anna in 1847. At long last, after more than twenty years, she made plans to travel back East to see her mother and sisters. She was full of both excitement and anxiety.

❧

4th mo 29th 1847
[addressed to Sarah Stabler]
My dear sister Sarah and all,

As letters sometimes are delayed a week, I thought it best to write this week to inform you of our present prospect. We expect to start on the 10th—that is, next 2nd day week. Our dear young friend Moore[1] rode up here yesterday and says they will be ready then. We shall travel in a buggy with one horse and take our own provision. Just to accomodate me with a way to get to see you, he will walk most of the way. They are exellent, kindhearted and very intelligent people. We expect to come by New Market [Maryland], and I expect it will take us 9 or 10 days. They have a great desire to be present at our meeting, and after all their kindness to me I know you will welcome them and give them one night's lodging before they go to thier friends. Anna (his wife) counts on almost as much pleasure in witnessing our reunion as in meeting her husband's relations.

I have a great deal to do yet, for I did not get the few little things absolutely needed till a few days since. Deborah has been working from home two weeks, the first week housecleaning, the last sewing. Caroline went out <u>last week</u> at 62 ½ [cents] per week. I don't know how long they will want her, but it will help her in the way of clothing while I am gone.

Granville and Richard sometimes talk of an intention away off in the future of paying you a visit, but it will not be for a year or two yet. Thomas is actively engaged in farming but says if his crops turn out well this season, before another year goes round he thinks he and wife will try to see you. He has his father's ploughing to do this season. They divided the farm. Thomas rents and has his own 20 acres to till. . . .

My own precious Sister Mary, how my heart thrills to picture the meeting with each one of you. Let us all strive to compose our feelings that rapture may not be almost agony. And I don't know but it may be as well to prepare you for the change time has made in my old countenance: gray, rough hair; an old yellow, wrinkled, withered, long phiz; a few black snags only in place of the white teeth I used to have; a stoop in my shoulders. <u>A very homely old woman the youngsters will all think me</u> at first, but I am pretty sure I will make them all love me and think me prettier when I come away—there is some sort of a <u>pickle</u> about my heart, that it has kept its <u>feelings</u> fresh.

Poor Sally Ann G's in a very deplorable state of mind. She seems in utter despair. Her reason is much impaired. I feel for her afflicted parents, her <u>mother</u> especially. She is entirely turned against her whole family and thinks they all hate her because she is so wicked. Well, I must leave this for Granville to finish and am your own, Anna.

1. It's impossible now to know which Moore this was, but there were Quaker Moores in Salem and Marlborough. Anna never hints that these Moores are relations.

~

Everyone knew how much this trip home meant to Anna, but the anticipation also affected the folks at Sharon. Awaiting Anna's arrival there, Elizabeth Briggs wrote to her brother Isaac, "We have heard within the last few weeks that sister Anna Bently has a prospect of visiting us sometime this mo. & it has produced a considerable excitement thou mayst be sure beginning with mother & displaying itself in various way with all the branches of the family. Sister Sarah has prepared a box of plants for her to take when she returns some blue & white sweet violets, chinquopin bushes, & a little budded Kentish Common Cherry tree. She is of a nature to prize them almost as much as if they had <u>human</u> life about them. Mother is kept in a state of restlessness on the strength of this information & could not be persuaded to accompany Uncle Roger & Aunt Sally [Brooke] to Baltimore yesterday on a visit to aunt Dolly [Hopkins] & family, which she has been much pressed to do, & she hurried home from Avondale [home of William and Henrietta Briggs] much sooner than they wd. under other circumstances have been willing to part with her. . . . Henrietta says she looks at all the Pedlars & Strangers who come there very <u>narrowly</u> lest in some one of them she might detect a brother in disguise. And mother does the same here at home."

Later in the same letter, Elizabeth went on, "Just as I was putting my letter away cousin Anna [Brooke] came in & she left here within the last half hour taking Mother home with her to spend the afternoon at Fulford. As they were getting ready to start we remarked on its being post day. And Mother said 'Cousin Anna <u>what</u> if we were to get a letter from Anna saying the plan for her coming was all knocked in the head!' Sister <u>S</u> replied <u>Well</u>, Mother, thee can just take <u>one</u> Anna (looking significantly at <u>cousin</u> A.) in the place of another. And I presumed to speak up & say 'We <u>have</u> already adopted thee as a sister cousin Anna.'"

As things turned out, Thomas and Ruth Anna accompanied Anna Bentley east.

~

Salem May 23 1847
[from Maria Garrigues to Anna Bentley]
My dearly loved Mother,

Does not something whisper thee this Sabbath afternoon, and all the overwhelming emotions of thy heart, that fond hearts in Ohio—at Green Hill and at Salem—are full to overflowing with hopefull pleasure & sympathy at the fruition of thy long-cherished wishes that we can hardly wait untill we hear <u>where</u> and how thee is? And yet how can thee think of anything but that thee is <u>there</u>? Oh, Mother, I hardly dare dwell upon it. Can it be as rapturous as <u>I</u> immagine it must be, to look into thy blessed mother's face, hear her voice so long dead to thy ear—<u>and smoke thy pipe</u> by her side? Then there is Aunt Mary's sweet face rises to my fancy, as when a naughty little girl I often bro't tears thereon; Aunt Sarah, a rosy girl with such long black curly hair, and so dignified, and so good; our Aunt Elizabeth, a pale-faced, curious, darling, comical young thing, a story teller that none could beat—Oh those stories! And dear little Aunt Margaret that used to get me to help make [the] garden, and give such good advice that I could never be bro't to follow. Oh, what a train of loved images arise from kind memory's dwelling place within my heart— and thou, dear Mother, art realizing all this. . . .

Then there is Uncle W Henry and little Auntie that I used to love so dearly in their little humble home in Lynchburgh. Wouldn't I love to see them, and introduce as my spouse of near eight years standing the Cousin Dick they used to teaze me about, and our son, a great big boy? Oh dear, oh dear. Mother, I never felt so strange about any event as about this visit of thine. Some w'd not understand it, but I know thee will—that I cannot trust myself to dwell upon it in conversation with anyone—my heart fills and I cry like a baby and often find myself expressing myself aloud in thanks to God who has preserved your lives thro' long years of separation to meet again this side of the grave. . . .

Frank and family were all out at meeting this morning and were well, of course. Frank is at work with Richard and shop work generally, and Richard finds it much more profitable than pattern-making. We have not heard from Green Hill since thee left. Nor from Ruth Anna's friends. Is Thomas nearly beside himself, or does his philosophy keep guard over his weaknesses and make him appear stoical? No, I know it is not so. His tender sensibilities must flow forth. Do not strive to force them back, dear Brother. . . . And Mother, do go with Thomas and Ruth Anna to see dear Dorcas—I need not remind thee of it—but I wish my especial love to be given her. Poor faithful Dorcas, how I used to love her. Now, do write—if thee had not already—to me and tell me as particularly as thee can. What thee knows, I want to know.

I have regretted sending Norman's likeness—it is not a good one, and we intend having it taken over. But did thee tell them that I am much prettier in substance than represented there? Do now—tell them all the good that will make them love me and keep shady on t'other side of how contrary I am—how red-peppered and all that. Now do warn Thomas & his wifey not to empty their bosoms too freely when on the subject of the elder sister and touch very lightly on the mischief, wilfulness &c &c of the "only one" nor spoil the picture his mother drew of him some 2 years ago—a truthful one then, if it did appear to my dear Uncle Farquhar not an impartial one.

But there is no use in my dictating to thee, Mother. I know thee will

just go and tell everything thee can think of to gratify their enquiries.
But thee ain't going to tell of the lassie's beaux, is thee? I don't know but
any husband will be eclipsed in thy good graces if Alice wins that "tall
youth" thee spoke of. I really must be after going down there very soon
to see how matters are progressing, and to cheer poor dear old Father up.
I do wish he would come up here and stay a week among the Books,
magazines, and papers. He might read, read, read, and when he was tired
of that we'd go and see Aunt Jane [Steer] and drink tea with her in her
nice new house. She seems to sympathize with thee very much and make
many affectionate enquiries after thee.

Aunt H Griffith[1] is not well and entertains strong fears that she had
a cancer of 8 months growth in her breast. She suffers very much from
some cause similar to that in symptoms, &c. I went to see her last week
and felt truly grieved at the thought of the acute suffering she must
endure if it should prove to be cancer. But she appears resigned either
way and is more cheerful than one could expect. . . .

Richard just by chance met Joel [McMillan][2] and his Mother and
they could'nt stop only long enough for him to run home and right back
to Main St., so that I could not even write farewel to thee nor send
anything I wished.

Yesterday I got home from the weaver's 24 yds of very pretty
carpeting, and I feel quite impatient to be fixing it in the place of the old
one in "the room." I feel doubly paid for all my labor when I think of
how nice and comfortable it will look & feel. It is striped with very
bright colors, and I'm pretty near being proud of it. . . . Thy tenderly
affectionate daughter,

Maria S Garrigues

1. Probably Hannah Griffith, age sixty-seven, who is listed in the 1850 census as living in
Salem with her husband, Reuben, and her two grown daughters. They were from Pennsylvania and apparently were related to the Garrigues family.
2. Brother and mother of Ruth Anna Bentley.

~

June 4th 1847
[to Thomas M. Bentley et al.. from Granville and Hannah]
Dear Brother, . . .

We have all had pretty good health since you left & have been getting
along very well, I think. And I have actually beheld with my own eyes
father mounted upon <u>Lady</u> and have hear'd of his riding out several

times. He and I took a ride to Lisbon and had our canal stock business arranged. Father succeeded in making a fixed settlement. And I have my case in a fair way of being settled sometime soon. I beleive it will do me some good, for I have mentally resolved that henceforth and forever more nobody corporate nor politic nor Kingdoms nor principalities nor republics nor power-that-be nor anything that <u>straddles</u> on horseback or vicusversa shall ever get me into just exactly such another scrape. . . .[1]

With much love to Ruth A and all, I am, as ever, Thy Brother, G. S. Bentley

[A hasty note from Elizabeth was interrupted by a summons to a sick neighbor. Then Franklin's wife, Hannah, contributed.]

. . . I expect Granville has told you who of us are here and how we come, but in case he has not I will just mention that Franklin & Brother Richard walked and hired a person to bring Maria, myself, and the children. We came day before yesterday and expect to stay a week. It is indeed pleasant to be here, but we miss you very much. William Henry & Margaretta [Garrigues][2] are here too but expect to leave today. They were very much in hopes that poor Cousin Sally Ann could stand to go home with them, but she thinks she cannot go. Perhaps you have not heard that Father was up to Salem to pay us a little visit, seem'd to enjoy himself very much, said he felt so lonely at home without dear Mother, tho the girls made out very well. It is now almost time for the mail. With much love to one and all, your Hannah H.

1. Unfortunately, the entries relating to this matter in the Columbiana County courthouse in Lisbon are nearly illegible. They probably had bought shares in the Sandy & Beaver Canal that required payment from them at this time. It must have been fairly clear by 1847 that the canal was never going to be the blue chip investment stockholders had anticipated.
2. Hannah and Richard's brother and sister.

~

Salem June 21st 1847
[to Anna from Maria]
My dear Mother,

Richard has gone to church, and I intend devoting the hour to thee, as I do not feel very well, shall not go to meeting this morning. I received a letter from Aunt Sarah and thee last 6th day week which was exceedingly welcome. We had just returned from Green Hill that day—where we spent a week very delightfully. . . . Father had been to Salem the week before and spent several days very pleasantly indeed with us. He said he

had lost his appetite and felt so lonesome he must come up here. How
glad we were to have him. I say <u>we</u>, for no own son could be more
affectionate & kind than my dear Husband is to him, and Father feels it
too, I know. I cracked away and got a first-rate supper—mackerel, coffee,
&c &c. Suffice it to say what with change of scene, our agreeable
company, plenty to read, <u>strange vittels</u>, and an easy mind, my beloved
Parent left us bright & early on Sabbath morning very much the better
of his visit. He gave Richard such glowing accounts of the fish caught &
to catch in the region round about Lynchburgh that he, Richard, and
Frank put their heads together and gave Father the promise that we
would be forthcoming. That same week on 5th day Father was at
Lynchburgh to welcome us and did seem so happy to have us there. I
went right up <u>home</u>, and staid there most of the time.

The next day Hannah [Preston] came up and staid till the next day.
Laura is certainly a very sweet babe. She is so good and lovely I fell to
love her more than any babe I know. Hannah and I spent a very happy
time together. I think she enjoys life much more than she ever has before
and is certainly very much improved since this new tide of deep
unfathomable tenderness had been opened up in her heart by the gift of
her darling child—bless the bright creature!—sent to make better and
kindlier feelings have sway in that dear mother's breast.

7th day . . . Sabbath morning we had the critter saddled and bridled.
Alice, Richard & I started a little after 8 o'clock for Holland's (we did'nt
all ride at once, mind). They seemed much gratified to see us. We dined
at the dear old Homestead, a most profuse meal. Mary & Matilda were
more agreable than I expected to find them. Indeed, I was rather pleased
with the latter than otherwise. Friend Holland is more deaf than when I
saw her before, making it difficult for me to talk with her at first. After
dinner we all went over to see Susan, had a real nice little visit with them.
Robert seemed very much <u>taken</u> with my spouse.[1] We had Aunt Sarah's
first letter with us, which was read and read and read by both Mother &
daughter. Friend Holland w'd say, "Well, well. The parting'll spile all, the
parting'll spile all. Yes, if I live to see the day when Anna Bently comes
home, I shall want to see her, oh dear." And then the glasses were taken
off, tears wiped away, & we would turn the subject, for I do not like to
see the dear old Lady weep. She seems so isolated from the rest of the
world thro' her great affliction. I never looked upon deafness as being
such a misfortune before, that I felt only a yearning desire to give her
pleasure.

We took Tea at Robert's and had a delightful ride & walk together to

Green Hill. 2nd day. Alice washed. Debby & I went to Granville's in the afternoon. The 3-year-olds were so outragious I got the sick headache and was glad to get back to my dear old home again 3rd day morning, according to appointment. Early, Debby & I went to see Hannah. Her little cot[tage] was sweet as cleanliness, green boughs, and gay flowers could make it. . . . We had an uncommon happy day there, we three sisters, talking, singing, laughing, romping, eating, drinking, kissing the baby, rummaging everything, admiring everything—especially the whitest of white cupboards, a very nice new braid bonnet for Hannah, parasol, baby frocks, &c &c. . . .

4th day, the whole kettle bile of us met at Green Hill, 15 children & grandchildren besides the immediate family. I stuck at the Brethren till they took the workbench to the barn, moved the vinegar barrel into the Pantry. By the bye, they titivated[2] the Porch and Pantry first—got them moved up close to the house, moved the soap trough into the shop, and then sat down to a long table profusely covered with good Bread, butter, fruit, pickles, ham, eggs, currant, apple, and custard pies, pudding, very good sweet cake of some kind, which with good coffee and plenty of cold milk made a meal fit for [any], too good by half for Jimmy Polk or Queen Vic either.[3]

5th day Richard staid all day at home helping the girls and I clean house. He scrubbed equal to 3 women. In the afternoon at Father's request I wrote a long circumstansial letter to Aunt Alice Hall, which highly pleased him.[4] It rained all day, that day, and thee would have smiled to have seen Father. He brought his little Desk down, opened all the little contraptions, showed Richard all his old Papers, &c. And the girls remarked they had never seen Father make so free with anyone 'cepting his daughters—he would ask him do little things for him &c &c. . . .

Norman had the [illegible] of a time while we were there. He did not go with me anywhere but staid close by Alban all the time roaming the woods "a-ground hockeying" getting service berries, scaring the big owls from their haunts, hunting flowers and everything else two little boys could think of to make the time pass happily. I saw very little of Caroline. She looks thin & pale. I went with Alice to see Sarah Coulson a little, but one evening she was suffering terribly with her breast, but got better before we left the neighbourhood.[5]

Well, I have endeavored to be as satisfactory as I could in giving thee some account of home and will now return to my own dear sweet little nest in Salem. We found our roses in the heighth of their beauty and fragrance, the sweet brier beginning to shed its rich wealth of blossoms with every gentle breeze, the grass knee-high, the Cat and Brindle well and glad to see us, and all our little kingdom in a thriving & peaceful state.

Williams, the "old Missionary," is here holding a protracted meeting in Salem and vicinity—attracts overflowing houses and gains a great many signers to the blessed Pledge.[6] He came up to Richard the first evening he was here & asked him if his Mother-in-law did'nt live 3 miles west of Hanover. Said he had promised her he would come down there and lecture in their schoolhouse—and he must do it before he returned home. It surprised me so little that a man who travels so much & sees so many people should have remembered it. There is to be a great mass meeting held in New Garden on the 4th July which he expects to attend. We expect to go and will in all probability meet Father & the girls there. . . .

I would like to write a long letter to my good dear Aunt Sarah in answer to hers, but cannot get it accomplished now. Give love abundantly to her first, then to all the rest from me. Rich[d] said the other day after reading your letter, "If I only had the means to spare, I would just write to Mother to stay over there till we come, and we'll bring her back. Would'nt that be fine? But then we can't come before next spring anyhow, so thee will have to get thy visiting done up this summer, I expect. One word now about your coming away: Don't let it into your heads you will see each other no more, for thy son Rich[d] is getting along in the world and we intend taking a trip every now & then over there, and we can maybe take thee back sometimes. And mind we want you back here pretty bad by this time, do not forget that as you go along.

Richard says he wishes to write some, therefore I will leave the ends for him to fill. He is growing more and more squire-like, yet will not restrict his appetite for good things all that I can say. Give my most affectionate love to dear Thomas & his Ruth Anna. I often think of the great pleasure they must have seeing great sights and making various observations on men & manners together, "with none to molest them" or cry & squall after them. I hope and believe they will improve the opportunity. Now fare you well, Mother, Brother, Sister, beloved Kindred all, farewell and believe me ever your wilful, crooked, very imperfect—but tenderly affectionate—Maria

2nd Day noon
Dear Mother,

Maria had left the ends of this long letter for me to fill up, which was necessary that I might undo the soft soaping that she has put on. Now thee knows I am not near so good as represented, & when Maria takes a loving spell she can lay it on. Now I have not room to branch out or I don't know what fine things I might say. Suffice it I love thee very much and thy kind friends and thy dear old mother & thy sisters & Brothers & all who have helped to make thee happy and that thy happiness may continue and any pain that might naturally arise from taking leave of such kind friends be softened by the reflection that thee also has near and dear friends in Ohio who shall look anxiously for thy safe return is the sincere wish of thy Son,

Richard

[reverts to Maria's handwriting]

I'll forgive the Squire for the insinuation thrown out above for the kind things he has said afterwards. Father & Mother Garrigues are at Frank's waiting the arrival of Aunt EHG from Philadelphia.[7] Hannah sent word for me to go there this afternoon, which I shall do presently. Clara is not very well, has a bad cold & cough. She grows very fast & is very good. . . . I did not tell thee how anxiously Father watched for mail day when we were down. Indeed, thee would be gratified to see how he pored over Aunt Sarah's letter giving a short account of your arrival—the girls are first-rate managers but they seem to miss thee very much. Debby had several little crying spells about [?] while I was there. MBG

[on address page]

Richard folded this letter and did'nt take notice of the place I had left for the seal so we have to stick it in the corner. M

1. Susan and Robert Miller and Susan's mother, Sarah Holland, Anna's old friend and neighbor.
2. Spruced up.
3. James K. Polk, eleventh president of the United States (1844–1848), and Queen Victoria.
4. Alice Hall was Joseph Bentley's sister.
5. Sarah Garrett Coulson, wife of Jabez Coulson, died on July 31, 1850, age sixty-seven.
6. The temperance movement remained popular for decades.
7. William and Margaret Garrigues of Marlborough were waiting for their sister-in-law, Elizabeth Magdalen Hill Garrigues, the wife of James Ralph Garrigues, Isaac Briggs's nephew.

~

The travelers returned to Ohio on the National Road, the busiest highway in the country at that time. It took them across the mountains of western

Maryland, from Frederick to Cumberland, before turning northwest through Uniontown, Pennsylvania, and Wheeling. They stayed in such modest taverns as they could afford, sharing space with drovers and workmen.

Even as Anna traveled by one-horse wagon, thrilled to have made her trip at all, however, a new form of transportation was pushing west that would make future journeys cheaper and faster. The Baltimore & Ohio Railroad reached Cumberland in 1844 and Brownsville, Pennsylvania, in 1847.

~

6th mo 30 1847
fourth day evening
[to Sarah Stabler from Thomas Bentley & Ruth Anna Bentley, with note
    from Anna]
Dear Aunt,

We expect to pass through Cumberland tomorrow, & I take this opportunity to redeem my promise to the precious Sharon folks—i.e. to put a letter in the office at Cumberland for you. Well, where does thee suppose we are tonight? I will try to inform thee, tho first we are well, have got along first-rate except—now guess: Why, the tyre came off of one of the wheels of our buggy today, & that ai'nt all. The first thing I saw of it 'twas going rattle-te-clatter over a stone-heap & splash into the canal three rods from the roadside. Now, I guess we had to stop & calculate a little. Well, now all hands are busy planning. Mother thinks, "Jim must be loosed from the buggy," but I think not. Ruth Anna is silently putting her plan into execution, which is to get a pole & fish it out, but she can't make it take. I, in the meantime, have learned of a black-smith hard bye & have proposed to start the women off there with Jim & our crippled buggy, while I try my hand at fishing. This plan takes, of course:

So off they trudge, poor things, trembling at every step for fear the wheel will come to pieces & let all our nice things down in the dirt! I obtain'd the asistance of a boy & skiff, took a long pole, found, & raised. The "neighbor" gave the boy a ten cent piece for his part of the fun, which was to take hold of the tyre when I raised it up & hoist it on his boat. He looked at the money & asked, "How much is this?" Ten cents, said I. "Well, hain't you got a sevenpence nor nothing?" No. that's money enough for all that you have done, but I am obliged to you. "Oh, you are welcum," & off the little urchin went, I don't know where.

We all arrived at the smith shop found a good-natured sort of person there who agreed to make "all right" in short order. I thought it best to have the tyre taken off of all the wheels and made less & put on tightly. This he agreed to do for three dollars, but I assured him I would not give more than two, alltho he told me I would have to pay four dollars for the job in town. He agreed to do the job at my price & in three hours had it all completed, & we were on our way again for the lovely west.

This catastrophe happened five miles east of Hancock. We are now 10 1/2 miles west of that place, have traveled 15 1/2 ms since 2 o'clock P.M. . . . But I must go back a little & tell how we got along the two first days of our journey, after we left Falling Green. We felt a little sort-of-blue, but all at once we came to a fine lot of rasberry's. We gather'd a lot of them & felt better. We next found cherrys, lots of them. We stopped four miles south of New M. T.[1] & ate plentifully of biscuit, ham, sausage, & pickles & rasberry's for desert: We then felt very comfortable, traveled to Frederick had to stop out of the rain, had a fine Shower. We only traveled 28 miles that day. Next day had to stop before twelve out of the rain. Waited one and a half hours but traveled in all 34 miles that day. Jim eats heartily & looks well. . . .
Your affectionate &c, TM Bentley

West foot of Sideling Hill, 5th day morning
Dear Sharon,

Thomas left a little room for me which I shall try to fill up some sort of fashion. He has told all the large things, so I must content myself with small. I was very tired last night for I walked a good deal. We all walked all the way up Sideling Hill[2] last night, and it is an awful long hill, being two miles in height. We have rested well the two last nights, but the first night was almost beyond endurance. We were storm staid at Frederic; and such a house and such beds I never saw, let alone trying to sleep in. The beds looked as if all the dirty waggoners and drovers that had come along in the last year had slept in them. And I guess the bed buggs had not been disturbed for some years, nor the floor washed for an age, so with the warm weather and all these things put together you may think we did not sleep much. Well, Aunt Lizzie, we drank out of that same delicious spring again, but I took good care not to hurt myself this time, and we clambered up the rocks just below, and gathered a pint of rasberries for dessert at dinner. Oh how I wish thee could have been with us, as we came up Sideling Hill. On one side of us was the mountain away above us, and on the other it was <u>down, down, down</u>. The tops of the forest trees were near a mile below us, and then these sweet springs and sweet flowers and sweet <u>rasberries</u>, food to refresh both mind and body. I will tell you more when I get home. Your <u>clever</u> neice, RA Bentley

5th day morning
Dear Mother and all,

We got along well in every respect. I felt well after the first day. I could not sleep one hour the first night in F. The folks were so dirty I would not give mother's love, though they were kind. . . . I expect I walked 8 miles yesterday, was tired but feel refreshed this morning. We have suffered with the heat but very little. It is quite cool this morning. We have had the road pretty much to ourselves, but from Cumberland is the great thouroughfare. . . . Thy own affectionate A

1. Probably New Market, on U.S. 40 east of Frederick.
2. In Allegany County, Maryland, east of Hancock, Sideling Hill has an elevation of 1760 feet.

∾

Lynchburgh July 9th 1847
[Granville and Elizabeth to Sarah Stabler]
My Dear Aunt,

The folks landed safely on 4th day evening the 7th inst, were in good health, fine spirits, and <u>mighty yaller</u>. They met with no mishaps on the way except losing a tire off one wheel. . . .

I enclose in this $15 for Uncle WH Briggs. Will thee please get it to him as soon as convenient and get him to let me know what the balance is, which I can send at any time? I will then be entirely out of debt except some few debts of gratitude which this kind of currency don't always pay. Please write often and believe me, Thy loving nephew, G.S. Bentley

Seventh day morning
My dear Grandmother and Aunt Sarah,

This evil spirit of Procrastination has left me but a few moments before
the mail arrives to assist in filling this blank space. We are all truly glad to
have Mother at home again, wish her visit with you could have been
longer. But the light shed upon her pathway has brightened the
atmosphere that surrounds her. She and Father seem to have renewed
their union. They are like young folks again. He enjoys so much hearing
of the happy and loving circle that surrounded her, and prizes every little
token of affection which her friends gave. I spent yesterday at Green Hill
and had a very interesting description of their journeyings. They seem
quite well, but Mother is fatigued as she walked a good deal and the
weather was so warm. I was glad they came directly home. . . .

Our friends here generally well—with the exception of poor Cousin
Sally Ann, who is very low. Her head seems a little relieved by copious
bleeding, but her mind no more comfortable that I can discover. I never
saw a more utterly despairing countenance. It is indeed sorrowful to hear
her hopeless agony. She condemns herself if she indulges in the least
gleam of light. Poor dear girl, I do not think she can continue long in
this way.

Our little folks have the measles. I think they are not very sick, but
complaining and fretful. I must say farewell now. This is not <u>the</u> letter we
were to write to thee, dear Aunty, but accept a great deal of love, dear
Grandmother, and Aunt Lizzie too, all my sweet little cousins. I feel
almost acquainted with all and am affectionately,
Your Elizabeth G Bently

∾

7th month 10th, 1847
My own dear Mother and all her tribe,

Well, here I am at home again, safe and well, though not quite recovered
from fatigue. I will not dwell upon my feelings when distance shut out
the last view of my 2 dear sisters and the last loved spot of Falling Green
from my eyes. Thomas drew closer to my side. Ruth Anna threw her arm
around me, clasped my hand, and, in a low, soothing voice, said, "Now,
Mother, think of home." With a strong effort I mastered my feelings and
in silence poured out my thanks to God who had permitted me to taste
of happiness as full as mortal could enjoy while shackled with the bonds
of earth.

We walked many miles, gathered a pint of raspberries for dinner, and, as a gust seemed rapidly approaching, stopped in Frederick at Hitteshew's—the filthiest tavern, dirty, buggy beds. I slept but little. The next night we had good accomodation and a sweet kind little hostess with whom I left Mother's love. She laughed and said she could well appreciate the dear old lady's feelings and sent her in return her name, Sally McLaughlan. The next night dirty, but kind, didn't leave Mother's love; there was no place clean enough to put it in.

We did not suffer as much with the heat as we expected. Jim performed well. I did not take any notice, cannot recollect in order when and where certain events occured, and I forgot till just now that we wrote to you the morning before we reached Cumberland. I think it was before we reached there a tire flew off the forewheel, bounded across the road into the canal. Ruth Anna and I took the buggy 1 mile to a blacksmith's on the road while Thomas got a skiff and fished the tire up. The smith took off all the tires and tightened them. It detained us 3 hours.

We met another little accident in Cumberland at this end of it similar to the one in going. Thomas went into a baker's, and Ruth Anna, against my advises, drove on. Well, after going a square, the National Road makes a turn down another street. She knew the right way (as she always did any spot we had passed in our journey). We went a considerable way, and as I could see nothing of Thomas, we stopped to wait for him before a tavern. We waited near 1/2 an hour and began to have misgivings. I told her I was certain he had taken the straightforward road. She could not believe he would be so simple.

Well, she fastened Jim to the signpost, left me in the buggy, and went back to the baker's 1/2 a mile, and by inquiry found he had gone over the bridge the wrong road. She came back. It was now sundown. Well, we drove on and met him. He had found he was wrong, cut across and got into the narrows and walked 2 miles. Not seeing us, he walked 2 miles back and met us. We were glad to meet, and I told Ruth Anna if Thomas stopped again I would get out and wait for him if she drove on.

We went 5 miles to the very nastiest, filthiest tavern yet. Fifteen Irish turnpike men boarded there. We could not have the same room. Two rooms filled with men. Between a dirty bed, half a chair on 3 legs the only furniture, the walls and floor covered with tobbacco spit. The outside of the house looked ellegant and the parlour fine. Well, there was no help for it. I spread my handkercheif over the pillow, locked my door, and was not affraid.

Those 3 nights were all the poor taverns we stopped at, the rest all elegant. We got to R's cousin W Griffith 1st day before noon, washed, dressed, and rested till morning. Wm Griffith discovered one of the houns of the buggy was broken and they got it mended 1st day. We got the next night to Isaac Griffith's (it was not Amos). They were glad to see us, as kind as ever. Gave Mother's love to her, which seemed to gratify her, and she said, "Why, bless her, give her mine in return."

Next day was the hottest day we had felt. We walked a great deal. My walking averaged 10 miles a day all the way. We crossed the river in good time, could have gone 5 or 6 miles further but thought best to stop as we were all tired and could easily reach home next day. The next day the hottest day I have felt this season, the 10th day of our travelling. We walked a great deal and got on safely to Lynchburg. (We did not go by Salem.)

The first sight in town was 2 huge cannal boats building there and hundreds of bushels of coal dug. Cousin RHG bowed to us from the store door and ran round to meet us at Granville's door. As we drove up, Caroline got a peep through the clustering rosebushes at the door where she was sitting, and I heard her exclaim, "Oh, Sister Elizabeth, it's Mother, it's Mother! Oh, it's Mother!" And she darted in the house to hide her tears. Then such a rush. Elizabeth with her sweet beaming face, little Willie and Joe, Cousin Robert and Rachel Wickersham all welcoming us cordially, every door filled with kind faces.

I could only stay a moment to speak with them. Cousin Robert said, "Well, don't let us keep them. Drive on, make haste and get rested and come to see us. Poor Sally Ann is a great deal worse. She raves at times till she exhausts herself."

Cary came with us. I got out and walked on. As I came on towards home, I heard Deborah and Alice talking. They were taking a walk, were in the woods on a high hill. All at once I heard Aliceanna say, "Oh, Deborah, somebody is coming down the hill. I do believe it is Mother." Deborah says, "Oh, it is, it is!" And they ran like the wind, and soon I felt thier clasping arms around me, thier warm kisses and tears on my lips and face. They laughed and cried, and with an arm of each to lean on and Cary to cary my pipe and fly brush, I arrived safely and was fondly welcomed by my dear companion, who has keenly felt my absence but who rejoices in the satisfaction it has afforded. He never wearys in hearing me talk of you.

I cannot pretend to give you all the different messages of love to all of you from all of us and the delight the distribution of all the many tokens of kindness has occasioned. Sister Elizabeth, I have concluded to do with the music box as thee told me at first—hold it in my own name and let all have a part in it.

This is a poor kind of letter, but my extreme fatigue prevented me from writing till this morning, and I have been so much hurried. I will do better another time. Love to you all individually and most tenderly and to all who enquire for me. You know I love you. Your own, Anna

I fear this will be too late now.

There was some talk of sending this to Aunt Sarah, but Father said it was not worthwhile to send it as we had written. I read and thought it worth ten cents to Grandmother, so here it goes.

Farewell. Elizabeth

~

Salem, the biggest town near Joseph and Anna, and the home of her children Maria, Franklin, and Thomas, was by now a city of almost two thousand people, with a large anti-slavery faction. The abolition newspaper, *The Anti-Slavery Bugle,* was published there, and the Underground Railroad had been active for many years. Leaders of the national movement, including William Lloyd Garrison and the escaped slave Frederick Douglass, as well as Quaker women such as Lucretia Mott and Abby Kelly, repeatedly crossed the fertile ground of the Western Reserve on the lecture circuit. They were wildly popular in Salem, where an anti-slavery rally might attract thousands.

Anna's cousin, Samuel Brooke, frequently wrote for the *Bugle* or shepherded visiting celebrities. He even paid for a huge tent used by visiting abolitionists. The Brooke brothers and their wives had been ardent and active in the cause for almost a decade by this time. At Abraham Brooke's house in Clinton County, where he and his family lived for some years, he had built a meeting hall on his farm styled "Liberty Hall" for gatherings of the faithful, and he opened his doors regularly to escaping slaves. He and his brother Edward were notorious for having been at the center of an uproar in Waynesville, Ohio, in 1841. They had participated in liberating an encampment of slaves whose masters were traveling through Ohio. The abolitionists told the slaves that because they were in Ohio they were automatically free, "whereupon they all decamped," according to a newspaper account. Edward and twenty other abolitionists were arrested, and the trial turned into political theater. Edward's activism cooled after a time, but Samuel and Abraham were never far from the center of action.

~

8th mo 1847
6th day evening a rainy day
My dearest mother first,
My precious sisters & thier offspring,

Oh, how plain I can seem to see you all. You don't feel to be half as <u>far off</u> as you did before I was with you. I do not think I ever shall feel lonesome when <u>alone</u> again, for constantly there are coming before my mental view so many dear, dear, kind, <u>dearly loved</u> forms, and I think of thier love and kindness to me. I look over the many mementos I have received with encreasing love to all who gave them. And Sister Sarah, the brown dress holds its due value amongst the rest. The sight of it always excites a smile. Mother's I fixed up elegantly and have <u>appeared</u> in it at meeting twice.

7th day morning the 14th. I began this last week, and, finding Thomas and Ruth Anna had written, thought I would leave it till this week, but yesterday Hannah sent for me to help her quilt, and it was too late when I got home, and I was too tired to write last night, so shall be hurried. I know as yet I have made poor returns for your goodness in writing, but please make allowance. It has taken some time to recruit the strength of mind and body. The dear kind neighbors almost think hard of me that I have not answered thier calls and pressing invitations, but I cannot yet. I have been to see poor Cousin MEG once, to Granville's, and twice to Hannah's.

Deborah and Alice have been working from home most of the time, and it leaves me as much care at home as I can get through with. Deborah has not been well for a week past, so that she had to leave her place and come home. Something like cholera morbus first and threatenings of billious fever, which is prevalent, but she is much better. Chamomile tea has helped her much. <u>Thomas and Granville are going to take Ruth Anna and our girls (in Thomas's waggon) to New Lime</u>[1] <u>near Cleaveland 60 miles to a great <u>Anti-Slavery Convention</u>. They start 2nd day the 16th, to be gone 1 week.</u> They are very busy fixing.

Ruth Anna's health has been good ever since we returned. She had for some years been subject to such sick spells as she had in Baltimore, but has had no return of it since. I have had a good deal of rhumatism in my shoulders ever since I returned.

We have had a great deal of wet weather this summer. There was no dry weather here of long continuance this season and consequently vegetation is very luxurient. We have some hay and some oats to haul in yet, and then harvest will be done. Joseph's corn is the finest ever raised at Green Hill, his buckwheat and potatoes also very fine. Thomas's harvest also is nearly done, and corn and potatoes good. Jim is in exellent health and spirits. If you had seen him the next day after we got home kicking up his heels and racing over the feilds in all the joy of liberty and home, you would have thought he did not seem much the worse of his long journey. And Thomas did not walk any more coming home than when we went in, but I did 3 times as much.

I wish you had some of our delicious plums. We have green gages and the large peach plum, some as large as appricots, now in perfection and abundance, the peach trees breaking down, but few apples.

Oh I do hope S[amuel] Wetherald will succeed in getting a good likeness of my dear mother. Sis Sarah, do get him to try—thy dear homely phiz, too. (What will my sweet pets, thy children, say to that speech? James: "I think Mother is quite as pretty as Aunt Anna." Lizzie S will grin and Francis pout and say, "Mother ain't homely.")

Dear gentle Sister Lizzie, come out of that little corner thee asked for in my heart and go up higher. There is room for thee in the first row near that cushioned seat; and Sister Mary, heaven bless my darling sister and her precious household. The first fond clasp of meeting, the last sad one of parting was there. Children, don't let Mother forget her promise to write, and you must set her the example. I would like to single each one of you out and address you individually, but time will not admit. I find it so difficult to write in a crowd, and as soon as I begin to write I am surrounded. There is Mother first and foremost with her pipe ready filled and her dear tender eyes looking at me. Here comes Bro and Sister Farquhar and tribe, the princess and her suite, the omnibus with its beloved freight, Cousin Phoebe. And I almost feel the arms and kisses of the dear children of my dear sisters, and they come round me.

Friends, dear friends, stand back a little. Indeed, you have made such a tumult, how can I write? Never mind. Bro WH Farquhar, I wonder at thy impudence. I have read the character thou dared to compare mine with and am at a loss for words to express my wrath at thee and Sister Sarah, but when I came to a particular scene among the Kenwigs's,[2] Cousin Anna's application of it to Sister Mary and children diverted me very much.

We had a visit from Cousin James B Garrigues's sweet little wife. She is a most lovely woman—indeed, is well-acquainted with Isaac Bond.[3] Richard and Maria paid us a very short visit. Both they and Deborah regret very much they did not give me leave to leave Thomas's likenesses with you. Richard and Maria still talk of paying you a visit before very long.

I expect to attend the yearly meeting in Salem the last week in this month. Tell dear Cousin E Lea[4] the children all insisted on my doing up the black silk dress to wear there, and I have made it look like a bran new. The difference in our size admitted of my cutting out all the parts worn, and there is not a darn in it, and the bonnet is neatly done up and looks like new. Bless her warm generous heart, I love her as a sister and her sweet children. Give my love to them all.

About the spoon: Perhaps Bro WH Farquhar would get <u>upon Kate</u> and ride over to Wilson's and try to get <u>possession</u> of it for me, as he has a fondness for such little comissions; or if any other plan should offer, I should be glad if you could get it into your possession, and then if Dr. Fries had it he would bring it out. I have but 8 of the dozen left.

Well, I find I shall have to stop abruptly. Alice gave me a long string of thanks, love, excuses for not answering her cousin's letter, &c. All send love. Mine is unmeasurable—to you all first and divide the rest in large parcels to all who love me.

<u>Sally Ann grows worse. Hers is a state of despair and hatred of</u> everybody. It is <u>monomania</u>. As her health is stronger, her mental malady increases. Her poor mother. How I feel for her. I must stop or this will not go. Dear ones, farewell. Your own, Anna
Tell Lizzie and Frances, kiss Cousin Phoebe twice a day for a week for me.

1. The "immediatist" William Lloyd Garrison was there, with Frederick Douglass, Stephen Foster (who later married the Quaker abolitionist Abby Kelley), and, in an uneasy union with the Garrisonians, members of the Liberty Party, the political abolitionists who hoped to end slavery gradually through compromise. The second day of the convention some four thousand people attended.
2. In Charles Dickens's *Nicholas Nickleby*, published in 1839, the Kenwigses were one of Dickens's big, happy, penurious families. Mrs. Kenwigs was characterized by her adoration of her children, her "olive branches," whom she found so beautiful she was sure they would die young.
3. Mary Brooke wrote in May 1846 that during a visit to Philadelphia she had visited with both the Isaac Bonds and the James Garrigueses. "James's wife is a <u>very</u> sweet woman," she reported.
4. Possibly Elizabeth Ellicott Lea, or Betsy Lea, a cousin through her mother, Elizabeth

Brooke Ellicott, James Brooke Jr.'s daughter. As a widow in 1845, Betsy published a famous book of recipes and domestic hints called *Domestic Cookery, Useful Receipts and Hints to Young Housekeepers.*

∽

9th mo 17th 1847
[postmark New Garden; address Sarah Stabler]
My dearest Mother,

All the rest of you, I have not <u>willfully</u> neglected you, but I had to get Carry and self ready to <u>attend our Yearly meeting in Salem</u>, which we attended. It was larger than any I ever was at in Baltimore. We had the celebrated <u>Lucretia Mott, Elizabeth Peert</u> from New York, Maria Kent (former Cook)—she was till her marriage a resident of Baltimore and knew Uncle and Aunt Hopkins. We had many other ministers with us. We had <u>much of good council</u> and much of an unChristian spirit, two parties each <u>wanting to rule the other</u>. But towards the close a quiet calm seemed to come over the turbulent spirit. I have to copy and revise the Epistles and minutes for printing.

Well, the meeting closed 6th day the 4th (it commenced 1st day 29th of 8th), and on 7th day the 5th there <u>was a great antislavery convention</u> held there. An immense and beautiful tent which cost 300 dollars (a present from Cousin Saml Brooke to the Society) was erected on an emminence. It is capable of holding 5000, but it could not anything like hold the vast multitude that poured forth from hill, and glen, city and cabin, from far and near. A raised platform held the speakers, who were <u>William Lloyd Garrison</u>—a most noble-looking man; I never saw such a head, all the moral and intellectual organs are very large, benevolence and firmness enormous—Frederick Douglass, the celebrated fugitive from slavery—his master was Thomas Auld of Baltimore; he escaped 9 years since, is now 29 years of age. I wish you could see and hear him, he is the <u>perfect, polished</u> gentleman in his appearance and manners, his language forcible, entirely correct, elloquent, touchingly so, and all his gestures so appropriate, natural, and graceful I do not wonder that he can enchain the attention of assembled thousands. By his side sat Lucretia Mott; another very talented, highly educated young gentleman, a Dr Peek[1] of Pittsburgh—he is the colour of Jaccob Hardesty—several others, but those I mention were the Lions.

A celebrated family of singers, a father and his two daughters (thier names Cowles), sat on the platform and sang.[2] Oh, such singing.

Douglass and Peek sang with them. It was the first meeting of the kind I
ever was at, and I was highly delighted and think any of you would have
been too, even Bro William Henry Farquhar, for here in our own free
state we dare to avow our loathing of the foul plague spot on our country's
glory.

Douglass made his home at Cousin Gove's (Sally Stroud).[3]

On 1st day the 6th Maria concluded to come home with us to spend
a week. Thomas brought us in his waggon—that is, Ruth Anna, Maria &
son, Alice, Carry, and I. We found Elizabeth very poorly with the Ague
and fever, which is very prevalent in the neighbourhood—several deaths.
Thyphus symptoms combine with it in many cases. She is pretty well
now, but weak, poor dear child. I am so engaged with drying my peaches
that I have not been with her much. Indeed, I have felt very weak and
good-for-nothing for some time past. Maria was quite poorly the last 2
days she staid (she left us 2nd day). I feel anxious to hear from her.
Deborah went with her.

Poor Sally Ann is not better. She is continually scolding or weeping.
Her poor mother seems to be the peculiar object of her dislike. Every
scoff and taunt that her diseased imagination can invent is lavished on
her. She won't suffer her to wait on her, and has struck her. She bears it
all with patience. Her lungs are much affected. She spits blood but
obstinately refuses to take anything, and though looking like a shaddow,
she will do the cooking, often gets up in the night and makes the bread
and pies. She has knit upwards of 40 ellegant cottons, N° 60 cotton. Will
not be idle a moment, often sits up all night, often gives directions about
her clothing, saying she must and will die that night, lifts heavy lifts that
you would not think possible, says she does it to break a blood vessel.
Her poor parents, how deeply I feel for them. . . .

A steam sawmill is building in Lynchburg, and the first cannal boat
was launched last 7th day.

Jos has been ploughing for a week past with Thomas's horses, the
first he has used horses. He has made great speed. Jim is in fine order and
is a darling horse. Lalie is larger than he—chestnut sorrel, fat and strong
and gentle, quite as good to work and easier to ride.

You remember Maria mentioned a tall young gentleman in connection
with Alice, and on your making some enquiry I told you I thought there
was a mutual attachment? She wishes me to assure you it is not the case
with her and that a warmer attachment than friendship he can never
inspire in her bosom, and you may depend on her word. But I will tell
you what a pair of loving black eyes looked into hers 2 years ago and an

impression was made on her heart by a young and noble-hearted man. They were separated without any avowal of attachment. He went to the Prairies of Upper Sanduskey [Ohio], 120 miles west from here, to tend some thousand sheep for his uncle. She struggled with feelings she thought it a folly to entertain as she had no evidence he reciprocated them. He returned not long since on a visit to his parents. They met and she found he had cherished her idea in all his toils and banishment, had never sought other female society. He offered her a heart which he said had never loved but her, and that the test he had determined to try his fate by was to leave her to act for herself till he acquired a competence, and then if he found her affections free, which sometimes he trembled to think of, he should know it was right.

Under such views when they met and he found her trusting heart his own, no wonder they soon stood in the tender relation of <u>betrothed</u>— but I do not expect they will be united very soon. He will return to the west to finish his contract with his uncle. That will take a year. He has just recovered from a spell of illness and looks so delicate to leave the care of his devoted mother and sisters to go among rude strangers. This much I will tell now, don't allude to it when you write. His name I will give you another time.

I have a fruit kiln to attend to and have commenced drying peaches, have dried 2 bushels begun 3rd day. Ruth Anna has a kiln and began yesterday. Her aunt, Ann Pearson, is with her. Thomas is carpentering at Lynchburgh at $20 per month and found they enjoy uninterrupted good health. We often talk of the happiness we enjoyed with you, Sister Mary. Now, my dear sweet sister, do please write. Henry, Hannah, Charlie and all the rest, say something. Do not forget to love me. When I begin to write messages here they all come clamouring among my heartstrings. My love warm and strong I send in a lump. Please take out a due portion at Sharon and spread the rest widely. . . . Tell me all you can about Bro Isaac. Oh, how we long to see him. Well, I fear this will be too late for the mail. Your own Anna

Alice says all accept her love, specially Uncle Isaac.

1. From Letter 209 of William Lloyd Garrison, August 15, 1847: "Saturday afternoon, at 4 o'clock, Dr. Peck, (he is a fine, promising colored young man, son of my old friend John Peck now of Pittsburgh, and formerly of Carlisle,) who has lately graduated at the Rush Medical College at Chicago."
2. Giles Hooker Cowles was a preacher who performed with his two daughters, Betsey and Cornelia, at abolition events such as this. Betsey, a graduate of Oberlin College, became an activist in the abolition, women's rights and education reform movements and was elected president at the nation's second women's rights convention in Salem in 1850.

3. Sally Stroud Gove, the wife of Moses Gove, was the granddaughter of Samuel and Sarah (Garrigues) Brooke of Marlborough. Her mother, Anne, had married Jacob Stroud.

~

11th mo 5th 1847
[addressed to Sarah Stabler]
My dear Mother, always 1st, Sister Sarah, and all of you,

I must first acknowledge the receipt of my dear Sister Sarah and Mother's letter. The mournful tidings were not unexpected to me, and I deeply sympathize with you to whom he was so dear.[1] Ah, what a sad autumn at Sharon after the <u>bright</u> joyous <u>Spring</u> and <u>summer</u>. Such is life! Is my beloved brother still with you? What are his prospects? My heart yearns for some intercourse with him, some little token of his affectionate remembrance of us, if it was only a message of love. His name is never spoken <u>alone</u> at Green Hill. Deborah and Alice talk of him almost every day and have an idea that he certainly is going to pay us a visit. And the thought flashed in my mind today what if he is coming and Sister Sarah or Lizzie with him? It made my heart jump. Oh, if it could be so.

Don't leave it long, for in March there will probably be another breach made in my family circle. Our darling <u>Alice expects to leave us</u> for a home in the <u>west 150 miles from he</u>re. The young man to whom she is engaged is named Josiah Griffith, of a very respectable family (his father and Ruth Anna's first cousins, his mother a most lovely talented woman, Maurice Miller's wife's sister[2]), his age 22, handsome, well-educated, intelligent, exellent disposition, very affectionate and easy in his manners, a Friend; and we hope and trust he is worthy of the precious treasure we have consented to bestow on him. But Oh, I shall miss her. None of my children ever waited on me as she always did. She is so cheerful. She is so beloved wherever she is known.

His mother and sister drove up in thier carriage a few days since. The mother is still mourning the death of a precious daughter aged 20 who had gone on a visit to Josiah, was taken ill, and died among strangers last 6th mo. She seems as if she wanted Alice to fill the void in her heart and treats her with the most endearing fondness. She said some might think it strange <u>her</u> <u>coming</u> here (it was our first acquaintance), but she had seen so much sorrow lately she did not mind these little things and her heart yearned for an acquaintance with Alice and her family. The dear child seems anxious to do all for herself she can. It is so little I can do to help her. My time and labour <u>is</u> in <u>my</u> power and that I most freely bestow, and she and I have worked early and late. She took in 5 bed quilts to quilt. In 3 weeks and 2 days we quilted 4 (which amounts to 7 dollars), have another ready to put in tomorrow which is to have considerable work on it. It will be 3 dollars more. Another she has to peice and quilt will be 3 more. And she has 6 ready to quilt for herself. She owes 3 dollars on her bureau, but the remainder will help get some little articles needful, and she has a fine cow worth 12 dollars which she expects to sell. Dear Lizzie G [Bentley] has furnished her wedding dress. It fits her beautifully with the other body.

Alice and I did work faithfully at the peaches. We dried 13 bushels with the skins on, a bushel and 1/2 pared. We made between 4 and 5 gallons of delicious peach jam, selling dried peaches to get the molasses, as much apple butter, besides preserved peaches, damsons, grapes, plum sauce, pickled cabbage, peaches, & tomatoes. A great lot of jams and dried peaches paid for all we had to buy (that is, jams spices and "sweetening," besides a paper of backy and pipe).

Deborah has been from home serving this 3 weeks. We expect her tomorrow. Poor Elizabeth has had a tedious time with the chill fever. Last week she had several chills but still went about her work, till this day week she was taken with violent palpitation of the heart and difficulty of breathing. Alice went down and staid 4 days. I sent stripped poplar bark and No 4 bitters at a venture, and she commenced taking with immediate good effect. Aliceanna came home 3rd day evening and Carry went down and will stay till Elizabeth gets stronger, though she was well enough to ride up here today with her brother Charles and his sweet young bride. They were married last week. Her father and Jesse Kersey's wife were brother and sister.[3] She is very pretty and amiable. They spent the day here. Charlie took Elizabeth home and after tea (or coffee, rather). They went down to Thomas's to spend the evening and night.

We have had so much wet weather it has been a difficult matter with farmers to get thier seeding done and clover seed in. But Joseph has got more seeding done than he has ever had and more clover seed, and his corn is very exellent, though not many acres. He has worked to the utmost of his strength, and I fear his feet are going to suffer as usual this winter. He has several of the worst-looking corns I ever saw. His tax this year amounts to 20 dollars.

Richard and Franklin and their families are well. Hannah and her sweet good little Laura M are well, were here yesterday. Hannah spoke of each one of you with the warmest affection, wanted her love given to you individually. She is a fond and rather good-looking mother, keeps her babe very sweet and nice as she does her house. Dear Sister Elizabeth, won't thee write some more? Do, Honey, bless thy dear, gentle, loving heart.

Carry has written and commenced half a dozen letters to her cousins which she has destroyed. . . . Cousin Phoebe, dear, don't think me ungrateful or willfuly neglectful of thy interesting letter. I intend to answer it when I can find time to do justice to it. Does thy health still continue better? Sister Mary, I am waiting patiently for something from thee; and Henry, Hannah, if you don't write I shall think you not much better than your mother. Alice sends love to all. Please give mine to all my beloved friends and every one of you. It is useless to try to express how much I love you. Your own, A

My own dear Aunt. Will you please excuse me for not writing more at this time? I just need this and am looking for the mail, and can only say that we truly sympathise with thee in thy bereavement. We had intelligence of Pleasant's death by a Baltimore paper before receiving thy letter. Please write often and remember me affectionately to uncle Isaac. Thy nephew, GSB

1. Sarah Stabler's stepson, Pleasants Stabler, had died.
2. Josiah Griffith was the son of William and Mary (Votaw) Griffith.
3. Charles Garrigues married Martha T. Coates in 1847. Jesse Kersey, the Quaker preacher, had married Elizabeth Coates, daughter of Moses and Mary Coates.

SIX

1850–1858

There is a break in the letters between 1848 and 1850. As Anna had hoped, her youngest sister, Margaret, and her husband, William Farquhar, visited Ohio in the spring of 1848. Elizabeth Briggs quoted from a letter she received from her brother-in-law at Green Hill dated May 19: "'We have been here several days,' he says, 'arrived safe & a little fatigued, I reckon, as every two persons were travelling the same distance. . . . At Salem ville I went into coal mines that extend 1/2 a mile under ground & saw some great salt works in operation, & heard about a well from which constantly issues a stream of inflammable gas; I mean to visit the place again. Margaret read while we passed through this angular kind of country (that's just the word for it) until we got within 3 miles of Lynchburg: then we found we did'nt want to read any more—Enquiring for Granville Bentley's, we drove up to the house: Alice Anna came out with open arms & heart ditto, she knew us by instinct, I suppose. In going in we found Elizabeth unable to rise from her chair from a severe attack of inflammatory rheumatism & evidently more excited than was for her good, by our arrival. Granville was sent for, he looked & behaved just as I expected he would.'" William Henry Farquhar also wrote that he found his brother-in-law, Joseph Bentley, a gentleman much like his uncle, Caleb Bentley, that Deborah had been "very agreeable" and Hannah and her eldest daughter, Laura, were "decidedly interesting."

In the 1850s, abolition was no longer a fringe issue. Slavery dominated the political debate, either directly or indirectly (through issues such as states' rights), and always profoundly. Abolitionists came in several flavors, rarely compatible with each other. Their different philosophies led to deep divisions in the movement. The followers of William Lloyd Garrison, such as the Brooke brothers, were immediatists. They rejected the Constitution, with its tacit acceptance of slavery, and the whole political process of compromise. As Northern politicians strained ever harder through the 1840s and 1850s to find common ground with the South and keep the Union together, the deeply moralistic Garrisonians took an uncompromising position. Their objective was nothing less than immediate emancipation. Salem, a hotbed of Garrisonianism, was the center of the Western Anti-Slavery Society, which published the *Bugle*.

Opposed to them in attitude and approach, political abolitionists believed in weaning the country from the evil institution through the political process. The Liberty Party was formed to represent Americans who believed in voting their way to a free United States. Eventually it gave way to the Republican Party in the middle of the decade.

The two main forces for abolition were divided by conscience and strategy. During the presidential campaign of 1856, when Republican John C. Fremont had captured the imagination of the political abolitionists, Daniel Hise of Salem wrote in his diary that Thomas Bentley had tried to get him to vote for Fremont, but that Hise, a staunch Garrisonian, "declined, having scruples about supporting a constitution that is pro-slavery."

As the country expanded, North and South tried to keep a balance of power. For every new state or territory designated free, the South demanded a corresponding pro-slavery state to maintain parity in the U.S. Senate. The price of Union seemed to get higher every year. The Fugitive Slave Act of 1850—which gave slave owners the right to travel in non-slave territories with their property and pursue runaways into Northern states with the full support of the law—caused widespread revulsion in the North. Passive resistance was practiced widely. Abolitionists played cat and mouse with federal marshals and slave catchers. In 1854, Salem abolitionists including Anna's cousin, Abraham, hearing that a Southern family had just arrived at the train station with a young slave girl, left an anti-slavery meeting and marched to the station, boarded the train, and seized the girl from her master and mistress. Abby Kelly Salem, as the black girl was renamed (after the popular lecturer of the day), went to live with Joel and Sarah McMillan.

In Sandy Spring, Maryland, farmers began to enjoy their first prosperity in many years, partly thanks to the interest in scientific farming that

Isaac Briggs Sr. and his associates had introduced decades before. The use of Peruvian guano as fertilizer starting about 1845 brought "magical" results, according to Maryland historian J. Thomas Scharf, and the 1850s reversed the local depression that had exiled so many of Anna's generation. But not everyone prospered.

Brother Isaac Briggs gave up the practice of Thomsonian medicine and started a second career. After studying photography in Baltimore, he took to the road as an itinerant daguerreotypist in 1849. Unfortunately for him, it was an overpopulated profession. Isaac's business never really flourished, as far as we can learn from family letters. At times he came close to being down and out.

During this period, some members of the family in Maryland and Ohio also began to drift away from the Society of Friends, which was going through yet another schism, between "Wilburites" and "Gurneyites." Richard and Maria Garrigues joined the Baptists in Salem. Hannah and Deborah had both been drummed out of the monthly meeting for joining other denominations in the 1840s. In 1849, Isaac Briggs was visited by a committee of Friends "on account of his intentionally absenting himself from our meetings." He breezily told them, according to the minutes of the monthly meeting, "that the charge was correct, and that for a considerable time his mind was fixed in opposition to belonging to any religious denomination whatever." He was disowned.

When the educator Alfred Holbrook, a staunch Methodist, took the reins of the Marlborough school in the early 1850s, however, he noted that the countryside was still made up "almost exclusively" of Quakers, especially Hicksites, whom he found to be "what were generally called 'Comeouters,' separating themselves from all religious associations and restraints." The Brookes seem to have been foremost among Freethinkers. Abraham's eccentricities became the talk of the family, if not the community. Caught up in the perfectionist movement of the day, which led to enthusiasm for vegetarianism, graham crackers and utopian communities, Brooke took his convictions a step or two further. While he allowed a group including his brother Edward and his cousin Elizabeth Luken to set up a communitarian society on his farm near Marlborough, Abraham himself refused to join because the communitarians didn't go far enough to suit him: They refused to reject the use of money.

Whatever Anna thought of all this religious and social ferment, she kept it to herself. She always maintained her Quaker dress and speech patterns, but held her tongue about the religious preferences of her children.

During gaps in Anna's letters, the plans for Aliceanna's wedding came to nothing. We can't know if Josiah Griffith left or died, jilted or was jilted. Perhaps to console Aliceanna, or just to broaden her horizons, Joseph and Anna allowed her to go to Maryland on an extended visit. It may be she accompanied her Aunt Margaret and Uncle William Farquhar back home after their stay at Green Hill. She never lived in Ohio again. In a letter she wrote from Sandy Spring in November 1849 to her cousin Henry Brooke, she said she had received a letter from home wondering when she might be returning. "But cousin Henry I do not think of returning to my native home to live for I certainly prefer this part greatly to the West. The Society in this immediate neighbourhood I have reference to," she wrote. One among that society was a cousin, John Stabler, son of Thomas Pleasants Stabler. A month later, John himself wrote to Henry that he had been to Falling Green to see "thy Cousin AA Bentley and the rest of thy family" and that he found her "one of the most lovely girls it has been my good fortune to meet with."

At home, Granville, Thomas, Franklin, Maria, and Hannah all were married and raising families. Anna delighted in her children-in-law and grandchildren, priding herself on getting along with the daughters-in-law and welcoming each successive addition to the family.

She continued to worry about Deborah's health, however. Poor Deborah had longed for her chance to visit back East ever since Hannah's unhappy trip in 1843, but poverty, bad timing, and bad health had kept her stuck at Green Hill and Salem. Behind Anna's letters one can hear the restless longing of her daughter for travel, culture, and a change of scenery. To Bentleys that inevitably meant Sandy Spring, Maryland, the object of Anna's nostalgia and doubtless the subject of many stories to her children. Her heart had yearned toward Sharon for years, so it should be no surprise that her daughters saw the old home as both exotic and comforting, where they might break out of their narrow country existence while still being in the bosom of family.

In the meantime, there was great relief that Hannah seemed to be maturing and flourishing as a young mother.

∽

2nd mo 6th 1850
1st
My own dear Sister Sarah,

My debts are accumulating, so I possitively must "make an effort" to get
some of them settled. Thank my stars I don't owe Sister Mary <u>nothin'</u>. I
do love to get a letter from thee. Thank thee for the rose seed. I planted
some of them. We have had 2 spells of intensely cold weather, and
notwithstanding all my care I fear last night has done for my lavender
and rose geraniums. My Japonica is splendid. Its glossy dark green leaves
look so fresh and cheerful in the dreary winter. I think it will bloom next
summer. I have 2 varieties of cowslips just ready to bloom, very flourishing,
a stockgilly cactus, orange and lemon trees. My only hybiscus was killed
last night. I <u>love</u> my plants. Will I see the "roses of Sharon" bloom next
summer? Who can tell!

I am occupying every moment of my time trying to get everything
done that is needful for my dear Jos and the rest in case the <u>right time for
me to go</u> should <u>once more manifest</u> itself. In my last letter to Alice the
9th of the 1st mo, she was commissioned to make some enquiries of thee
which we were anxious to have answered soon. I suppose it had not come
to hand when Sister Margaret wrote, for she did not mention it. I wish I
had thy letter by me, but I sent it to Salem and Debby forgot to bring it
back. She has been paying us a visit of a few days, left us last evening.
Her health is very good, she likes her employment, has made several
coats all herself. She has learned tell of several songs (from a Washington
lady, Mrs. Gary—"Napoleon's Grave," "The Blue Juniatta" (a wild
Indian song—beautiful), "The Spotted Fawn," "Love Not Be Kind to the
Lov'd Ones at Home"). She has improved in singing. She does make
melody. She has no prospect now of paying you a visit soon.

I have not seen Maria and family since the 8th month, was down to
see Elizabeth [Bentley] and Hannah Preston last week, divided the day
between them, the 2nd time since last fall, and have been nowhere else. I
wish you could see Hannah's very lovely little girls. Laura always was
good, but Almeda is the best child (<u>except one or two of my own</u>) I ever
saw. Now, I was just going to say something about Elizabeth's little boys,
but she has room to tell about them and can do it better. And Hannah
don't write to tell you this is Carrie's birthday, 16. She has gone to
Geography school with Thomas and Ruth Anna, and it is dark, cold, and
windy. I wish they had not gone. Thomas has 2 schools <u>afternight</u>. He
keeps them alternately.

I am almost uneasy about Alice. I want her to be happy, to enjoy herself among her friends, but when there is <u>so much</u> visiting and company, how does my darling manage to attend to her <u>more</u> important <u>duties</u>? (Does she neglect them? I hope not.) Watch over and counsel her. She has a loving heart and will listen. <u>Don't let anybody</u> gain her affections that is <u>not</u> worthy.

This is fourth day night. This won't go till 7th day, but so often when I leave it I am prevented. I thought I would begin when I <u>could</u>. Poor Joseph has suffered all winter very much with his feet. This winter has been hard on them, but the most favourable for grain that we have had for many years, great crops. . . .

5th day. Well, it has moderated some. Jos and Alban <u>have gone</u> to Hanover with a load of wheat and clover seed which <u>will pay several debts there</u>, but poor Joseph's feet will pay for it. <u>I have been working hard all day</u> and that is not favorable to writing agreeably. I have <u>all the housework except washing, milking, and getting breakfast, and though</u> there is but 4 of us, we eat and make a litter considerably, besides all the making and mending, knitting, and a considerable amount of the SCOLDING. I have exellent health, only Jack Frost took a notion to bite severely both my heels and <u>little toes</u>, with which I have suffered much; and when I shew them to Jos, he says, "Poo, that's nothing." I have not been down to Cousin R's for a great while. Sally Ann is not better.

I believe I must divide this sheet between thee and Sister Margaret. I will leave room for Granville to pay his respects to thee. I know he loves thee. Please give my love individually to all the household at Sharon. Thy own sister, A

[continuation of above]
Dear Sister Mary,

Thank thee for thy letter, if it did communicate a portion of its sadness to my heart and make me almost sorry to look at the enclosed. I hope our dear Alice is at home now, her <u>reaction</u> over, and performing her <u>duties</u> cheerfully. Oh, dear Sister, watch over my child and warn her of danger when thy <u>more</u> experienced eye detects it, and I sincerely hope she may not add to thy cares instead of lighten them. I want her deeply to consider the influence her example will be likely to have on Ellen and let it be such a one that may make her a blessing to her parents. I am affraid, tell her, she is <u>rayther</u> too fond of company for a portionless girl situated as she is. I don't want to check her social affections, dear child. Her early life was one of toil and restriction, cares beyond her years, few associates, few congenial spirits. No wonder she should feel like a new being, in a brighter sphere, I want her to love and be worthy of the love of all her friends, but temperance and moderation in pleasures secures its long continuance.

Do thee tell me if any of the gentlemen whose names I so often see—thee is so good at guessing what I want to know. Fancy the question asked and form thy answer.

6th day. Hannah and her sweet little pets came up last evening, are here now, and a long letter from Alice giving an account of her visits. She is enjoying herself—highly. . . .

Oh it is such a dreary, rainy night. Hannah could not go home as she intended but is sitting just opposite to me with Almeda asleep in her lap. She is piecing a quilt. Every now and then she grins and gives me some queer message for you I can say for her. She is very judicious and very successful in the management of her children—firm, but gentle.

When I was coming away from Granville's last week, after I had kissed Elizabeth, I offered to kiss little Joe. He turned away with a cunning look and said, "No, I haven't got one for thee, but I will take the one thee give my mother." He held up his mouth to her and said, "There's one of Grandmother's kisses in thy mouth. I want it." He took it laughing and looking so quizzical but would not give me one. He talks very sweetly and very plain, is a very pretty, rosy-cheeked little darling. Willie can read right smartly, is very fond of his books, has a great turn for calculation. He has never gone to school. He will make a smart man some day, if he lives. Elizabeth is just a darling, and so is Granville. They don't seem proud or stuck up, though Granville is Postmaster, Merchant, and waggon maker of Lynchburg and farmer of Green Hill.

Please give love to all my beloved friends.

Thy loving sister, Anna

P.S. Alice, darling, write soon and tell much. Don't take hard what I have said in Aunt's letter. It is not to censure thee but from love. Continue to write freely of all that concerns thee.

Thy own mother.

My Dear Aunt Mary,

Please accept the Ribbon Aunt Sarah chooses to leave. And don't feel jealous that she should have first choice. I don't know that she is any

<u>prettier</u> or <u>cleverer</u> than thyself but she is a <u>good deal older</u>. If thee don't choose to wear it, pin it under Ellen's chin.
Much love to Aliceanna and all.
Thy own Nephew,
G.S. Bentley

Anna's initial trip home to Sandy Spring in 1847 seems to have broken the dam of her pent-up need for her family. She <u>thereafter paid</u> visits every couple of years or so, perhaps with financial <u>help from her children.</u> In July, Brother Isaac wrote to her in Sandy Spring—addressing her as "Dear Stranny"—from Prince Edward Court House, where <u>"extreme penury"</u> had caused him to stop and set up a photo studio in the abandoned courthouse. His letter was a typical catalog of misfortune told with broad strokes of humor. He vented his bitterness against people in Sandy Spring. While he "doats" on a few people there, "I <u>spises many</u> others <u>infernally</u>." And, by the way, he also hated the "self righteous" Pharisees who attended at the "<u>accursed</u> old brick Synagogue."

In his present situation, his makeshift studio was so damp and windy and the local water so full of minerals he couldn't develop pictures properly. Furthermore, the courthouse was being used as a privy, and he claimed that the rotting bones of a dead body occupied a whiskey barrel outside the window. An over-indulgence in unripe cherries had stricken his digestive system, and while he lay ill in bed, a number of customers had gone away disappointed. As he writes, "things have gone <u>wrong, wrong, wrong</u> ever since I have been here."

October 25th 1850
[from Granville to Sarah Stabler]
My Own Dear Aunt, . . .

Mother appears to have spent the time most delightfully amongst you. There was nothing could have given her more real happiness than such a visit. Some of you must return the visit and let us welcome you to Ohio. I hear that Aunt Lizzie talks of coming sometime hence, with Alice. Think she ever will? Tell her that her likeness was shown me suddenly and I bore it well. She is better looking than I expected, and I love her enough.

Thee asks what I think of the folks moving to Salem? Well, I am not so sanguine in my expectations as some of the rest. I give them six months to tarry in Salem. Father may be satisfied there for a longer time if he gets into business of some kind. If not, he will absquatulate[1] before that time expired—And then he'll never undertake another move. This is not what I wish or hope for. I shall be very much pleased to hear of their being comfortably situated there and satisfied with it. Father has been used to an active life, and I don't think any other would suit him. In fact, I look upon this as an experiment and desire it may prove a successful one, if it adds to their happiness. They have sent some things on and I expect will be ready in 2 or 3 weeks for their new home. We expect to occupy the house they leave for a time indefinite, perhaps 3 or 6 months or as many years. Maria writes that the house is ready and looks very nice and comfortable. She thinks they will never wish to leave there. Don't thee think we will feel rather lonely being the sole occupants of Green Hill when so lately we numbered the 3rd family?[2] . . .
Thy loving nephew
G.S. Bentley

1. According to the Oxford English Dictionary, a jocular word meaning to decamp.
2. With his parents and Franklin's family.

~

Joseph, Anna, and the remaining children moved into Salem that winter. Deborah and Caroline were able to take some advantage of living in a town, but Joseph became restless. And Deborah yearned to join her sister in Maryland.

In the meantime, Aliceanna once again was making plans to marry.

~

Salem 1st mo 28th 1851
after 9 oclock
My beloved Mother and all of you,

Does the wind howl so dismally around Sharon as it does here tonight? What are you all doing? Does a thought of me steal into your hearts often, tenderly making excuses for all my faults, even excusing me when I don't write to tell you how much my thoughts dwell with you, how I have treasured up every scene, your kind, loving words and looks and

every spot and object—bright, precious, beloved pictures in my memory's
storehouse gathered in my recent visit to you? I cannot describe to you
the vivid distinctness of these pictures. It is as if they were daguerotyped
into my brain. Mother, when I think of our dear little room, every
minute article is there. I see always even the lantern that shewed through
the crack over the closet door, Sister Elizabeth's basket of patches, even
the <u>blot</u> in the picture of the bird on the box under the glass, our pipe
box, the spool handle to the drawer, &c. It is so with all the rest, and
your dear selves. I can dress you at pleasure in anything I ever saw you
wear, and the very folds are the same. The tones of your voices, your very
words, I can never feel lonely while I have such treasures.

We have had a most unusual winter, so mild and pleasant. We had
one snow that made good sleighing for a week or two, and I never saw as
many sleighs. (All have bells.) It was quite musical. I have to quit
tonight, I believe.

5th day night. The Northwestern did not blow for nothing night
before the last, a very sudden change from our pleasant springlike
weather to below zero. I don't know how much exactly the coldest night
last night was, that we have had this winter and tonight will be colder
still. I have fixed up the flannel thee gave me, Mother, in 2 nice garments
with sleeves that are such a comfort to me. You would scarcely think how
busy I have to be. I'm blessed with good health.

Oh, just while I think of it, Sister Sarah, please tell me how many
peices it took to form the squares of patchwork in that quilt we saw at
Cousin Roger's, how many of dark. I remember the peices of dark on the
corners of the light. I think thee wisely took a memorandum. Please
don't forget.

How does our dear little "Jim Crack" get on with his tools? Always
tell me of any accessions to his stock. And Lizzie, dear, has she got hair
enough now to keep her head warm this cold weather?[1] Oh, I must go to
bed, for the fire has got so low and no more wood in. It is after 10. Bless
you all, good night.

31st. Ugh! what a cold morning, and last night was severely cold.
Debbie got a letter last night which put the finishing stroke on her long
fondly cherished hope of seeing you ere long. Cousin Letitia Gilpin[2] had
sent her word to be sure and get ready to go with her in the early spring,
so that good company seemed provided, and as with the feelings and
news of things thee have grown with her growth she cannot understand
<u>why</u> it would not be <u>respectable</u> to earn in Maryland with her <u>needle</u> the
means to return, and to keep her while there from being a burden to the

beloved friends whose limited means she would never be willing to
encroach upon. And as she only had laid by sufficient to <u>get</u> there, she
now, entirely and forever, abandons the idea.

Oh, I did not intend to say one word about all this. Why did I? I am
so apt to let my feelings just run out at the end of my pen, and if it
troubles me to see my child look sad, I should not be so selfish as to
inflict the least portion of it on you. <u>She</u> has had bitter <u>trouble</u> of heart
for some months past that increased her desire to be with you and her
beloved <u>sister</u>— but enough of that. Don't allude to this in your letters.
Oh, I keep doin' it. I will stop and get dinner for them————

PM. Sister Lizzie, darling, I see thee in the kitchen—and, strange to
tell, got on the old green, when I thought it was upstairs in the big
trunk—making biscuits for supper: Darling sister, heaven bless thee for
all thy gentle kindness to me. I often think of how thee gave up thy place
by Mother's side at night and slept on the lounge, and I often wonder I
did not do more for you all when I was there. I want you to tell me <u>every</u>
thing about yourselves, when any bundles come with "clothes," &c.
Sister Sarah, I can't just make out how to dress thee just now—not as I
have seen thee sometimes, draggled to thy knees and <u>squishing</u> in the old
gum shoes, but primmed up in <u>that cap</u>; and I can't fix her in any dress
but the plaid silk. She has got her desk and just commencing a letter—
"My dear sister Anna"—and she is going to write some poetry in it.
Mother is smoking, and as she happens to think of me, a great round
sigh comes out all blue and nearly smothered in the smoke!————

I wish you could see how snug we look here. I am seated in our little
kitchen as there is no fire in the parlour. On the table before me is a
flourishing pot of cowslips almost in bloom. It is a species of great beauty
and sweetness. An orange tree, a pot of violets, a rose geranium. My
splendid silver-edged Euonymus is in the parlour. It is a little round tree
more than 3 feet high with bright glossy green leaves large as orange
leaves, only darker green, more round at the point, and indented like a
rose tree leaf. But I do not expect we shall stay here longer than till
spring, pleasant as it is to me, for Jos cannot be contented without
employment and none has offered yet. Will you let me write to Alice a
little seperately on this and tell her she is to pay half the postage and I do
wish I could write something better worth it. It seems as if my talent, if I
ever had one, is departing, but I know I write to those who love me
enough to overlook deficiencies.
Most tenderly, your loving A

1. "Jim Crack" and Lizzie were Sarah's children, James P. Stabler Jr. and his sister.
2. Letitia probably was related to Lydia Gilpin Brooke, the wife of William Brooke of Marlborough, and may have been visiting her there.

~

My dear Alice,

In thy last to me thou made a request for the "written consent" which shall be forthcoming as soon as the certificate can be proccured. If given, it is immediately to be forwarded to us and we will promptly attend to it.

"Thee art a saucy baggage," as old Seth used to say. When I came to that part in thy letter where thee spoke of something in my letter that had made thee unhappy and would not say what it was, I was troubled and bewildered, for all my recollection and feelings refused to aid me in throwing any light on what it could possibly be. I have always been in the habit of writing just as the thoughts came, and as I never write but to those I love, I never expect they could possibly beleive I would think an unkind thing, let alone write it. So, my naughty pet, kiss its mother and be good. It was not pretty either to say what thee did at the close. Thee "concluded it was most pleasant to us to hear but little on the subject," &c. There is nothing too trivial to interest me that concerns your interest. And would thee "just as leave I would keep quiet," too, on the reverse side of opinions? Which with me are not "pretence"? I would that my judgement had never been listened before I met thee, precious one.

Well, thy long-looked-for letter to Debbie came last night. She did not get it till this morning. She has been suffering with tootheache for several days and yesterday afternoon went to the dentist's to get it extracted. She took chloroform, was insensible more than an hour. They broke the toothe and got out part of the root without her being conscious of it, but she fainted and laid so long, 15 minutes, they were scared and desisted. She walked home and attended her writing school in the evening. She suffers much pain and soreness from the remains of the tooth and operation and is nervous and drowsy. But is engaged on a fine sack coat, which father helps her with (and we all think none the worse of them for it).

Alice, dear, I remember well when thy dear grandmother used to be glad to get work from the tailor's and took in all the sewing she could, even in Maryland; and she was then and will be as much honored and respected as if she had been too proud or idle to do so. And with these feelings do not be surprised that thy parents did encourage her [Deborah].* But if I thought going there would instill that kind of pride in her, then I should have opposed it. But it is all over now, and after a time I hope she will be reconciled to her disapointment. She has not been happy lately and longed for thy company. Thou wouldst not know her hand-writing or Caroline's, they have improved so.

Now, Honey, I have only been lovingly writing for thy good in all tender feeling. Don't take it wrong. If thee should, get Grandmother or Aunt Sarah to explain it all. Oh, I must take another bit of paper for I have more to say but must get supper first.

Well, I baked lots of biscuits. Supper is over. [letter breaks off]

*beleiving none whose opinion she need value would think the less of her

❧

In May, having obtained a certificate of removal from the New Garden Ohio Monthly Meeting to Sandy Spring [Maryland] Monthly Meeting, Aliceanna married thirty-one-year-old John Stabler, the fourth child of Thomas Pleasants and Elizabeth Stabler. Within the month beloved Isaac Bond, Sharon's adopted son, married Anne Wetherald in Sandy Spring.

Deborah Bentley attended her sister's wedding. Having waited years for her opportunity to go back East, Deborah made the most of it. She was a big hit with the family at Sharon. Hannah wrote to Isaac, "She is very lively and very funny, makes us laugh untill our sides ache sometimes." Aunt Elizabeth, who often spared no criticism when writing to her brother, had nothing negative to say about this niece when she wrote him in May 1851. "She is already quite a favorite with all who have made acquaintance with her," Elizabeth conceded. "Cousin Betsy Lea says 'she has the true dignity of a woman about her.' Almost every one thinks she looks like her grandmother. We feel very warmly attached to her & consider her a good girl. I think it quite probable she 'may scratch up a husband' here. If she meets with a suitable character I shall be glad if she does."

As Granville had predicted, Anna and Joseph didn't stay in Salem. Her next letter came from Green Hill.

❧

8th mo 19th 1851
My own dear sister Sarah,

Oh, how thee can weild that ready weapon of thy wit. If I did not know the shafts were never dipped in venom, but love that causes no smart, I should dread them and take <u>some pains</u> to avoid them, but I love to provoke them. A <u>very</u> few times they have hit in a tender place. Now, thee may just enjoy making fun of my helter-skelter style of writing as much as thee pleases; it is pure envy. Mother says I write interesting <u>letters</u>, and <u>Cousin Betsey Lea</u> says my letters remind her of Anna Grant's!!![1] And thee, to pretend to immitate, and laugh because the thoughts come tumbling from the pen and don't take time to be <u>STOPPED</u>, but nearly run over each other. Well, thee has wit enough to untangle them and set them up straight in thier places. And I don't expect to do much better, but I do wish, dear Sister, thee would tell me about thy plans and prospects. Which of thy cows did thee lose and how? Tell me when anybody is kind and helps thee. Tell me when it goes rough with thee. I would share with thee in joy or sorrow. Tell me of thy farm prospects: garden, fruit, and flowers.

Those wild sensitive plant seed I gathered at Sharon have produced plants which are <u>beautiful, much</u> larger than thier <u>parents</u>. I have several and 1 in a flowerpot, and somehow I always think of Sister Lizzie when I look at it. I have several perriwinkles from Cousin Betsey Lea in bloom, and the plant from the Capitol I can't describe. It is rather a coarse-looking plant now in bloom. It is 2 or 3 feet high. Oh, mercy, I tried to draw something [and here she inserts a picture of a plant] in shape of the leaf but it's more like a spider. They are 6 inches long, some of them, and have [illegible] on the undersides. The blossom is singular but not very pretty; I can't describe it, <u>let alone draw it</u>. And about the lady slipper seed I gathered so carefully from the most beautiful and marbled of thine: They are very few, say 4 or 5 among hundreds, the least spotted. But Cousin MEG told me if I would in the spring in transplanting twist the roots of any two together, they would always be variegated.

Is Aunt H Bentley going to remain at Richard's? How is the property divided?[2]

Well, I must get dinner.

Afternoon. In the spring we had an army of rose bugs that destroyed all our grapes and many other things. They were succeeded by a countless host of ugly striped (some yellow- and some white-striped) bugs that first appeared on the potatoe vines and then the beets and tomatoes, riddling the leaves completely. They act like cantharides on the skin. And myriads of grasshoppers, which have destroyed all the clover seed—and we never had a better prospect before. They laid it waste. In some places they have destroyed oats, buckwheat, and corn. I never saw anything like it.

Thy friends have gone, and I am disapointed. Cousin Margaret did not get over to see me.

Poor Cousin Mary Miller. Had she a younger than Freddie?[3] I wish when Cousin Ann writes she would give my love to her and tell her if she wishes to add to the circle of her acquaintance in St. Louis, my daughter Elizabeth's brother Edward [Garrigues] and wife (a very amiable woman) board at her sister's, Mrs Harriet Blakely's, boarding house. They have 2 children, Gertrude and Josephine. I think an acquaintance would yield mutual pleasure. They have lost one (Isabella, thier second child). We all loved Margaret when she visited us.

I wish Debbie would go and see Cousin Betsey Thomas when she is well enough [prudently?] to do so. I do not expect <u>she</u> would receive pleasure from it other than the thoughts visiting the sick and soothing the poor, helpless, afflicted sufferer of so many long weary years would give; and it would so gratify Cousin Margaret to hear some account of her. Sally Ann never forgave me for not going oftener. Write particularly about Debbie's throat, what thee thinks about it.

And now I will try <u>once more</u> and <u>never quit</u> till I do get the desired information <u>about that quilt</u> we saw at Cousin Roger's. I do really wish <u>very much</u> to know the number of peices in each block, dark and light <u>each</u>. I think thou took a memorandum. I regret I did not, then I would not have had occasion to bother thee <u>so often</u>, and make thee feel so ashamed, as thee <u>needn't</u> feel when thee reads this. . . .

Ah, no daguerreotype was ever so distinct, as lovely & beloved Sharon and all its inmates, its furniture. (Oh, tell, is the grease spot gone in the carpet? It is bright as ever in my view.) Bless you, one and all. Thy own sister, [paper fold]. There's a kink here; fix it right.

1. While this must have meant something either shocking or amusing to Anna and Sarah, I have been unable to identify Anna Grant or her writing style.
2. Henrietta Bentley's husband, Caleb, had died on July 13, age ninety.
3. Freddie Miller, age one, died on July 1 in St. Louis. The Millers were a Sandy Spring family.

∾

The happiness at Sharon was shattered in December of that year when Hannah <u>Briggs died, age eighty-two</u>. Anna's brother-in-law William Farquhar described her last few days: "On Sunday evening last (the 21st)

M & I walked over to Sharon, & found them all laughing very merrily, Mothers voice with the rest. Warwick Miller & Mary were there, and had been telling some wonderful accounts of the spiritual knockings, in which Mary partly believes. Mother looked very well & pleasant, but when they were gone, she got up & put on a cloak, saying she was chilly." Nausea and back pain were followed by a restless sleep. The Farquhars went home "feeling a deal uneasy." The next day, afflicted with diarrhea, she grew steadily weaker. Although in some pain, she remained coherent until she died at 10:45 the morning of December 26.

~

1st mo 11th 1852
1st day night
[addressed to Sarah Stabler]
My own Sister Sarah & all the dear household of Sharon,

Oh, could the wings of the spirit waft the poor mortal clogs that surround it, I should be with you all these long, long, weary days of mourning. It would be such a relief to my heart to have some one to talk to continually of our dear mother, to speak of her love, her gentle kindness. But it always is the case with Joseph when death has drawn the curtain between any loved one and us, his lips are sealed, thier names even never pass them, and he avoids all conversation that alludes to them. Oh, if I could be amongst you, there is so much yet I wish to hear, dear precious sisters and my own loved children. Oh, give me that proof of your love and sympathy as to commune with me often, very often, and the only way now in our power, by letters. Oh, did she miss me, her first-born, in the loved circle of her anxious children that gathered round her, privileged to do something for her, though agonised to see her suffer?

I remember once saying to Deborah, "If it should be that my blessed mother should be called away while thee is there, consider thyself as my representative and supply my place with all tender attention." And when the pure spirit burst its bond and was clothed in immortality (but alas to be seen by us no more on earth), you wept together over her venerated form, over her closed grave. I know you thought of poor Brother Isaac and of me; our tears are shed afar off, and alone.

Thou asked me, dear Sister, if I had "no premonition of the coming of a great affliction" all that week. I had great heaviness of spirits. I several times stood at the west window in a deep reverie following with my eye the course of a slow funeral procession all along our lane up to our little place of graves, but my own form was the one to be laid there. On 6th day morning Elizabeth was here. We were talking of Mother. I told her that Caroline the day before had said, "Mother, would thee greive <u>much</u> to hear of Grandmother's death? For it is what thee might expect to hear at any time." I replied, "Oh, Caroline, I never could bear to dwell on the idea. I allways put it from me, and yet I would far rather she should go now than for the hand of time to shatter the intellect, the freshness of feeling, that makes my mother so loving and beloved."

On New Year's night I was sitting sewing and alone, Jos in bed. Carrie came home from Geography school and said, "Oh, Mother, here is a letter from Sis Maria Cousin Robert brought. Open it and read out loud, for I want to hear." She called to her father, who answered. I commenced it and read a few lines. It enclosed Debbie's to Maria, with the most tender lines from herself and entreaties for me to come to her as she could not come to me—I will not dwell longer on my own feelings. Tell me of yours, of dear Sister Lizzie's. I am now the oldest of the Sharon family. Oh Mother, Mother, let thy mantle of love descend to me, let me be unselfish as thou.

Joseph and Caroline were very anxious for me to go to Salem to spend 2 or 3 weeks, and Richard had spoken to Ezra Reeder to bring me up last 7th day as he was going up with an empty sled. I had got all ready, Granville had taken my trunk to his house, was going to take me to Lynchburg, when Thomas came up and told me he had just heard Ezra was going to hitch 2 colts unbroken. Well, that settled the matter. They did get there and back, but had a time of it. The colts were very unruly, ran away and were very near running the sled backwards in the canal. I did not feel easy either about leaving Father. If Deborah has received my letter directed to Geo[rge]Town she will know about his feet being so badly frosted he is not able to wear a shoe yet. Oh, they seem a little better for 2 days past so that we have discontinued poulticing and applied greased rags. One heel is raw where the black spots came the skin comes off. Thy overshoes have done good service. I never saw any feet so bad as his.

Carrie has had all the feeding to do. The day before New Year I was coming downstairs with a box to chop mince meat on the steps, one very narrow, and had ice on all of them, and my shoes very smoothe. On the 2nd step they slipped, and I fell all the way down 10 or 11. My back, hips, arms, and legs were dreadfully bruised, one on my leg—the back part from the ancle up—is as large as this mark. The leaders sore, and I think it a mercy no bones were broken. So with a wounded spirit and bruised flesh it is hard to arouse my energies.

I had a very satisfactory letter from dear Hannah yesterday. She desired her most tender love to all of you, says she loves you as well as she ever did, wishes Deborah and Alice would write to her. Tell Alice <u>please</u> do; her address is Frederick Town, Knox County, Ohio. Her boy sat alone at 3 months, is large of his age, very good.[1] Almeda, they say, is a beauty. They talk of visiting us in the spring. Debbie, tell Alice her old friend Eliza Smith (Preston) has a son 2 weeks old, Martha Garrigues a young son.[2]

We received a letter from Alban yesterday. He is improving, writes quite a good letter, is very happy and a great favorite at Cousin William Brooke's, where he lives. In addition to poor Father's other suffering, he has had tootheache since yesterday. But I fixed a mustard plaister on his face, put <u>my night cap</u> on him, and he is asleep. No news of Matilda.* She is lost, no doubt. How heartless! to desert her only child, but better far for it.

Please write to me. Debbie and all, my dear sister Margaret, I feel that it looks like <u>neglect</u> in me not to have written to thee long ago, but there is none of the <u>feeling</u> of it in my heart, only I have so many to write to now my children scattered about so. How I would love to see thy little boy—yes, all of you. How does brothers WH Briggs and WH Farquhar get on with thier schools? Forgive me if I can't fill the blank. I can't tell the love, the encreased tender love I feel for you all. <u>She</u> loved us all and taught us to love each other. Give my love to dear Lizzie when thee writes to her. And sharing your joys and sorrows, I am your affectionate sister and mother,
Anna Bentley

*Since writing the above we have heard she went off with Milton Coffee (not the one in Salem). He came to see her before she was married. She is in Ohio City in a <u>disreputable boarding house</u>. She had agreed to go off with another man, but renewing her acquaintance, changed her mind.

2nd day. Please tell me what gown our mother was dressed in. Please send me a scrap of it. Did Aunt Dolly get up?[3] Oh, do among you give me every minute detail concerning her and yourselves individually, how each one bears it. I am with you in thought continually and in the past "long, long ago." You are together there at Sharon, a spot her living love and death has sanctified.

2nd day night. Dear Sister Mary will write soon. Oh, don't let us feel it such a task to give each other so much pleasure and comfort. We have here a severely cold winter but favourable to the grain as it has been protected by snow all the hard freezing spells.

3rd day morning. Father is better, though he had a suffering night with his head. His feet are better, though they do look bad—so purple, with raw places and dark spots. The weather is most intensely cold with a keen northwest wind that fills the air with the drifting snow. As soon as it moderates enough to be prudent, we are going to wrap up and Charles Reeder[4] will take us in his sleigh to Salem where dear Maria will assist me in nursing Father up and there we can get worming medecines. Granville will assist dear Carrie tending to the stock, and E Reeder be with her every night. Granville cuts wood plenty for us, but we can't keep warm.

Most affectionately, you're A

1. Probably Horace Bentley Preston, her fourth child and first son. Almeda was born in 1846.
2. Eliza Preston had married Joseph B. Smith on October 10, 1850, and Charles Garrigues (Robert and Margaret's son) had married Martha Stackhouse on April 13, 1843.
3. This would be Aunt Dorothy Hopkins from Baltimore.
4. A neighbor, age about forty-six.

~

Elizabeth Briggs Luken of Marlborough remembered Hannah Briggs lovingly in a letter she wrote in February 1852. For more than twenty years she had kept a letter Hannah had written her on the death of Elizabeth's son, Samuel, age sixteen, in 1830: "She compared our situations—each had lost a husband and a child. It brought back memories of our trials many years ago."

Debbie's health remained precarious. She was sick in her room for nine weeks in the spring of 1852, while her sister Aliceanna, who gave birth to her first child, Florence, that year, was described as "smart" and "blooming." A teenage cousin, Deborah Stabler, described finding Deborah at one point "sitting on the floor suffering the most intense agony; she had the cramp and is still in a very critical condition. I sat up with her all night; and never did I see anyone suffer as much as she did." In August, Isaac responded to more dreary news about Deborah with a bit of characteristic philosophizing: "Poor niece Debbie! were Greek mythology true, I would believe she had swallowed at least half the contents of 'Pandora's box'—her case as regards physical suffering is certainly anomalous & my heart would bleed, & I could weep tears of blood for her—were I only a devout heathen." As it was, however, Uncle Isaac ascribed to the "doctrine of compensation" in which Debbie would get some spiritual reward for her suffering. Anna traveled to Maryland that November to bring her home, where she moved in with Richard and Maria Garrigues, who had lost their toddler, Harold, in July.

This was also the year Granville's youngest child was born. Julia Alice, who never married, would prove to be one of Anna's stalwarts in old age. And it was the year the Cleveland & Pittsburgh railroad was built, spelling the end to any hope that canal shipping would bring lasting prosperity to villages like Lynchburgh. One of the local resources the railroad took east from Hanover was coal. This was the beginning of serious coal mining in the area, far from the small-time enterprise of farmers like Joseph Bentley who took their coal to market by the bushel. Not least, the linking of the railroad with Pittsburgh opened unprecedented possibilities for Anna to travel back east. And she did, with increasing frequency.

In Salem, some notes from Daniel Hise's diary introduce another social issue of the time, one in which the Salem Quakers were naturally at the forefront. In May, Hise noted that his wife Margaret had gone to Akron with Joel and Sarah McMillan for a Women's Convention.

The women's rights movement grew out of the abolition movement. Women took a more and more active role in abolition, from their first tentative steps onto a speaking platform before other women, to assertion of their opinions in open meetings, to signed articles arguing the cause of anti-slavery, to (in a few cases) extensive travel and public lectures in cities and villages all over the North. Women stepped forward in large numbers to participate in the great movement, and over time they felt their power and exercised their skills.

Their self-assertion caused a rift in the movement. Radicals such as Garrison embraced feminism, extending his arguments for the equality of all men to the equality of the sexes. Others, men and women alike, were repelled by the idea of women breaking out of their domestic realm. Quaker women were among the most forward of the early feminists. Naturally, Salem, Ohio, harbored a coterie of women in the vanguard. The nation's second women's rights convention was held there in 1850.

So closely were the women's rights and abolition movements inter-twined that the call for the convention appeared in an edition of the *Anti-Slavery Bugle*. Hannah Brooke of Marlborough (Cousin Edward Brooke's wife), Hannah Wileman (Cousin Samuel Brooke's future wife), and Maria Garrigues all signed the document, and Maria was named to an organizing committee. Betsey Cowles, an Oberlin College graduate and abolitionist, was elected its president.

Jane Trescott wrote to her friend Sarah McMillan in 1851 that no one had yet seen a Bloomer dress in Salem, but "I would like to have one with the skirt some 6 or 8 inches shorter [than] I wear my dresses now but I don't think I would like them to come above the knee." In July of the following year, Daniel Hise recorded that he and his wife had walked into town, she in her Bloomer dress.

On the lighter side, when they weren't attending lectures by famous abolitionists such as Sojourner Truth or William Lloyd Garrison or smug-gling escaping slaves, Salemites shared a widely popular interest in spiritu-alism. The Hises spent an entertaining evening with their friends Isaac and Jane Trescott and three mediums. Over in Marlborough, as Alfred Holbrook reported, Hannah Wileman (later Brooke) claimed to be harassed by some errant apparition who threw objects around the room and spilled a pitcher of water on her and a friend. Traveling circuses came to town, theatricals were performed, and social calls were paid.

Tom, Frank, and Maria all made their homes in Salem, although the restless Tom, maybe taking a leaf from his Uncle Isaac's book, wasn't to stay put. He and Ruth Anna had two sons, Emerson, born in 1850, and Lin-den, born in 1852. Maria's youngest child, Harry Bentley, was born in January 1853. Frank and Hannah Bentley had two young children, Walter and Clara. Down at Green Hill, Granville and Elizabeth were raising their brood, William, Joseph, and Julia. Hannah Preston's fourth child—after Laura, Almeda, and Horace—was Charles Sumner, born in 1853 and named for the famous abolitionist politician. Anna, her childbearing years finally well behind her, had only two children at home, the teenagers Caroline and Alban. Joseph, now over sixty, with bad feet and other, more serious, health problems, worked constantly.

∾

11th mo 28th 1853
My beloved sister & precious neice, Lizzie,

You will think it an unseasonable hour to commence a letter and regret
the cause of my being up. I am watching the heavy sleep that Morphine
has produced in its successful aleviation of the intense agony of billious
colic with which my dear Joseph suffered since yesterday morning. It
would not yield to my remedies and was becoming so alarming I ran for
Granville and got him to go about noon for Dr Swearingen (at
Lynchburg). While he was gone I was alone with him. He could not lie
down. He had a chill and was in such agony the blood settled round his
mouth, and fingernails purple. And he looked so ghastly Granville was
back soon. The Dr sent a portion of Morphine, which relieved him in a
few minutes. The Dr came in 10 minutes after, pronounced it a billious
attack, says his system is very much out of order, highly billious. He is
very weak. I have given him all the 3 powders he left and 1 spoonful of
castor oil and no opperation, yet he has had but little pain since; has
vomited twice but slept most of the time and has had profuse perspiration
and a violent itching all over him.

   Last 6th day he walked in much suffering to his lame feet to
Rochester, 3 miles, and back and then to Alexander, 3 ditto, and back,
the next day to Hanover 3 and back again. He says for 2 or 3 weeks he
has suffered much pain at times in his breast and stomach, but still he
worked on trying to get all fall work done that he might take rest with an
easy mind and that Alban might not miss a day at school.

   He has made up his mind when he recovers from this to have the
toes next his great ones on each foot taken off! The Dr examined them
today, says it would not be very painful and would relieve him of much
suffering. They are crowded entirely out of thier place, have dreadful
corns on them and make corns on the others and hurt him every step he
takes. My poor, toil-worn companion, what wonder is it that he should
be irritable and impatient.

   Before I finish this I hope I can tell you he is much better, as I must
attend to giving him the oil every 2 hours till it operates and wait on
him. I had rather keep wide awake all the time, and it was something of
an effort, as I was on my feet all day, added to anxiety. So I got your dear
letters and read them over and they warmed up and invigorated my old
heart. Now, if my disjointed tedious scrawls can ever give one half the
comfort, the pleasure, that they have given me, why it would be almost
wicked in me to withold them. Precious, very precious to my soul is your

love, your sympathy, but I ought not to be selfish enough to burden your loving spirits with complaints or despondency. I could not help it when I wrote last, I had no other material to work with. My health and spirits are both much better now. I feel like another being. I do my own washing and ironing in the first-rate style and with less fatigue. I have to be constantly busy and always at home, but it is becomeing easier.

Sister Sarah, I do think thy letter was the most interesting one thee ever wrote me, not a line too much.

Now stop a bit and let me try
To write a little po-e-try,
To tell you since my last sad letter
I kind a feel a little better.

Now ain't that fine? So simple, nothing studied, no insinuations like many folks to an old hen "scratching," "hopping," &c.

My muse has mostly dwelt in the Cypress shade, and the chords of her harp were formed of severed heart strings. They have seldom sounded to a merry lay but have sometimes given forth a wailing dirge o'er departed friends and joys.

Well, it is after 2. Given all the powders and 3 doses castor oil. No effect. I must lie down awhile to gather strength for my duties.

Noon, 29. He [Joseph] is free from pain but very weak, very little action from the bowels, his skin very yellow. I feel so anxious. Never saw him look so bad.

Night. He is better. The medium has acted some but not as effectually as we could wish from the highly billious state of his system. This afternoon he mentioned while Granville was here he did beleive he could eat mush if we had meal to make it. Granville made no remark but soon went home, and soon after dear Elizabeth stepped in with a dish of mush she had made for him. He enjoyed it, the first nourishment he has taken since 1st day morning except a little beef tea and toast water. He is better and I am truly thankful.

It is a stormy night. The driving rain is beating on my window pane, and wildly roars the howling wind, as if Old Scratch was close behind! That'll do, Aunt Anna, thinks Lizzie G. Try as much as thou will, Mother can beat thee. What is she (by her own admission) but an owl, and I think a hen is much the better fowl. Good night.

6th day night, Dec 2nd. Father is much better though weak. He is

<u>about</u> again. He looks badly, but I hope will gather strength. I had to put off washing till yesterday, and then I did a large wash and today I baked bread, did my ironing <u>elegant</u>, roasted beef, &c., cleaned, starched, and ironed 10 caps, with my other housework. So, Miss Lizzie, thee needn't cry about me. I don't beleive thee has an aunt of <u>my age</u> that <u>could</u> do as much as I do, <u>because I has to</u>. Oh, I wish some of you would come out and see us.

One piece of news I just thought of. You heard May Holland[1] took his wife to California? Well, she and his partner, Frank Hastings, have gone off together!! Alice knew him. There has been queer accounts of her conduct in letters from several individuals. One said she was a great pet among the gentlemen. There one had given her a 50 dollar rocking chair. Let her go. I hope May may not find them, for he threatens vengeance. Says he will come home next spring.

Please don't say Granville is "bad." He does love you, but it has been the busiest summer with him. He has built a large barn doing a great part of it himself: quarried all the stone for the cellar wall, hewed all the timber, made most of the shingles, attended his farming himself with very little hired help; and dear Elizabeth had masons and carpenters to cook for. So they have been very much overwhelmed with toil this summer. When Granville read thy letter he laughed and said, "Bless her dear old heart, I wish I could get 10 bushels of our exellent potatoes to her. She would be heartily welcome to them." He had a great crop. He tried an experiment. He put leaves from the woodeuther [?]—under or over, I don't know which—as he planted, and it was new ground.

I read a receipt the other day which I copied and intend to try it. It is a Chinese mode of propagating fruit trees, and I reckon it would do for flowering shrubs. Wait till tomorrow; I must go right to bed.

2nd day night. There was no chance to get this to the P office today. Josey EB got up this morning early, made fire, called me, and when I came out found he had decamped <u>without his breakfast</u> to Alexander. He wanted to find sale for beef. Our old ox buck is in fine order, the market overstocked. He got back weary a little before 11. In 15 minutes I had him a nice little meal: good coffee, roast beef, pickles, peach jam, preserves (greengages), stewed peaches, nice toast. And he did ample justice to it, rested 15 minutes, and then trudged off to Hanover, had no success there. We have not engaged but one quarter.

Hannah and children are going to Granville's tomorrow, and I will try to meet them there. Father and Alban have to be 2 or 3 days helping Reeder with the threshing machine as they helped us. I shall have to get breakfast by daybreak. Richard paid us a pleasant little visit 2 weeks since, came on the cars 7th and left 2nd day. He brought the most exact likeness of their angelic little <u>lump of sweetness</u>, Harry, another <u>idol</u>, I fear. Norman and Walter are making <u>great</u> progress in thier learning. They receive premiums every examination. Thomas has been very successful in his new employment moving buildings.[2] Richard says he has cleared $1,000 this summer, has a very convenient, roomy, and handsomely finished house all paid for, house and palings white, latticed porch upstairs and down, papered, carpeted, and comfortable furnished and 2 little "limbs" of mischief as ever a poor mother was ever blessed with.

I have not half room to say all I would like to but make haste and write and I will do better next time. We expect to butcher hogs next week, 4 of the largest. I shall have all the greasy work and cooking for hands to do myself.

Oh, I love you all, and you know it. Please send this to Alice. Your loving sister and aunt,

Anna

[written around page 1]: Tell Alice and John I will write soon and my request is always send my letters to Sharon. Oh, I forgot the receipt: Strip a ring of bark an inch wide from a bearing branch, and surround the place with a ball of fat earth or loam bound fast to the branch with a peice of matting. Over this suspend a vessel of water having a small hole in the bottom just sufficient to let the water drop so as to keep the earth constantly moist. The branch throws new roots into the earth just above the place where the rind was stripped off. The operation is performed in the spring and the branch is sawed off and put in the ground at the fall of the leaf. The following year it bears fruit.

1. Samuel May Holland had owned the land that William Holland and Robert Miller laid out as Maysville in 1852 along the Cleveland & Pittsburgh Railroad. Later it became the village of Kensington. In November 1846, he had married Matilda Ann Higgins, the daughter of Benjamin and Mary Higgins. After Mary Higgins's death in 1837, described so movingly by Anna, Matilda had been taken in by the Holland family.
2. Daniel Hise noted in his diary that he had put on a gravel roof for Harry Ambler (a Salem lawyer) and Tom Bentley, presumably on a building they had moved. He also wrote that Tom had tried to borrow $6; maybe business wasn't quite as good as Anna believed.

❧

Feb. 5th 1854
[from Granville]

. . . As to our mode of getting along, making a living, &c, it has been done so far pretty much by reasonably hard labour. And from the prospect ahead we have not much reason to expect any very great relaxation of effort. We are not farming on a large scale but raise considerable to dispose of and all we need to live upon. The part of the farm we purchased was principally woodland, which requires much hard labour to make it ready for farming. We have been unusually busy this last season building a barn of which we stood much in need. It is nearly completed and best of all nearly paid for. The present seems very favourable for the farmers—who instead of selling their wheat for from 60 to 70 cts. as has been the case in this region for 2 or 3 years past—can now readily obtain 1.50 cts. But it is very hard for the labouring man who has to buy his grain and whose wages do not advance in proportion. There will, no doubt, be a reaction.

Thee asks in one of thy letters "why Granville and Elizabeth could'nt pay you a visit." It may be that we can in the distant future. Indeed we often speak of such an event as among the possible and probable things we <u>sometimes</u> <u>dream</u> of. We certainly think it would give us more pleasure than any other visit we could make. You have, I think, had a pretty good share of visitors of the Green Hill tribe within the last few years. <u>We</u>, for <u>our</u> parts, think we must have the honour of a delegation from Sandy Spring before Green Hill is again represented there.

It seems strange, "passing strange," where I think of the number of <u>our</u> cousins, I have only *two, of whom have I ever seen: Isaac Bond and Cousin Hannah Brooke and she was a <u>mighty small affair</u> then, too. And I don't remember whether she was <u>pretty</u> or not, but suppose she <u>was</u>, and <u>is</u>—and what is of more consequence, amiable, agreeable, and intelligent, all of which I <u>intend</u> to believe will apply in an especial manner to thy daughters. And all the rest of my cousins, as if nam'd. Please give our love in an especial manner to Uncle WH Farquhar and Aunt Margaret. Tell them we often think and talk of them and their visit to us. Our best love also to Aunt Mary, Aunt Lizzie, Uncle WH Briggs and wife, and <u>all</u> their families. And last but not least, my <u>little pet</u> sister, Alice. And I wish to tell her and all the rest of you that you need'nt expect to get <u>out</u> of answering my wife's letters by saying how "<u>sweet</u> she is." And what a "<u>sweet</u> letter that last one was." She has been quite familiar with such expressions, and likely it don't make the impression it would on some. Believe me, thy precious Nephew,

G S Bentley

*A mistake. Cousin Mary Briggs, another <u>small affair</u> when I saw her.

~

In January 1854, the play *Uncle Tom's Cabin* was performed at Salem Town Hall, no doubt to sympathetic audiences, for many Salemites were increasingly absorbed with the business of ending slavery. In October, after some escaped slaves had been hurried through on their way north by members of the Western Anti-Slavery Society, a U.S. marshal came to town. "His movements were closely watched," Daniel Hise noted in his diary.

At Green Hill, attention was focused on Granville's wife, Elizabeth, who was so sick that in August, when she was sent to Salem, she was almost too weak to sit up. Likewise Deborah continued with her same off-and-on medical problems. Aliceanna gave birth to her second child, a daughter, christened Alice Evelyn, in 1854. In 1857, Alban married Amelia Walton, who gave birth to their first child, Frank, the same year.

~

5th day 27th 1855
first day night
My beloved sister Sarah and all the Sharon tribe,

Some of you are naughty to me about writing. I know you are all busy, but then there are so many of you. Have you all felt it such a relief to get the old critter off home that you want to shake off all bother with me? No no, bless you. I know you all think of me often and love me as much as I deserve. And if I may claim as much as I give, it is a full measure running over. How does my child come on? Has she got you all "under her thumb," or like a good girl submitted like a daughter to thy gentle rule? Please, dear sister, urge her to write oftener.

It has been several weeks since Alban wrote to us. J Reeder got a letter from him last week. He was well, very busy, and in fine spirits. Albert, Ed, and John are going after harvest. . . .

Susan Miller came up last week and brought me a candle plant and a perfectly beautiful pheasant breast cactus. Now if I could not get another I would not take a silver dollar for it, but still I would give one of my two gold dollars to have it safely transported to either Sister Mary or thee. Sister Mary gave me a black, hard, shining seed the size of a small pea. It has come up and I wish I knew what it was. I never had as many kinds of flowers as have come up from seeds, and Carrie, thee never saw our garden look as it is going to. Father works in it most of his time, and he has not made a cucumber patch of my flower bed but helped me fix them up. More than half the currant bushes were killed by the drought

and severe winter, but he has cut out the dead wood, worked about them
well, leveled and made a broad fall all along the north side and a nice
walk below it, cleared out every weed, sprout, and grass, trimmed all the
trees, cut down the peach tree next the barn, half the gooseberry and
apple tree, made a nice straight walk, planted all but the cabbage ground,
and that is most ready. The prettiest walk is along the south. He has dug
it down, levelled it, making a high fall of the garden above. He fixed up
the asparagus bed so that we have had great abundance and to share with
Granville and others. I have trained and tacked up the roses, sweetbriar,
Washington bower, and snowberrys till they look beautiful. I never saw
such peonys—so large.

Jos mowed the yd 6th day. It was much more than knee high, no
little feet to tramp it down. We were astonished at the quantity of hay it
made. The ivy <u>is</u> growing, Carrie. I must tell of the singular circumstance
about our peach trees. The first I noticed was the one in our front yard,
and since that I have noticed the same with most of the others though
not in so great a degree. <u>Not</u> one 1/4 of the number of peaches on the
whole tree are single—2, 3, and 4 coming from the same blossom and
joined. Jos says he read something in the papers about it. . . .

Dear Elizabeth is up nearly every day. She works in her garden.
Granville has fixed it up nice. She bakes and cooks and <u>whitewashes</u> and
sometimes goes abroad, and she is a darling. One of Guy Ball's daughters
lives with her; she is about 13. She does her washing and what she can
between whiles and goes to school. Dear Granville comes up night and
morning and milks our cow. Every other morning he leaves the milk here
and they send us butter enough to do us.

I think I have the best washerwoman I <u>ever had</u>, and she always does
the ironing, & I never would wish it done better. I often look with
satisfaction at father's clothing, &c. And she is an old woman. She always
cleans up everything, wipes up the floor, gets supper, sprinkles and folds
down the clothes, and makes no charge!!! Guess who is it. Father brings
up the water.

Well, I have worked hard this spring. Or not <u>hard</u>, for I have
cheerfully done it, taken a real comfort in it, and when I have really been
so stiff and sore I could scarcely get up when I sat down, I only regretted
my power was not equal to my will, and we do have <u>plenty</u>, and very
good provision for our table: first-rate bacon. Our pie plant is so luxuriant,
and I make pies, puddings, custards, biscuit cakes, &c.

Oh, I was moving a firkin that I use for a pickle tub. Well, this
summer 3 years ago I packed in salt a quantity of cucumbers, and forgot

but what I had used them. When lo, there were 5 or 6 dozen as firm as when put away. I took out a dozen for Elizabeth, 2 for myself, and put them in a bucket under the spout, let them stay 3 or four days, then put them in a jar with seasoning and vinegar cold, intending to scald when I had time. Well, they don't need it, but are as good pickles as I ever made.

And now I must tell of my exploits last week and the week before. I made 40 gallons of soft soap and about 20 lb of hard, purified in lye all my grease, have better than 5 gallons of fat that looks like lard, all safe from the flies. Had to fill the barrel 3 times; Jos did it twice. I emptied and filled 1 and for 4 days I carried 10 buckets water a day, had to boil it (the water to run the lye); and then, when the soap was done, I had to carry it in a pan that only held a gallon to the smokehouse and get up and down that high step.

There, have I soaped you enough? Don't thee wish thee had some? I do. I expect to undertake the whitewashing next week, couldn't get lime sooner. Granville's cottage is snow white, Carrie. He has a peach orchard on your mountain tea bank cleared even with the springhead, a road running up that hollow, P Taylor's in sight. Did I mention E Wooly and D Reeder were married?[1] If thee <u>does</u> laugh, Sis Sarah, <u>I just will</u> put down things as they come in my mind and mix up soap and whitewash and peach orchards, mountain tea and weddings in one mess—and add for poor Carrie a dead Oleander; yes, Honey, I would not tell thee till I thought the roses of Sharon were beginning to bloom to comfort thee.

I wish I knew if thee was a good girl and happy and giving satisfaction. Sister Sarah, please thee write about her, and all the rest add to it. Don't fret about us. We are getting on <u>very</u> comfortably. I gathered up treasures of love, memories to dwell with, and I am not alone anymore. A new life seems given me, a contented spirit and hopeful heart. Oh, it did do me good to be with you.

Well, what are you going to have for dinner? I am going to set my table now and put on it part of a boiled ham (better we never had), a plentiful dish of asparaguss, first-rate pickled cucumbers, ditto biscuits, ditto butter, ditto pie plant, pie, ditto <u>custard pie</u> (that's what they call custards in a crust here). I often get the most affectionate letters from Maria. Debbie is much better so that they take her out. She says she never loved Maria so well for she is so good to her. She speaks with affectionate interest of Carrie, and I do wish she would write to Debbie. She does feel neglected, and her great suffering, mental and physical, calls for all the kindness of all her friends.

1 PM. Dinner all done and cleared up, a few minutes before I go to

my sewing the 2nd French linen vest for Joseph—2 inside breast pockets. He helped me make the 1st. And he does like it, so cool and light. . . .

Now, Sister Lizzie, we all expect thee this fall with Carrie, and won't we have fine times? Jos expects to go to Iowa this fall, and "when the cat's away the mice will play." How is Bro Willy and family? . . .

I have not mentioned darling Fanny's name or dear Jemmy's, but I do love them. And Therese must not forget me nor Holly. Dearly I love you all. Jos sends love to all. Good-bye. Write very soon.

I ain't done yet. It is all the way I can talk to you now. Frances, honey, do get 2 large sheets of paper and every one of you write, Therese too. Don't try to write pretty, but let it tell of everyday life and Sharon. And Carrie, my darling, talk to me. Tell of how happy thee is and how prudent Aunt Sarah has taught thee to be and careful of thy health. . . .

And now say, dear, when the TIME is fixed please let Aunt Anna know. I do wish I had Charley's likeness even as friend Snook's on the pitcher face. Do thee give my love to him and to his parents.[2]

Carrie, that beautiful grapevine east of the house is dead to within a foot of the ground. The live part is sending up new shoots. Oh, I wish you all could see my colored man, Bill. I have with black cambric made the most complete body I ever did make, have fastened the face on so that it don't shew, made a nice white shirt, plaid pants, a complete fur hat out of Father's, made him a red pocket handkerchief. He is the admiration of the neighbourhood. Dear William, how it reminds me of him. . . .

Oh, how I would like to see the babies—my little pet, Evelyn, and the little sprite, Florence. How has the ice kept? I have scalded my right hand, the back of it. I tried flour, the best remedy in the world. Well, now I am done, and nearly asleep. Farewell, beloveds all.
AB

1. Eliza Woolley and David W. Reeder married on April 26, 1855. She was the daughter of Taylor and Mariah Woolley, and he was the son of William and Lydia Reeder (or Reader) of Hanover Township.
2. Nephew Charles H. Brooke, Sister Mary's son, age twenty-three.

$\backsim$

2nd mo 23rd 1856
My own dear sister,

In my heart I have not neglected thee or been unmindful of thy two dear letters, one written so long ago, but I have found it impossible to get out of <u>debt</u>. 'Bleive I'll take the benefit of the act of Insolvency and take a fresh start. I owe 5 letters now and I have no paper but this note paper.

I have so much to occupy me and have suffered so much in various ways this most intensely severe winter. Our old house is so open, and Father has not felt able to repair it. It has been very hard for me to do the necessary work of our family this winter. <u>My back has been so weak</u> washing is very hard for me; and the week before Christmas a son of Jos's nephew came and for five weeks I had to wash and do for him. We should have suffered still more if we had not got a new coal cook stove (the first cooking stove we ever had). We had done with an old 10-plate.

In this room I could keep comfortable, but just going upstairs to make John's and Alban's beds my heels and 4 of my toes got so badly frosted that I could not wear shoes for 5 weeks except loose overshoes and hobbled about in suffering. I then was taken sick like I was last spring, and for 2 weeks my lungs were considerably affected, my cough very bad. I still cough some but am able to do my work without suffering. Indeed I had to do all that was done <u>all the time</u> when I was not fit to be out of bed. And poor Father has been confined to the house in great and continual suffering all winter, unable to do anything but tend the fire and read. His feet become more and more crippled. He often gets discouraged and no wonder.

Thy last letter came when I was getting a little better, and at Father's request had just written a letter to Alice to enclose $10 for John on Dr Riggs'[1] account; 10 more are due him. And our poor suffering child needs a Dr's services every 2 weeks and often between. Her poor helpless arm to the elbow bound fast to her side, a still spring on the joint of her shoulder to keep it in place. She <u>cannot</u> help herself, and it is grief to me that we are not able to do more.

1. The Riggs family of Sandy Spring produced four brothers who became doctors.

∼

5th mo 22nd 1858
My dear sister,

I don't know but I had best take the benefit of the act of insolvency, for I have so many creditors I feel quite puzzled which claim to settle first, feeling also a desire to do justly by all. I believe there stands first on the list dear sister, and thou art the representative of Sharon and a <u>grandmother</u> too, consequently more on an equality with me. Sister

Mary, son Thomas, daughters Alice & Hannah, Ellen Farquhar,[1] Sally
Lea, Cousin Martha Tyson I owe letters to, and how will I ever find
leisure and a quiet time to give each as satisfactory a letter as I wish?
Sp'ose I write everything pretty to thee and copy <u>off</u> to the rest to save
trouble? If I write of passing events, why I can't afford a new dress for
each.

Did thee remember the 18th was <u>my 62nd birthday</u>? That day I did
a very long washing, 2 tubs full of white clothes, Carrie having been ill
for more than a week with Neuralgia in her Ear and Head. It happened
fortunately that sweet Annie Walton, Amelia's sister, aged 22, was here
on a visit, and being fully qualified for a teacher (has taught 3 terms), she
took charge of Carrie's school for 9 days, and then she <u>would</u> go. Her
school is very large—60 scholars. In a day or two she was delirious with
nervous headache, and we insisted on her dismissing the school for one
week; and Maria, who had been spending two weeks with us, took her
up to Salem last 2nd day to see Dr Spear and get some medicine and
linnament—that always arrests it if taken in time. I heard from her this
evening (7th day). She is well and expects to be back tomorrow, and go
on with her school 2nd day.

See how I flew out of the washtub. The big wash was all to iron and I
did it. Carrie begged me not to do the washing, but I was not going to
leave it for her to do after she comes tired from school. Then I have made
a most grand corn broom as neat, strong, and workmanlike as those in
the stores. I pride myself on my brooms. Yesterday I swept all over the
house and pottered about, today have made lots of pies, churned such
golden butter, scoured and cleaned everywhere. I have a good deal to do
and have not felt as strong since a spell of sickness I had in the spring. I
lack the energy, get weary sooner, and for 2 or 3 weeks I was so lame in
my feet and ankles but have not felt that much this last week.

Dear me, I suppose I have set Alice and some of the rest in the
fidgets about Carrie and her beaux so that I verily believe the little puss
thinks something serious of what I said in joke, partly to provoke Carrie
to write and explain and partly to watch Alice for pretending to think a
few words I said in praise of a young <u>man</u> she knew as an awkward <u>boy</u>
implied I would have no objection to him for a <u>son in law</u>. Depend on it,
I should apprize you of any such a change.

After her first school closed she wrote to her kind friend Augustine
James, maiden aunt to the Townsend children she taught, to discover if
she still remained at Paul's so that she might know where to send $12
which she had lent her, speaking of her grateful affection and the great

pleasure she felt in being able to return it. Such a beautiful kind answer came entreating her not to return it but use it in getting books she so much loved, said she had never intended to have it returned for she did not need it, said all the children's likenesses had been taken and were waiting for her direction to be sent to her. Some weeks since she was in Salem and was going to the bookstore to get a book. Norman said, "Don't, Aunt Carrie. Just give me thy dollar. I am making up a club to send to Phil^d to Evans Gift bookstore. Well, she did, and the book soon came, and a most splendid Cameo breast pin and Ear drops worth $10. . . .

Now, I would dearly love to trudge with thee over to Riverside to see the dear children and the grandchild.[2] Well, I sympathize with thee in thy fond tender joy, but wait till thee has 20 here and 2 in heaven, see how thy heart will have to expand to hold them all. Two of mine thou hast not been introduced to: Thomas's Alonzo and Alban's Frank, the latter a sweet, blue-eyed, healthy boy. His mother [Amelia] is very amiable, gentle, and quiet, so affectionate and attentive to us. She is too diffident to write or I would urge her to speak for herself. She is well-educated, perfectly correct in her language. Her sister Annie is a very superior girl, finished her education at Millersville Normal School, pleasing, unaffected, modest manners, talented & cultivated, the sweetest smile, dress tastefully and neat. She is smaller, if anything, than Hannah Brooke. . . . Carrie and she are warmly attached to each other. Amelia is a very great favourite with Father. Her quiet manners exactly suit him. And I believe Frank is going to be a fine affair for him.

Jos's general health is pretty good for as old a man,[3] but he does still overtax his strength.

Dear Sister Mary sent me some nice flower seed. Do thou likewise, that is a dear.

25th. Raining and dull. We have only been able to plant one small field of corn, have 4 acres waiting for the weather to become suitable. Carrie's friend and winter partner in the school went up to Salem and brought her home first day. She looks pale and thin for [?] is very weak and still suffers at times with her head. She has medicine which relieves her some. If she does not get better soon she must quit the school. The Dr says her nervous system is all out of order and such a large school of such pupils is entirely too much for her in her present state of health. She will give her whole soul to the undertaking, dear precious child. She came home last night looking so pale and weak and her head so bad she went right to bed, and after 3 hours good sleep got up to a nice little supper and her beloved brother Granville's ever-welcome society, both of which she enjoyed. This morning she has gone again through the rain.

And dear Debbie, who had been for some time past better than for years, has been suffering for 2 or 3 weeks with diarhoea, I hear.

7th day. It was dysentery. Jos went up yesterday to spend a few days. Maria sent me (by Carrie) a birthday gift of a nice dress pattern, calico (brown), and Carrie's gift, a nice buffaloe hair comb, and pr of fine stockings. Those 2 and Thomas while in reach always have noticed my added years by some little token. Frank <u>began</u> with it last year and maybe has forgotten it this.

Amelia's sister Annie has been a great comfort and help at this time. She is a first-rate nurse, firm in the faith of the Botanic system. Amelia fared very well throughout.

It does look a little like clearing off, and I hope it may. Do write soon, dear sister, and tell me of thy prospects and of each member of thy own dear family. Where is our brother Isaac, and what is he doing? How does Lizzie's health stand the duties and cares of a mother? Tell of the little one, in prose and verse, and I won't do as <u>some have done</u>, dish up an old fable of Cat and Owl, or Crow and young, to throw cold water on the Heaven-lit flame of pure love that warms a parent's heart, for I <u>know</u> all about it. There, old thing, I remember thy wicked acts of old—not in malice. No, nought bordering on that could ever arise in my heart for any of Sharon born.

And now with tender love to all I must conclude. I fancy Sister Elizabeth would not care for any particular message from me which might put her to the trouble of replying to it. I will give it up.

Thy truly affectionate sister, Anna

All branches of our tribe with the exceptions specified are well.

---

1. Her sister Margaret's oldest child, born in 1836.
2. Riverside, overlooking the Patuxent River, was the home of Elizabeth (Lizzie), Sarah Stabler's oldest daughter, and her husband, Charles Augustus Iddings.
3. Joseph Bentley was sixty-nine.

~

SEVEN

The Later Years

While never politically active, Anna was politically aware. She would have shared in the excitement generated by John Brown's raid on the federal arsenal at Harper's Ferry in 1859, followed by the trial and hanging of Brown and his men. Not only was there a great deal of sympathy in Salem for the aims of "Martyr John Brown," as the diarist Daniel Hise termed him, but one of Brown's young followers, Edwin Coppock, was a local boy of Quaker origins. After Coppock was hanged, some anti-slavery Friends paid for his body to be returned to Salem for burial. About six thousand attended his funeral, and his monument is one of the largest in Salem's Hope Cemetery.

Of more immediate interest to Anna, at long last her sister Elizabeth, and maybe Brother Isaac as well, traveled to Ohio for a visit. They probably were there for the marriages of Caroline on April 13, 1860, to James Heston, the eldest son of David and Ruth Armstrong Heston, a nearby Quaker family; and Deborah on June 9 to Isaac Trescott, a Salem stationer and well-known abolitionist. Both ceremonies were performed by Maria's husband, Richard, a justice of the peace.

At thirty-five, Deborah brought to her marriage a history of ill health. Her husband was a kindly middle-aged widower with several children still at home. He had long been a fixture in the abolition movement, and, with his brothers-in-law Richard Garrigues and Granville Bentley, a leader of Salem's temperance movement for a time. He did not cut a glamorous figure, and he never made much money—in fact, his house was sold at a sheriff's auction in 1874—but he was well respected. He gave Deborah a stable relationship and great patience. Deborah wasted no time starting a family. Her first child, Lilian, or Lily, was born the following September.

Along with a flood of pioneers, the young Hestons soon emigrated to the Kansas Territory. At least one of Caroline's cousins, Jane Grey (Brooke) Northrup, the daughter of Cousin James Brooke, preceded them in 1853 with her husband, Lorenzo, a doctor and abolitionist. They were prominent citizens of Valley Falls, Jefferson County, when the young Hestons may have passed through on their way farther west to Ogden, in Riley County.

A lot of folk went west in those years looking for cheap land or a fresh start. Some went for political reasons, too. In 1854, Congress passed the Kansas-Nebraska Act, which allowed popular sovereignty to determine if the new territories would be free or slave states. People on both sides of the question poured across the Kansas border. By the time the Hestons arrived, the state had been in turmoil for years as each side tried to get a majority. In May 1856, a pro-slavery mob attacked Lawrence, Kansas, a bastion of abolition, and burned the governor's house.

James and Caroline stayed in Kansas more than twenty years, producing seven children and barely surviving dreadful seasons of drought and grasshoppers in a sod house built around a spring.[1] The news from them was often as miserable as it could be. Anna fretted, "I know they do not tell me all. Why did they go so far?" no doubt echoing her own mother more than thirty years before. Anna was called upon more than once to help out with money and supplies.

Only two letters written by Anna during the Civil War were saved among her papers. One is undated. On the whole, the war was a worry for her, but not a tragedy. Her sons Franklin, Thomas, and Alban, and her three eldest grandsons, William and Walter Bentley and Norman Garrigues, all served, and all survived apparently unscathed.

Franklin, forty-four, signed up in October 1861 for a three-year hitch with the Nineteenth Ohio Volunteer Infantry. He was assigned to the regimental band along with his eighteen-year-old son, Walter. Both were mustered out with their whole company the following September.

---

1. The sod house built around a spring was the only secondhand memory of Kansas that still survived among Heston grandchildren at the turn of the twenty-first century.

Anna's son Thomas, nearly forty, enlisted as a private in the Fourth Wisconsin Infantry (later the Fourth Wisconsin Cavalry), as he and Ruth Anna and their four sons were living there in Jefferson County. Thomas had earned the title "Doctor," and as a medical practitioner and dentist he most likely wielded a scalpel and saw in the war rather than a gun. His regiment took part in the capture of New Orleans and Baton Rouge. He was discharged in January 1863 in Carrollton, Louisiana, in order to pursue a government contract—so said his discharge papers.

He remained in Louisiana for the rest of the war, serving in various capacities in the Union occupation government. His oldest son, Emerson, kept a diary in 1864-1865, when the whole family took part in efforts by various religious and social service organizations to make Louisiana a model of Reconstruction. The entire family, including fourteen-year-old Emerson and his younger brothers, Linden and Milan, became involved in teaching freed slaves.

Although deeply unpopular with the local planter population and other white people, Northern carpetbaggers such as the Bentleys suffered more than insults and social ostracism. They also risked their health and their lives from outbreaks of yellow fever, smallpox, and other life-threatening diseases. Malaria sapped their energy. In early 1864, several members of his household, including Ruth Anna, having come down with varioloid, the preamble to smallpox, Thomas sent his wife and children by river steamer to Ohio.

Sadly, they didn't all make it. On the boat, five-year-old Alonzo came down with a fever. When telltale pustules made it clear he had smallpox, the river boat captain put the family off at Cairo, Illinois to seek shelter in a pest house. There little Alonzo died a week later. He was buried in a cemetery at the edge of town with a small wooden cross on which Emerson wrote "AB" in pencil, and the family departed for Ohio the next day. A family friend brought Alonzo's body to Salem for reburial months later.

Ruth Anna and the children stayed in Salem almost a year, until Thomas summoned them back to teach in Black schools in and around Donaldsonville, Louisiana. It was a life-changing move for them. Thomas died of yellow fever in 1867. Emerson and Linden, who had led independent lives from an early age, chose to stay on after Ruth Anna and Milan moved back to Ohio.

Maria's son, Norman Garrigues, served first with the Fifth Independent Company Ohio Volunteer Cavalry in Missouri, then with the Eighty-fourth Ohio Volunteer Infantry, eventually rising to the rank of sergeant. If, as Anna wrote, he served for a time in the flashy bodyguard surrounding Gen. John C. Fremont, it would have been a point of great pride for the family, for Fremont was admired by abolitionists for his outspoken opposition to slavery. Fremont was so popular that the Salem diarist Daniel Hise reported that some 25,000 to 30,000 people showed up in Massillon, Ohio, to hear him speak in August 1856. As a general, however, Fremont did little but irritate his Commander in Chief. Lincoln relieved him of command after only one hundred days, when Fremont exceeded his powers by declaring the slaves within his jurisdiction to be free.

Alban, age twenty-six, joined the same regiment as his nephew, Norman, in June 1862, but by August he had been mustered out because of a disability.

Granville's son, William, had the longest Civil War service of the six. He enlisted on August 9, 1862. As part of the 104th Ohio Volunteer Infantry, he saw action in Kentucky and Tennessee, then took part in Sherman's siege of Atlanta, including the engagements at Kennesaw Mountain and Pine Mountain, before being sent back to Tennessee with Gen. George Thomas, where the Union forces destroyed General John Hood's Confederate army. William ended his service in North Carolina, and was discharged on June 7, 1865.

In Maryland, Elizabeth Briggs suffered from a lingering illness, punctuated by several operations. Aliceanna, who now called herself plain Alice, lived near Sharon with her growing family. Anna's sister Mary was widowed when Richard Brooke died in 1862.

War reached the quiet backwater of Green Hill, Ohio, only once, when the thrilling raid of John Morgan's Confederate cavalry ended in Columbiana County, but it came a bit closer to the folks in Sandy Spring. In the slave state of Maryland, loyalties were divided from the beginning. The enrollment at Fair Hill Quaker school for girls, on the old estate of the Revolutionary warrior Richard Brooke, plummeted in the early days of the war as Southerners withdrew their children. On the couple of occasions that the Confederate army took the war into the North, Maryland was on its route.

In the summer of 1863, the cavalry of Confederate general J.E.B. Stuart passed through the area, stripping the farms of horses as they went on their way to Gettysburg, Pennsylvania. According to the *Chronicles of Sandy Spring*

Friends Meeting and Environs, the big guns of the battle that raged there at the beginning of July could be heard clearly at Sandy Spring some fifty miles away.

In June 1864, while Gen. Ulysses Grant and his forces were massed outside Petersburg and Richmond, Virginia, Confederate general Jubal Early and fifteen thousand rebel infantry swept into Maryland through the Shenandoah Valley and threatened Washington. They pillaged and burned their way across Maryland, much like Sherman was to do later that summer on his march from Atlanta to the sea. They extorted large sums of money from the towns of Hagerstown and Frederick, and burned Chambersburg, Pennsylvania.

Sarah Stabler wrote to her brother about what happened in Sandy Spring:

Perhaps thou hast been thinking of us since we have been infested with <u>vermin</u> but being happily rid of them, for the present we are rather more fit to take pen in hand than we were a week since.————About two weeks since we heard reports of the critters crossing the river for their Maryland invasions and as we were expecting James [Stabler Jr.] we wrote to him not to come but he did not heed us and came on 7th day. We enjoyed his visit in fear and trembling until first day evening, when cousin George came up to tell him to get off as soon as possible before the way was closed, for the Rebels were in Rockville where a skirmish was said to have taken place.

So James, Isaac Bond (who was up), and James Hallowell all put off directly in James H's carriage to go by Laurel—Next day (July 11th) the Rebs were all around us by thousands, no one knows exactly how many, their principal mission seeming to be to get horses and rob stores, which they succeeded in to a considerable extent. They evidently had been well informed about where their chance was best. Indeed they had a number of Maryland traitors with them to guide and inform them. They did not get here at all although they were all around us.

The first of our friends who came in contact with them were Charles H Brooke & Tom Stabler who did not believe rumors of their coming and rode as far as Monrovia and found themselves suddenly within the Rebel lines & prisoners for awhile. But on telling them they were citizens who had nothing to do with the war they were suffered to pass on without losing their horses. One of the Rebs told them to keep to their saddles or they would lose them. . . . They stopped at John Stabler's and asked for horses. Alice told them there were none there. "Where are they?" "I hope they are in a place of safety!" said Alice. "You are a Yankee woman." "No," said she, "but I am a good Union woman"————They went to the Stablers' and told some one what Alice had said—confessing they liked an outspoken woman like that.

Many people in the neighborhood had horses confiscated. Passing Confederate soldiers came upon Cousin Benjamin Hallowell, a well-known educator and the founder of a famous school in Alexandria, Virginia, and demanded his workhorse. Hallowell told them he had been Robert E. Lee's teacher. Impressed, the men withdrew. But a general made of sterner stuff ordered his men to take the horse. "They forthwith loosened the girth and left cousin Benjamin in the road with his saddle—grieving for [his] pet horse which had been his companion of the road for hundreds of miles. He put his saddle on the fence, walked home, and sent some one for it, but it was gone also."

"Rumors are plentiful as blackberries," Sarah wrote, including one that Washington had been taken. But Grant sent seasoned troops to guard the capital, and Early backed off.

In October, some of Mosby's Raiders swooped down on the Sandy Spring store owned by Richard Bentley, ransacked it, and took off, a local posse on their heels. In a confrontation the next day, one of the raiders was killed before the rest got away.

By the spring of 1865, while huge armies fought just to the south, Anna traveled to Maryland for the wedding of her nephew James P. Stabler to Alice Brooke. While there, she also nursed Elizabeth, now nearing the end of her long illness. "She helps me more than anybody else could, for I feel quite easy, while she is taking care of Aunt Lizzie, to spend all the time necessary about kitchen affairs," Sarah wrote.

But Anna was summoned home with news that Joseph's health had taken a turn for the worse. "Poor sister Anna seems in a good deal of trouble," her sister Mary wrote. "I pity her very much, but feel in a hurry for her to go."

The end of the war brought joy to the North and devastation to the South. Robert E. Lee's Army of Northern Virginia surrendered on April 9. Daniel Hise wrote on the next day that he had raised $300 for fireworks for

a "Great Day of Rejoicing in Salem." The Confederacy collapsed soon after. Then on April 15, Hise recorded the arrival of a telegram reporting that
President Lincoln had been assassinated.

Public events never moved Anna as much as private joys and sorrows.
At this period, her heartbreaks were closer to home. In July, Granville's
wife, Elizabeth Bentley, died, followed in August by Elizabeth Briggs, age
fifty-eight, and the worn-out Joseph Bentley, age seventy-six, in October.
The following February, Eliza Brooke dropped in on Aliceanna Stabler and
heard of Hannah Preston's death in Lynchburg, Virginia, "after only a week's
sickness." Wrote Eliza's mother, "She leaves a family of children who will
deeply feel the loss, so distant as they are from her family & friends." She
left her husband, John, and seven children.

In 1867, Thomas Bentley, who had stayed on in New Orleans after the
war with his wife and boys, was struck down like his great uncle had been
by one of the city's periodic yellow fever epidemics. He died there on September 18.

Aliceanna, who had lost her nine-year-old daughter, Alice Evelyn, in
1864, remained in Sandy Spring until 1868 with her husband, John, and
their growing family of daughters and a son. A favorite of her Aunt Mary
Brooke, Alice was known for a sweet disposition and fine singing voice.
When they moved to Chicago, her Aunt Mary wrote that she "seems cheerful & hopeful,—feeling anything preferable to the way she has been living
lately." But just three years later they came back east to Philadelphia.
Aliceanna wrote to Sally Stabler in November 1871 on the stationery of
the Gunpowder Pile-Driver Company, "I cannot tell thee dear sister how
thankful I am to be here with my Husband and children. It seems much
more pleasant to me to think of raising our children here than in Chicago."
She went to meeting once again, something she said she hadn't done since
her daughter Elsie was a baby. Until they found a more permanent address,
the family lived in a boarding house, where Aliceanna had to wash and
dress the children three times a day to appear for meals.

Maria's son, Norman, had married Daniel Hise's niece, Nina, in 1864,
and they settled in Salem. Anna reported in 1869 that their three-month-
old son, Leon, whom they "idolized," had died of cholera infantum. Anna
added with this news that "57 years ago I was a bride of 16."

The Civil War abolished slavery, but it didn't end the involvement of
civic-minded members of Anna's family in various causes, including the

temperance movement. Thomas's oldest boy, Emerson, went a good deal further than his uncles in Salem. Like his father, he threw himself into Reconstruction.

The nineteen-year-old continued to teach black children at the Freedman's Orphans Home started by John Baldwin, the radical Methodist educator who had run the school in Berea, Ohio, attended by Emerson's father and other Bentley children in the 1840s. Emerson also became the English editor of the bilingual *St. Landry Progress* in Opelousas. He used the newspaper as a bully pulpit for his religious and political ideas. As a Radical Republican, he advocated the complete reformation of the political and social hierarchies of the Old South. During the heated Louisiana elections of 1867, disaffected whites, who had formed gangs to intimidate blacks and reconstructionists, smashed his presses and caned him in front of some of his black pupils. When blacks armed themselves and began to assemble for their own protection, the white gangs went on a rampage of murdering and lynching. As many as two hundred black people were killed in the weeks following Emerson's beating. The violence failed to quell Emerson's passion, however. He wrote to the *Salem* (Ohio) *Journal* in July 1868, "Tramp! Tramp! Never stop! Or the Ku Klux will go marching on, and anarchy prevail."

Throughout her later years, Anna's passion was her flowers. Her daughter-in-law, Ruth Anna, wrote in 1870, "She spends a great deal of time among them, does a great part towards cultivating them." Her letters were full of references to the abundance and beauty of her flowers and the quaintness of the novelty plants that she acquired, like "Animated Oats." As she explained to Sister Sarah, "I just dip them quickly in water, not wet them too much, and lay them on a dish, table, or chair and watch their strange motions when they straighten out like dead. They will perform no more till thoroughly dried and wet again. I am afraid thier legs will get broken. I would send a lot if I knew how to fix them. Anyhow, I could send the grains for thee to plant. I had 8 seed, and I raised a bandbox full."

Her pipe was another pleasure. As she joked to her brother, Isaac, "My pipe is not a common clay, thankee, but a venerable Powhattan which cousin Wm Hopkins gave me on the day Richmond was taken, and its first smoke mingled with that of the booming cannons that spoke a nation's rejoicing. It never descended as low as some meerschaums I have heard of!!"

Debbie was raising her young daughters in Salem and growing increasingly stout. Cousin MEG nearby suffered from dropsy, but Anna was too lame herself to walk down and pay a visit. Increasingly, Anna depended on members of younger generations to carry the load for her. Among her favorites were her granddaughter, Julia, and Lydia Alice Wickersham, the sister of grandson Joseph Bentley's wife. Both made their home on the farm and waited hand and foot on the old woman, to her delight.

Alban, the youngest, moved to Wisconsin sometime after the war with his wife and sons. Franklin visited his young brother there in 1869 and described an exciting run-in with a mother bear and two cubs, the kind of adventure a man didn't find in Ohio at that late date. Alban, like his father, worked too hard, Anna thought, and farming was as hazardous in Wisconsin as it had been in Ohio. Alban was laid up for weeks after being gored by an ox.

In the summer of 1870, Emerson and Linden Bentley visited Green Hill, where Ruth Anna was helping out the family. This was the beginning of a relationship that would last the rest of Anna's life. As Lydia Wickersham married and moved away after three years with the Bentleys, Anna transferred her dependence to her daughter-in-law. Thereafter Ruth Anna grew more and more indispensable to the workings of the Bentley household. Whenever she left on visits to her blood relatives, things seemed to go awry at Green Hill. During one extended visit, Julia fell sick and Granville telegraphed Ruth Anna, who arrived at 9 P.M. having walked from Hanover, though the temperature was six below zero, "and next morning commenced straightening out things that had got in dreadful confusion."

Life had become easier for the Bentleys in many ways. Ruth Anna reported that the whole family had gone to Cleveland "for a pleasure excursion" while she stayed behind to care for the livestock for both Granville and Joseph. "To help the fun along," she wrote, "the bees swarmed and I hived them, something I never did before."

At the age of seventy-four, Anna still worked hard and "cannot be idle." At Julia's behest, she helped cut up old clothes to make forty pounds of rag strips for a sitting room carpet. Then she sewed up a coat for Granville after a tailor measured and cut out the pieces. Granville spent the winter mending chairs and making baskets.

Aliceanna Stabler and her children also visited from Chicago. In these years Green Hill became a magnet for the scattered children and grandchildren, many of whom whiled away summer holidays on the farm, especially Aliceanna's girls, who in turn became a magnet for their cousin, Milan Bentley, who worked in a hardware store in nearby Alliance.

As her grandchildren married, Anna became a doting matriarch and great grandmother. Franklin's son Walter Bentley married Marcia Clemmer; they moved to Chicago, where he became a newspaper reporter. Milan's brother Emerson Bentley took a young Louisiana bride, Joan Purcell, in the spring of 1871. Emerson then purchased the *Attakapas Register* in Brushear Parish for $2,000. The newlyweds sent the Green Hill family some of their wedding fruitcake decorated in gold and silver. Emerson, once the hated firebrand, was apparently developing better relations with his Southern neighbors. "Emerson said that a 'Seymour Knight' who had threatened to shoot him in Opelousas made him a present of a very nice beaver hat, before his wedding," Ruth Anna wrote. The precocious Emerson became a justice of the peace and a member of the state legislature, continuing his work as a journalist as well. Linden also stayed in Louisiana and worked as a journalist, eventually becoming owner, publisher, and editor of the *Donaldsonville Chief.*

The news from Carrie and Alban generally wasn't good. They were in poor health. Carrie had lost her second child, Maud, at age two, and Alban had been advised to stop working in the lumber business because he had injured his back a few years before. Both families struggled financially.

The neighborhood around Green Hill continued to produce human interest stories for Anna's letters. In 1871, she wrote, "Last week a neighbor of ours, Mahlon Hole, aged 79, took his axe and went to the woods to chop something. He was gone longer than they expected and someone went out, found him lying dead. They supposed it was an affliction of the heart. He was uncle to Hannah's husband (JA Preston)." Granville bought the house of one of the Reeder family, and his son Joseph moved in.

At some point in the early 1870s, Granville lost his sight. Although he underwent an operation, his blindness was permanent. Whatever caused it—cataracts, perhaps?—Granville seems to have been patient about his affliction. His mother admired him all the more.

Ruth Anna wrote to her niece, Alice McMillan, encouraging her to come down from Salem for a visit: "We have hills and woods and plenty of good water, and bread and butter and milk, and a nice little dog that would like to run with you." Milan, Alice's frequent correspondent, reported to her in July that he had been helping his older cousin, Joseph, with the harvest. The Bentley farm had five milk cows, a herd of cattle, about eighty Brahma hens and pigs for butchering, as well as beehives, an abundant garden, and an orchard. There was always plenty of canning, pickling, preserving, and sausage-making to be done. During one of the extended summer visits of Aliceanna's girls, granddaughter Cora was taught to piece a quilt and Franklin's daughter, Clara, taught Fannie to crochet "tidies" for the washstand.

Anna wrote, "Such happy times they had before the winter set in, rambling through the woods after chestnuts. They gathered near a bushel, out in the cornfield with their uncle husking corn, feeding chickens, calves, &c. And at night such merry games of blind man's buff, grunt, my ships come in, &c, &c, Granville and Julia and Ruth Anna always taking part. And they seemed to love to wait on Grandmother."

Joseph and "Sennie" Bentley named a daughter after Anna, which pleased her greatly. Unfortunately, the namesake Anna Bentley died in young womanhood as a schoolteacher in Lisbon.

In July 1871, Anna's nephew Isaac Bond, son of her sister Deborah, the baby who had been taken in by the family at Sharon after his mother had died in 1825, himself died in Sandy Spring of tuberculosis. According to William Farquhar in his *Annals of Sandy Spring*, Isaac had come back to the town of his kin "but to die" in the place "where all his affections were fastened."

In 1872, Anna's youngest brother, William Henry, lost his wife, Henrietta. He had been struggling for years to make ends meet while preaching the gospel and taking occasional teaching jobs. At one point he reported that he was peddling Fink's Magic Oil. But if WHB never gave up on life, life offered little financial reward in return. He and his unmarried daughters, Sarah and Hannah, who took in sewing, often relied on the kindness of relatives, while another daughter, Mary, went out to work. William wrote in December 1886 that they had been taken in by relatives for the winter but had no idea what would become of them next.

In 1873, Isaac Briggs lived in a boarding house near the docks in Baltimore and worked the night shift as a ship's inspector. In October, he wrote to his niece Frances Stabler that he had gone on the sick list with a bout of fever and jaundice. "How quick 2 or 3 good Thomsonian courses would set me all right again," he wrote. "—but alas! There are no

Thomsonian practitioners left in Balt. that I can hear of—all dead that I formerly knew."

"However," he went on, "if thy religious prospect is fulfilled, thou might arrive here in time to put the Coppers on my eyes when they are set & "kick the [stick figure of a person kicking a bucket]. But perhaps thou may think I am not worth the coppers. In that case I suppose 2 lumps of stove coals would do as well." It was his final little sally of wit. On the envelope of this letter, there is a note: "The last letter written by Uncle Isaac—1873."

∼

11th mo 25th 1873
My dear sister,

One common sorrow draws our hearts together in sympathy and a renewed desire for communion with each other, and as I could not be with you in the sad days when our beloved brother was removed from the cares and toils of life on earth and laid to rest amongst the many dear ones gone before, I shall be so thankful for <u>any</u> reminiscence of him. Did he seem conscious of his approaching death? Dear, loving, generous-hearted brother, how I loved him, and never thought he would go before me.

I received thy dear letter in due season, and thank thee for making the effort, for I know the days have come to thou and I when it is an effort to write letters. Yet it is a great comfort to receive them. It is a dark, dreary day, has been raining since yesterday, has taken off entirely some inches of snow which fell last week. I find I cannot see the lines in this paper, and thee will have to excuse it.

It is 11 AM. My dear son sits with his poor bandaged eyes (still in midnight darkness) before the open stone grate. He is talking cheerfully, sometimes laughing with Ruth Anna and Julia. No apparent change since my letter to Brother and Sister Farquhar. It would be vain for me to attempt to describe my feelings on account of his great and unlooked-for affliction; only look in the face of thy darling son, and judge for me. It has had one effect, to take any thoughts from <u>myself</u> and my increasing infirmities. I am more hard of hearing than our mother was, my sight good for my age, my general health better for some weeks past, the soreness in my side and back nearly gone. I am highly favoured with the strength to keep down <u>despondent</u> feelings, and to trust <u>all</u> to Him who is all-wise.

Yes, dear sister, Clara is sweet and lovely. I am glad you had a chance to know her better. She is a pure-minded, good girl. I have not heard if she has left Maryland or when she will come home.[1]

One thing I will mention: Last spring I received a package of seeds from the Agriculture Department which I took for granted I was indebted to my dear nephew JPS [James P. Stabler Jr.] for, and I did in my heart thank him over and over again, but whether I ever gave it expression to him I cannot remember. I know I fully intended to. The china asters were the most beautiful and perfect I ever saw, the snapdragons splendid, & all did well. I had a large collection of beautiful flowers last summer, and they were medicine Mentally and Physically. I could not bear to stay in the house. Granville was away at Salem nearly 3 months after the first dreadful operation, part of the time ill and we in anxious suspense between the letters that once a week came. I don't know what I should have done without my flowers and the exercise the care of them gave, and I spared no pains to have his dear home look lovely, but they faded and withered, and though he never saw them, he did sit in the shade and inhale thier perfume. . . .

Cousin Robert H Garrigues, now past 80, walks up to see us at least once a week—twice if the weather is good. He is very kind and affectionate, feels much for Granville. Cousin MEG has a bad cough of long standing, very hard of hearing, her sight very dim—can't see to thread any kind of needle with her best glasses. She seldom goes from home.

I forget if I mentioned in my letter to Brother and Sister Farquhar the death (on the 15th of Oct) of our tenant's wife, a terrible cancer in her mouth and throat. Starvation at last released her from lingering torture. They expect to move away this week. . . .

Anna Bentley

Dear Sister Mary. Won't she ever write to me? I love her.

1. Clara was Franklin and Hannah's younger surviving child, born in 1846. She died, unmarried, at age eighty in Massillon State Hospital in 1927.

∽

Granville did not regain his sight. To his mother he was "an example of patience." In 1878, she wrote, "He has a path in the yard worn smooth where he walks for exercise. There is a white wire line on one side, the palings on the other, the middle a grass plot. He knows how many steps around will make a mile, and he walks many miles a day." Isaac Trescott saw his own homestead sold at sheriff's auction, yet was considered by Deborah "so good, so brave." And so patient with her "irritability," Anna added.

Maria's husband, Richard Garrigues, died in September 1874 and was buried in Hope Cemetery after a large funeral. The usually acerbic Daniel Hise, who attended, wrote that he was a man of "many friends and few enemies," adding more characteristically that black people "have lost a friend of whom they were not worthy."

Aliceanna and her two girls visited again that fall. Ruth Anna's son, Milan, went down to Green Hill in November, walked from the Hanover train station to Green Hill, took his aunt and cousins back to Hanover in the wagon and from there to Alliance to put them on the train. He said his whole trip down and back took only three and a half hours.

At the end of 1874, Anna wrote to her sister that during her visit Aliceanna had begged her mother to come east for a time, but Anna cautioned Sarah, "Whatever she may tell you, don't expect me. I never <u>expect</u> to go further from my dear Granville than to Salem."

In the meantime, Caroline, the mother of six, and her family were going through some of their worst times on the prairie in a period of drought and grasshoppers that has gone down in Kansas history. The family was reduced to a diet of bread and water. Like Anna many years before, Carrie appealed to her relatives back east for help.

∼

I have had to feel deeply for my dear Carrie & family. The grasshoppers, drought, and chinch bugs destroyed all they had planted —choice fruit, the trees loaded for the first time, a vineyard of 500 grapevines. All gone and no money in circulation.[1] James has enough owing him to supply thier wants but can't get a cent, and she expecting every hour to add another helpless one, her 7th. Snow a foot deep and the 4 youngest neither shoe or stocking and very bare of others. She could stand it no longer and wrote this statement to me without her husband's knowledge. Next day I sent it to Maria with a request they would immediately forward $10 on my account. (They had 40 or 50 dollars of mine.) It was sent next morning, and Maria, her two daughters, Hannah, and Clara, went to work and packed a valuable collection of clothing and sent it a few days later; and I sent from here 7 dollars more. She received <u>both</u> letters with the money on the 18 last month. On the 19, she says, "We each had a new pr of shoes and stockings. Oh, Mother, what a comfort." Next day afternoon sent for Dr—at 10 PM a boy weighing 9 lb.[2] Next day a dear old woman that has always been like a mother drove up with a feather bed, bolster, and pillows and blanket, said she had come to take care of her. The bed was to stay till she got about. We among us packed a large box in which were 20 pr of stockings all sizes.

1. According to W.F. Pride in *The History of Fort Riley*, "1874 is known to all the old settlers in Kansas as the 'Grasshopper Year.' The grasshoppers came from the northwest in clouds and devoured everything in their path. . . . Practically all the crops were destroyed and a great deal of hardship resulted from this wholesale devastation. Many relief committees and societies distributed rations to the settlers throughout the winter and until the next crop could be harvested." The following three years the blight continued, although not as bad as the first year. Grasshoppers were just one of the challenges. Carl Frederick Kraenzel wrote in *The Great Plains in Transition*, "The winter of 1880-81 was called the hard winter, but only until those of 1885-86 and 1886-87. The school children's storm of 1888 is also well-remembered, as are the dust storms of 1889 and the river floods of 1881."
2. Paul Llewellyn, born on November 20, 1874, the youngest of Caroline's children.

~

A month later, Milan reported that Anna and Ruth Anna were both in Salem for a visit. Anticipating the arrival of his cousins Cora and Anna Stabler in July, Milan wrote to Alice McMillan that he expected Green Hill "will be our place for fun." Indeed, the attentive young man went down and played croquet with his pretty cousins and squired them to Cleveland to see the sights, including Euclid Avenue with its millionaires' row. The girls remained at Green Hill through August, while Aliceanna stayed at a resort hotel in the mountains of western Maryland, trying to recover from a nearly fatal bout of pneumonia six months before. It was not the last of Aliceanna's health problems over the next few years.

As she approached eighty, Anna preferred the comforts and familiarity of Green Hill. She no longer looked forward to a trip to Salem, much less the impossible journey east to Maryland. After writing "home" to Sandy Spring for almost fifty years, she seemed to find her relatives there less real than the children and grandchildren immediately around her. The death of her sister Mary Brooke seemed of passing interest compared to other, closer deaths, like that of Plummer Taylor, Lydia Alice Wickersham's husband, who passed away after three years of invalidism in 1875.

Children in those days were still carried off suddenly by illness. In quick succession her grandsons Harry Bentley and Norman Garrigues lost children. Anna considered Harry's wife, Dolly, "not capable of any depth of feeling" when the infant Richard died in 1875, but her heart went out to Nina: "Her lovely little Edwin, 7 months old, sat at the table in his high chair apparently well at 7 PM. Nina put on his night dress, put him in the cradle, gave him his bottle. He took all the milk, in 15 minutes threw it up, seemed deathly sick and in violent pain. The Dr came, but all they could do was of no avail. Before 3 AM he was gone, sweet angel."

Once again Green Hill threw open its doors to one and all. Anna wrote, "All summer we have had a constant stream of visitors, 7 different sets spent a week, and many others days. I counted till I got 46 in a few weeks that had spent days. Our spring wagon and 2 horses had been 18 times to the station 3 1/2 miles to bring and take visitors," among them, Aliceanna's daughters Cora and Anna.

Milan continued to write regularly to his cousin Alice McMillan in Salem. In December, he reported that the infamous woman's rights activist Victoria Woodhull had lectured in Alliance, and that his brother Emerson had moved into the same Congressional district as Linden, about eighty miles from New Orleans, "and they control the two best papers in it."

Milan stayed in close touch with the Stabler cousins. In 1875, Fannie sent him for Christmas the motto "Friendship, Love & Truth" worked in perforated cardboard. The following April, Milan left Wright & Pennock hardware store in Alliance after seven years, shipped his belongings to Green Hill, and moved to Philadelphia, where he joined a marine insurance firm. After his grandmother's eightieth birthday in May 1876, he wrote to her that he had attended the Centennial Exhibition in Philadelphia, courtesy of the *Donaldsonville Chief,* his brother Linden's Louisiana newspaper. He also had been to a temperance meeting and had heard of "base ball" being played "a good deal."

In August, Linden and his wife buried their newborn son, Thomas Beale. In September, Milan noted of his Aunt Aliceanna and her family, "Those nice cousins of mine are still among the living—inhabitants of the Quaker City, and are just as nice as ever."

Milan didn't put down roots in Philadelphia quite yet. In January 1877, his cousin Fannie mourned that "our much beloved cousin" had just left for a job in Van Wert, Ohio. After he left, Fannie wrote, the Stablers' next-door neighbor in Philadelphia remarked, "It's not likely, Miss Fannie, that you will get anybody else to <u>cart you around</u> as he has done."

The plight of Carrie and her family continued to cause the most anxiety. Eva, her oldest daughter, though only twelve, assumed the burden of the housekeeping while Carrie was ill and exhausted after nursing her children through diphtheria. Neighbors took over the care of five-year-old Gertrude, but Carrie wouldn't give up three-year-old Paul. Norman, sixteen, became indispensable on the farm.

Closer to home, common ailments of the late nineteenth century took their toll among the neighbors. Anna wrote in 1878, "The day before yesterday Tamer Reeder's granddaughter, Tamar Smith, was buried. They live in sight of here. One year ago her mother died with rapid consumption. She then was a bright, beautiful girl, the picture of health, 20 years old. She took cold and the fell destroyer fastened on her lungs. Her father married in six months after his wife's death a nice woman of suitable age. She nursed Tamar most tenderly."

In August 1877, "the 65th anniversary of my wedding day," Anna recorded that the farm at Green Hill had received eighty-two visitors since the beginning of the year who had stayed at least overnight, including Aliceanna and her youngest daughter, Marion, who spent a month in the summer. Oddly, however, Anna had not seen Maria for almost a year and a half, though she was only fifteen miles away in Salem, because Maria was afraid to travel alone.

That same month, when Ruth Anna's brother Joel died, leaving his family grief-stricken and in financial straits, the ever-faithful Ruth Anna rushed to Salem to care for her ailing sister-in-law, Sarah. As Milan noted to his cousin Alice, "Will Bentley will miss her help in many ways, poor fellow. Poor Grandmother will take it the hardest, to be separated from her Ruth Anna! Dear old woman! She is getting <u>along</u> in years, to an age, when cheerful companionship is a necessity almost. I hope that Aunt Maria will make up her mind to stay there this winter, and try to fill the vacuum that Mother will create." A year later, Anna wrote to her sister that Ruth Anna was very tied down by Sarah McMillan, "a nervous invalid." Unself-consciously, Anna added, "Ruth Anna is slavishly confined there."

William Bentley, his wife Dora, and their child Howard lived at Green Hill for three years, until William was elected Columbiana County Treasurer and moved to Lisbon to take office in 1878. Anna enjoyed the company of small children, although she was well past eighty.

~

I have been minding baby[1] ever since I have been writing this disjointed letter and have had to stop so often, for he is the busiest little mortal. No cushion, or my <u>spectacles</u>, can stay in place an instant when in his reach. Yet he looks so cunning and will kiss me and say "Poor Ma ma ma" when he jerks them off. I can't be out of patience. He says many words, understands everything, is extravagently fond of flowers and pictures. I have to watch him from the stove. Our nearest neighbor had a little boy just his age, thier firstborn, that a few weeks ago was burned to death. The parent had left him playing, first securing, as they thought, everything. She lit the lamp with a splint, blew it out, felt the end, saw that no fire was on it, placed it on the mantel and hurried out. A neighbor coming soon after heard its screams, looked in the window. It was all in flames. He had to run round the house before he could get in, smothered the flames and tore off its upper garments. A spark must have fallen from the splint when she lit the lamp and smouldered in its calico dress.

1. Howard Bentley, born in 1876, her great-grandchild. He was the son of William and Dora Bentley.

~

During the breathlessly hot July of 1878, Anna complained that her sight and hearing were failing. She could scarcely hear the songs of the birds that built nests on the porch.

Joan Purcell Bentley and her two sons visited Green Hill the following April, and Milan was shocked to see that she was as short as Cora Stabler but weighed 172 pounds. Milan probably saw most of the world in relation to Cora Stabler in those days. His relationship had changed from cousinly to something much more. He and Cora announced their engagement in 1879. In Louisiana, Linden and Ella had a new baby, Eugene Preston Bentley. Like his brother, he did not survive infancy.

Cora spent part of the summer at Green Hill, then returned to Philadelphia, where she and Milan got married on November 20. Less than three months later, <u>Aliceanna died at the age of fifty-one.</u> Cora wrote to

Alice McMillan, "She was so good, so lively, and now she is gone from us forever. I cannot bear it." She drew comfort from the fact that her mother had been at her wedding to Milan, and "she died with her head on his breast."

Milan and Cora had their first child, Raymond, in June 1881. In Louisiana, Emerson and Joan had three boys and a girl. Ruth Anna, fifty-two, continued to make Green Hill her home and her major life project. "She has so little society," Milan complained. But she obviously assumed great importance to Anna Bentley, who was at a stage of life where the shades of the departed began to outnumber the living of her generation. Each passing was a spiritual blow that left her with an array of physical symptoms.

In June 1880, she wrote that Margaret E. Garrigues, her friend and cousin MEG who had lived down the road for fifty years, was dead of dropsy and paralysis and had been laid to rest next to her husband Robert in the Sandy Spring Quaker cemetery outside Hanover. MEG's last sad suffering and death had had a "depressing and debilitating" effect on Anna's spirits, she wrote.

❧

After the terrible shock of the death of my darling Alice my strength left me and my liver become much out of order with <u>all</u> the attending symptoms: loss of appetite and sleep, nightmare, depression, extreme soreness in my side, back, and shoulder; could not wear a garment fastened round my waist for 6 weeks, and the touch of my clothing to my side felt like tow linnen. Then the dreadful blow to my poor Carrie in the death of her noble first-born son, Norman. His father wrote, "Just as his character was formed and we had begun to look up to him as a model of all that was good and noble and manly, we had to give him up. He had graduated in the College, had received a full Teacher's Certificate, was just about to commence teaching. He took the measles followed by Pneumonia. Carrie was utterly prostrated." He was 19 years old. He was buried on the 16 of April. On the 22nd of May Carrie had not been able to sit up. That is the last I have heard. . . .

Shall I tell thee of the beautiful bright birds that have generally been considered wild but this summer built thier nests and raised their young in the vines and trees close to our house? & a beautiful red bird raised 4 in a grape vine that shades my west window and another like it raised a family in the syringa bush dear Sister Lizzie brought me from Cousin A

Brooke's. Bright Orioles, catbirds, robins, yellow birds have raised their young in our household trees. One red bird roosts every night in a vine <u>close</u> to the front porch, and another hopped in at the door and gazed at me the other day.

~

She added to this letter a postscript to her beloved correspondent, Sarah Stabler, "Thy letters are so <u>refreshing</u> to me, a real comfort."

Anna wrote <u>her last letter, dated November 7, 1881,</u> "a dark, cloudy, rainy morn." Sixteen-year-old Eva Heston had been spending a few weeks at Green Hill. Her aunt Julia wrote that she had been away from home already nearly four years, yet Carrie and James were willing for her to stay on. In the meantime, she was one of the numerous grandchildren and great grandchildren who accumulated a host of childhood memories on the farm under the amused and loving observation of the old woman in the white cap with her pipe at the ready.

~

My beloved sister, . . .

Dear sister, no lack of interest or warm sisterly love causes my long intervals of silence, but the failing powers of nature, great dimness of sight. My black eye has given out <u>entirely</u> and I cannot read without the aid of Bro Isaac's magnifying glass held between my spectacles and book or paper, but I can still knit. Oh, how I <u>do</u> knit.

And dear Ruth Anna and Julia are so good about reading aloud to dear Granville and Grandmother. They are very pleasant readers and so good and kind to me. My heart overflows with thankfulness to the good Father who has led me to this blessed retreat where loving hearts and willing hands administer to all my wants and <u>no</u> jarring discord comes. My memory fails me too, as it regards recent events. The "long ago" is still bright before me. Many fair pictures are treasured in my gallery. Those which are not I pass over till they are fading out. 85 1/2 years wanting a few days.

On the 20th of last mo sister Alice Hall died aged 92—my Joseph's sister, the last one of that family.

I am <u>now</u> in <u>usual</u> health having passed through a spell of disordered liver & kidney and billious symptoms, sleepless nights, nervous depression, &c &c. I could not write while so.

Dear patient Granville is also much better after a trying spell of sick headache for two days previous. The rest well, our housecleaning all done except the sitting room. We had to wait for the man who is to paper it. Such lovely paper and border. He will come on the 10th.

We had a long drought in the summer which burned up the pastures. We had to feed the stock like winter. Sometime in Sep nice rain came and the grass revived like a second spring. Our lovely hills and yard that were quite brown are still as bright and green as June. And such sweet golden butter as Ruth Anna turns out, over 25 lbs a week. Our potatoes were a failure, corn much better than they expected.

Maria suffers much with rheumatism. Harry is attending college in New York. His wife and children moved to Cleveland to her sister Trescott's. And Frank's well now.

I have left telling of the great and unspeakable comfort and happiness we have been permitted to enjoy in a visit from our good and loving Alban. Oh, what a change in him. I felt that my earnest prayers for him had been answered, he is so gentle, loving, and earnest. All his relatives <u>felt</u> the change and gave him such love and <u>respect</u> as they had never felt before. He is highly respected and trusted in Cadott where he now lives. He has been Justice of the Peace 9 years, is Notary Public, Land Agent, Coroner, and Postmaster; says he thinks he must give up the Justice of Peace office as he has too much on hand. He is doing well. His son Frank, he says, is an <u>exellent</u> young man with no bad habits except <u>SMOKING</u>. He speaks so lovingly of his dear wife. "Oh, Mother," he said, "she is one of the best of women. She is so earnest in what she believes right. She is so unselfish. My true helpmate. She is loved and respected by all. In sickness and sorrow she is a faithful help and comforter."

We had a card from Salem telling of his probable arrival. The hour for the hack had passed and the rest gave him out and we had supper. I sat at my knitting but still looked for him. Joseph, who lives on the road near us, had stopped him to supper and came up with him. I heard his voice in the next room and stood up to meet him. "Oh, Mother, my dear Mother," as he put his arms around me, and I could only say, "My dear dear son. Oh, thank the Lord!"

I then led him to Granville's chair. He dropped on his knees beside him, laying his face in Granville's hands which he covered with tears and kisses, saying, "Oh, my dear dear brother, how I have longed for this meeting." Granville spoke low words I could not hear.

Amelia sent the most beautiful rug I ever saw of the kind, her own work. Have I tired thee? I see I have only left room for love to all, every one of thy dear ones. All here dearly love thee, and thou never doubt the love of Sister Anna.

~

Epilogue

After a long old age at Green Hill, the matriarch of her extended family, Anna left the world quietly, age ninety-four, on August 1, 1890. "She was a remarkable woman in several respects," said her obituary in the *Salem Republican-Era*. "Mrs. Bentley was a lady of more than ordinary intellectual ability, and being a great reader, possessed a vast fund of general information, and her faculties remained unimpaired until near the close of her long life. She was a lady of fine colloquial powers, being at one time, without doubt, one of the finest conversationalists in Columbiana county."

She is buried next to Joseph and her granddaughter Julia under a spruce tree in Hope Cemetery, Salem. Nearby are other children and grandchildren. Of her thirteen children, five were still living at her death.

In the melancholy way of people who reach a great age, Anna outlived many of her loved ones, including all but one of her seven younger siblings. Only William Henry, the baby, survived her. Anna's sister Sarah died in 1886; her youngest sister, Margaret, her son Franklin, and her grandson Emerson in 1889. Her Ohio Brooke cousins, William, Samuel, Abraham, Edward, and James, all predeceased her. With the passing of the next generation of Brookes, many of whom died young or never married, the family disappeared from Marlborough. Eventually their farms were inundated by the Dale Walburn Reservoir.

Franklin's daughter Clara died unmarried in 1927 at Massillon State Hospital. Franklin has descendants through his son Walter, who became a journalist in Chicago.

Maria died in Salem in 1895, age eighty, leaving two sons, Norman and Harry Garrigues. Her obituary noted that she died a member of the Baptist church and that she had been a "great reader." Norman, who had taken over his father's machine shop and also served as Columbiana County

Auditor and Salem fire chief, followed just two years later, "a victim no doubt to nicotine poisoning," wrote his Aunt Ruth Anna. His and Nina's daughter, Mabel Virginia, married J.W. Burrows of Pittsburgh. Harry Bentley Garrigues, a homeopathic doctor in nearby Massillon, died in 1932, leaving an unmarried daughter. His obituary said he was a member of the Presbyterian Church. The Bible that Maria and Richard had received as a wedding present and in which they had recorded family births and deaths was found in an antiques store in the 1970s. The births, marriages, and deaths recorded in it were reprinted in a genealogy collection.

Two of Thomas's sons made their permanent homes in Louisiana. Emerson flashed through the world like a comet, brilliantly but quickly. He served in the state assembly and edited New Orleans newspapers, including the *Morning Chronicle,* before he died at the age of thirty-nine, leaving six children: Alonzo, Emerson, Pearl, Edith, Arthur, and Ralph Waldo. Emerson Jr. became a prominent Shreveport lawyer specializing in rail transportation law. Linden had a long career as the founding publisher of the *Donaldsonville Chief.* When he died at the age of ninety-one in 1944, the *New York Times* ran his obituary. His daughter Ella, friend and secretary of the famous newspaper lovelorn columnist Dorothy Dix, married Stanley Clisby Arthur, a writer, naturalist, archivist and Louisiana social historian.

Thomas's youngest son, Milan, died suddenly in Philadelphia in 1895, age forty, leaving Cora Lea with two children, Aliceanna and Raymond. Ruth Anna, whose competence and hard work bore up the Bentley household for years, stayed on at Green Hill in her old age, rarely leaving the farm. In 1900, she was listed among Civil War pensioners, suffering from Bright's disease.

Hannah Preston left seven children when she died in 1866. Those I was able to trace lived in Michigan and Iowa. All married, and all but one had children. Her husband, John, remarried and had three more children before he died in Guthrie County, Iowa.

Deborah's husband, Isaac Trescott, was killed by a train in Alliance, Ohio, in 1887. His funeral attracted a large crowd in Salem, where he had been well known as a merchant, abolitionist, and temperance leader. Deborah remarried Charles Rice—a farmer from Hanover Township whose son was a prominent dentist in Alliance—and joined the East Goshen Monthly Meeting in Damascus, Ohio. Having suffered years of ill health in her youth, Deborah outlived her second husband, too, and died in 1905. Her descendants are numerous.

Aliceanna left a large family of daughters and one son. Her daughter and namesake Alice Anna married Ernest Tompkins and had three sons. The eldest, Warwick Miller Tompkins, became a famous yachtsman whose book *From Fifty South to Fifty South* recorded his 1936 voyage around Cape Horn in the restored 1883 pilot boat *Wander Bird.* Known in her family for her strong character, Alice Anna the younger kept the thee's and thou's of her Quaker heritage until her death in California at age 105.

Caroline and her husband, James Heston, left Kansas for Palatka, Florida, in the 1880s. Caroline died in 1917. They are buried in Jacksonville, and most of their descendants still live in the state. It was this branch of the family that inherited Anna's photo album, which included some of the photos reproduced in this book. Their daughter Eva, who was sent back east to live as a young girl, never fully reconnected with her family, according to family lore. She remained aloof from her siblings the rest of her life.

Alban and Amelia left Wisconsin sometime after 1880. Anna's obituary noted that Alban was living in Louisiana in 1890, although at least one of his four sons stayed on in Wisconsin.

The "noble" Granville, the eldest Bentley child, never regained his sight. He spent his last years, increasingly feeble, at Green Hill. After he died in 1898, the farm passed successively to his son, Joseph, and his grandson, also Joseph. Granville's daughter, Julia Alice, one of Anna's caretakers in old age, died unmarried in 1923, age seventy. The homestead is still in family hands, although much altered. According to the family, Anna's original house, which had been raised with great exertion in 1826 by those "39 sturdy sons of the forest," was dismantled sometime in the 1880s. Her grandson's farm became the center of family gatherings for many years. Eventually, family members moved away from the immediate neighborhood, and the house was occupied by a tenant farmer and his family. Green Hill continued to be used for summer reunions for many years.

Sadly, in the 1990s, arsonists burned down the unoccupied house and the barn in separate incidents. All that remain today are the dressed sandstone foundations, the stone footprint of a barn with the tile silo rising next to it, and, among the weeds and trash that have accumulated in the burnt-out wreckage, the rusted skeletons of milking stalls.

Over the years, many farms in southern Columbiana County gave way to strip mines, which tapped rich veins of coal like the one Joseph E. Bentley himself had exploited. One hundred and seventy years after Jos first chipped coal out of the ground by the bushel, the land over which Anna Briggs Bentley gazed in 1826 and wrote, "A feeling of thankfulness arose in my heart as I thought, here <u>is</u> my home, here <u>is</u> an inheritance for my children where they <u>may</u> earn their bread if it <u>is</u> by the sweat of their brow," was crisscrossed with bulldozed trails in preparation for a modern strip mining operation. On a ridge overlooking the property is the old family burial plot, obscured by myrtle. There lie the remains of Anna's three children who died in 1842.

Appendix One

The Children of Roger Brooke IV and Mary Matthews Brooke

Samuel (Uncle Sammy) (1758–1846);
m. (1797) Sarah Garrigues

Mary Matthews (Mary Jr. or Aunt Polly), (1760–1840);
m. (1791) Thomas Moore Jr.
Their house: The Retreat, also called Longwood

Deborah (1764–1844);
m. (1783) Richard Thomas Jr. of Brookeville;
parents of Margaret Thomas Garrigues (MEG)
and Elizabeth Thomas (Cousin Betsy)

Margaret (1765–1830)

Sarah (1767–1805);
m. (1791) Caleb Bentley of Loudoun Co., Virginia,
the uncle of Joseph E. Bentley.
Caleb married Henrietta Thomas, his second wife, in 1807.

Hannah (1770–1851);
m. (1794) Isaac Briggs (1763–1825)

Roger Brooke (1774–1860);
m. 1) (1804) Mary Pleasants Younghusband,
and 2) (1840) Sarah Gilpin

Dorothy Brooke (Aunt Dolly) (1776–1857);
m. (1796) Gerard T. Hopkins

Appendix Two

The Children of Isaac Briggs and Hannah Brooke Briggs

Anna (1796–1890); m. (1812) Joseph E. Bentley (1789–1865)

Mary (1798–1875); m. (1824) Richard Brooke
(son of Gerard and Margaret Thomas Brooke) (1790–1862).
Their house: Falling Green

    Henry Briggs (1827–?)

    Hannah Briggs (1828–1914)

    Charles H. (1831–1915); m. (1865) Anna Farquhar

    Eliza (1834–1919)

    Margaret (1838–1919); m. (1866) Dr. William Magruder

Deborah (1799–1825); m. (1824) Joseph Bond

    Isaac B. (1825–1873)

Sarah Bentley (1801–1886); m. (1830) as his second wife, James
Pleasants Stabler (?-1840), son of Thomas Pleasants Stabler.
(James P. Stabler had a son, Pleasants, by his first wife, Elizabeth Gilpin)

    Elizabeth (Lizzie) (1834–1932); m. (1851) Charles Iddings

    Frances D. (1837–1930)

    James P. (1839–1925); m. Alice Brooke

Isaac (1803–1873); never married

Elizabeth (1807–1865); never married

Margaret (1812–1889); m. (1834) William Henry Farquhar (1813–1887). Their house: The Cedars

> Ellen (1837–1927)

> Arthur B. (1838–1925)

> Edward (1843–?)

> Henry (1851–1925)

William Henry (1815–1902); m. (1836) Henrietta Eliza Thomas (1810–1872)

> Mary (c. 1837–?)

> Edward H. (1839–1925); m. (1861) Frances P. Beckwith

> Hannah (c. 1842–?); m. John Parks

> Sarah E. (c. 1848–?)

Appendix Three

The Children of Joseph E. Bentley and Anna Briggs Bentley

This listing of descendants includes only the grandchildren of the older Bentley children, i.e., those great-grandchildren Anna Bentley may have known.

1. Granville Sharp (1813–1898); m. (1842) Elizabeth Garrigues
   (c. 1818–1865) of Marlborough, daughter of William and
   Margaret (Humphrey) Garrigues
   William G. (1843–1914); m. (1875) Dora L. Bean
      Howard V. (1876–1914); m. (1902) May Dickinson;
        no children
      Nina E. (1880–?); never married
      Joseph E. (1883–1967) m. Ione Dole (1884–1956)
   Joseph E. (1846–1925); m. (1868) Asenath Wickersham
      (1846–1916)
      Elizabeth Martha (Lizzie) (1869–1946);
        m. William Henderson (1865–1942)
      Anna B. (1871–1896); named after Anna Bentley
   Julia Alice (1852–1923); never married

2. Franklin Hamilton (1815–1889); m. (1841) Hannah Garrigues
   (1819–1893)
   Clarence (1842–1843)
   Walter B. (1844–1910); m. (1870) Marcia Clemmer (1847–1927)
      Lotie Maude (1876–1957); m. Frederic Smith Niles (1875–
        1902)
   Clara (1846–1927); never married

3. Maria (1817–1897); m. (1839) Richard Humphrey Garrigues (1816–
   1875), son of William and Margaret (Humphrey) Garrigues
   Norman B. (1840–1897); m. (1865) Nina Hise, niece of Daniel
      Hise of Salem

Leon (1869–1869)
Mabel Virginia (1872–1945), m. John W. Burrows
Edwin (d. 1875, age 7 months)
Harold R. (1849–1851)
Harry Bentley (1853–1932); m. 1) (1873) Caroline "Dollie"
    Webster (1855–1893)
    Richard (1874–1875)
    Lyndon W. (1876–1903)
    Mary Alice (or Alice Mary) (1879–1966); never married
2) (1899) Emily Leighton (?–1950)

4. Edward (1819–1824)

5. Thomas Moore (c. 1821–1867); m. (1846) Ruth Anna MacMillan
        (1827–c. 1900)
    Emerson B. (1850–1889); m. (1871) Joan Pursell/Purcell
        (c. 1852–?) of New Orleans.
        Alonzo Charles (1872–?)
        Emerson ("Bud") (1875–1947); m. 1) Marie Louise Connolly,
            2) Sue Eleanor Watson
            Pearl (1879–?); m. William Hurley
            Edith
            Arthur
            Ralph Waldo (1882–1962); m. (1905) Katie R. Hicks
    Linden E. (1852–1944); m. (1874) Ella Donnaud
        (c. 1856–1900)
        Thomas Beale (1876–1876)
        Linden A. (1877–1880)
        Eugene Preston (1879–1880)
        Ella (1881–?) m. Stanley Clisby Arthur
        Granville D. (1883–1966); m. (1905) Heloise Simms
    Milan (1855–1895); m. (1879) Cora Lea Stabler (Aliceanna's
        daughter)
        Alice Anna (c. 1880–?)
        Raymond (1881–1970)
    Alonzo (c.1858–1864)

6. Hannah B. (1823–1866); m. (1845) John Alexander Preston
        (1824–1899)
    Almeda (1846/47–?); m. 1) Lewis Penwell and 2) Jack Mast

Laura Maria (c. 1850–?); m. William Hall
Horace Bentley (1851–?); m. Louise Richmond
Charles Sumner (1853–1915); m. Irene (Rena) Martin
Lindley Franklin (c. 1858–?); m. Tryphena Blackman
Mary Janette (c. 1860–?); m. Frank A. Wilson
Elmer E. (1861–1925); m. 1) May McGilvary, 2) Lillian Edwards

7. Deborah R. (1825–1905); m. 1) (1860) Isaac Trescott (1817–1887)
    and 2) (1889) Charles H. Rice
    Lilian, or Lily (1861–1919); m. (1883) John Ross McArtor
    Lola G. (1869–1938); m. Frank H. Sage
    Ernest B. (1870–?); m. Grace Thornburg

8. Aliceanna (1828–1880); m. (1851) John Stabler, the son of Thomas P.
    and Elizabeth Stabler
    Florence (1852–?); m. (c. 1870) P.D. Blackman
    Alice Evelyn (1854–1864)
    Cora Lea, (1857–?); m. (1879) her cousin, Milan Bentley (son of
        Thomas, see above)
    Anna B. (1859–?)
    Fannie (1860–?)
    Eliza Brooke (1863–?)
    John Jr. (1865–?)
    Alice Bentley (1868–1973); m. Ernest Tompkins
    Evangeline (Eva) (c. 1871–?); m. William Gilpin
    Marion (1873–?); m. Sprague

9. Edmunds (1831–1842)

10. Caroline Elizabeth (1834–1917); m. (1860) James Heston (1831–
    1904)
    Norman (1861–1880)
    Maud (1862–1865)
    Eva (1865–?); m. Butler
    James Hardel (Harold) (1868–1948) m. Jennie Donnelly
    Claude (1870–1942); m. Catherine Cecelia Gallager
    Gertrude (1872–c. 1973); never married
    Paul Llewellyn (1874–1943); m. Lillian Holden

11. Alban (1836–1923); m. (1857) Amelia M. Walton (1834–1913)
    Franklin Hamilton (1857–1939); m. Margaret Jethson/Jellison
    Edgar Walton (1863–1937); m. Anna DeLong
    Granville Sharp (1875–1916); m. Alfreda Laura Anderson
    Arthur
    Howard (1884–1977); m. 1) Blanche; 2) Anna Rath

12. Margaretta (1839–1842)

13. Joseph Garrigues (1842–1842)

Bibliography

I drew on several collections of family papers for this book. Foremost among them were the sixteen boxes of miscellaneous documents that make up the Briggs-Stabler Family Papers, 1793–1910, in the collection of the Maryland Historical Society. This is where Anna Bentley's letters have been preserved, as well as many letters by her father, Isaac Briggs, and other family members, including Isaac Briggs Jr. and Elizabeth Briggs. I reprint letters from that collection and others with permission.

The correspondence of Anna's sister and brother-in-law, Mary and Richard Brooke, are in the Brooke Family Papers in the archives of the University of Maryland Libraries.

The Jordan and Stabler Family Papers, 1807–1916, including letters of the family of Aliceanna Bentley Stabler, are in the collection of the Virginia Historical Society.

For insights into Anna Bentley's later years and life on the farm at Green Hill, I found the papers of Alice McMillan, niece of Ruth Anna McMillan Bentley, in the collection of the Ohio Historical Society, to be invaluable. They include letters by Ruth Anna and Milan Bentley. Likewise, from the same archive, the diaries of Daniel Hise give a somewhat acerbic account of daily life in mid-nineteenth-century Salem, especially relating to the community of anti-slavery activists including Brooke, Garrigues, Luken, and Bentley family members.

Equally helpful in sorting out the family relationships and tracing the comings and goings of a generation of Sandy Spring, Maryland, Quakers were the minutes of the Sandy Spring and Indian Spring Monthly Meetings in the archives of the State of Maryland in Annapolis.

Among the local Ohio newspapers of Anna Bentley's day, with obituaries, marriage announcements, and other items of moment, were the *New Lisbon Western Palladium, Ohio Patriot, Salem News, Salem Daily Herald, Salem Era, Salem Republican-Era, Alliance Review, East Palestine Reveille Echo, East Palestine Daily Echo, Canton Repository* and *Anti-Slavery Bugle,* all in original or microfilm in the extensive Ohio newspaper archive of the Ohio Historical Society, as are the Ohio censuses that record the families of Columbiana and Stark counties through the decades.

Finally, there is the Internet, which brought to bear on this project a whole new level of research and human interaction. The U.S. Library of Congress has made available on its Web site scanned reproductions of the correspondence of Thomas Jefferson, including letters to and from Isaac Briggs that were invaluable to me in researching this book.

Numerous family and genealogy Web sites, while they often are works in progress, nevertheless repeatedly pointed me in the right direction in making complicated family connections, and they led me again and again to Anna Bentley's descendants, with their family lore and photos. It would be impossible to cite all the Web sites I consulted that offered bits and pieces of useful information.

Manuscript Collections

Briggs-Stabler Family Papers, 1793–1910. MS 147. Maryland Historical Society, Baltimore.

Brooke Family Papers, 1650–1954. University of Maryland Libraries, College Park.

Hise, Daniel Howell. Diaries, 1849–1883. 6 vols. MSS 981. Ohio Historical Society, Columbus.

Jordan and Stabler Family Papers, 1807–1916. MSS 1J7676a. Virginia Historical Society, Richmond.

McMillan, Alice. Papers, 1847–1903. MSS 591. Ohio Historical Society, Columbus.

Minutes of Sandy Spring and Indian Spring Monthly Meetings. Maryland State Archives, Annapolis.

Other Sources

Abernethy, Thomas Perkins. *The Burr Conspiracy.* New York: Oxford University Press, 1954.

"Abraham Brooke," *American National Biography.* New York: Oxford University Press, 1999.

Anderson, George M., S.J., "The Montgomery County Agricultural Society: The Beginning Years, 1846–1850," *Maryland Historical Magazine* 81, no. 4 (Winter 1986): 305–15.

Anthony, Katharine. *Dolly Madison: Her Life and Times.* New York: Doubleday & Co., 1949.

Barbour, Hugh, and J. William Frost. *The Quakers.* New York: Greenwood Press, 1988.

Barnes, Robert William, comp. *Maryland Marriages, 1778–1800.* Baltimore: Genealogical Publisher, 1978.

———. *Maryland Marriages: 1801–1820.* Baltimore: Genealogical Publisher, 1993.

Barrow, Healan, and Kristine Stevens. *Olney: Echoes of the Past.* Westminster, Maryland: Family Line Publications, 1998.

Barth, Harold B. *History of Columbiana County Ohio.* 2 vols. Topeka: Historical Publishing Company, 1926.

Bear, James A., Jr., and Lucia C. Stanton. *The Papers of Thomas Jefferson.* Second series, *Jefferson's Memorandum Books: Accounts, with Legal Records and Miscellany, 1767–1826*, Vol. 2. Princeton: Princeton University Press, 1997.

Bell, Carol Willsey, ed. *Columbiana County, Ohio Newspaper Abstracts.* Youngstown, Ohio.: Bell Books, 1986–87.

———. *Columbiana County, Ohio and Vicinity Bible Records.* Apollo, Pennsylvania: Closson Press, 1992.

Bell, Carol Willsey. *Columbiana County Ohio Marriages, 1800–1870.* Youngstown, Ohio: Bell Books, 1990.

Briggs, Isaac. Letter regarding working on the New York Canal, 16 January 1819, *Annals of Cleveland—1818–1935*, 1 (1819): 356–58. Cleveland: Cleveland WPA, 1937 <http://web.ulib.csuohio.edu/SpecColl/annals/An1819r787.htm>.

Brinton, Howard. *Friends for 300 Years: The History and Beliefs of the Society of Friends Since George Fox Started the Quaker Movement.* New York: Harper, 1952.

Burke, James L., and Donald E. Bensch. *Mount Pleasant and the Early Quakers of Ohio.* Columbus: Ohio Historical Society, 1975.

Canby, Thomas Y., ed. *Sandy Spring Legacy.* Sandy Spring, Maryland.: Sandy Spring Museum, 1999.

Coulter, Harris L. *Divided Legacy: The Conflict Between Homoeopathy and the American Medical Association.* Vol. 3, *Science and Ethics in American Medicine, 1800–1914.* Berkeley: North Atlantic Books, 1982.

Doherty, Robert W. *The Hicksite Separation: A Sociological Analysis of Religious Schism in Early Nineteenth Century America.* New Brunswick: Rutgers University Press, 1967.

Dumond, Dwight L., ed. *Letters of James Gillespie Birney: 1831–1857.* New York: Appleton-Century Company, 1938.

Elliott, Errol T. *Quakers on the American Frontier: A History of the Westward Migrations, Settlements, and Developments of Friends on the American Continent.* Richmond, Indiana.: The Friends United Press, 1969.

Farquhar, William Henry. *Annals of Sandy Spring, or Twenty Years History of a Rural Community in Maryland.* Baltimore: Cushings & Bailey, 1884.

Farquhar, Roger Brooke. *Historic Montgomery County, Maryland: Old Homes and History.* Silver Spring, Maryland, 1962.

Filler, Louis. *The Crusade Against Slavery: 1830–1860.* New York: Harper & Brothers, 1960.

Foley, John P., ed. *The Jeffersonian Cyclopedia.* New York: Funk & Wagnalls Company, 1900.

Foner, Eric. *Reconstruction: America's Unfinished Revolution: 1863–1877.* New York: Harper & Row, 1988.

Fossier, A.E. "History of the Yellow Fever in New Orleans," *The Louisiana Historical Quarterly* 34, no. 3 (July 1951): 205–15.

Franklin, William M. "The Tidewater End of the Chesapeake and Ohio Canal," *Maryland Historical Magazine* 81, no. 4 (Winter 1986): 289–304.

Furin, Terrance L. "Berea, Ohio: Change in a Covenanted Community." Ph.D. diss., Case Western Reserve University, 1974.

Gamble, Douglas Andrew. "Moral Suasion in the West: Garrisonian Abolitionism, 1831–1861." Master's thesis, Ohio State University, 1973.

Gard, R. Max, and William H. Yodrey, Jr. *The Sandy & Beaver Canal.* East Liverpool Historical Society, 1952.

Gibson, Langhorne, Jr. *Cabell's Canal: the Story of the James River and Kanawha.* Richmond: The Commodore Press, 2000.

Gunn, John C. *Gunn's Domestic Medicine, or Poor Man's Friend.* Xenia, Ohio, 1837.

Hackett, Mary A., ed. *The Papers of James Madison.* Secretary of State Series, Vol. 4 (8 October 1802–15 May 1803). Charlottesville: University Press of Virginia, 1998.

Hageman, Jane Sikes and Edward M. *Ohio Furniture Makers, 1790–1860.* Vol. 2. Cincinnati: J.S. Hageman, c. 1984.

Hallowell, Benjamin. *Autobiography of Benjamin Hallowell.* Philadelphia: Friends' Book Association, 1884.

Hicks, Elias. *Journal of the Life and Religious Labours of Elias Hicks, Written by Himself.* New York: Isaac T. Hopper, 1832.

Hinshaw, William Wade. *Encyclopedia of American Quaker Genealogy.* 7 vols. Ann Arbor: Edwards Bros., 1936– .

History of the Upper Ohio Valley. 2 vols. Madison: Brant & Fuller, 1891.

Holbrook, Alfred. *Reminiscences of the Happy Life of a Teacher.* Cincinnati, 1885.

Horsman, Reginald. *The New Republic: The United States of America, 1789–1815.* Harlow, England: Longman, 2000.

Howe, Henry. *Historical Collections of Ohio.* 2 vols. Cincinnati: C.J. Krehbiel, 1900.

Hunt, George B. *History of Salem and the Immediate Vicinity.* Salem, Ohio: by the author, 1898.

Ierley, Merritt. *Traveling the National Road: Across the Centuries on America's First Highway.* Woodstock, N.Y.: The Overlook Press, 1990.

Ingle, H. Larry. *Quakers in Conflict: The Hicksite Reformation.* Knoxville: University of Tennessee Press, 1986.

Jacob, Caroline N. *Builders of the Quaker Road.* Chicago: Henry Regnery Company, 1933.

Janney, Samuel M. *Memoirs of Samuel M. Janney.* Philadelphia: Friends Book Association, 1890.

Jefferson, Thomas. *Papers. Series 1: General Correspondence, 1751–1827* [letters to and from Isaac Briggs]. U.S. Library of Congress <http://memory.loc.gov/ccgi-bin/ampage>.

Jeffrey, Julie Roy. *The Great Silent Army of Abolitionism: Ordinary Women in the Antislavery Movement.* Chapel Hill: University of North Carolina Press, 1998.

Joint Committee of Hopewell Friends, comp. *Hopewell Friends History: 1734–1934.* Strasburg, Virginia: Shenandoah Publishing House, Inc., 1936.

Jones, Rufus. *The Later Periods of Quakerism*. 2 vols. London: Macmillan & Co., 1921.

Kersey, Jesse. *A Narrative of the Early Life, Travels, and Gospel Labors of Jesse Kersey, late of Chester County, Pennsylvania*. Philadelphia: T. Elwood Chapman, 1851.

Ketcham, Ralph. *James Madison: A Biography*. New York: Macmillan & Co., 1971.

Kocher, L. Richard. *A Listing of Entrymen on Lands in Columbiana County, Ohio*. Columbus, Ohio, 2000.

Kraenzel, Carl Frederick. *The Great Plains in Transition*. Norman: University of Oklahoma Press, 1955.

Lampe, Gregory P. *Frederick Douglass: Freedom's Voice, 1818–1845*. Lansing: Michigan State University Press, 1998.

Lehman, John H., ed. *A Standard History of Stark County*. Chicago: Lewis Publishing Co., n.d.

Loveland, Anne C. "The 'Southern Work' of the Reverend Joseph C. Hartzell, Pastor of Ames Church in New Orleans, 1870–1873." *Louisiana History* 16, no. 4 (Fall 1975): 391–407.

Mack, Horace. *History of Columbiana County, Ohio*. Philadelphia: D.W. Ensign & Co., 1879.

Maizlish, Stephen E. *The Triumph of Sectionalism: The Transformation of Ohio Politics, 1844–1856*. Kent: Kent State University Press, 1983.

Manuel, Janet Thompson. *Marriage Licenses Montgomery County, Maryland, 1798–1898*. Silver Spring, Maryland: Family Line Publications, 1987.

Marks, Bayly Ellen, ed. "Correspondence of Anna Briggs Bentley from Columbiana County, 1826." *Ohio History* 78, no.1 (Winter 1969): 38–45.

Marrin, Albert. *1812: The War Nobody Won*. New York: Atheneum, 1985.

Mattern, David B., et al. *The Papers of James Madison*, Secretary of State Series, Vol. 5 (16 May-31 October 1803). Charlottesville: University Press of Virginia, 2000.

Mayer, Henry. *All on Fire: William Lloyd Garrison and the Abolition of Slavery*. New York: St. Martin's Press, 1998.

McCord, William B. *History of Columbiana County, Ohio and Representative Citizens*. Chicago: Biographical Publishing Co., 1905.

McCullough, Lel Hamner. *Emerson Bentley: A Personal Crusade in Louisiana Reconstruction.* The Amistad Research Center, Tulane University, New Orleans. Typescript, 1975.

McPherson, James M. *Battle Cry of Freedom: The Civil War Era.* New York: Ballantine Books, 1988.

Merrill, Walter M., and Louis Ruchames, eds. *Letters of William Lloyd Garrison.* Vol. 3, *No Union with Slaveholders: 1842–1849.* Cambridge: Harvard University Press, 1973.

Nesbitt, Martha C., Mary Reading Miller, et al. *Chronicles of Sandy Spring Friends Meeting and Environs.* Sandy Spring Monthly Meeting of the Religious Society of Friends, 1987.

Perrin, William Henry. *History of Stark County, with an Outline Sketch of Ohio.* Chicago: Baskin & Battey, 1881.

Peterson, Merrill D. *Thomas Jefferson and the New Nation: A Biography.* New York: Oxford University Press, 1970.

Pitch, Anthony S. *The Burning of Washington: The British Invasion of 1814.* Annapolis: Naval Institute Press, 1998.

Rohrbough, Malcolm J. *The Trans-Appalachian Frontier: People, Societies, and Institutions, 1775–1850.* New York: Oxford University Press, 1978.

Scharf, J. Thomas. *History of Western Maryland, Being a History of Frederick, Montgomery, Carroll, Washington, Allegany, and Garrett Counties.* 2 vols. Clearfield Company & Family Line Publications, 1995.

Scheiber, Harry N. *Ohio Canal Era: A Case Study of Government and the Economy, 1820–1861.* Athens: Ohio University Press, 1969.

Shaw, Francis E. *Francis E. Shaw and Relatives, with Other Matters.* Garretsville, Ohio: Francis E. Shaw, 1921.

Siebert, Wilbur Henry. *The Mysteries of Ohio's Underground Railroads,* Columbus: Long's College Book Co., 1951.

Sigourney, Lydia Huntley. *Poems; by Mrs. L.H. Sigourney.* Philadelphia: Key & Biddle, 1834.

Smith, H.E. *The Quakers, Their Migration to the Upper Ohio, Their Customs and Discipline.* Marietta, Ohio, 1928.

Sterling, Dorothy. *Ahead of Her Time: Abby Kelley and the Politics of Antislavery.* New York: W.W. Norton & Co., 1991.

Trelease, Allen W. *White Terror: The Ku Klux Klan Conspiracy and Southern Reconstruction.* Baton Rouge: Louisiana State University Press, 1971.

Tunis, Edwin. *Frontier Living: An Illustrated Guide to Pioneer Life in America, including Log Cabins, Furniture, Tools, Clothing, and More.* New York: The Lyons Press, 2000.

Walker, Pearl Ada. *The Story of Salem Friends from 1803 to 1973.* N.p., 1973.

Wall, James T. *The Boundless Frontier: America from Christopher Columbus to Abraham Lincoln.* Lanham, Maryland: University Press of America, 1999.

Webber, Judge A.R. *Life of John Baldwin.* [Cincinnati?]: The Caxton Press, [c. 1925].

Wilson, James D. Jr. "The Donaldson Incident of 1870," *Louisiana History* 38, no. 3 (Summer, 1997): 329–45.

INDEX